Exam Number	MCSE Course Title	Course Number	M(	
70-59	Internetworking with Microsoft TCP/IP on Windows NT 4.0	688	TCP/IP MCSE Study Guide Bulette, 0-7645-3112-3	E
70-14	Supporting Microsoft System Management Server 1.2	732	SMS 1.2 MCSE Study Guide Bulette, 0-7645-3163-8	E
70-87	Implementing and Supporting Microsoft Internet Information Server 4.0	936	IIS 4.0 MCSE Study Guide Dillon, Linthicum, 0-7645-3118-2	E
70-81	Implementing and Supporting Microsoft Exchange Server 5.5	771	Exchange Server 5.5 MCSE Study Guide Robichaux and Glenn, 0-7645-3111-5	E
70-88	Implementing and Supporting Microsoft Proxy Server 2.0	836	Microsoft Proxy Server 2.0 MCSE Study System Simmons, 0-7645-3336-3	E
70-79	Implementing and Supporting Microsoft Internet Explorer 4.0 by Using the Internet Explorer Administration Kit	956	Internet Explorer 4.0 Administration Kit MCSE Study System Sullivan, 0-7645-3279-0	E
70-80	Implementing and Supporting Microsoft Internet Explorer 5.0 by Using the Microsoft Internet Explorer Administration Kit		Internet Explorer 5.0 Administration Kit MCSE Study System Sullivan, 0-7645-4648-1	E

INTERNET EXPLORER 5 ADMINISTRATION KIT
MCSE STUDY SYSTEM

INTERNET EXPLORER 5
ADMINISTRATION KIT
MCSE STUDY SYSTEM

Chris Sullivan

® IDG Books Worldwide, Inc

An International Data Group Company

Foster City, CA ● Chicago, IL ● Indianapolis, IN ● Dallas, TX

IDG BOOKS WORLDWIDE

**Internet Explorer 5 Administration Kit
MCSE Study System**

Published by
IDG Books Worldwide, Inc.
An International Data Group Company
919 E. Hillsdale Blvd., Suite 400
Foster City, CA 94404
www.idgbooks.com (IDG Books Worldwide Web site)

ISBN: 0-7645-4648-1

Printed in the United States of America

10 9 8 7 6 5 4 3 2 1

1L/SX/QU/QQ/FC

Distributed in the United States by IDG Books Worldwide, Inc.

Distributed by CDG Books Canada Inc. for Canada; by Transworld Publishers Limited in the United Kingdom; by IDG Norge Books for Norway; by IDG Sweden Books for Sweden; by IDG Books Australia Publishing Corporation Pty. Ltd. for Australia and New Zealand; by TransQuest Publishers Pte Ltd. for Singapore, Malaysia, Thailand, Indonesia, and Hong Kong; by Gotop Information Inc. for Taiwan; by ICG Muse, Inc. for Japan; by Intersoft for South Africa; by Eyrolles for France; by International Thomson Publishing for Germany, Austria and Switzerland; by Distribuidora Cuspide for Argentina; by LR International for Brazil; by Galileo Libros for Chile; by Ediciones ZETA S.C.R. Ltda. for Peru; by WS Computer Publishing Corporation, Inc., for the Philippines; by Contemporanea de Ediciones for Venezuela; by Express Computer Distributors for the Caribbean and West Indies; by Micronesia Media Distributor, Inc. for Micronesia; by Chips Computadoras S.A. de C.V. for Mexico; by Editorial Norma de Panama S.A. for Panama; by American Bookshops for Finland.

For general information on IDG Books Worldwide's books in the U.S., please call our Consumer Customer Service department at 800-762-2974. For reseller information, including discounts and premium sales, please call our Reseller Customer Service department at 800-434-3422.

For information on where to purchase IDG Books Worldwide's books outside the U.S., please contact our International Sales department at 317-596-5530 or fax 317-596-5692.

For consumer information on foreign language translations, please contact our Customer Service department at 800-434-3422, fax 317-596-5692, or e-mail rights@idgbooks.com.

For information on licensing foreign or domestic rights, please phone +1-650-655-3109.

For sales inquiries and special prices for bulk quantities, please contact our Sales department at 650-655-3200 or write to the address above.

For information on using IDG Books Worldwide's books in the classroom or for ordering examination copies, please contact our Educational Sales department at 800-434-2086 or fax 317-596-5499.

For press review copies, author interviews, or other publicity information, please contact our Public Relations department at 650-655-3000 or fax 650-655-3299.

For authorization to photocopy items for corporate, personal, or educational use, please contact Copyright Clearance Center, 222 Rosewood Drive, Danvers, MA 01923, or fax 978-750-4470.

Library of Congress Cataloging-in-Publication Data

Sullivan, Chris.
  Internet explorer administration kit MCSE study system / Chris Sullivan.
     p. cm.
  Includes index.
  ISBN 0-7643-4648-1 (alk. paper)
  1. Electronic data processing personnel--Certification.
  2. Microsoft software--Examinations--Study guides.
  3. Microsoft Internet Explorer. I. Title.
QA76.3. S83 2000
005.7'13769--dc21   00-023394

ABOUT IDG BOOKS WORLDWIDE

Welcome to the world of IDG Books Worldwide.

IDG Books Worldwide, Inc., is a subsidiary of International Data Group, the world's largest publisher of computer-related information and the leading global provider of information services on information technology. IDG was founded more than 30 years ago by Patrick J. McGovern and now employs more than 9,000 people worldwide. IDG publishes more than 290 computer publications in over 75 countries. More than 90 million people read one or more IDG publications each month.

Launched in 1990, IDG Books Worldwide is today the #1 publisher of best-selling computer books in the United States. We are proud to have received eight awards from the Computer Press Association in recognition of editorial excellence and three from Computer Currents' First Annual Readers' Choice Awards. Our best-selling *...For Dummies®* series has more than 50 million copies in print with translations in 31 languages. IDG Books Worldwide, through a joint venture with IDG's Hi-Tech Beijing, became the first U.S. publisher to publish a computer book in the People's Republic of China. In record time, IDG Books Worldwide has become the first choice for millions of readers around the world who want to learn how to better manage their businesses.

Our mission is simple: Every one of our books is designed to bring extra value and skill-building instructions to the reader. Our books are written by experts who understand and care about our readers. The knowledge base of our editorial staff comes from years of experience in publishing, education, and journalism — experience we use to produce books to carry us into the new millennium. In short, we care about books, so we attract the best people. We devote special attention to details such as audience, interior design, use of icons, and illustrations. And because we use an efficient process of authoring, editing, and desktop publishing our books electronically, we can spend more time ensuring superior content and less time on the technicalities of making books.

You can count on our commitment to deliver high-quality books at competitive prices on topics you want to read about. At IDG Books Worldwide, we continue in the IDG tradition of delivering quality for more than 30 years. You'll find no better book on a subject than one from IDG Books Worldwide.

John Kilcullen
Chairman and CEO
IDG Books Worldwide, Inc.

*Eighth Annual
Computer Press
Awards ≥ 1992*

*Ninth Annual
Computer Press
Awards ≥ 1993*

*Tenth Annual
Computer Press
Awards ≥ 1994*

*Eleventh Annual
Computer Press
Awards ≥ 1995*

THE VALUE OF MICROSOFT CERTIFICATION

As a computer professional, your opportunities have never been greater. Yet you know better than anyone that today's complex computing environment has never been more challenging.

Microsoft certification keeps computer professionals on top of evolving information technologies. Training and certification let you maximize the potential of Microsoft Windows desktop operating systems; server technologies, such as the Internet Information Server, Microsoft Windows NT, and Microsoft BackOffice; and Microsoft development tools. In short, Microsoft training and certification provides you with the knowledge and skills necessary to become an expert on Microsoft products and technologies — and to provide the key competitive advantage that every business is seeking.

Microsoft offers you the most comprehensive program for assessing and maintaining your skills with our products. When you become a Microsoft Certified Professional (MCP), you are recognized as an expert and are sought by employers industry-wide. Technical managers recognize the MCP designation as a mark of quality — one that ensures that an employee or consultant has proven experience with Microsoft products and meets the high technical proficiency standards of Microsoft products.

As an MCP, you receive many benefits, such as direct access to technical information from Microsoft; the official MCP logo and other materials to identify your status to colleagues and clients; invitations to Microsoft conferences, technical training sessions and special events; and exclusive publications with news about the MCP program.

Research shows that organizations employing MCPs also receive many benefits:

- A standard method of determining training needs and measuring results — an excellent return on training and certification investments

- Increased customer satisfaction and decreased support costs through improved service, increased productivity, and greater technical self-sufficiency

- A reliable benchmark for hiring, promoting, and career planning

- Recognition and rewards for productive employees by validating their expertise

- Retraining options for existing employees, so they can work effectively with new technologies

- Assurance of quality when outsourcing computer services

Through your study, experience, and achievement of Microsoft certification, you will enjoy these same benefits, too, as you meet the industry's challenges.

Nancy Lewis
General Manager
Microsoft Training and Certification

FOREWORD TO THE MCSE SERIES

Certifications are an effective way of "selling your skills" to prospective employers, since they represent a consistent measurement of knowledge about specific software or hardware products. Because of their expansive product line and tremendous marketing efforts, Microsoft certifications have become the gold standard in the exploding certification industry. As a Microsoft Certified Professional, you are recognized as a "Subject Matter Expert" as defined by objective standards. As a training organization, we recognize the value of offering certification-level training. In fact, approximately 55 percent of students in our Microsoft classes are working toward certification, and I expect that number to continue to rise.

Studies have been conducted that show increased productivity among Microsoft Certified Solutions Developers versus non-certified programmers. Additionally, compensation for Microsoft Certified Systems Engineers and Microsoft Certified Solutions Developers averages higher than for those without certification. For individuals looking for a career in these areas, there is no better metric of legitimacy that can be placed on a resume than Microsoft certification credentials.

Information Systems/Information Technology (IS/IT) decision makers for ExecuTrain clients worldwide increasingly require certifications for their IS employees. Often, individuals are required to be certified or find that certification was their competitive edge in landing the job. Conventional wisdom and every study you read indicates these trends will continue as technologies become more a part of daily business in corporations.

Microsoft recently certified the 100,000th Microsoft Certified Professional. I expect this number to balloon as corporations make certification part of IS staff job descriptions. I predict certified candidates can expect better-paying jobs and positions with more technical responsibility to match their hard-won certification. Although the number of MCPs rises daily, that population is eclipsed by the more than 200,000 open IT positions reported today. Microsoft tracks these open positions and would like to fill each of them with an MCP. My bet is that if anyone can make the math work, they can.

Kevin Brice
Vice President/General Manager
Technical Training
ExecuTrain Corporation

CREDITS

ACQUISITIONS EDITOR
Jennifer Humphreville-Fusilero

PROJECT EDITOR
Robert MacSweeney
Brian MacDonald

TECHNICAL EDITOR
Art Brieva, MCSE, CNE, CCNA

COPY EDITOR
Chandani Thapa

PROJECT COORDINATOR
Linda Marousek
Marcos Vergara

GRAPHICS & PRODUCTION SPECIALISTS
Robert Bihlmayer, Jude Levinson,
Michael Lewis, Victor Perez-Varela,
Ramses Ramirez, Dina F Quan

QUALITY CONTROL SPECIALIST
Laura Taflinger

BOOK DESIGNER
Kurt Krames

ILLUSTRATORS
Mary Jo Richards, Shelley Norri

PROOFREADING AND INDEXING
York Production Services

MEDIA DEVELOPMENT SPECIALIST
J. Kiempisty

PERMISSIONS EDITOR
Lenora Chin Sell

MEDIA DEVELOPMENT MANAGER
Stephen Noetzel

ABOUT THE AUTHOR

Chris Sullivan is the Chief Technical Officer of Network Data Systems, Inc., a Washington, D.C.-based Application Service Provider. Chris has been involved in the computer industry for eight years as a network administrator, support engineer, and manager of many large-scale network and platform integration projects for federal and Fortune 500 companies.

Chris has been working with Microsoft products since the early versions of DOS, and currently holds the Microsoft Certified Systems Engineer + Internet certification as well as several other industry certifications. Over the years, Chris has developed technical training and documentation material for many large companies, such as Allstate, America Online, Lockheed Martin, U.S. Department of Housing and Urban Development, and the Office of the Comptroller of the Currency. You can contact Chris at chriss@netdatasys.com.

To my friend and mentor, Roy Kapani. Roy typifies what we all strive to be in this industry, a successful IT professional with an honest, hard-working, successful past.

PREFACE

Welcome to the MCSE Certification Series! This book is designed to help you acquire the knowledge, skills, and abilities you need to pass Microsoft Certified Professional Exam No. 70-080: Implementing and Supporting Microsoft Internet Explorer 5.0 by Using the Microsoft Internet Explorer Administration Kit.

If you're *not* planning to take the Internet Explorer Administration Kit (IEAK) exam, but you want to develop a comprehensive working knowledge of how to administer Internet Explorer, then this book is also for you. The book covers all of the applications covered in the Internet Explorer 5.0 suite of software, how to configure them, and issues related to the operations and deployment of the Internet Explorer suite of software.

This book is designed to be the only book or course you need to prepare for and pass the IEAK 5 exam. The focus of the book is to give you the knowledge and understanding of all of the pieces of the suite so that you can pass the exam and know how to use the IEAK to deploy Internet Explorer 5.

HOW THIS BOOK IS ORGANIZED

This book is organized in four parts, followed by a Resources section that contains appendixes and supplemental materials, as well as a CD-ROM. Within these major parts, each chapter begins with an overview of the topics that will be covered in that chapter. Then, pertinent information on each topic is presented. An Exam Preparation Summary, summarizing the preparation strategies for the exam, and a Key Point Summary, summarizing the chapter highlights and reviewing important material, follow. At the end of each chapter are Instant Assessment questions to make sure you understand and can apply what you've read. Additionally, at the end of many chapters are Hands-on Labs to help you master the specific tasks and skills tested by the exam.

Hands-on Labs present physical, computer-based activities for you to work through and are designed to provide you with practical experience with the concepts in the exam objectives. Hands-on Labs may cover hardware/software installation and configuration, in addition to any activity that requires you to sit at the computer and use the mouse and/or keyboard.

Part I: The Overview

Part I covers the applications within the Internet Explorer suite. In this Part, I talk about the basics of the Internet Explorer browser, the browser's capabilities, and technologies behind the scenes. I then move on to the electronic mail client, Outlook Express, and discuss the basics of e-mail and how to configure the client.

We will proceed to talk about data conferencing using Microsoft NetMeeting, and how you can bring real-time collaboration to the desktop using this powerful tool. I conclude Part I with a discussion of Microsoft Windows Media Technologies using Microsoft Media Player 6. You will cover the configurations and other important information about sound and video technologies using the Media Player tool.

Part II: The Nuts and Bolts of Internet Explorer

Part II starts with an in-depth discussion on how the installation of the software works. You will learn about the algorithms used to install the software, migrating from other browsers, and other considerations. You will also learn about event logging, basic troubleshooting, and how to recover a failed installation.

Part III: Managing Internet Explorer Using the Administration Kit

In Part III, I discuss the Internet Explorer Administration Kit, the applications that you will learn to use to deploy the Internet Explorer suite. You will learn about licensing the products, how to get them, and what to do with them once you are ready to deploy your browser.

Once I have covered the basics, I walk through all of the configuration options you have for the Wizards and talk in depth about the tool you will use to maintain the browser configuration, the IEAK Profile Manager. You will learn about how to deploy the browser using a variety of methods, ways to maintain your configuration, and other means to manage your browser configurations.

Finally, I cover the tool you will use to build dial-up configurations for your users, the Connection Manager Administration Kit. Using this tool, you will custom configure proxy settings, phone books, protocols, realms, and other options for your dial-up users.

Part IV: Tying It All Together

In Part IV, I cover planning your installation in detail and point out things you need to think about when deriving your configuration options. Also covered are lessons learned from engineers who have deployed the software and also taken the exam.

I then walk you through a sample deployment of Internet Explorer from soup to nuts. Using the tools that you have learned about up to this point, we will undertake a sample implementation of Internet Explorer.

Part IV concludes with a chapter on troubleshooting the various pieces of the suite and common issues that have come up concerning deployments, and also Microsoft's lessons learned.

Resources

The Resources section at the back of the book contains a wealth of information. In addition to a detailed glossary and thorough index, you'll find exam preparation tips, answers to chapter Instant Assessment questions and labs, a Mini-Lab Manual that features all of the labs in the book, and a description of the CD-ROM contents. Appendix A contains the exam objectives for the IEAK 5 exam, and includes a detailed Exam Objectives Cross-Reference Chart for study purposes.

CD-ROM

The accompanying CD-ROM contains the following materials:

- BeachFront Quizzer exam simulation software
- An electronic version of this book in Adobe's Acrobat format
- Adobe Acrobat Reader
- Microsoft Internet Explorer 5.0
- *Micro House Technical Library* (evaluation copy)

How to Use This Book

This book can be used either by individuals working independently or by groups in a formal classroom setting. For best results (and, of course, the only acceptable results are passing scores on the MCSE exam), I recommend the following plan of attack as you use this book: First, read the chapter and the Key Point Summary at the end. Use this summary to see if you've really got the key concepts under your belt. If you don't, go back and reread the section(s) you're not clear on. Then do *all* of the Instant Assessment questions at the end of the chapter. Finally, *do* the Hands-on Labs.

Don't be afraid to go beyond the confines of the labs once you feel like you understand the basic concepts in each chapter. Remember, the important thing is to master the tasks that will be tested on the exams. Your testing experience will be much more pleasant if you have the confidence that comes from practice working the IEAK. You will be amazed at how much you can learn from making mistakes.

The flow of the book was carefully designed to take you from simple concepts in the beginning to advanced concepts and techniques at the end. Most of the labs can be done out of order, but your study time will be a little less complicated if you work through the chapters and the labs in sequential order.

After you've completed your study of the chapters and reviewed the questions and labs in the book, use the BeachFront Quizzer product on the CD-ROM to take the practice tests. Many of the Instant Assessment questions mimic some of the questions for other exams, but the practice tests will help familiarize you with the type of exam questions you'll face when you take the real exams. They will also help you identify weak areas that need more work.

The important thing to remember about practice tests is that they *resemble* the exam, but they are not exact copies of it. I have found from my own studies that it is more important to know *why* the answer is correct than to know the answer itself, especially on practice exams. That means that if you can answer all the questions in the Instant Assessment and the practice exams without even a single guess, you are probably ready to take the test.

If you are the least bit unsure about an answer, go back and study the related sections. Appendix A contains a table that maps the objectives on the exam to the chapters and sections in this book. Use that table to correlate the objectives listed in the practice exam with the appropriate part of the book, then read the entire section before you try to take the practice exam again.

Prerequisites

This book is a mix of basic information and advanced concepts, but my explanations depend on your having some experience. In order to get the most out of this book, at a minimum, you should have these prerequisites.

- Networking knowledge or experience equal to the scope required to pass the Networking Essentials exam (70-058).
- Experience using Windows 95, 98, or NT.

    If you meet these prerequisites, you're ready to begin this book.

Determining What You Should Study

Your individual certification goals ultimately determine which parts of this book you should study. Whether you want to pass the Microsoft Certified Professional Internet Explorer 5 Administration Kit exam or you just want to develop a comprehensive working knowledge of how to administer Internet Explorer 5 and its components using the Administration Kit, I recommend you study, in sequential order, the entire book.

ICONS USED IN THIS BOOK

Several different icons used throughout this book draw your attention to matters that deserve a closer look:

 **This icon points you to another place in this book (or to another resource) for more coverage on a given topic. It may point you back to a previous chapter where important material has already been covered, or it may point you ahead to let you know that a concept will be covered in more detail later.**

 Be careful here! This icon points out information that can save you a lot of grief. It's often easier to prevent tragedy than to fix it afterwards.

 This icon identifies important advice specifically for those studying to pass the IEAK exam.

I know this will be hard for you to believe, but sometimes things work differently in the real world than books or software documentation say they do. This icon draws your attention to the author's real-world experiences, which will hopefully help you on the job, if not on the Microsoft Certified Professional exams.

 This icon points out an interesting or helpful fact, or some other comment that deserves emphasis.

 Here's a little piece of friendly advice, or a shortcut, or a bit of personal experience that might be of use to you.

That should be enough to get you started. With a lot of study, some adventurous exploration of the IEAK, and some prematurely gray hairs, you should be ready for the exam. Good luck on your way to becoming an MCSE!

ACKNOWLEDGMENTS

There are a lot of people to thank for this book, first of all Jennifer Humphreville-Fusilero, who worked closely with me to get this project over with. Jennifer cut me a lot of slack on this difficult book while I had a lot of things going on. Thanks to Bob MacSweeney, one of the best editors I have ever worked with. Bob edited the first parts of the book and Brian MacDonald and Chandani Thapa joined the project to bring everything together. Thanks also to Michael Kimes, the Technical Editor who provided some great insights on the subject. Thanks to Lenair Ballard who helped throw some of the developer's perspective into the book. Finally, thanks a million to my best friend and wife Susan, who was very patient while I dedicated a lot of my time to writing this book.

CONTENTS AT A GLANCE

Contents

The Overview

Here you are, ready to study for the Internet Explorer 5.0 exam. The book is broken down in four parts to help you understand the complexities of the Internet Explorer suite of software and the Internet Explorer Administration Kit (IEAK). Part I covers the applications within the Internet Explorer suite. In this part, we are going to talk about the basics of the Internet Explorer browser, the browser's capabilities, and technologies behind the scenes. We will then move on to the electronic mail client, Outlook Express, and discuss the basics of e-mail and how to configure the client.

We will proceed to talk about Data Conferencing using Microsoft NetMeeting. We will talk about how you can bring real-time collaboration to the desktop using this powerful tool. We will then conclude Part I with a discussion of Microsoft Windows Media Technologies using Microsoft Media Player 6. You will cover the configurations and other important information about sound and video technologies using the Media Player tool.

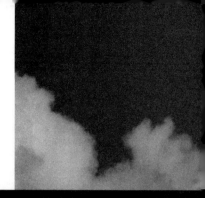

Internet Explorer

1

About Chapter 1

Microsoft's Internet Explorer has undergone several major upgrades in the last few years to evolve as one of the most powerful development platforms in the market today. Since the introduction of Internet Explorer 4, Microsoft's Web browser has become an integral part of the Windows Operating System platform.

The features of the browser will become very important when you have to bring all of your lessons together to utilize the Internet Explorer Administration Kit (IEAK), the tool you will use to deploy your customized version of Internet Explorer 5. The IEAK enables you to customize the Internet Explorer browser and all of the applications accompanying the suite when you deploy the software to your enterprise. The Internet Explorer platform is very flexible and allows you to customize the interfaces, options, and other configuration information with IEAK to maximize the deployment of the software. Before you can get into the IEAK and its features, you need to gain a clear understanding of the software, how it works, and the configuration options that you have available to work with, which is the purpose of Part I.

In Chapter 1, we are going to talk about the features of the Internet Explorer browser and ways that the Internet Explorer browser can be best utilized by your users. We will talk about the interface, technologies, and other important features that you should be aware of as an Internet professional. While studying to take the Internet Explorer 5 exam, keep in mind any specific points made by the Exam Preparation Pointer. These references in the book are important because they point to specific exam objectives that you must master in order to pass the exam.

PLATFORMS

The Internet Explorer browser is designed to run on a multitude of operating system platforms. This integration enables the browser and the browser's associated development tools to be utilized in a variety of different scenarios. Sun Solaris, for example, is a widely utilized UNIX platform for high-end computing environments. Microsoft has made the Internet Explorer browser available to the following operating systems for end users:

- Windows 95

- Windows 98

- Windows 3.1, 3.11

- Windows NT 3.51

- Windows NT 4.0

- Sun Solaris 2.5.1 and 2.6

- HP-UX

- Mac OS 7.1 and above (this is for the current Internet Explorer 4.5 version; Internet Explorer 5 should be released shortly with the same requirement)

You are probably asking yourself, "Why do I care about other platforms; everyone runs 95 or NT." In most environments, this is a true statement. Sooner or later, however, if you haven't already, you are going to be exposed to situations where other tools are the best or only choice due to the customer's requirements. As a well-rounded professional, it is only prudent that we know what is going on in other environments.

The most important idea you should take away from this section is that Internet Explorer's code base runs on platforms other than Windows. This is important to remember as the target audience of this Microsoft application has a more broad base than most other Microsoft applications. The ability to deploy the browser to your UNIX and MAC communities allows you to standardize your browsing platform across your network. This enables content developers to write code for Web applications and Web sites to one interface instead of multiple interfaces.

Table 1-1 denotes the hardware requirements to run Internet Explorer 5.

TABLE 1-1 INTERNET EXPLORER 5 HARDWARE REQUIREMENTS				
PLATFORM	*VERSION*	*DISK SPACE REQUIRED*	*MEMORY REQUIRED*	*PROCESSOR REQUIRED*
Windows 95/98	95 OSR1	45MB minimum	16MB	486DX/66
Windows NT 4.0	NT4 w/ Service Pack 3	45MB minimum	32MB	486DX/66
Windows 3.1 for Workgroups	3.1, 3.11	45MB prior	16MB	486DX/66
Windows NT 3.51	3.51	45MB prior	32MB	486DX/66
Macintosh	7.1 and above	45MB	16MB	68030

exam preparation pointer **Table 1-1 is very important to know for the exam. Also, the current version of Internet Explorer for the Mac is 4.5. Version 5.0 is under development at the time of this writing. Version 4.5 is what you will need to know for Mac questions on the exam.**

THE INTERNET EXPLORER INTERFACE

The interface of Internet Explorer has not changed much since Internet Explorer 4, as you can see in Figure 1-1.

The browser buttons are very similar to that of the Internet Explorer 4 interface. The big changes to the browser are under the cover and in the accompanying applications to Internet Explorer.

Internet Explorer 5 is more than just a browser. It is also a suite of applications that have intricate "hooks" to each other in functionality and performance. For example, you can launch Outlook Express right from the Internet Explorer browser by clicking the Mail button. Functions are also related such that you can double-click a Web link in an e-mail message and launch the Internet Explorer browser.

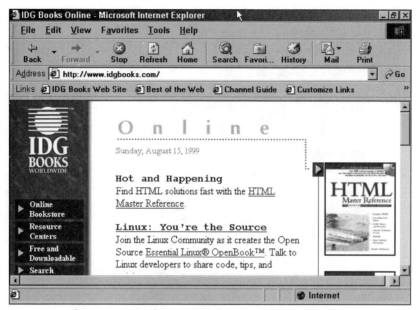

FIGURE 1-1   The Internet Explorer 5 interface

The suite of applications that can be installed with Internet Explorer is as follows:

o Microsoft Outlook Express 5 — E-mail client

o Windows Media Player — Sound and video player

o Microsoft NetMeeting — Videoconferencing software

o Microsoft Front Page Express — HTML (Hypertext Markup Language) editor

o Microsoft Chat — Online chat client

History Bar

You can easily return to sites you visited previously by using the History bar. Figure 1-2 shows the History bar and menu in Internet Explorer 5.

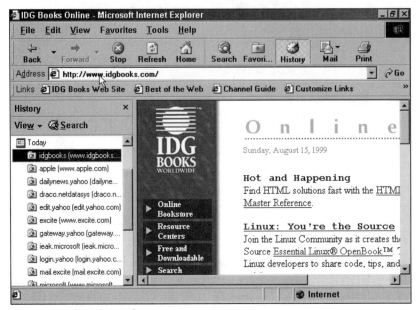

FIGURE 1-2 The History bar

The History bar actually views data stored in your C:\Windows\History folder, where it is categorized by the day, week, and month for easy reference. You can configure the amount of days to retain pages in your history by selecting the Tools ⇨ Internet Options ⇨ General Page.

 tip **Don't confuse the History folder with your cache. The History folder merely records the URLs that you visited and are not the actual files themselves.**

Favorites Bar

Many Web sites exist out there, and we all have our favorites. The Favorites bar enables you to save the URL to your favorite Web site to return to the site. You can also use the Favorites bar to point to a local HTML document. Figure 1-3 shows the Favorites bar.

A lot of organizations are using the Favorites bar to point to intranet sites and local Web applications used by their employees. Usually, these Web servers are maintained within the company's internal network and have various selections such as a company directory, human resources information, and other Web applications. For example, the Favorites bar could be used to point your users to another organization's extranet. Extranets are used by organizations that want to share information, and are usually secured so that only permitted domains or users can view information on the Internet. Various methods are used to secure these sites, such as encryption, certificates, special user IDs, passwords, and many others. Extranets allow companies, such as an auto parts chain, to share information with suppliers, such as an auto parts wholesaler, to improve communication and marketing.

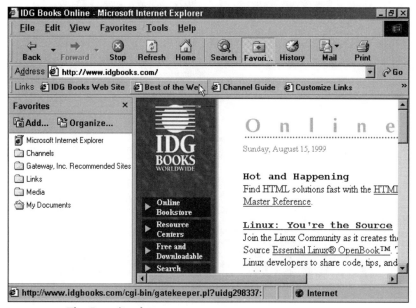

FIGURE 1-3 The Favorites bar

Search Bar

The Search bar is a pre-configured pointer to a search site. Search sites contain powerful Web site indexing engines that enable you to find information. You can configure the Search bar for any search site you find the most useful.

To use the Search bar, click the Search button on the toolbar. Once the Search bar is displayed, click on the customize option to launch the search assistant. The search assistant will enable you to search more than one search site for your criteria. While this is not covered on the exam, this is something good to know.

Figure 1-4 shows the Search bar and demonstrates the usefulness of the Search tools.

 tip **Did you know that you can search for information directly from the URL field? Instead of typing** `www.excite.com`, **just type GO EXCITE; it's a real time saver.**

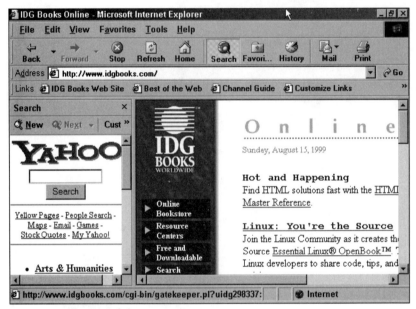

FIGURE 1-4 The Search bar

The Links Bar

Do you or your users have a site or Web location that you use frequently? The Links Bar enables you to place frequently used Web sites right on the Internet Explorer interface. These references are merely Internet shortcuts that point to a destination of your choice. You can add a link by dragging a link from the desktop to the Links bar, for example. You can create icons on your desktop for the Web by right-clicking the desktop, and selecting New ⇨ Shortcut. In the shortcut, specify the Web location for your link, such as `http://www.idgbooks.com`.

These links are very helpful where frequent navigation is a part of your work. In Figure 1-5, we use the IDG Books link to go to the IDG Books Web site.

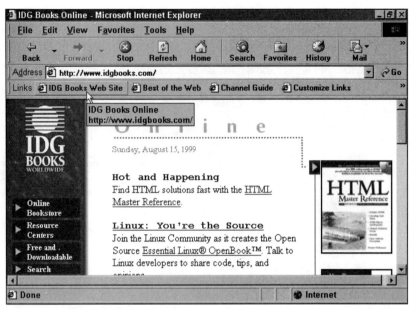

FIGURE 1-5 The Links bar

Radio Stations Bar

Do you surf while listening to the radio? The new Radio Stations bar enables you to select a radio station to listen to over the Internet. You can select the stations as shown in Figure 1-6 and listen to live radio content over the Internet. To navigate to the channel guide, click on Radio Stations, and Radio Channel Guide.

in the
real world

This is a feature that you may want to disable during your IEAK deployment. If a lot of your users decide to use this feature on a regular basis, it may use a substantial amount of bandwidth. To find out how much bandwidth this uses on your network, check out the Network Monitor tool that I cover in Chapter 13. Multiply the throughput used while you are using the radio feature times the number of users in your organization. Then, estimate that ten to fifteen percent of users will use this on a regular basis as your guide.

It is important to remember that radio broadcasts are by nature, live audio streams over the Internet, thus you must be connected to the Internet in order to utilize this feature.

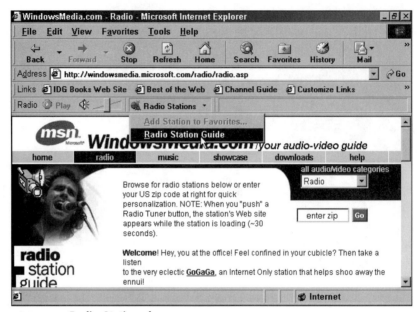

FIGURE 1-6   Radio Stations bar

OFFLINE BROWSING

An increasing number of users are connecting to the Internet, affecting download times and performance on the Internet, especially during the workday. Internet Explorer 5 enables offline browsing which, when enabled, allows the user to view Web information and HTML documents when the user is not connected to the Internet. While online, the user browses the information that he or she wants to view offline. When the user visits a site, the graphics and HTML content are cached locally on the user's hard drive. Then, when the user wishes to view the content offline, the information is already on the user's computer. The purpose of the feature is to view the content only. It is not meant for user input or changes to the content itself.

A new service has been added to Internet Explorer 5 called the Windows Synchronization Manager, which adds even more functionality to offline browsing. The Synchronization Manager enables you to select Web content on your favorite Web sites and synchronize the files on the site with the files you have in your cache. This feature enables you to look at the content when you are not connected to the Internet. This is a great feature for mobile users that only connect for a few minutes a day, but, would like to look at Web sites, intranet sites, and extranet sites while traveling or when Internet access in not available.

exam preparation pointer

This feature only applies to static content, such as HTML. Dynamic HTML, streaming video, and audio cannot be synchronized as the body of the code changes frequently based on user input. You may be asked about this on the exam.

In addition to synchronizing files, the user can also use this feature to send a Web page to another user in an e-mail message attachment. This handy feature enables the user to send the body of the page in its entirety, unlike previously where the user would have to cut and paste the text into the message after extensive editing.

Depending on the Internet bandwidth your organization has available during the day, you may want to consider using this feature as a part of an overall bandwidth utilization strategy. In this manner, you can effectively utilize all of the tools available to ensure that your users have access to the information they need more effectively.

concept link

We will cover the Synchronization Manager in more detail in Chapter 7.

CONNECTION ENHANCEMENTS

Internet Explorer 5 has included a major enhancement to connectivity for the browser. The browser has built-in code to now detect the type of connection that you are currently using. For those of us who are laptop users, this will be a huge timesaver. This feature also applies to proxy servers. You can build specific connections with corresponding Proxy settings. This feature enables you to not have to change Proxy settings for different environments dependent on your personal preferences. This can also dramatically reduce the support required for your laptop users as well.

AUTO-COMPLETE

Auto-complete was a feature introduced in Internet Explorer 4, but it deserves mention once again in Internet Explorer 5. Auto-complete enables the browser to type in information for you such as Web site addresses, user names, passwords, and other data entry tasks. Internet Explorer remembers the addresses that you have previously visited, as well as other features, such as user names and the like. This feature, shown in Figure 1-7, enables you to type in only part of the Web site name and still be able to navigate to the site. You can disable this feature with the Internet Explorer Administration Kit, which is discussed in Chapter 7. You can also disable it manually through the Tools ➪ Internet Options ➪ Advanced function.

tip **As a developer, you can control the caching of user names and passwords to control the security of your Web site. Check on the Microsoft Site Builder network for more information and search on the "no-cache HTML tag."**

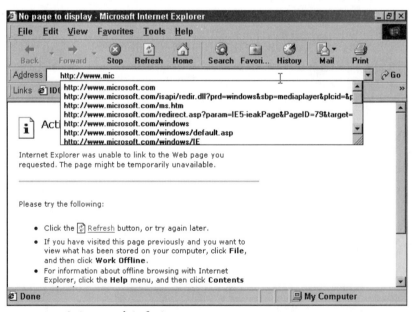

FIGURE 1-7 Auto-complete feature

WEB FOLDERS DRAG-AND-DROP

How many times have you wished for a single interface for publishing, File Transfer Protocol (FTP), and Web tasks? Internet Explorer 5 has answered your requests and has integrated these features into a single interface. Now, you can FTP files from a Web server down to your workstation and vice versa without leaving the Internet Explorer 5 interface. This feature, know as webDAV (Web Distributing Authoring and Versioning), is a standards-based enhancement that allows this functionality to browsers and Web servers that support this standard.

Standards-based enhancements are updates to software provided by the vendors that comply with agreed-on, industry standards, such as RFCs (Requests for Comments) or by the W3 consortium. The consortium meets to discuss new technologies relating to the Web and provide agreed-on strategies for the development and deployment of new technologies.

Figure 1-8 is an example of the drag-and-drop feature. I am accessing one of my company's FTP servers and am preparing to FTP down a directory.

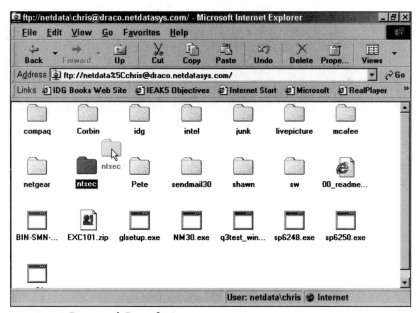

FIGURE 1-8 Drag-and-Drop feature

As you can see in the figure, I can choose the directory that I am going to copy the files to on my local hard drive just as if I were logged into a local server or my own hard drive. This feature truly integrates the Web and the workstation into a single, navigable interface.

HELPFUL ERROR MESSAGES

Let's face it, error messages are annoying. But, the reality of it is that most of the error messages that we see point to user errors. In the past, errors seen in applications, such as a browser, gave explanations that only the developer or the most hardcore of geeks could possibly understand. Microsoft heard these complaints and created a smoother interface to ease our frustration in Internet Explorer 5. Error messages tell you what the error was and also give helpful hints on what the possible problem could be. For example, the famous white screen and bell yelling at you saying the server is not available has been replaced with a kinder, gentler error message, as shown in Figure 1-9.

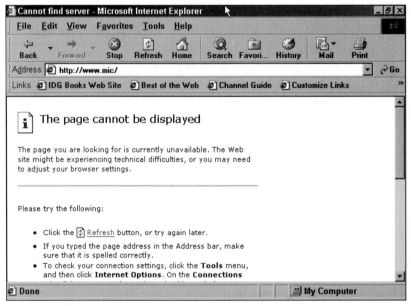

FIGURE 1-9 New error message

MULTI-LANGUAGE SUPPORT

Internet Explorer 5 includes support for over 26 languages. Internet Web sites viewed though the browser can be viewed using the language the page was written in. In most cases, the page developer will tag the page with the language and character set that the page was authored in. In the event that the page was not tagged or was improperly tagged, Internet Explorer will detect this problem and correct it before presenting the content to the user.

 tip **Downloading language packs from Microsoft's Web site can perform updates to Internet Explorer's languages. For more information, check out Internet Explorer's home page at** `http://www.microsoft.com/windows/IE/`.

START MENU AND TASKBAR UPDATES

The Start menu now hosts the Favorites folder for quick access to your favorite and frequently used Web sites. The Favorites folder in the Start menu is the same one you see in Internet Explorer. Figure 1-10 shows the new look of the Start menu.

FIGURE 1-10 The new Start menu

As you can see, a new log off option (for Windows 95) has been added to enable you to log off from your local area network. Several new options have been added to the Find menu of the Start menu, shown in Figure 1-11.

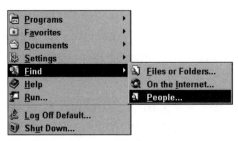

FIGURE 1-11 The new Find menu

New features include a Lightweight Directory Access Protocol (LDAP) people finder on the People option. The LDAP protocol enables you to use the Find On the Internet option to access a search site to look for information on the Web. Examples of sites that rely of the use of LDAP are `bigfoot.com`, `four11.com`, and `switchboard.com`.

The taskbar, shown in Figure 1-12, has been improved with some new features, such as:

o Quick Launch bar

o Address bar

o Desktop bar

o Quick Links bar

FIGURE 1-12 The new taskbar

Now, let's look at some of these new features in more detail.

Quick Launch

The icons for a user's most commonly used applications can be dragged onto the Quick Launch bar. When a user is accessing an application and needs to run another application, such as Internet Explorer, the user can merely click the Quick Launch icon to open the application. This saves time by avoiding the need to task-switch using Alt+Tab and locate the application on the desktop or Start menu. This feature helps clean up the desktop and lets the user be more productive. Figure 1-12 shows some quick launch icons, such as Internet Explorer, Outlook Express, and QuickTime for Windows.

Address Bar

The Address bar, shown in Figure 1-13, enables the user to enter a URL and auto-open Internet Explorer to the specified URL address. It performs the same function as the Address window in the Internet Explorer browser. This is a time-saving step for users because they don't have to wait for the browser to launch before they enter the URL.

 tip **You can also run programs from the Address bar in the same manner that you do from the Start ⇨ Run feature. In the Address bar, type the location and filename to launch the application, such as** `C:\windows\explorer.exe`.

FIGURE 1-13 The Address bar

Desktop Bar

The Desktop bar shows all of the desktop icons on the toolbar. This feature enables users to access all the applications on the desktop from the taskbar. This is similar to Quick Launch in that users can run other desktop applications without exiting or minimizing the currently open application. You can enable the Desktop bar by right-clicking on the taskbar, and then selecting View.

concept link

You can enable the Desktop bar in the IEAK as well. This is discussed in Chapter 7.

The Desktop bar is shown in Figure 1-14.

FIGURE 1-14 The Desktop bar

Quick Links

The Quick Links feature enables the user to add frequently used links to the
taskbar for quick access. Quick Links can provide access to regularly visited Web
sites, such as Internet or intranet Web sites. Quick Links enables you to quickly
navigate to Web-based services, much in the way icons enable you to navigate to
an application. You can add links to the Links bar by dragging a desktop link onto
the Quick Links bar. Figure 1-15 shows the Quick Links bar.

FIGURE 1-15 The new Quick Links bar

Single Explorer

The introduction of Internet Explorer to the operating system also brings with it a
feature called Single Explorer. The Windows Explorer interface has merged with
the Internet Explorer interface to provide a similar interface for user navigation.
From the Internet Explorer browser, the user can access local or network drives by
typing the path into the URL window of the browser. In Windows Explorer, the
user can also navigate to Web sites, intranet sites, or other Web-based services.
This, combined with the other applications in the Internet Explorer suite, provides
a similar interface for navigation, which enables the user to work more efficiently.

Figure 1-16 shows my local machine while I am getting ready to navigate to
the Web.

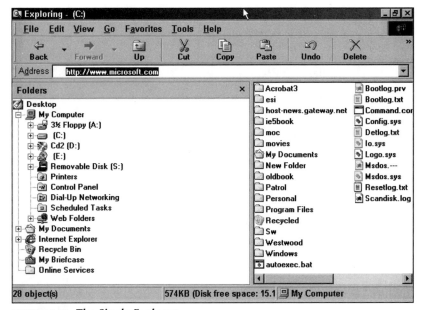

FIGURE 1-16   The Single Explorer

KEY POINT SUMMARY

In this chapter, we covered the enhancements and many new features of the Internet Explorer 5 browser. We talked about the new connectivity features, navigation features, and the visual enhancements that will enable your users to use the Web to the fullest.

- The Internet Explorer browser is designed to run on a multitude of operating system platforms. This integration enables the browser and the browser's associated development tools to be utilized in a variety of different scenarios.

- The most important feature described in this section is that Internet Explorer's code base runs on other platforms than Windows. This enables content developers to write code for Web applications and Web sites to one interface instead of multiple interfaces.

- Internet Explorer is more than just a browser. The suite of applications that can be installed with Internet Explorer are Microsoft Outlook Express 5, Windows Media Player, Microsoft NetMeeting, Microsoft FrontPage Express, and Microsoft Chat.

- The History bar lets you view data stored in your `C:\Windows\History folder`, where it is categorized by day, week, and month for easy reference.

- The Favorites bar enables you to save the URL to your favorite Web site to return to the site. You can also use the Favorites bar to point to a local HTML document.

- The Search bar is a pre-configured pointer to a search site. Search sites contain powerful Web site indexing engines that enable you to find information, like `yahoo.com` or `excite.com` for example. You can configure the Search bar for any search site you find the most useful.

- The Links bar enables you to place frequently used Web sites right on the Internet Explorer interface. These references are merely Internet shortcuts that point to a destination of your choice.

- Internet Explorer 5 enables offline browsing which, when enabled, allows the user to view Web information and HTML documents when the user is not connected to the Internet.

- The browser has built-in code to detect the type of connection that is currently in use.

- You can FTP files from a Web server down to your workstation and vice versa without leaving the Internet Explorer 5 interface. This feature, known as webDAV (Web Distributing Authoring and Versioning), is a standards-based enhancement that allows this functionality to browsers and Web servers that support this standard.

APPLYING WHAT YOU'VE LEARNED

This section is an opportunity to use what you've learned in this chapter. The Instant Assessment questions here will help you practice for the exam.

Instant Assessment

1. The _____ bar enables you to set up pointers to your most commonly used Web sites.

    A. Favorites

    B. Radio

    C. History

    D. Links

2. _____ is a new feature that enables you to view Web content while not connected to the Internet.

    A. The Address bar

    B. Connection Wizard

    C. Offline browsing

    D. Quick Links

3. You can only use one language at a time with Internet Explorer 5.

    A. True

    B. False

4. The minimum disk space available to install Internet Explorer on SCO Unix is:

    A. 45MB

    B. 40MB

    C. 50MB

    D. None of the above

5. The minimum processor speed to run Internet Explorer 5 is a:

    A. 486SX/66

    B. 486DX/100

    C. 386 w/ math co-processor

    D. 486DX/66

6. Which application is included with Internet Explorer 5 as the e-mail client?

A. Microsoft NetShow

B. Internet Mail and News

C. Microsoft Outlook

D. Microsoft Outlook Express

7. WebDAV is an acronym that describes:

A. an annual Web conference for Microsoft professionals.

B. an Internet Explorer navigation bar.

C. standards design that enables drag-and-drop in the browser.

D. navigational help within the browser.

8. Offline browsing also offers the capability to use the radio features of Internet Explorer 5.

A. True

B. False

9. A user calls you and asks what tool the user should use to edit an HTML document without installing another tool. The user has a full installation of Internet Explorer 5. Which tool would you recommend?

A. Microsoft Office 4.0

B. Microsoft FrontPage Express

C. Microsoft FrontPage

D. Microsoft Page Editor

10. To properly develop a Web page in a language, the developer should insert a _____ to specify the language that the page was written in to ensure that the user has the correct character set.

A. return code

B. language pack

C. insertion string

D. tag

11. You can enter the URL of an Internet site in the Windows File Explorer
(`explorer.exe`) and navigate directly to the site if Internet Explorer 5 is
installed.

    A. True

    B. False

12. A user logs into two different networks that have completely different proxy
settings. The user asks for your advice in configuring these settings in
Internet Explorer 5. What is the best answer you could give the user?

    A. Make the settings changes every time the user logs in.

    B. Write the user a `.reg` file to click on when logging in.

    C. This feature is already included in Internet Explorer 5.

    D. Tell the user not to do this.

13. The other day, you found a great Web site for troubleshooting Internet
Explorer, but you cannot remember that address. Where could you find
this information quickly?

    A. At `msn.com`

    B. In your History folder

    C. Favorites bar

    D. Windows Explorer

14. The Quick Launch feature enables you to navigate to frequently used
Web sites.

    A. True

    B. False

15. The _____ allows you to enter a URL and automatically launch
Internet Explorer.

    A. Quick Links

    B. Search bar

    C. Address bar

    D. Multi-language support

16. The _____ protocol enables you to find people on the Internet using sites that supports this feature.

A. LDAP

B. POP3

C. IMAP

D. IPX/SPX

17. If you wanted to author a Web site designed to share information with your business partners regarding inventory, support, and other services generally not available to the public, you would create a/an _____ site.

A. intranet

B. Internet

C. extranet

D. publicnet

18. If you wanted to listen to a `.wav` file that contained a favorite song, you would use the _____, which is included in Internet Explorer 5.

A. Microsoft NetShow

B. Windows Media Player

C. Outlook Express

D. Internet Explorer Browser

19. Under Windows 3.0, you must have at least 45MB of free disk space to run Internet Explorer 5.0.

A. True

B. False

20. You can use the Favorites feature in Internet Explorer 5 to point to a local intranet site even if you are not connected to the Internet.

A. True

B. False

Outlook Express 5

About Chapter 2

In Chapter 2, we are going to cover the Outlook Express 5 mail and news client included in Internet Explorer 5. We will cover the Outlook Express 5 mail client from basics to advanced configurations to ensure that you have an expert level of configuration knowledge for the Outlook Express 5 application. This chapter is meant to enable you to move forward into IEAK with the required information to configure and deploy the Outlook Express 5 mail client in most scenarios. First, let's start out with some mail basics.

OUTLOOK EXPRESS OVERVIEW

The Internet Explorer 5 suite of software comes complete with a next-generation electronic mail and news client called Microsoft Outlook Express 5. Outlook Express 5 is the successor to Outlook Express 4.0, which was included in Internet Explorer 4, and Microsoft Mail and News, which was included in Internet Explorer 3.

E-mail is one of the most widely used features of the Internet and of networking in general. Similar to network protocols, high-level mail protocols have been established for e-mail communication through various Requests for Comments (RFCs). Outlook Express 5 includes configurations for the following mail and news protocols:

o *SMTP (Simple Mail Transport Protocol).* SMTP is the de facto standard for sending e-mail on the Internet.

o *POP3 (Post Office Protocol 3).* POP3 is the standard for receiving e-mail on the Internet. Messages are stored on a POP server and remain on the server until downloaded by a mail client. Options for downloading include downloading and deleting messages or leaving messages on the server.

o *IMAP (Internet Mail Access Protocol).* IMAP is the successor to POP3. IMAP offers more efficient mail access capabilities that enable a user to view the message's header, instead of downloading the entire message as POP mail does. This handy feature enables more efficient mail management so the messages the user does not want to view can be deleted on the server. The POP protocol process would have been to download all messages and then delete the messages the user did not want from the user's mail file. Using IMAP, the user can view and use mail services from the home, office, or any other remote location.

- *NNTP (Network News Transport Protocol).* NNTP is the standard for posting and reviewing messages from a news server, such as Usenet. News servers store news postings by individuals; these postings are stored in a hierarchically based database referenced by topic, such as `microsoft.public.inetexplorer.ie4.setup`. This is an example of a newsgroup. In Outlook Express, you can subscribe to a newsgroup by using syntax such as this to specify the topic that you would like to join. To add a newsgroup, select the control key, hold it down, and hit the W key. This will bring up the dialog to edit and add newsgroup subscriptions to Outlook Express.

- *LDAP (Lightweight Directory Access Protocol).* LDAP support is included in Outlook Express 5 for locating people, places, and things. Many commercial organizations have set up LDAP-based servers that contain a variety of searchable data, such as e-mail addresses, names, and organizations. Outlook Express 5 uses the LDAP functions of these servers to locate data specified by the user.

- *HTML (Hypertext Markup Language) Mail.* HTML is the standard programming language used on the Internet. Outlook Express 5 supports the use of HTML mail messages both for the body of the text and for the stationery. You can use any HTML editor to create an HTML message and use Outlook Express 5 to send the message. You can also use Outlook Express 5 itself to create text-based HTML messages.

You need to gain an understanding of these protocols to both pass the exam and also to do your job if you work with this software on a daily basis. Get familiar with the explanations here. Now that we have talked about some of the protocols, let's get into the nitty-gritty on the Outlook Express 5 Mail Client.

THE OUTLOOK EXPRESS 5 MAIL CLIENT

As you can see in Figure 2-1, Outlook Express 5 has an interface similar to that of Internet Explorer. The familiar interface enables easy navigation of the mail client for the end user.

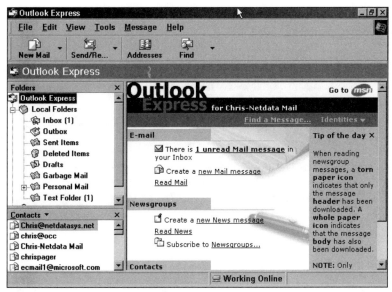

FIGURE 2-1   The Outlook Express interface

As you have probably learned as an IT professional, the more familiar you can make things for the end user, the fewer headaches you will have to deal with later on. Let's talk about the features of the interface in more detail.

tip   **Unlike Outlook Express's parent application, Microsoft Outlook 2000, Outlook Express still retains the naming convention of older versions of Outlook Express. Outlook Express is launched by select-**
ing msimn.exe **located in the** C:\Program Files\Outlook Express **directory. Outlook 2000, 98, and 97 are launched by selecting the** outlook.exe **file.**

New Mail

The New Mail option enables you to start or create a new mail message to send to another party. Click on the new mail button to create a message. As you will see, the new message windows will open as shown in Figure 2-2.

tip You can use the Ctrl-N combination as a shortcut to create a new mail message.

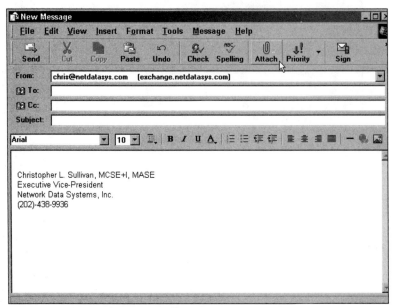

FIGURE 2-2 Composing an e-mail message

Note that the From address shows your default mailbox. You can select a mailbox to be your default mailbox when creating an e-mail message. When you select the new mail button, your default in the From line will be your default mailbox. If you want to change the From line, note the drop-down box in Figure 2-3 that shows all of the mailboxes you have currently installed on your workstation. You can select any of these mailboxes to send a message from.

 note Sending a message requires that your SMTP server is properly configured. We will cover configuring SMTP in Outlook Express later in the chapter.

As you know, you can also use HTML as stationery in mail messages. Outlook Express includes stationery for you or you can create your own. The New Mail drop-down box shows you the available stationery for you to use (Figure 2-4).

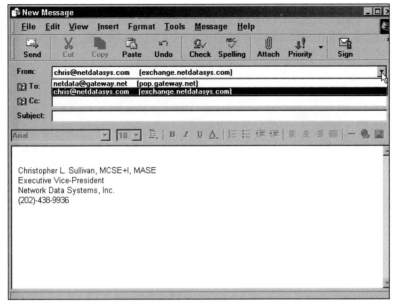

FIGURE 2-3 Changing the From line

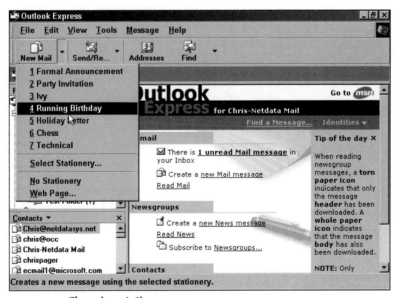

FIGURE 2-4 Choosing stationery

Sending and Receiving Mail

You can choose a variety of options in sending and receiving mail. You can perform the following actions using the Send/Receive button as shown in Figure 2-5.

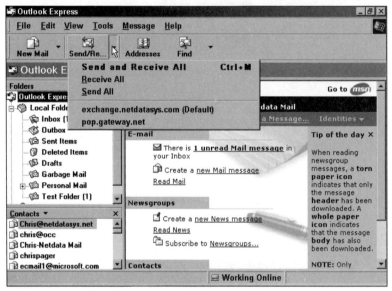

FIGURE 2-5   Send/Receive options

- *Send and Receive All.* Accesses and downloads all mail in POP accounts and sends all pending mail in the Outbox.

- *Receive All Mail.* Accesses and downloads all mail in POP accounts.

- *Send All.* Sends all pending mail in the Outbox for all accounts.

- *Send and Receive on Specific accounts.* Accesses and downloads all mail in specific POP accounts and sends all pending mail in the Outbox for a specific account.

Address Books

The Addresses button enables you to view and edit your Address Book. Your Address Book allows you to save a variety of information about friends, colleagues, and co-workers in a central location for easy retrieval. This information, shown in Figure 2-6, enables you a single point of reference for contact information for another individual.

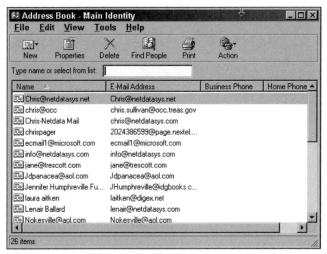

FIGURE 2-6 The Address Book

You can create new contacts, delete, and create new mail messages right from this interface. The Address Book also includes a handy feature called Find People that enables you to search the Address Book for a contact, or you can select an LDAP server on the Internet for further searching capabilities.

tip **You can launch the Address Book separately by creating a shortcut to the** wab.exe **(Windows Address Book), located in the** C:\Program Files\Outlook Express **folder. You can also convert other address books, such as Netscape mail, by choosing the** wabmig.exe **application.**

To get a better idea of the information you can store in the Address Book, highlight one of your entries or select New. There is a lot of information that you can keep on a specific contact. In addition, you can categorize the information in a variety of ways, as the following tabs demonstrate.

The Summary tab

The Summary tab enables you to grab a quick snapshot of the information contained in the Address Book. You can get the most utilized information on this tab and it is the primary tab you will use. The Summary tab is shown in Figure 2-7.

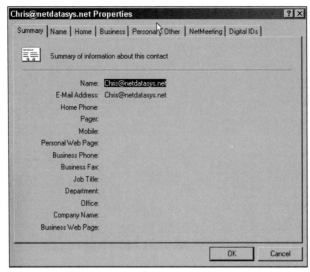

FIGURE 2-7   The Summary tab

The Name tab

The Name tab enables you to enter the user's name, the way you want their name displayed in your Address Book (Display Name), and their e-mail addresses. The most important entry on the page is the default e-mail address. This is the primary address you will use for the user in 90 percent of your mail communication with the user. The Name tab is shown in Figure 2-8.

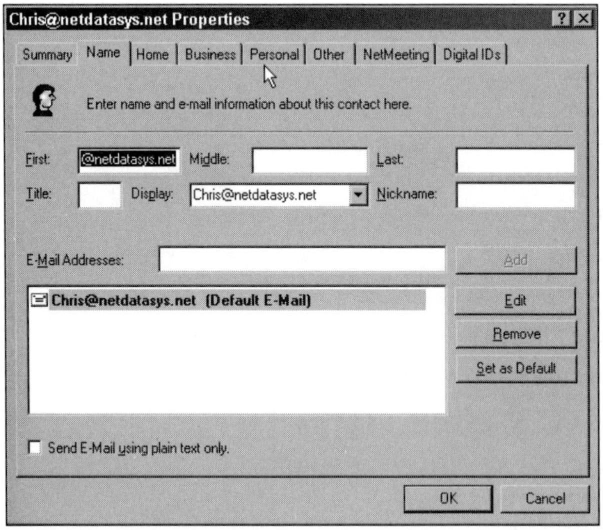

FIGURE 2-8   The Name tab

The Home tab

To access the user-specific information, double-click the user's name in the Address Book, or select the user's name with the mouse and select Properties. When the user's properties are displayed, select the Home tab. The Home tab enables you to store the user's home address, phone number, cell phone, and personal Web page information. You can also store gender and contact information such as address, phone, fax, pager, cellular phone, and a business Web site in the Address Book, as shown in Figure 2-9.

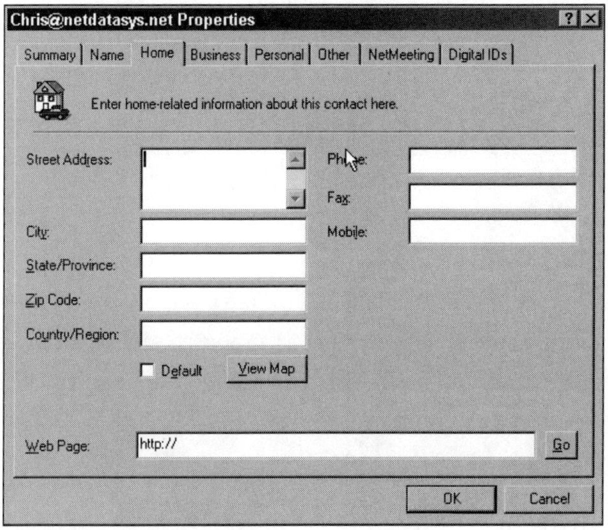

FIGURE 2-9 The Home tab

The Business tab

The Business tab enables you to store information about the user's work contact information. Take a look at Figure 2-10, there is a lot of basic information there about addresses, phone, fax, URLs, and so on. There is also one new entry that is of interest, the IP Phone. IP Phone enables you to call the user over the Internet using the Voice over TCP/IP technology. This new technology is expected to be widely introduced over the next few years and is expected to dramatically reduce the cost of long distance phone calls.

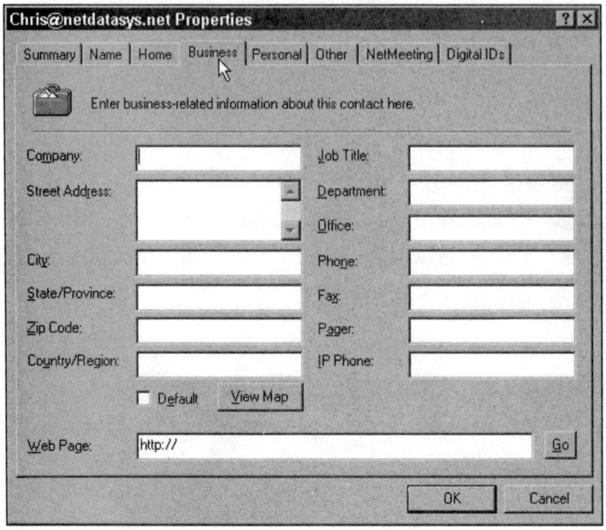

FIGURE 2-10   The Business tab

The Personal tab

For those sales folks out there, the Personal tab is a must (see Figure 2-11). You can keep information about a contact, such as a spouse's and children's names for later use. Gender, birthday, and anniversary information are also tracked here for even better, more personal communication.

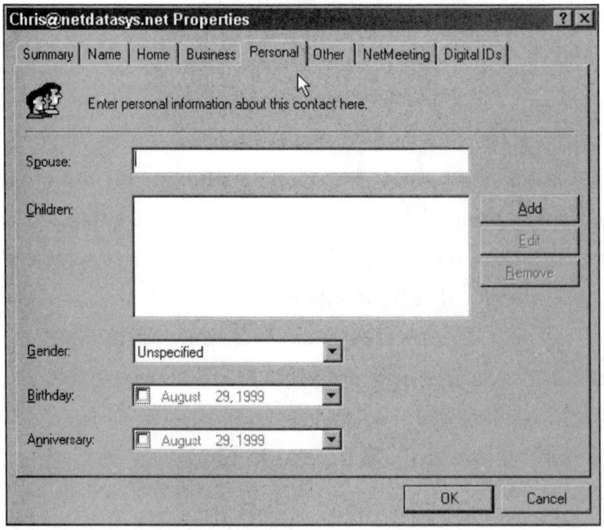

FIGURE 2-11   The Personal tab

The Other tab

You may also want to keep notes about information that is specific to that contact, and update this information frequently. You can do this in the Notes section of the Other tab, as shown in Figure 2-12.

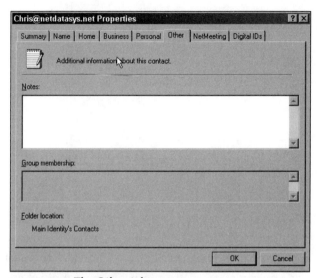

FIGURE 2-12 The Other tab

The NetMeeting tab

Do you remember when I talked about the software programs in Internet Explorer 5 being integrated with each other? The NetMeeting option in the Address Book enables you to store NetMeeting contact information for an individual so you can quickly access the individual online.

NetMeeting allows the user to collaborate with other users in real time using video, audio, and other data collaboration features, such as whiteboards. Using NetMeeting, you can connect to another user and see the user in real-time video and audio (provided the user has a camera and microphone configured).

concept link

We will talk more about NetMeeting in Chapter 3.

This is yet another option that removes a step for your users in their everyday work. Figure 2-13 shows NetMeeting contact info.

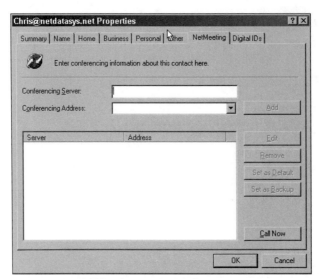

FIGURE 2-13 NetMeeting contact info

The Digital IDs tab

The Digital IDs tab in Figure 2-14 shows the digital IDs you have for various contacts in your Address Book. Prying eyes can easily intercept a standard e-mail message traveling across the Internet with a variety of products. Secure e-mail is becoming as important as securing the Web server due to the proliferation of mail forgery. "Spoofing" is when a hacker or other individual sends a mail message that appears to come from someone else. Outlook Express 5 includes support for a variety of mail security options to avoid activity like spoofing; here are a few important features to remember.

Digital IDs enable you to encrypt mail sent to another party using a technology called key encryption. The keys contain an encryption and decryption algorithm that enables secure e-mail messages to be transferred between individuals. A digital ID has three basic key functions: the public key, the private key, and the digital signature. The user sends the public key to an individual to whom the user intends to send an encrypted message. When a public key is sent, two IDs are created: one is the public key itself, and the other is the private key. The private key is used by you to decrypt responses to messages you receive from individuals to whom you have sent your public key. You designate who receives the public key, and only this recipient can use the public key.

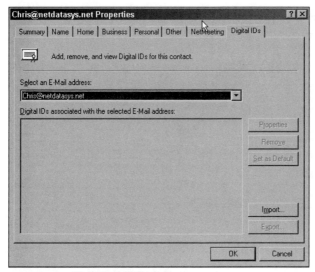

FIGURE 2-14 The Digital IDs tab

The digital signature on the key ensures that when a response is received from an encrypted message that was sent to another party, the key is authentic. This system of checks and balances ensures that the key is not forged or altered in any way. If the key is altered, an alert notifies the user of the anomaly.

For even more secure transactions, you can obtain a digital certificate from organizations such as VeriSign, Inc. The certificate ensures that you are who you say you are. The independent organization verifies your identity and provides the stamp of approval to the recipient of your message. In most cases, digital certificates are used only in commerce-based e-mail applications that involve monetary transactions. So much for the Address Book; let's get back to the Outlook Express Interface.

The Find Option

The Find option, shown in Figure 2-15, enables you to find messages, newsgroup postings, and other information retained in Outlook Express.

You can choose a variety of methods to perform your search, including LDAP searches on the Internet, local searches, and many others. The widest use of the Find option is to find specific mail messages you have received, such as in the search performed in Figure 2-16.

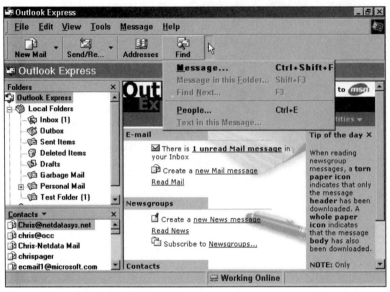

FIGURE 2-15 The Find option

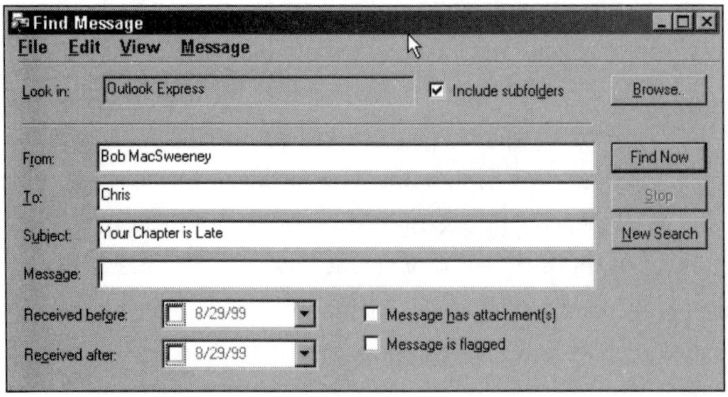

FIGURE 2-16 Finding a mail message

In Figure 2-16, I am looking for my latest nasty-gram from my editor while I was writing this book. As I am sure you will agree, using this feature is faster than going through every one of your folders looking for a mail message. Does the term "needle in a haystack" sound familiar?

The Outlook Express 5 Inbox

Read messages are in plain text, whereas unread messages are indicated by bold text. The envelope icon next to the message itself also indicates whether the mail is read or unread. The two read messages in Figure 2-17 show an open envelope, whereas the unread messages have a sealed envelope.

Mail messages always include the sender's name, subject header, and the time that the user sent the mail message. You can preview the message in the preview pane, which is located at the lower right corner of Figure 2-17.

 tip   **You can configure Outlook Express to automatically display images in the preview pane for faster editing in the Tools ➪ Options feature.**

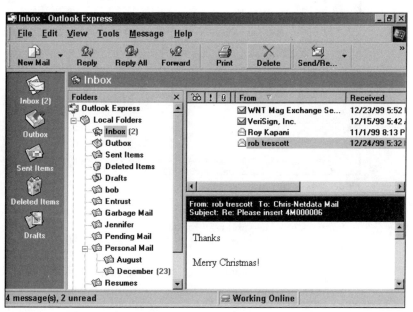

FIGURE 2-17 The preview pane

This pane enables you to preview the text within a message so you can decide whether you want to open it now or later, depending on the urgency of the message.

The Outlook Bar

The Outlook bar, shown in Figure 2-18, enables easy navigation within Outlook Express 5. The following list describes the various features of the Outlook bar in detail.

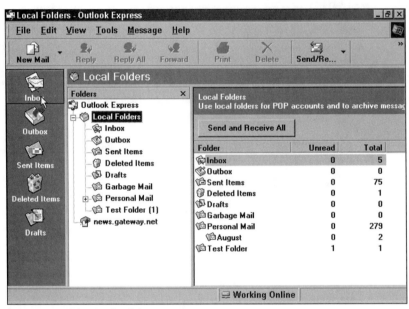

FIGURE 2-18 The Outlook bar

- *Inbox.* Stores new and read messages that have not been moved to another folder.

- *Outbox.* This folder acts as a queue for outgoing mail in case an Internet connection is not present. Mail can be composed offline and sent all at once when the user connects to the Internet.

- *Sent Items.* Outlook Express 5 can maintain copies of all of your sent e-mail in the Sent Items folder. This prevents you from having to blind copy yourself on all messages to maintain a copy of what you've sent.

- *Deleted Items.* Stores messages you delete until the folder is purged. This feature is very similar in function to the Windows 95 and Windows NT Recycle Bin.

- *Drafts.* The Drafts folder provides a place to store mail messages that are not ready to be sent yet. Some messages can be very long, and the user may want to take time to compose the message. The user can store the message in the Drafts folder until he or she completes the message. This is also a good place to store frequently sent messages, such as a list of who is out of the office on any particular day.

The remaining folders in the Outlook bar are self-explanatory and can be removed if you wish. Outlook Express 5 also enables you to "nest" directories within folders. With this feature, you can create your own folders to better organize your mail. In Figure 2-18, I have created a nested folder within my personal folder called August. Within the August folder, I have two mail messages that I am working on.

Message Rules

Junk e-mail has become one of the biggest problems for Internet service providers and their customers. Businesses, both large and small, have started using e-mail to advertise their products and services inexpensively. This mail, sometimes called "spam," comprises an estimated 40 percent of the total electronic mail traffic on the Internet today. Outlook Express 5 includes a useful feature called Message Rules that enable you to filter incoming e-mail based on the sender, size, and other information.

In Figure 2-19, I have set up a rule for any mail coming into my mailbox from `spamking@spamemall.com`. To set up a rule, select the Tools menu and then Message Rules. Once you've accessed the Message Rules, select Add to set up a new rule.

If this individual, `spamking@spamemall.com`, sends me any mail, Outlook Express 5 will automatically move the mail to a folder I have created called Garbage Mail. In addition, Outlook Express 5 will send the individual a mail message I've created, requesting that I be removed from the individual's mailing list.

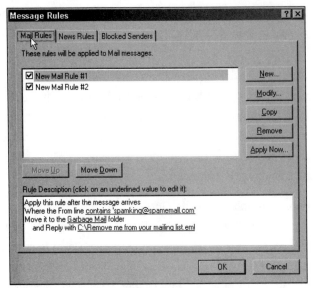

FIGURE 2-19   **Message Rules**

As you can see by my example, you can combine many of these features for quite a few actions depending on the sender's name. A wide variety of applications exist for this feature; use your imagination and you can come up with a few.

Newsgroup Rules

Newsgroups are a great source of information on a variety of subjects. Newsgroups can provide you, as an IT professional, with valuable information about issues that affect you directly in the computer industry. Like e-mail, newsgroups are also plagued by spam from individuals who are advertising products and services, or who just want to be annoying. Outlook Express 5 enables you to apply rules to your news messages to filter out unwanted mail from newsgroups to which you subscribe. Factors such as subject, originator, message age, and number of lines within the message can be used to filter news messages. Figure 2-20 shows the Newsgroup Rules option.

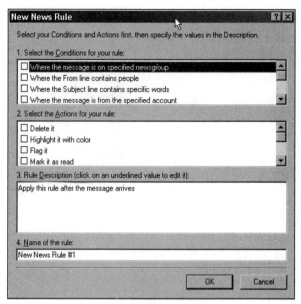

FIGURE 2-20 Newsgroup Rules option

Internet Accounts

The Internet Accounts option, located in the Tools/Accounts menu, enables you to set up multiple users in Outlook Express 5, as well as multiple e-mail accounts. In Figure 2-21, my corporate e-mail account and personal gateway.net accounts are shown. Each account can be set up with different preferences and options, including different rules in the Inbox Assistant. One of the most widely heard complaints from early e-mail clients was the lack of individuality in mail configurations. Some users, both private and corporate, have to share computers due to a lack of equipment or rotating shifts. Outlook Express 5 overcomes this problem with the capability to create and configure multiple accounts, servers, and LDAP-based services.

For users who maintain several e-mail accounts, such as personal and business accounts, the Accounts option enables you to create an account for each mailbox. You can then use Outlook Express 5 to send and receive mail from each account at the same time. For example, if you have three different POP mail accounts, you can retrieve your mail from all three mail servers using Outlook Express. You can then answer all of the mail from Outlook Express and the replies will appear to have come from three different POP addresses. This feature provides the user with a timesaving tool that allows mail to be compiled and distributed from a single mail client.

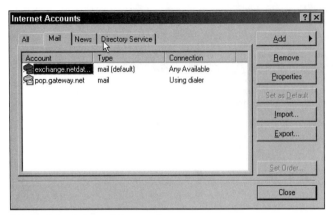

FIGURE 2-21   Internet Accounts

REPLACING OTHER MAIL CLIENTS

The Outlook Express 5 installation is written to help the user migrate from other popular mail clients. Several factors should be considered when migrating a mail client:

- Address books
- Mail currently in the Inbox
- Mail configuration (server names, types of servers, and so on)

Outlook Express 5 will import address books, mail, and mail configurations from the following mail clients during the Outlook Express 5 installation:

- Microsoft Exchange
- Microsoft Outlook
- Windows Messaging
- Eudora Light and Eudora Pro
- Netscape Mail (versions 2 or 3) and Netscape Communicator

After you install Outlook Express 5, you can import and export an address book as frequently as you need to. The import and export tools are located on the File menu under Import and Export. You can also import a name and address book from a comma-delimited text file (also known as a comma-separated value, or CSV, file). Microsoft Exchange Server enables you to import addressing data from the Exchange directory using LDAP Data Interchange Format (LDIF). For more information on Exchange and LDIF, consult the Microsoft Exchange Server Resource Guide in the BackOffice Resource Kit.

CONFIGURATION OPTIONS

Outlook Express 5 offers a variety of configuration options to enable you to configure the mail client for given scenarios. As an IT professional, you will find that many different configurations are required, even within just one organization. For example, take the case of an ISP.

The user joins your service and gets a new e-mail account from you, called joeuser@rockinisp.com. The user needs to pull down mail from other locations that he has mail accounts at, such as his work or other mailboxes. Using Outlook Express, you can set up multiple mail profiles for the different accounts so that the user can send and receive mail from all of the accounts at the same time. For each account, the user would have to add the profile through the Tools ➪ Accounts ➪ Mail option in Outlook Express.

As another example, suppose the user has an e-mail account in the POP server and also monitors five other mailboxes that serve as general mailboxes for receiving inquiries from the public. You can create six profiles in Outlook Express for this user and set the option on the five general mailboxes to not delete the messages when checking mail. This way, other employees checking this mailbox will still be able to view the new mail. To leave copies of the messages on the server, select Tools ➪ Accounts ➪ Properties on the Account-Advanced page. As you will see, the bottom of the tab shows an option to leave mail on the server. You should consider using this feature for general mailboxes.

Outlook Express 5 offers nine different category tabs for customization. To access the configuration options select the Tools option from the menu and then choose Options. Let's start with the General tab.

The General Tab

The General tab focuses on overall Outlook Express 5 configuration options that are not specific to any particular function. Figure 2-22 shows the options available on the General tab.

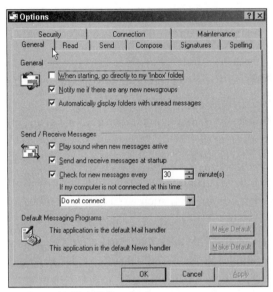

FIGURE 2-22 The General tab

- *When starting, go directly to my 'Inbox' folder.* This option enables you to navigate to your Inbox automatically when you launch Outlook Express.

- *Notify me if there are any new newsgroups.* This option enables Outlook Express to notify you when new newsgroups are added to your subscribed news servers by providing a dialog box notification. For technical newsgroups, this feature is invaluable.

- *Automatically display folders with unread messages.* This option enables Outlook Express to display all folders with unread messages. This option also assists in notifying the user when messages have been filtered.

- *Play sound when new messages arrive.* Allows a sound file, such as a .wav file, to be played when new messages arrive after an update.

- *Send and receive messages at startup.* This option forces Outlook Express to send all messages in the Outbox when Outlook Express is launched. This option also forces Outlook Express to check all configured mail accounts for new mail as well.

- *Check for new messages every ____ minute(s).* This option enables Outlook Express 5 to check for new mail messages at selected intervals. Outlook can use a modem or a LAN connection to check for messages, and can do so at the interval you select. Unchecking this option requires that the user selects the Send and Receive option every time the user wants to check mail.

- *This application is the default Mail handler.* Allows Outlook Express 5 to be the default client for reading and sending mail. For e-mail enabled applications, such as browsers, this is the default application that is launched on any mail-related API (Application Programming Interface). An example of this is when a user clicks on a mailto: link on a web page, Outlook Express will be launched if this option is selected.

- *This application is the default News handler.* Allows Outlook Express 5 to be the default client for reading newsgroups, such as Usenet. You can also use Outlook Express 5 to view internal news servers.

The Read Tab

The Read tab, shown in Figure 2-23, enables you to customize the options available for reading mail and news. The options include message markings, download options, fonts, and character sets.

- *Mark message read after displaying for _____ seconds.* The preview pane enables you to look at a mail message without actually opening the message itself. This option allows the message to be marked as read once it is highlighted for a specified amount of time.

- *Automatically expand grouped messages.* Grouped messages are also known as conversation threads. Conversation threads in newsgroups are basically replies to replies to an original message. The user starts off with a topic, and several people provide opinions and feedback based on the subject matter. This option allows for the entire thread to be expanded, once the thread is selected.

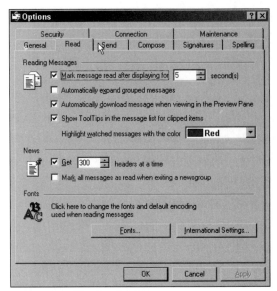

FIGURE 2-23 The Read tab

- *Automatically download message when viewing in the Preview Pane.* This option allows Outlook Express to download the message in the background while you are viewing the message. This option is primarily used for newsgroups and IMAP-based mail servers.

- *Show ToolTips in the message list for clipped items.* Specifies whether ToolTips are used when items are cut off in a column.

- *Highlight watched messages with the color _____.* In Outlook Express 5, you can select Inbox messages and newsgroups to watch by selecting this option. This enables you to pay attention to specific conversation threads that you are interested in.

- *Download _____ headers at a time.* Specifies the number of message headers downloaded at any one time. You may remember that message headers include the originator's name, the subject, and the date on which the server received the message. By simply viewing the header, you can sometimes determine which messages are good and which are spam.

- *Mark all messages as read when exiting a newsgroup.* If you are manually browsing newsgroups, you can simply mark all messages as read upon exit, rather than marking the messages manually. In this configuration, a user can easily identify and download new messages that are posted at a later date.

- *Font Settings*. You can change the character set and default font settings for Outlook Express 5 with this option. This feature is mainly used for incoming messages.

- *International Settings*. For users who are bilingual or plan on sending e-mail in languages other than English, this option enables you to change the character mappings for your e-mail. In most cases, you will not have to change this option at all. The actual character sets for Outlook Express 5 are determined by the character sets chosen in Internet Explorer. You can add more languages to Explorer and allow those configurations to port over to Outlook Express 5, if you wish.

The Send Tab

The Send tab enables you to configure the options for sending mail and also posting to newsgroups. The following options are available as shown in Figure 2-24.

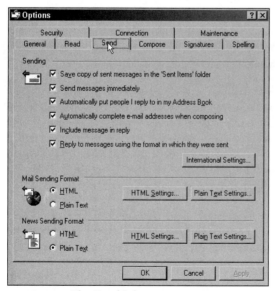

FIGURE 2-24 The Send tab

- *Save copy of sent messages in the 'Sent Items' folder*. The Sent Items folder can retain copies of all e-mail correspondence you send. This is a very good idea and I highly recommend using this feature rather than blind copying yourself on every message. Blind copying wastes valuable bandwidth and creates unnecessary overhead on the SMTP and POP servers.

- *Send messages immediately.* This is an option that users choose most frequently when they have a constant Internet connection. In a modem-based scenario, Outlook Express 5 automatically dials up to the ISP every time the user completes a mail message.
- *Automatically put people I reply to in my Address Book.* This enables Outlook Express to add reply addresses of the people you've replied to directly to your Address Book.

 caution

This option can get out of hand if your users answer mail from the general public. Every time a mail message is answered, its reply address is added to the Address Book. Think about disabling this option for your users that get a lot of public mail.

- *Automatically complete e-mail addresses when composing.* Outlook Express 5 can check the e-mail address you are typing against the Windows Address Book for a match. If a match is found, the address auto completes in the To, Cc, and Bcc windows for you. This is a fantastic feature, especially when you are composing a large message to a large number of different people.
- *Include message in reply.* This option enables you to include the body of a mail message when you reply to a message. Including the body of the message makes correspondence much easier for the person or persons to whom you are sending the message. The entire message you received, including mail routing information, is sent back to the originator of the message.
- *Reply to messages using the format in which they were sent.* This option allows for a message reply to be sent in the same format in which the originator sent the message. For example, Mary Doe sends you a message in plain text. If this option is selected, Outlook Express 5 will respond to Mary in plain text as well. Outlook Express 5 is installed by default with HTML mail as the standard. If this option were not selected, the response to Mary's message would be in HTML mail.
- *Mail Sending Format/HTML.* Enables you to configure the HTML mail settings. You can send mail messages in the HTML programming language to other Outlook Express 5 users. The Settings option enables you to configure MIME (Multipurpose Internet Mail Extensions) settings that let you compress your mail message size and encode the message.

- *Mail Sending Format/Plain Text.* Enables you to configure the plain text message format. You can also use binary encoding for plain text messages, as you can with HTML messages.

  One of the biggest complaints about Outlook Express 5 is that the default message type is HTML, and not plain text like other mail clients. When you are setting up Outlook Express 5 for a large distribution, this is definitely something to consider. If you use the Internet Explorer Administration Kit (IEAK) to deploy Outlook Express 5, you can change the default message type and create your own installation. I cover the IEAK in Chapter 7.

in the real world

Not all e-mail clients support HTML messages. You should consider using plain text and allow the user to choose whom to send an HTML-based mail message to.

- *News Sending Format/HTML.* You can use HTML to post messages to supporting newsgroups as well. You can also use binary encoding to compress the size of your posting, which some newsgroups require.

- *News Sending Format/Plain Text.* The majority of newsgroup postings are in plain text. As with HTML, you can use binary encoding for large text postings.

The Compose Tab

The Compose tab (Figure 2-25), allows for configuration of the default mail message types when you send mail to another user.

exam preparation pointer

The Compose tab is new in Outlook Express 5.

- *Compose Font/Mail.* This enables you to select the default font for mail.

- *Compose Font/News.* This allows you to select the default font for news.

- *Stationery/Mail.* This selects the default stationery you want to use for your mail messages.

- *Stationery/News.* This selects the default stationery you want to use for your news messages.

- *Create New.* This allows you to create new stationery.

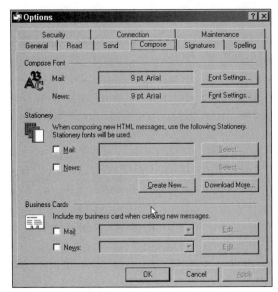

FIGURE 2-25   The Compose tab

   Using the "Download More" button, you can download more stationery templates from Microsoft. Even if you do not use them, they can give you some ideas on how you can create your own.

- *Business Cards/Mail.* This allows you to attach a V-Card to all outgoing mail messages. V-Cards are a standard that is supported by a variety of operating systems. V-Cards enable you to share information about yourself with others. The format of a V-Card is very similar to that of the Windows Address book. Some users will attach their V-Card to their mail messages to make it easier for you to send them mail. The V-Card allows for more information about the user, such as address, phone numbers, and so on. You can also import a V-Card into your address book by dragging and dropping the V-Card onto your contact list.

- *Business Cards/News.* This enables you to attach a V-Card to all outgoing news messages.

The Signature Tab

The Signature tab enables you to set up and configure the signature that goes out on your e-mail messages. This option automatically adds text to the bottom of your mail messages, as shown in Figure 2-26.

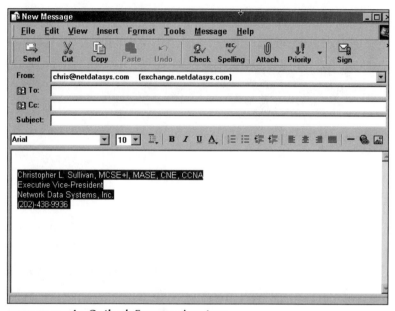

FIGURE 2-26 An Outlook Express signature

The Signature tab is shown in Figure 2-27. There is a variety of ways you can configure your signature.

- *Add signatures to all outgoing messages*. This adds your custom signature to every new message that you send.

- *Don't add signatures to Replies and Forwards*. This feature allows Outlook Express to disable adding your signature when replying to a message or forwarding a message.

- *Signatures.* This is the where you create new signatures and manage existing signatures. If you have work e-mail and personal e-mail from the same work-station, you may want to have multiple signatures.

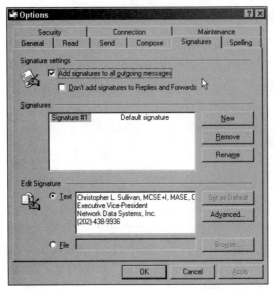

FIGURE 2-27   The Signature tab

- *Edit Signature/Text.* This allows you to edit your signature right in the window in the event that you would like to make changes.

- *Edit Signatures/File.* This allows you to edit your signature in a file, such as a `.txt,` `.rtf,` and `.html` files.

The Spelling Tab

Outlook Express 5 includes a spell checker for your e-mail messages that can be configured in a variety of ways. The Spelling tab enables you to configure options for the spell checker, including spell checker defaults, words and conditions to ignore, and custom dictionaries. The Spelling tab is shown in Figure 2-28.

- *Always check spelling before sending.* This option runs the spell checker automatically before you send a mail message — a good check-and-balance system in case the user forgets to run the spell checker before sending mail messages.

- *Suggest replacements for misspelled words.* The spell checker can suggest replacement words for a word you may have misspelled.

- *When checking spelling, always ignore/Words in UPPERCASE.*

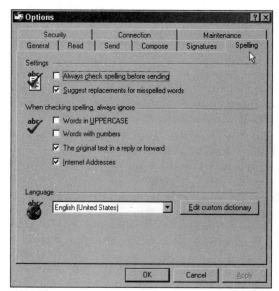

FIGURE 2-28   The Spelling tab

- *When checking spelling, always ignore/Words with numbers.*

- *When checking spelling, always ignore/The original text in a reply or forward.*

- *When checking spelling, always ignore/Internet Addresses.* Instructs Outlook Express 5 to ignore e-mail addresses, such as johndoe@noone.com, when running the spell check function.

- *Language.* Specifies the type of language you wish to use with the spell checker, such as U.S. English or UK English.

- *Edit custom dictionary.* Enables you to add and subtract words from the customized dictionary.

 tip **When using IEAK to deploy custom versions of Internet Explorer, this feature is helpful to the user if you include words commonly used in or specific to your organization, such as abbreviations, slang, and quick references.**

The Security Tab

The Security tab enables you to configure settings to protect and secure your users' mail messages. This option enables you to configure various options, including digital IDs, security zone configurations, and encryption-based configurations. The Security tab is shown in Figure 2-29.

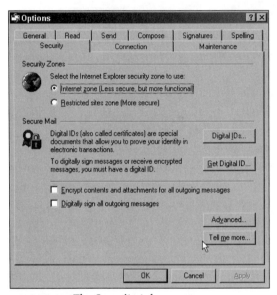

FIGURE 2-29 The Security tab

Security Zones. The security zones in Internet Explorer are also used in Outlook Express 5. The Security tab enables you to make changes to the security zone configuration as necessary, to accomplish the task at hand.

There are two choices in Outlook Express for mail security.

o *Internet zone.* Medium security level that is applied using Internet Explorer.

o *Restricted sites zone.* Highest security possible applied from Internet Explorer.

exam
preparation
pointer

In Outlook Express 4.0, you were able to choose from the four security zones in Internet Explorer 4.0. In addition, you were also able to change the default security settings as well, which was a popular complaint amongst administrators. Just remember that there are only two options to choose from now, as opposed to four.

- *Get Digital ID.* Enables you to navigate to a commercial site to obtain a digital ID.

- *Encrypt contents and attachments for all outgoing messages.* For all outgoing messages, this option allows the encryption of the body and attachments of all messages that are sent.

- *Digitally sign all outgoing messages.* Using the public key that I previously discussed in this chapter, you can sign all mail messages with a digital ID. This option adds your digital signature to the message and sends the public key to the recipient. This option works hand in hand with the next option.

- *Advanced settings.* Enables you to make very specific configuration options for mail encryption. You can use this option to make changes to the algorithm that is used to encrypt the message. The algorithm is essentially the method by which the text and attachment are encrypted.

- *Tell me more.* This option is a quick way to view the online help for Outlook Express 5.

The Connection Tab

The Connection tab enables you to configure various telephony capabilities with Outlook Express 5. Figure 2-30 shows the Connection tab.

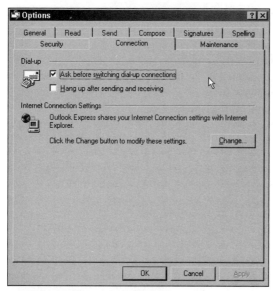

FIGURE 2-30 The Connection tab

- *Ask before switching dial-up connections*. Enables the user to be notified when the dial-up profile is changed. The most common use is for multiple phone access numbers. Some organizations may have local and long-distance numbers configured, and this option can notify the user that they are changing numbers so the user knows when a particular number may become significantly more costly.

- *Hang up after sending and receiving*. This option is used to disconnect the modem after update activity has ceased. For example, this configuration option can be used when mail needs to be accessed while unattended. That is, Outlook Express 5 can be configured to dial up and check for mail periodically while the user is not using the workstation or is away from the workstation. If the user were to stay logged on to the Internet for a long period of time, some time-based and long-distance charges could be incurred.

- *Internet Connection Settings*. Specifies the dial-up profile that should be used when Outlook Express 5 dials up for updates.

The Maintenance Tab

The Maintenance tab, shown in Figure 2-31, is used mainly for message file management, but is also used for the logging options.

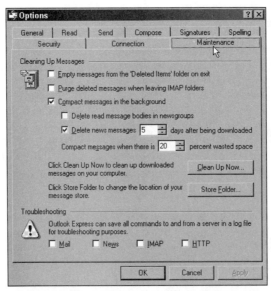

FIGURE 2-31 The Maintenance tab

The Maintenance tab was known as the Advanced tab in Outlook Express 4.0.

- *Empty messages from the 'Deleted Items' folder on exit*. Deletes the contents of the Deleted Items folder when the user shuts down Outlook Express. The action itself actually clears the contents of the Deleted Items .dbx file. If drive space is a big consideration in your network, you may want to select this option. The ramifications of this are that all deleted messages will be unrecoverable once the user closes Outlook Express.

- *Purge deleted messages when leaving IMAP folders*. Allows Outlook Express to delete local copies of IMAP messages to conserve space offline.

- *Compact messages in the background.* The easiest way to understand this option is to think of the mail or news file as a spreadsheet. When you create a spreadsheet, the sheet has some blank cells. The blank cells enable you to add more data as needed. When you clear data in any cell, the cell becomes blank. Blank cells, overall, increase the size of the spreadsheet file. Mail stores are similar in that any unused space becomes available within the mail file itself when messages are deleted. Compacting the mail file causes the blank space to be eliminated and reduces the overall size of the mail store to improve speed and efficiency.

- *Delete read message bodies in newsgroups*. This clears messages from your offline news store to make navigation through large newsgroups more effective.

- *Delete news messages ____ days after being downloaded*. This automatically deletes news messages based on the age of the message. Space is always a consideration for end users. This option specifies the interval at which news messages should be deleted once they are downloaded. As you learned previously, newsgroups hold hundreds, sometimes thousands, of messages. This option enables Outlook Express 5 to delete news messages after a certain number of days to preserve valuable disk space.

- *Compact Messages when there is ____ percent wasted space*. This option kicks off the compaction process when the mail store has a specified percentage of wasted space.

- *Delete news messages _____ days after being downloaded*. Don't keep read messages. Enables Outlook Express 5 to automatically delete messages that have been viewed.

- *Clean Up Now.* This tool allows you to clean up your own mail store. There are four features available.

  - *Compact.* Initiates an immediate compact request.

  - *Remove Messages.* This will deleted the bodies of every message cached locally on your machine.

  - *Delete.* This will delete all messages stored locally on your machine.

  - *Reset.* This will reset the headers and read marks on all messages so that they are downloaded again.

- *Store Folder.* Shows the location of your message store.

- *Troubleshooting.* Creates a log file for Mail, News, IMAP and HTTP. This tool is very valuable for troubleshooting mail.

CONFIGURING ACCOUNTS IN OUTLOOK EXPRESS 5

One of the nicest features of Outlook Express 5 is the capability to configure all of your e-mail accounts, LDAP servers, news servers, and other information from a single utility. From the Tools menu, choose Accounts.

The All Tab

The All tab in the Accounts box displays all the accounts that are configured for Outlook Express 5 by type. Figure 2-32 shows the All tab.

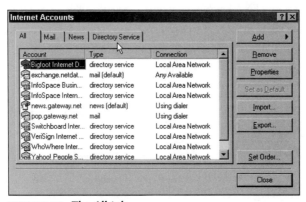

FIGURE 2-32 The All tab

This window provides you with a single interface to manage all the accounts in Outlook Express 5. From this window, you can add, delete, and manage all the accounts you have configured. Sometimes, these lists can become very large and unmanageable from a single view. Outlook Express 5 provides three other views to view information. These views break down the accounts by account type, such as mail accounts, news accounts, and directory service accounts.

- *Mail accounts.* E-mail accounts for one or several mailboxes you may use. You can also configure the accounts option for several users.
- *News accounts.* NNTP accounts for newsgroups to which you subscribe on the Usenet or on a local news server in your organization.
- *Directory Service.* LDAP-based directory servers, such as Bigfoot. These provide you with powerful search tools to find people, places, and things.

The Mail Tab

Let's take a closer look at each tab and the configurations available within each account type. As you can see from Figure 2-33, I have mail configured on my workstation. Let's take a look my mail server configurations.

The Mail tab controls the configuration of all of your e-mail accounts. You can add multiple user accounts in the Mail tab for multiple users if you so choose. Let's talk a little bit about configuring mail accounts.

The Mail/General tab

The Mail/General tab, shown in Figure 2-33, is how you configure your mail address. You can get to this tab by selecting the properties of any mail account in the Tools/Accounts/Mail option.

First of all, you have to define a name for this account to be referenced in the Mail and the All tabs. This name does not affect the sending and receiving of mail; it merely assigns a unique name to this account. This name should be something easy to distinguish so you know which mail server you are accessing with this entry.

The User Information enables you to append a name and organization to your e-mail messages so that you are easily distinguished. Lastly, you specify your e-mail address and your reply address.

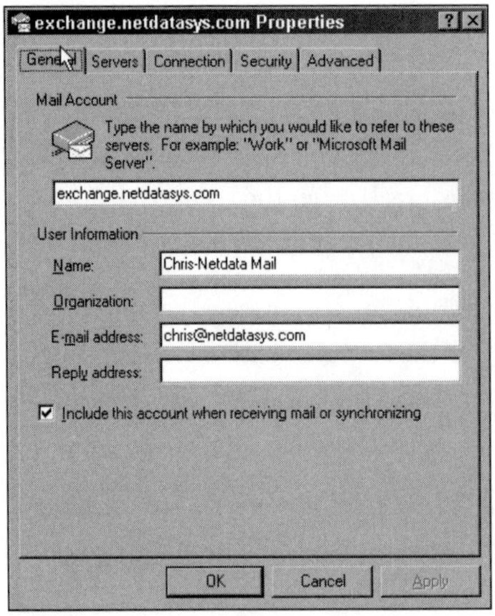

FIGURE 2-33   The Mail/General tab

The Servers tab

The Servers tab enables you to configure the outgoing and incoming mail server name. In this field, you can use a host name, TCP/IP address, or a NetBIOS name. This tab also displays the type of incoming mail server—POP3 or IMAP—that is in use. The Servers tab is shown in Figure 2-34.

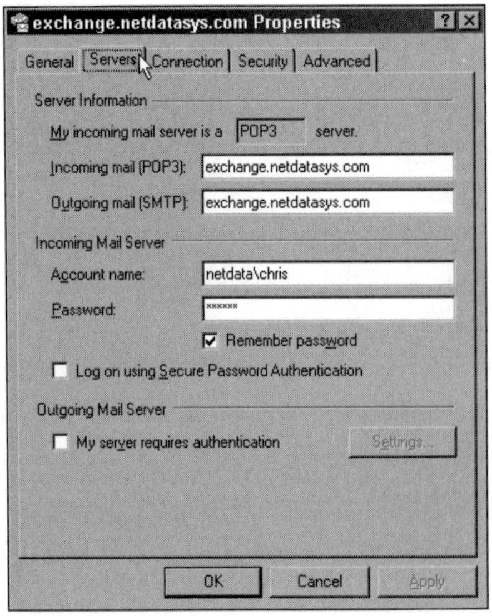

FIGURE 2-34   The Servers tab

You must also specify an incoming e-mail server account name and password in this tab. This information enables Outlook Express 5 to log into the mail server for you to send and receive mail messages. This logon can use the secure password authentication as well. In some cases, SMTP servers may also require a user ID and password to send e-mail. You can configure this option by selecting the checkbox, and then selecting Settings.

You can also use Log on using Secure Password Authentication for your e-mail logons as well with Outlook Express. This allows for your user name and password to be encrypted when sent to your mail server.

The Connection tab

The Connection tab merely specifies the connection profile that should be used with this mail account. Many accounts use different access numbers, user names, and passwords for authentication. The Connection tab is shown in Figure 3-35.

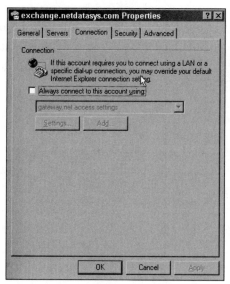

FIGURE 2-35 The Connection tab

The Security tab

The Security tab, shown in Figure 3-36, enables you to configure digital IDs to be used with your mail messages.

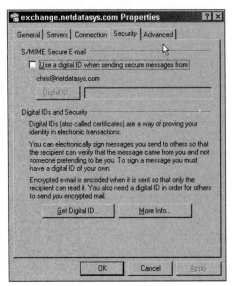

FIGURE 2-36 The Security tab

A digital ID can prevent unauthorized viewing of your mail messages. You can browse for the latest digital ID vendors by selecting the Get Digital ID button. This button launches Internet Explorer and navigates you to a Microsoft site where all the recommended digital ID sites are listed.

The Advanced tab

The Advanced tab enables you to configure the ports used in Outlook Express 5 for sending and receiving mail. You can also configure a timeout interval for Outlook Express 5 so an error message is displayed in case the mail server is not available.

The Advanced tab also enables you to configure Outlook Express 5 to leave copies of the mail messages on the mail server. This option is shut off by default so your mail store is cleaned out every time you send and receive mail. You can also configure Outlook Express 5 to break down mail messages over a certain size. This option allows for a more modular download of your mail. Figure 2-37 shows the Advanced Tab.

Other options include the capability to change the TCP/IP ports for POP- and SMTP-based mail. In general, you should not change any of the settings on this page unless told to do so by the server administrator.

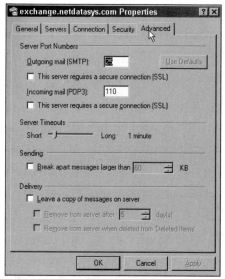

FIGURE 2-37 The Advanced tab

The News tab

Figure 2-38 shows the properties of news.gateway.net on my system.

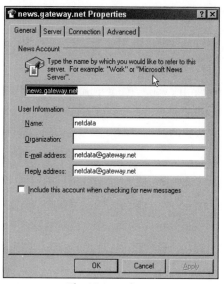

FIGURE 2-38 The News tab

The News Account dialog box shows the account name, which can be whatever you choose. This name should be something easy to distinguish, so you know which news server you are accessing with this entry. You can also rename the entries in this dialog box.

When you post a message to a newsgroup, your e-mail address is attached. The e-mail fields enable you to enter your e-mail address and a reply address where other users can respond to your news postings. The Organization field enables you to enter your company name or any other organizational reference that makes it easier for others to find you.

If the Send and Receive option is selected, you can configure Outlook Express 5 to check your newsgroups for new messages by selecting the checkbox shown at the bottom of Figure 2-38.

 The General and Connection tabs for news and mail messages are exactly the same. The only difference is the content that appears in each tab.

To configure different news servers, choose the Server tab. The Server tab, shown in Figure 2-39, enables you to configure the server name.

The News Server tab

The Server name field specifies the server name that hosts your newsgroups, such as news.widgets.com. This field can contain a host name, NetBIOS name, or a TCP/IP address. Some news servers require user IDs and passwords. If your news server requires that you have an ID, you can enter that information on this tab. If your news server requires secure password authentication, as Microsoft Exchange Server can be configured to require, choose this option. The News Server tab is shown in Figure 2-39.

The Connection tab

The Connection tab, shown in Figure 2-40, is almost identical to that of Internet Explorer.

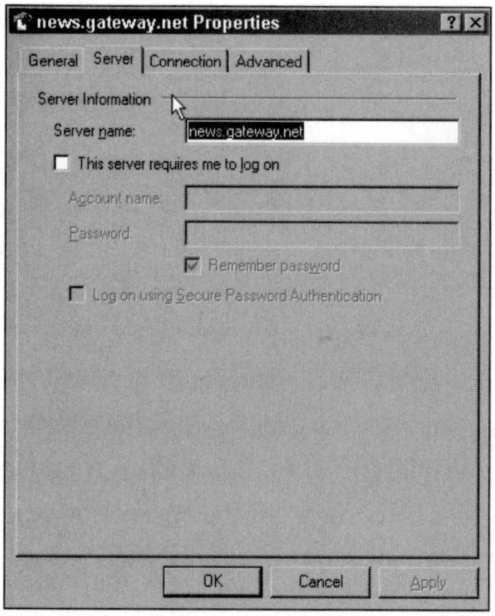

FIGURE 2-39 The Server tab

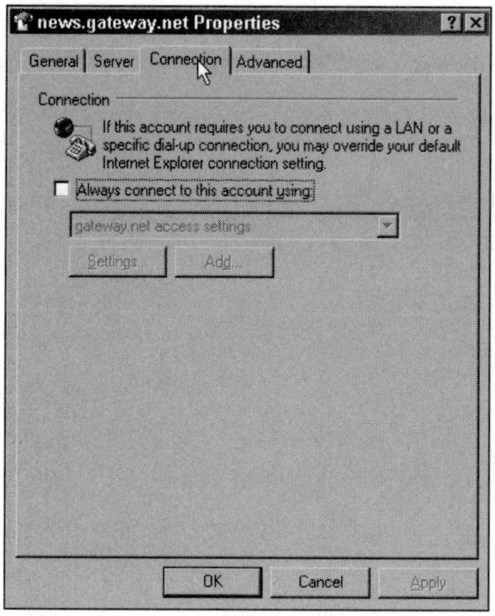

FIGURE 2-40 The Connection tab

In this tab, you can configure the type of connection with which this account is accessed. You can choose from three options: dial-up, LAN, or Internet Explorer or a third-party dialer. The modem section enables you to select your dial-up profile, and also to configure the profile you choose, by selecting the Properties button.

The Advanced tab, shown in Figure 2-41, enables you to configure options for the News account.

The Advanced tab

You can change the TCP/IP port for your news server by changing the decimal entry in the News (NTTP) field. Some news servers require that you use a secure connection to use and view sensitive information. If your news server requires SSL, select the SSL checkbox under this field.

In attempting to connect to a news server, your client may "timeout" occasionally due to a down server, network traffic, or other reasons. The Server Timeouts section of this tab enables you to configure a period for Outlook Express 5 to wait for a connection to a news server. If the connection is not established after a certain period of time, Outlook Express 5 displays an error message indicating the timeout has occurred.

The last two options in this tab enable you to download brief paraphrases of the content of the newsgroup, and also to break up news messages that are larger than a preset size. By breaking down the size of the messages, you can reduce the chances of missing the download of a certain newsgroup item. The Advanced tab is shown in Figure 2-41.

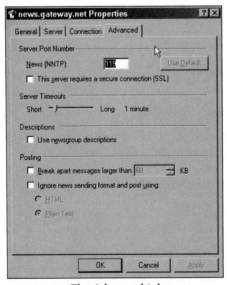

FIGURE 2-41 The Advanced tab

Directory Services

LDAP-based searching is becoming one of the hottest development trends in the Web marketplace. LDAP is a directory services protocol, much like that of X.500, which is the foundation for many directory-based products, such as Microsoft Exchange Server. LDAP is designed to be a small, fast database for querying information, such as names, e-mail addresses, and other simple data queries. LDAP provides the means for powerful and dynamic searching over the Web with Outlook Express 5. To use LDAP services, you must select an LDAP server to perform your searches.

Directory Service General tab

You can assign a descriptive name to your LDAP server and also change the name in the Account name field. In the Server name field, you specify the server's host, NetBIOS, or TCP/IP address. Some commercial LDAP servers require a user ID and password, which you can enter in the fields provided.

Outlook Express 5 also provides a nice feature that enables the LDAP-based directory list to be checked before you send a mail message. The recipient is checked against a dynamically created database through LDAP and against the mail address you specified. Figure 2-42 shows the Directory Service General tab.

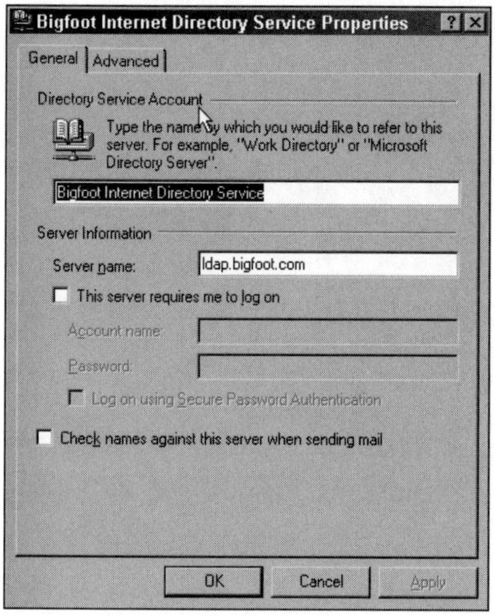

FIGURE 2-42 The Directory Service General tab

The Directory Service Advanced tab

The Advanced tab enables you to change the port number in which LDAP services are used. Some organizations opt to change the port on the LDAP server for security reasons. If your organization changes this port, you must also make these changes on your clients.

You can also use a timeout in the LDAP searches, which comes in handy when you use very popular LDAP servers. When you perform LDAP searches, the database returns the results to you as the server locates the information. With Outlook Express 5, you can limit the number of return matches for your search criteria by specifying the number you want returned in the Maximum number of matches to return field.

The Search base field enables you to specify the path on the LDAP server in which you would like to start your search. Most commercial sites tell you where to set up your search base. Search filters enable you to fine-tune the search based on the criteria you provide. This feature enables you to get more accurate hits on the criteria you specify. Figure 2-43 shows the Directory Service Advanced tab.

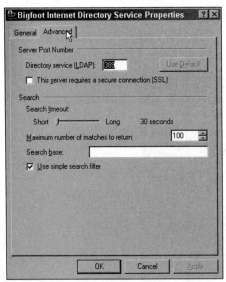

FIGURE 2-43   The Directory Service Advanced tab

KEY POINT SUMMARY

In Chapter 2, we covered the enhancements and many features of the Outlook Express Mail client. We talked about the mail features, navigation features, and the new visual enhancements that will allow your users to use Outlook Express 5 to the fullest.

- SMTP is the de facto standard for sending e-mail on the Internet.

- POP3 is the standard for receiving e-mail on the Internet. Messages are stored on a POP server and remain on the server until downloaded by a mail client.

- IMAP offers more efficient mail access capabilities that enable a user to view the message's header, instead of downloading the entire message as POP mail does.

- LDAP support is included in Outlook Express 5 for locating people, places, and things. Many commercial organizations have set up LDAP-based servers that contain a variety of searchable data, such as e-mail addresses, names, and organizations.

- NNTP is the standard for posting and reviewing messages from a news server, such as Usenet. News servers store news postings by individuals; these postings are stored in a hierarchically based database.

- Your Address Book enables you to save a variety of information about friends, colleagues, and co-workers in a central location for retrieval.

- Digital IDs enable you to encrypt mail sent to another party using a technology called keys. The keys contain an encryption and decryption algorithm that allows secure e-mail messages to be transferred between individuals. A digital ID has three basic key functions: public key, private key, and digital signature.

- The All tab in Tools/Accounts provides you with a single interface to manage all the accounts in Outlook Express 5. From this window, you can add, delete, and manage all the accounts you have configured.

- LDAP provides the means for powerful and dynamic searching over the Web with Outlook Express 5. To use LDAP services, you must select an LDAP server to perform your searches.

APPLYING WHAT YOU'VE LEARNED

This section is an opportunity to use what you've learned in this chapter. The Instant Assessment questions here will help you practice for the exam. The labs that follow provide you with important real-world practice using the skills you've learned.

Instant Assessment

1. What does HTML stand for?

    A. Hypertext Machine Language

    B. Hypertext Markup Language

    C. Hyperterminal Markup Language

    D. Hyperweb Machine Linguistics

2. You can change your "From" address after you have started compiling a new message.

    A. True

    B. False

3. You can preview the body of a message without actually opening the message in the:

    A. Outlook bar

    B. Channels bar

    C. Explorer bar

    D. Preview pane

4. A(n) _____ key is sent to another party to decrypt messages.

    A. integrated

    B. digital

    C. public

    D. private

5. You receive a call from a user who complains that several hundred e-mail addresses appear in his Address Book. The user knows the addresses contained in the book are from previous correspondence, but does not need most of the addresses for future use. The user also knows that he did not add the addresses to the Address Book. What is the most likely cause of the large number of addresses?

   A. The user's public key is corrupt.

   B. The user has a mail virus.

   C. The Windows Address Book is corrupt.

   D. The Automatically put people I reply to in my Address Book option is selected.

6. You can recover deleted mail messages in the:

   A. Recycle Bin

   B. Deleted Messages folder

   C. Deleted Items folder

   D. Outbox

7. A user calls and complains that Outlook Express spell checks each message she receives, including text that was created by others. The spell checker is annoying, according to the user, and she wants you to do something about it. Is there something you can do?

   A. Yes, tell the user to select Reply to All before running the spell checker.

   B. Yes, tell the user to change the applicable option in the Spelling tab.

   C. No, there is nothing you can do.

   D. Reinstall Outlook Express because the dictionary is corrupt.

8. You change the Internet zone security level to the Internet Zone. This will give the user more flexibility in sending messages to other Internet users, and affects only the security configuration of Outlook Express.

   A. True

   B. False

9. A multinational company to which you provide technical support wants to be able to send mail messages to their counterparts in Europe. The company wants to be able to send the messages in the language that the recipient speaks as well. The user can add more languages just to Outlook Express.

    A. True

    B. False

10. A user complains that he is having problems sending and receiving mail. The problem is sporadic, and the user cannot give you any specific circumstances in which the problem occurs. How could you change the configuration of Outlook Express to better assist you in troubleshooting the problem?

    A. Reinstall

    B. Enable logging in the General tab

    C. Run Regedit32 from the command line

    D. Enable logging in the Maintenance tab

11. You can configure Outlook Express to open automatically to the Inbox.

    A. True

    B. False

12. The spell checker always attempts to correct misspellings in e-mail addresses.

    A. True

    B. False

13. The file `custom.dic` is used to:

    A. store Outlook Express user profiles.

    B. store mail messages.

    C. customize dictionaries for the spell checker.

    D. customize settings for Outlook Express.

14. You can configure Outlook Express to display graphical attachments in the preview pane.

    A. True

    B. False

15. In order to completely clear deleted messages, you have to clear the Deleted Items folder or select Empty Folder by right-clicking the folder itself.

   A. True

   B. False

16. Which of the following words could be configured to be ignored by the Outlook Express mail spell checker? (Choose two.)

   A. THISWORD

   B. Thatword

   C. `noone@nowhere.com`

   D. Dictionary

17. You cannot configure Outlook Express to respond to a mail message with the same message format type.

   A. True

   B. False

18. An outgoing mail message uses the _____ protocol.

   A. IMAP4

   B. POP3

   C. NNTP

   D. SMTP

19. Unread e-mail messages are denoted by: (Choose two.)

   A. Bold text

   B. Unread Marker notice

   C. Closed Envelope icon

   D. Open Envelope icon

20. What is the standard protocol used to access newsgroups?

   A. IMAP4

   B. NNCH

   C. NNTP

   D. IPX/SPX

21. In order to retain a copy of messages you send, you must add your own e-mail address to the Cc line or the Bcc line.

  A. True

  B. False

22. You can save a mail message for later use before sending it, by dragging and dropping the message in the _____ folder. (Choose the best answer.)

  A. Windows\System

  B. C:\Personal

  C. Inbox

  D. Drafts

23. Newsgroups are automatically configured and added by Outlook Express.

  A. True

  B. False

24. What enable(s) you to encrypt mail that you send to another party with Outlook Express?

  A. SSL

  B. Cryptographs

  C. Digital IDs

  D. Digital signatures

25. The _____ enables you to take a quick glance at a mail message before opening the message itself.

  A. Subscription bar

  B. Status pane

  C. Inbox

  D. Preview pane

26. You can create new folders for your messages and also create subfolders.

  A. True

  B. False

27. The _____ key is sent to another individual so he or she can decrypt messages you send.

   A. Private

   B. Public

   C. Master

   D. Door

28. The _____ application is integrated into the Windows Address Book so you can easily contact another _____ user.

   A. FrontPage

   B. NetShow

   C. NetMeeting

   D. ActiveX

29. You can view digital IDs that you receive from another user.

   A. True

   B. False

30. This protocol provides search capabilities that enable you to find other users on the Internet.

   A. NNTP

   B. H.323

   C. LDAP

   D. NetBEUI

31. A user is receiving mail from a spam site and has requested that the individual stop sending mail on several occasions. You must provide a solution that enables the user to work a bit more easily with this inconvenience.

   Required Result:

      ○ The user's Inbox cannot be cluttered with spam from this site.

   Optional Results:

      ○ The user's mail client must forward a copy of the message to a preconfigured address, that of the Webmaster of the site from which the mail is coming.

      ○ The message sent to the Webmaster must carbon copy your mail account.

Solution:

o Using the Inbox Assistant, configure the sender's name in a rule.

o Configure the mail to be placed in a folder automatically.

o Configure the mail messages to be forwarded to the Webmaster of the spammer's site.

A. The solution meets the required result and both of the optional results.

B. The solution meets the required result and one of the optional results.

C. The solution meets the required result and none of the optional results.

D. The solution does not meet the required result.

32. A user is receiving mail from a spam site and has requested that the individual stop sending mail on several occasions. You must provide a solution that enables the user to work a bit more easily with this inconvenience.

Required Result:

o The user's Inbox cannot be cluttered with spam from this site.

Optional Results:

o The user's mail client must forward a copy of the message to a preconfigured address, that of the Webmaster of the site from which the mail is coming.

o The message sent to the Webmaster must cc your mail account.

Solution:

o Using newsgroup filters, configure the sender's name in a rule.

o Configure the mail to be placed in a folder automatically.

o Configure the mail messages to be forwarded to the Webmaster of the spammer's site.

o Configure the mail messages to be cc'd to your e-mail address.

A. The solution meets the required result and both of the optional results.

B. The solution meets the required result and one of the optional results.

C. The solution meets the required result and none of the optional results.

D. The solution does not meet the required result.

Critical Thinking Labs

Lab 2.1 *Troubleshooting Outlook Express*

Your boss comes to you and complains that she is unable to get to her e-mail using Outlook Express. She asks you to assist her in troubleshooting why she gets errors connecting to the POP server. She states that the error she receives says that the host cannot be found and something about POP Port 110. This is the only error message she receives. What configuration options would you check to see why she is having problems accessing her mail?

Lab 2.2 *Creating a Hotmail account*

Using Outlook Express, you are going to create a Hotmail account for yourself. Make sure that you are connected to the Internet and have installed Outlook Express 5. Select Tools ⇨ Accounts ⇨ Mail. Click Add and select Mail. Type Hotmail Account in the next field and click the Next button. At the next dialog box, select I'd like to sign up for a new account from Hotmail (there is no charge to do this). Click Next to continue to the sign up screen, and you will be asked to provide your information and create a unique ID for Hotmail. Once completed with the sign up, you will have created an account for Hotmail. Once you have created your account, send a hello e-mail message to `ieak5@netdatasys.com`. What happened?

Hands-On Labs

Lab 2.3 *Using Client-Side rules*

1. Create a folder called Test Folder.
2. Select Tools ⇨ Message Rules ⇨ Mail.
3. Create a Rule that copies any mail message received from `ieak5@netdatasys.com` to your test folder. Ensure that you only copy, not move, the message.

Lab 2.4 *Sending a mail message with Outlook Express*

1. Open Outlook Express.
2. Select New Mail.
3. Send a mail message to `ieak5@netdatasys.com`.
4. Check your Inbox again in about five minutes; did you get a reply? Who was the reply from? (Do not delete the message, you will use it again later in the labs.)

Lab 2.5 *Creating an Address Book entry*

1. Open the Address Book in Outlook Express.

2. Create an Address Book entry for a user; first name is Test, last name is User. For the e-mail address enter `testuser@nowhere.net.`

3. Open a new message and type **testuser**.

4. What happened when you typed testuser?

Lab 2.6 *Changing Read Marks on a mail message*

1. Select the mail message that you received in Lab 2.4.

2. Select Edit ⇨ Mark as Unread.

3. Select another mail message.

4. What changed in the view of the unread message?

Lab 2.7 *Performing LDAP searches in the Internet*

1. Using the appropriate feature, you are going to find a user on the Internet. The user's name is Bill Gates.

2. Using the Yahoo People Finder, how many e-mail addresses contain Bill Gates? (Do not delete the message, you will use it again later in the labs.)

Lab 2.8 *Recovering a deleted message in Outlook Express*

1. Find the message you received from `ieak5@netdatasys.com.`

2. Highlight the message and select Delete. Select Yes to delete if prompted.

3. You need to recover this message; how would you do that?

Lab 2.9 *Setting up another mail account*

1. Choose Tools ⇨ Accounts.

2. Select the Mail tab.

3. Choose Add.

4. Select Mail.

5. Enter Test Account.

6. Enter your e-mail address.

7. Select whether your incoming mail server is IMAP or POP.

8. Enter your e-mail server's POP and SMTP addresses.

9. Enter your user name and password.

10. Enter Test Account again.

11. Select the I will establish my Internet connection manually option.

12. Select Finish.

13. Is the Test Account appearing in the Mail tab?

Lab 2.10 *Changing port and mail server names*

1. Select Tools ⇨ Accounts.

2. Click the Test Account and select properties.

3. Click the Servers tab.

4. What are the server names?

5. Select the Advanced tab.

6. On which ports are SMTP and POP3 running?

Lab 2.11 *Creating and deleting folders*

1. Right-click the Inbox.

2. Select New Folder.

3. Call the folder Test Folder.

4. Select OK.

5. Right-click Test Folder in the Outlook bar.

6. Select New Folder.

7. Call the folder New Subfolder.

8. Did a plus sign (+) appear next to New Folder?

9. Right-click Test Folder again.

10. Select Delete.

Microsoft NetMeeting 3.0

About Chapter 3

Microsoft NetMeeting 3.0 is the latest video/data conferencing package from Microsoft. NetMeeting enables you to conference with other NetMeeting users over the Internet, a local area network, and dial-up. Using the NetMeeting software, required hardware, and a medium for connectivity, you can communicate with other users in real time using audio, video, and real-time collaboration. NetMeeting enables you to share applications over the Web, whiteboards for group discussions, and many other powerful features. In this chapter, we will cover the various features of Microsoft NetMeeting 3.0 and how you can configure the software for optimum performance.

NETMEETING: AN OVERVIEW

This section discusses how NetMeeting works from the point of view of the standards for videoconferencing. I then discuss the hardware you'll need to get NetMeeting up and running, and give a description of what you can do with it once it's working.

Video/Data Conferencing Standards

Before we delve into the bells and whistles of the NetMeeting application, let's take a look at the hardware required to run NetMeeting and the industry standards that make videoconferencing possible.

Using the H.323 protocol standard

The H.323 standard governs a variety of services that apply to videoconferencing, including the CODEC. CODEC is an abbreviation for compression/decompression. The CODEC basically compresses the video to be transmitted over the wire, such as a modem or network, to the destination. The CODEC also works at the destination to decompress the video to be viewed on the destination device. You can also use NetMeeting without video support, if you so choose as NetMeeting supports audio-only connectivity through the use of a standard sound card. Major sound card manufacturers support two modes:

- *Full duplex*. Enables audio to be sent and received simultaneously.

o *Half duplex.* Enables only transmission or only reception to occur at any
  one time.

Most of the latest sound cards support full-duplex audio; this is usually only
a consideration if you are working with legacy hardware. Because sound is the
basis for this technology, speakers (or headphones) and a microphone are necessary to transmit and receive the audio signaling.

**in the
real world**

**While not applicable to the exam, here's some additional informa-
tion to note. There is a misconception about this standard that
seems to be confusing for some people. The H.323 standard was
developed to provide multimedia content over packet switched networks that are not guaranteed, such as Ethernet. Non-guaranteed
networks do not provide a QOS, or quality of service, that ensures
packets arrive when they should. This results in dropped frames
and choppy video in some cases. The H.323 standard was developed to provide the best quality of multimedia for these types of
networks. Quality will be improved in the future with the introduction of RSVP (Resource Reservation Protocol). This new technology
allows for a segment of the available bandwidth to be held back for
multimedia.**

The T.120 data conferencing standard

The International Telecommunications Union (ITU) has established standards for
data conferencing that allow consistent development and expansion for future
needs and technologies. Microsoft NetMeeting fully complies with the ITU standards. Data conferencing is supported in NetMeeting with a variety of features.
These standards are important to you because they ensure that applications will be
able to interact with one another without causing major problems. If you are on
the other end of a call where two applications are stepping on each other, you can
further appreciate this.

The Hardware for Videoconferencing

Videoconferencing is one of the most popular features of NetMeeting. Using a
video camera attached to the workstation configuration, Microsoft NetMeeting
transmits a video image to other NetMeeting users via the Internet, an intranet, or

a local area network. There are several methods by which video support can be added to the workstation configuration.

Parallel cameras

Parallel cameras are very small cameras that connect to the workstation via the workstation's parallel port. The camera itself comes with software configured to translate the video signal into bit streams capable of being transmitted via the network connection. Parallel cameras are the most popular form of video encoding. The camera costs between $80 and $150 and is available at most computer stores. The positive features of parallel cameras are the cost and the widespread use of this type of camera. The negative features are that you lose the ability to use the parallel port on many PCs, or you have to share the port with other devices, which causes support problems in most cases. Other negatives include the speed, integration, and video quality as compared to the following two types of video encoding methods.

tip **If you are unsure as to which camera to get, select Help within the NetMeeting application and the Get Camera Selection. This feature will navigate you to the NetMeeting Web site where a list of compatible cameras will be listed.**

Capture cards

The capture card is an ISA (Industry Standard Architecture), PCI (Peripheral Component Interconnect), or PCMCIA (Personal Memory Card International Association) card that is configured within the PC to enable the digitization of video. Capture cards enable you to digitize video from a variety of sources such as VCRs, handheld video recorders, and television signals. When the capture card is present, a video camera must be attached to the video card to allow the use of the camera and capture card with Microsoft NetMeeting. Normally, you can connect any camera that has an RCA, S-Video, or composite video connector to the video card. Capture cards are generally the most expensive solution—they cost anywhere from $250 to $2,000, depending on the quality of the capture card itself. A camcorder must also be added to the configuration to allow the video. The main advantage of the capture card is that it's flexible enough to use for other tasks besides videoconferencing.

Universal Serial Bus

The Universal Serial Bus (USB) is a class of hardware that makes it easy to add serial devices to your computer. USB support is built to specifications that will allow future updates of Windows to support current drivers. Using USB ports, you can chain together a series of devices, such as printers, cameras, drives, and other hardware on the same chain, which is similar to SCSI capabilities. The advantage that USB has over SCSI is the number of devices that can be connected to USB. Up to 127 devices can be connected to a single USB chain, whereas SCSI is limited to three to nineteen depending on the manufacturer and hardware. You can plug multiple devices into a single hub, similar to that of Ethernet data networks, which is then connected to the USB port on the PC. This enables you to connect and disconnect devices in one quick, easy, and painless step.

In addition to the amount of devices on a single chain, USB is much closer to a Plug and Play type setup than SCSI. USB devices are very simple to configure as the manufacturer includes the necessary device drivers. All you have to ensure is that you have a USB port on the back of your PC. Check the following before installing USB devices:

o Make sure that you have Universal Serial Bus controllers enabled in your Control Panel. An example of what this looks like is shown in Figure 3-1.

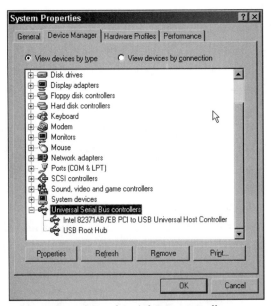

FIGURE 3-1   Universal Serial Bus controllers

- Make sure that USB is enabled in your system BIOS. If you find that USB is not enabled, refer to the PC manufacturer's documentation for more information on changing BIOS settings.

- Make sure that you are running Microsoft Windows 95 OSR2 (Operating System Release 2) or Windows 98 (preferred). Early versions of Windows 95 do not support USB, check to make sure that your version is compatible before installing your USB device.

 note **USB is not supported natively in Windows NT 3.5 and Windows NT 4.0 (through service pack 4). Windows 2000, however, will fully support USB standards and features.**

Once you make sure that the USB interface is configured on your PC, installing your USB device is literally as simple as plugging it in. There are many other features besides ease of use that makes USB attractive. USB supports a higher transfer rate than previous methods of connecting videoconferencing equipment for applications such as NetMeeting. Table 3-1 shows some of the various Intel-based connectivity methods for peripherals and average transfer rates.

TABLE 3-1 PERIPHERAL TRANSFER RATES

CONNECTION TYPE	TRANSFER RATE
Serial port	115Kbs (.115Mbps)
Standard parallel port	115K/sec (.115MB/sec)
USB	12Mbps (1.5MB/sec)
ECP/EPP parallel port	3MB/sec
IDE	3.3–16.7MB/sec
SCSI-1	5MB/sec
SCSI-2 (Fast SCSI, Fast Narrow SCSI)	10MB/sec
Fast Wide SCSI (Wide SCSI)	20MB/sec
Ultra SCSI (SCSI-3, Fast-20, Ultra Narrow)	20MB/sec
UltraIDE	33MB/sec
Wide Ultra SCSI (Fast Wide 20)	40MB/sec
Ultra2 SCSI	40MB/sec

Continued

TABLE 3-1 *(continued)*	
CONNECTION TYPE	TRANSFER RATE
IEEE-1394	100–400Mbps (12.5–50MB/sec)
Wide Ultra2 SCSI	80MB/sec
Ultra3 SCSI	80MB/sec
Wide Ultra3 SCSI	160MB/sec
(Fibre Channel Arbitrated Loop) FC-AL	100–400MB/sec

To install a USB device, plug the cord from the device into any USB port on your computer.

NetMeeting System Requirements

NetMeeting, like any other application, has baseline requirements for optimum application performance. The following Tables 3-2 and 3-3 outline the minimum hardware platform for running NetMeeting 3.0 in various configurations.

TABLE 3-2 DATA CONFERENCING AND AUDIO ONLY	
COMPONENT	REQUIREMENTS
Processor/Memory — Windows 95 & 98	90MHz Pentium Processor & 16MB of RAM
Processor/Memory — Windows NT	90MHz Pentium Processor & 24MB of RAM (Microsoft Windows NT 4.0 Service Pack 3 or later is required to enable sharing programs on Windows NT)
Browser	Microsoft Internet Explorer version 4.01 or later
Connection Speed	28,800bps or faster modem, integrated services digital network (ISDN) or local area network (LAN) connection (a fast Internet connection works best)

COMPONENT	REQUIREMENTS
Hard Disk Space Free	4MB of free hard disk space (an additional 10MB is needed during installation only to accommodate the initial setup files)
Sounds	Sound card with microphone and speakers (required for audio support)

TABLE 3-3 VIDEO, AUDIO AND DATA COMMUNICATIONS

COMPONENT	REQUIREMENTS
Processor/Memory – Windows 95	Pentium 90 processor with 16MB of RAM. (A Pentium 133 processor or better, with at least 16MB of RAM is recommended.)
Processor/Memory – Windows NT	Pentium 90 processor with 24MB of RAM. (A Pentium 133 processor or better, with at least 32MB of RAM is recommended.)
Hard Disk Space	4MB of free hard disk space. (An additional 10MB is needed during installation only to accommodate the initial setup files.)
Connection Speed	56000bps or faster modem ISDN or LAN connection.
Sound	Sound card with microphone and speakers. (A sound card is required for both audio and video support.)
Video	Video capture card or camera that provides a Video for Windows capture driver (required for video support).

What You Can Do With NetMeeting

Once you have all the hardware components in place, you'll probably want to do something with NetMeeting. Different users need different tools to conduct meetings, so NetMeeting offers a variety of tools. These include the whiteboard, for sharing images; file transfer, for sharing files; chat, for simple discussions; and application sharing, for looking at application data.

Whiteboard

The whiteboard is the electronic version of the school "blackboard." It is similar to Microsoft Paint. The whiteboard enables you to collaborate with other NetMeeting/whiteboard users to make pictures, drawings, and text. It also enables you to maintain several different pages of drawings at one time so participants in your meeting can view multiple drawings. The whiteboard is shown in Figure 3-2.

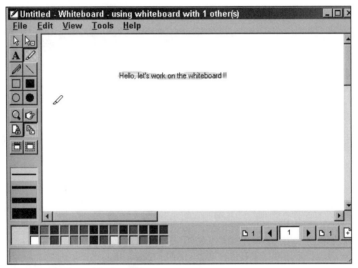

FIGURE 3-2 The whiteboard

File transfer

NetMeeting enables any conference user to transfer the file of his or her choice to all of the meeting's participants or to a single NetMeeting user (see Figure 3-3). A standard does exist for file transfer; it is actually a subset of the T.120 standard, called T.127.

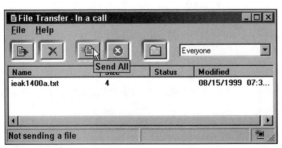

FIGURE 3-3 File transfer

Chat

As many commercial online services have done, Microsoft has provided a text-based chat function for Microsoft NetMeeting called Microsoft Chat (see Figure 3-4). In certain instances, NetMeeting users may not have the capability of audio, or may not wish to use audio. Chat enables the user to communicate with other NetMeeting users via text. With Chat, you can participate in a discussion with one user, multiple users, or just one user among multiple users.

FIGURE 3-4 Microsoft Chat

Application Sharing

NetMeeting participants in a meeting can share the use of an application on one user's workstation. The application is run on the host workstation and is displayed to all the other NetMeeting participants. Other NetMeeting participants can also control the application. Application Sharing is an excellent tool for presentations and end-user support, and for getting feedback on applications that are under development. Using this feature you can also share your desktop with other NetMeeting participants.

The NetMeeting Interface

Now that we have covered the basics for Microsoft NetMeeting, let's talk about the NetMeeting interface and how to configure the NetMeeting application. NetMeeting has changed since the 2.*x* interface; the interface is much more con-solidated and has the look and feel of Windows Media Player.

concept link **Windows Media Player is discussed in Chapter 4.**

Microsoft NetMeeting is included with Internet Explorer 5, as you know, and accentuates the browser with audio, video, and data collaboration. The NetMeeting interface is shown in Figure 3-5.

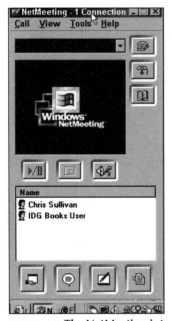

FIGURE 3-5 The NetMeeting interface

Companies spend considerable time and money on travel so their employees can meet and share information. NetMeeting can help save these resources by enabling users to communicate with one another right from their desks. Companies both large and small are looking to such MDC (Multipoint Data Conferencing) programs to provide a faster and more reliable means of communication. In addition to communication services, NetMeeting provides development tools that enable developers to write powerful applications that incorporate the NetMeeting functionality.

The latest Software Development Kit for NetMeeting, NetMeeting 3.5 SDK, allows you to NetMeeting–enable web applications.

Let's walk through some of the configuration options available within Microsoft NetMeeting.

Call features

The Call menu enables you to configure, guess what, your call options. Figure 3-6 shows the choices available to you.

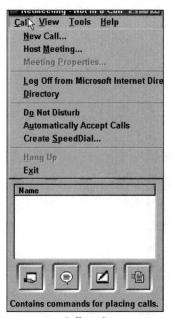

FIGURE 3-6 Call options

New Call

The New Call option allows you to connect to another party by their name as listed on the ILS (Internet Locator Service) server you are connected to. You can also use the user's TCP/IP address, e-mail address, or host name. When selected, the Place a Call window will be displayed (Figure 3-7).

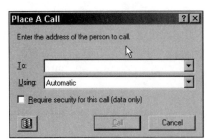

FIGURE 3-7 The Place a Call window

tip **You can initiate a call from the command line (Start/Run) by typing callto:** *email address.* **If you know the ILS server name, you can type callto:** *ILS Server\e-mail address.*

Host Meeting

This feature allows you to set a meeting for other participants to join. When selected, the Host a Meeting dialog box will be displayed (Figure 3-8).

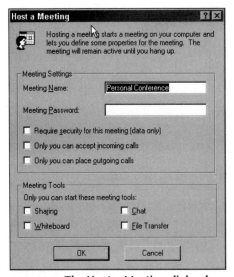

FIGURE 3-8 The Host a Meeting dialog box

In the Host a Meeting window, you can configure various options for your meeting as well.

- *Meeting Name.* Allows you to assign your own personalized name to your meeting.

- *Meeting Password.* Allows you to assign a unique password to your meetings. When set, your meeting participants have to enter the password to gain access to the meeting. As a security measure, the password is encrypted when sent by NetMeeting.

- *Require security for this meeting.* Forces the participants to use secure channels to participate in this meeting.

- *Only you can accept incoming calls.* This option allows you to control who enters the meeting. If not selected, anyone can allow access to your meeting. This also disallows others from receiving incoming calls during the meeting.

- *Only you can place outgoing calls.* This allows only you to place outgoing calls while the meeting is going on. This feature helps keep the participants focused on the meeting.

- *Meeting Tools.* This option allows you to specify the applications which only you can start. This helps to keep control of the meeting so that participants don't get sidetracked.

Meeting Properties

The Meeting Properties option enables you to view and configure the options for a meeting that you have set up and are participating in. You may want to make changes to the meeting configuration during the meeting; the window is the same as the Host a Meeting window.

Log On/Log Off from Microsoft Internet Directory

The Microsoft Internet Directory is an ILS-based LDAP (Lightweight Directory Access Protocol) directory that enables you to look up NetMeeting users. This directory enables you to search for specific users and connect to the user you are searching for by clicking on a link , and is much like a huge NetMeeting phone book.

The Microsoft Internet Directory Search dialog box is shown in Figure 3-9.

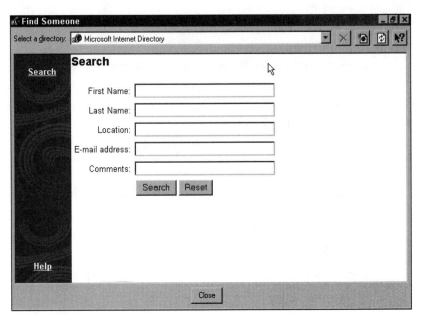

FIGURE 3-9 Searching the Microsoft Internet Directory

As you can see, you can search by the registered first name, last name, location, e-mail address, and comments.

Directory

The Directory option enables you to connect to other ILS servers on the Internet. By default, only the Microsoft Directory server is installed. You can enter different ILS servers if you know the host name of the server by changing the directory name as shown in Figure 3-10.

This ILS server, `ils.quicknet.net`, shows the current users that are logged on to their LDAP server. This is the default view for all ILS servers when you connect. You can connect to other users on this server by double-clicking their entry in the directory.

 tip **You can get a list of the most current ILS servers on the Internet at** `http://www.netmeet.net/bestservers.asp`.

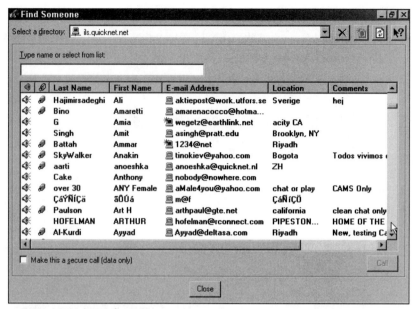

FIGURE 3-10 Using other ILS servers

The directory is the key to connecting to other users if you do not know the user's TCP/IP address. If you are setting up your own directory within your firewall, Microsoft has the ILS server service for Windows NT that you can install to host your own directory. Check out more information on this at `http://backoffice.microsoft.com`.

NetMeeting connects to an ILS by default to locate other NetMeeting users. The ILS server provides the LDAP services that store dynamic lists of users who are currently logged on. In Figure 3-10, you can see that several NetMeeting users are currently logged on to `ils.quicknet.net`. After a period of time, these users will log off and the list will no longer be current. By selecting F5, refresh, you obtain a new list of users directly from the ILS server.

Do Not Disturb

The Do Not Disturb button enables you to disallow others from connecting to you when you are in a meeting. This also can be used when you are busy working on something else and do not want to accept calls until such time as you specify. This is a lot easier to enable than to shut down the NetMeeting application.

Automatically Accept Calls

When you receive a call request from another NetMeeting user as shown in Figure 3-11, you are prompted to answer the call. You can configure NetMeeting to answer all calls if you choose by enabling this option.

FIGURE 3-11 Accepting a new call

Create SpeedDial

This feature enables you to use the SpeedDial list to connect to another user. The SpeedDial list allows you to save user information to a database located locally on your workstation for use in the future, and is a master list of NetMeeting users that you frequently talk with. This list is similar to that of the Windows Address Book. To view the Windows Address Book, type WAB from the command line to view your address book. Once you start saving addresses to the list, you can reconnect to your favorite users whenever you want, provided that the other user is logged on as well.

The View menu

The View menu on the toolbar enables you to select the manner in which you view NetMeeting. You may prefer certain settings when using NetMeeting that other users may not. This enables you to customize your use of the application to best suit your working style. The selections available in the View selection are shown in Figure 3-12.

Status Bar

The Status Bar option enables you to see the current status of your connection. This tells you whether you are in a call, not in a call, and so on. This is a nice feature that reminds you whether you terminated your last call or users are still "lurking." Lurking is a slang term in the NetMeeting world that is meant for people who sit in the directory to watch but never speak or take any action.

FIGURE 3-12 The View menu

Dial Pad

The Dial Pad enables you to dial a phone number. The phone number that you dial can be another NetMeeting user so that you can call the user directly without having to use the Internet to connect. The other reason for using the Dial Pad is to connect to a gateway. A gateway is a server that connects other conferencing computers together over a dialup session or over the Internet. In some configurations, allowing NetMeeting connectivity through a firewall is not allowed due to security reasons. In these types of implementations, a gateway controls the connectivity between the user and other users or to the outside world. Other implementations include specific hardware components called Gatekeepers, which are addressed using TCP/IP, that act as the gateway. The Gatekeeper controls communications between internal NetMeeting users and the outside world. Gateways and Gatekeepers are sometimes referred to as a *multi-point conferencing unit* (MCU).

Picture-in-Picture

Picture-in-Picture enables you to view the video that you are sending within the video you are receiving. This is similar to the picture-in-picture that is used in many popular television sets so that you can view two video images at the same time.

My Video (New Window)

This enables you to view the video you are sending in a separate window.

Compact

Shown in Figure 3-13, the Compact view enables you to shrink the NetMeeting window so that you can participate in meetings and still retain useable desktop space. This enables you to work in other applications and still participate in the meeting.

FIGURE 3-13 Compact view

Data Only

This feature enables you to remove the video window from NetMeeting for conferences that only allow chat, whiteboards, and other T-120 based communications. If video is not going to be used in the meeting, you can use this to save space on your desktop. The Data Only view is shown in Figure 3-14.

FIGURE 3-14 Data Only view

Always on Top

The Always on Top feature allows you to keep your NetMeeting call in the foreground while you are working. This is a nice feature, especially if you are like me and have a lot of windows open at the same time.

The Tools menu

The Tools option allows you to provide configurations for the NetMeeting application itself. Hardware, software, and many other features can be tuned and configured in this selection. Let's take a look at some of the things that you should be aware of. Figure 3-15 shows the Tools option.

FIGURE 3-15 The Tools option

Video

This enables you to configure and tune your video settings. There is not much you can change here, but it deserves mention as an option.

Audio Tuning Wizard

This feature is very important to you and your users as it controls the volume settings for your speakers and microphone. This handy wizard enables you to configure these options and gives you tips on how to best configure your audio settings. If you are supporting Microsoft NetMeeting in a large organization, this is a tool you will most likely be pointing your users to frequently. The tool is very self explanatory, just make sure that the user has the microphone plugged in before proceeding.

Application Sharing, Chat, Whiteboard, File transfer

You can launch any of these applications by selecting the appropriate option on the menu. These features were covered earlier in the chapter.

Remote Desktop Sharing Setup

Shown in Figure 3-16, this wizard enables your users to configure the remote desktop-sharing feature within NetMeeting. This is a really nice feature for support organizations where remote support is necessary. This enables you to connect to a user's desktop remotely to instruct, troubleshoot, or perform other support-related activities.

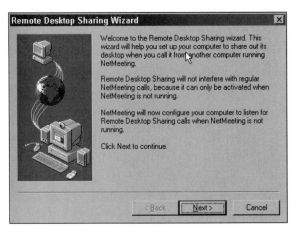

FIGURE 3-16 Remote Desktop Sharing wizard

You can password-protect this feature using the wizard so that only people you provide with the password can connect to your desktop. This feature is shown in Figure 3-17.

FIGURE 3-17 Password protection

You can also password-protect your screen saver in the event that the remote session is interrupted. If the session is interrupted, this may leave your workstation vulnerable to intruders. Enabling the screen saver password provides an additional layer of protection to your workstations. The screen saver protection is shown in Figure 3-18.

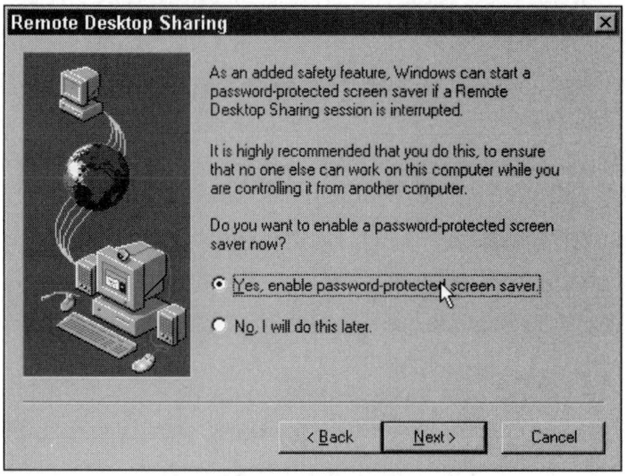

FIGURE 3-18 Screen saver protection

Once you have completed this step, the remote-sharing configuration is complete.

The Options selection

The Options selection is where you will find most of the configuration options for NetMeeting. This option is broken down into four key tabs.

o *General*. Provides configurations for personal information, such as name, address, and so on.

o *Security*. Specifies the security for various types of calls, inbound and outbound.

o *Audio*. Detailed configuration settings for the audio portion of the application.

o *Video*. Detailed configuration settings for the video portion of the application.

Let's talk a little about each tab so you can get more familiar with configuring Microsoft NetMeeting.

General tab

The fields in this tab are mostly self-explanatory. The Comment field enables you to enter personal information that will be displayed when other NetMeeting users are browsing various ILS servers. You should be aware that any NetMeeting user could view the information entered into this tab. With this in mind, you may want to educate your users about this option for personal security reasons. The General tab is shown in Figure 3-19.

o *Directory*. You can specify the default ILS server in the Directory Settings so that this is the server that is first contacted when the NetMeeting application is launched.

o *Do not list my name in the directory*. Do not list information in the LDAP directory on the server.

o *Log on to a directory server when NetMeeting starts*. When unchecked, NetMeeting does not contact your default ILS server. You have to manually initiate this when you launch the Directory option in the Call view.

o *Run NetMeeting in the Background when Windows starts*. Automatically starts NetMeeting with the default options. You can see that NetMeeting is running by looking for a globe with two arrows in your system tray.

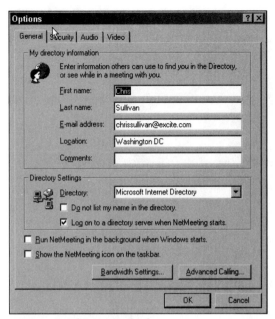

FIGURE 3-19 The General tab

- *Show the NetMeeting icon on the taskbar.* Allows you to use the NetMeeting icon in the system tray instead of using an icon on the taskbar. This feature is used to save space and to avoid accidentally shutting down the NetMeeting application.

- *Bandwidth Settings.* The Bandwidth Settings option enables you to optimize Microsoft NetMeeting for the maximum bandwidth available in your given situation. You can choose from several selections, including 14,400bps (Modem), 28,800bps or faster modem, Cable, xDSL or ISDN (Integrated Services Digital Network) 110,000bps, and LAN (Local Area Network) 5,000,000bps and over.

- *Advanced Calling Options.* Allows you to specify your gateway or Gatekeeper settings if applicable.

Security tab

The Security tab enables you to control how secure your communications are within the NetMeeting application (see Figure 3-20). You can opt to use only secure connections within NetMeeting to ensure that no one is eavesdropping on your calls.

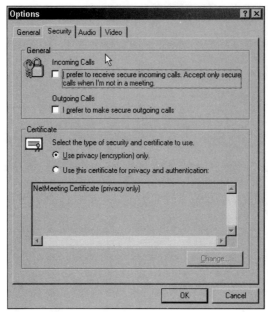

FIGURE 3-20 The Security tab

- *Incoming Calls.* Allows you to specify that you only receive secure calls.

- *Outgoing Calls.* This option is similar to the previous option, but secures outgoing calls.

- *Certificate/Use privacy (encryption) only.* Allows you to use the standard NetMeeting privacy certificate included in the installation.

- *Certificate/Use this certificate for privacy and authentication.* This option allows you to create your own connection using a certificate from Microsoft Certificate Server or from VeriSign at http://www.verisign.com.

 If you want to learn more about Certificate Server, check on Micro-soft's online seminar at http://www.microsoft.com/NTServer/appservice/deployment/training/appssemionline.asp.

Audio tab

This tab allows you to control and configure your audio settings. There are several features and selections for you to choose from. The audio tab is shown in Figure 3-21.

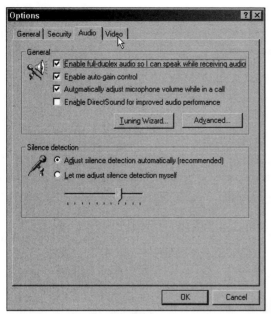

FIGURE 3-21 The Audio tab

- *Enable full-duplex audio so I can speak while receiving audio*. As I discussed earlier in the chapter, some sound cards cannot send and receive audio at the same time. These cards are called half-duplex sound cards. If your sound card supports full-duplex audio, this option enables audio transmission and reception at the same time.

- *Enable auto-gain control*. The auto-gain control allows your microphone volume to be adjusted dynamically depending on your speaking volume.

- *Automatically adjust microphone volume while in a call*. This option enables NetMeeting to configure itself automatically. The sensitivity affects how much background noise your microphone will pick up. This is also a handy option when you are not in close proximity to the microphone.

- *Enable DirectSound for improved audio performance*. This feature enables you to shorten the amount of time between transmitting and receiving audio streams. This improves performance, but sometimes has issues with certain sound cards.

- *Tuning Wizard*. This tool enables you to configure your microphone with NetMeeting. The Tuning Wizard is used to calibrate your microphone. We discussed the Tuning Wizard earlier in this chapter.

- *Advanced.* This option enables you to configure the audio CODEC configuration. Usually, this option is not needed unless you opt for a special configuration for NetMeeting.

- *Adjust silence detection automatically/Let me adjust silence detection myself.* Allows you to set up the baseline for the microphone silence. Silence is the baseline or starting point at which the volume is set. This is a simple concept if you think in terms of numeric volume. If silence is judged as one and maximum volume as ten, how can you judge whether the signal is in fact at ten if you do not know the scale?

Video tab

The Video tab enables you to control various video-related options. This tab is shown in Figure 3-22.

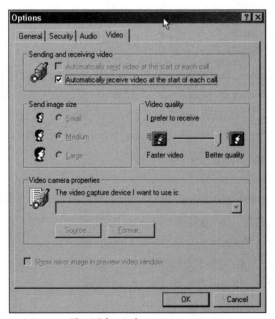

FIGURE 3-22 The Video tab

- *Automatically send video at the start of each call.* Enables NetMeeting to begin video transmission when initiating a NetMeeting call. The Video tab is shown in Figure 3-22.

- *Automatically receive video at the start of each call.* Enables NetMeeting users to receive video transmissions when initiating a NetMeeting call.

- *Send image size.* Allows the video image that you transmit to be small, medium, or large. This option configures the size of the video image that other NetMeeting users will see when you videoconference with them.

- *Video quality, I prefer to receive.* This option enables you to configure the frame rate that Microsoft NetMeeting will use during a session. The faster you configure the video, the more frames will be displayed, allowing a more real-time video experience.

- *Video camera properties.* This option enables you to select the video capture device to be used with Microsoft NetMeeting.

NETMEETING AND FIREWALLS

As you know, illegal entry and tampering can occur both inside and outside your network, and network abuse should be a serious consideration for any IT professional. The best defense against tampering is a documented and enforced security policy. This security policy governs the configurations of all the hardware and software attached to your network. The policy also establishes requirements for your protection against entry from the outside world, namely, through the Internet.

The Internet connection is the most likely place you will experience a breach in your security. One of the most popular defenses against this type of intrusion is a firewall. Firewalls can comprise software and many types of network-related hardware, such as proxy servers and routers. Most organizations use a combination of equipment and software to provide the security defenses necessary to secure their network.

Firewalls can be configured to allow and disallow TCP/IP ports. Most commercially developed IP-based applications use specified ports for communication. Standards organizations, such as the Web Consortium, agree on standard port numbers for applications to use. With a firewall, you can configure the software and/or hardware to allow or disallow traffic through the specific port. The reasons for doing so are many, but most are related to security and to preserving bandwidth.

...discussed earlier in the chapter, NetMeeting has several features that ...the application, including security features. NetMeeting has several fea-...elating to firewalls that you, as the administrator, need to be aware of. Let's ...a look at the ports that NetMeeting uses.

These ports may be covered in the exam, so get to know them as well as you can.

Table 3-4 gives a summary of ports and protocols necessary to support Microsoft NetMeeting through a proxy server or firewall. Remember that these ports must be allowed for inbound and outbound traffic.

TABLE 3-4 SECURITY PORTS AND PROTOCOLS FOR NETMEETING

SERVICE	PORT	PROTOCOL
ILS (Internet Locator Server)	389	TCP (Transmission Control Protocol)
ULS (User Locator Service)	522	TCP
T.120 MDC (Multipoint Data Conferencing)	1503	TCP
H.323 Call Setup (video and audio)	1720	TCP
Audio Call Control	1731	TCP
H.323 Call Control and Streaming	1024–65535	TCP and UDP (User Datagram Protocol)

Internet Locator Server requires that port 389 be allowed on the firewall. As you know, ILS acts as the meeting place for Microsoft NetMeeting. If you intend to allow your users to connect to Internet-based ILS servers, port 389 must be open.

If your intention is to deploy NetMeeting only within your network and not allow connectivity to the Internet with NetMeeting, you may want to verify that these ports have been allowed on your internal routers as well. A good method to test this is to use the Telnet utility to access a server on the other side of the router. If your connection request is unsuccessful, then you may have to do some investigating. To see if the port is open on your firewall, try to telnet to the ILS server using the server's name and port 389, for example. An example is shown in Figure 3-23. If your connection fails for any reason, your firewall is probably blocking this port.

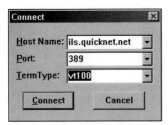

FIGURE 3-23 The Telnet test

User Locator Service (ULS)

If you are connecting to Internet Locator Server's predecessor, ULS, port 522 must also be open. If you do not have direct access to the server itself, you may have difficulty determining whether the server is an ILS server or a ULS server. You may want to attempt the Telnet trick for verification.

Multipoint Data Conferencing (MDC)

Multipoint Data Conferencing requires that port 1503 be open. Whiteboard, Chat, and Application Sharing are features that require the use of port 1503. These three utilities are examples of Multipoint Data Conferencing applications. In most cases, these ports are disabled on firewalls, proxy servers, and border routers to reduce the amount of non-business throughput on your external links. When deploying technology such as NetMeeting, educate yourself on the configurations of the network that have occurred and continue to occur. The more information you can gather, the better off you will be when it comes time for your users to click the setup button.

Call Setup and Call Control

NetMeeting negotiates dynamic ports to exchange video and audio streams. In order for NetMeeting to initiate the negotiation process, two ports must be open for the negotiation phase. Port 1720 allows the H.323 call setup phase, and port 1731 allows the audio call control. Once the negotiation phase is complete, a dynamic User Datagram Protocol (UDP) port is assigned for each feature on both sides of the connection.

Other Concerns

When choosing a firewall product or evaluating your NetMeeting implementation, you should be aware of compatibility issues between NetMeeting and some firewall products. Some proxy server configurations include virtual TCP/IP addressing, which enables you to assign IP addresses behind your firewall in any manner you choose. When a request is made to the Internet for data, the proxy server translates the IP address into a real IP address that can be used on the Internet. Some proxy servers cannot perform the packet translation necessary to function with NetMeeting.

KEY POINT SUMMARY

In this chapter, you learned about the Microsoft NetMeeting application and the configuration options that are available to you.

- Videoconferencing is one of the most popular features of NetMeeting. With a video camera attached to the workstation configuration, Microsoft NetMeeting transmits a video image to other NetMeeting users via the Internet, an intranet, or a local area network.

- The H.323 standard governs a variety of services that apply to videoconferencing, including CODEC. CODEC is an abbreviation for compression/decompression. The T-120 standard, data conferencing, is supported in NetMeeting with a variety of features. These standards are important to you because they ensure that applications will be able to interact with each other without causing major problems.

- Parallel cameras are very small cameras that connect to the workstation via the workstation's parallel port. The camera itself comes with software configured to translate the video signal into bit streams capable of being transmitted via the network connection.

- Capture cards enable you to digitize video from a variety of sources such as VCRs, handheld video recorders, and television signals. The Universal Serial Bus (USB) is a class of hardware that makes it simple to add serial devices to your computer. USB support is built to specifications so that future updates of Windows will support current drivers.

- The Audio Tuning Wizard controls the volume settings for your speakers and microphone. This wizard allows you to configure these options and gives you tips on how to best configure your audio settings.

- The Microsoft Internet Directory is an ILS-based LDAP directory that allows you to look up NetMeeting users. The Directory option allows you to connect to other ILS servers on the Internet.

- Firewalls can be configured to allow and disallow TCP/IP ports. NetMeeting has several ports that the application must be able to use in order to function properly.

APPLYING WHAT YOU'VE LEARNED

This section is an opportunity to use what you've learned in this chapter. The Instant Assessment questions here will help you practice for the exam. The labs that follow provide you with important real-world practice using the skills you've learned.

Instant Assessment

1. The _____ feature allows you to initiate a NetMeeting session with another user with whom you have previously held a NetMeeting session.

   A. Properties

   B. Current Call

   C. SpeedDial

   D. Hang Up

2. You can share an application with another NetMeeting user or multiple NetMeeting users.

   A. True

   B. False

3. The _____ defines the standard for video and data conferencing.

   A. IEEE

   B. IETF

   C. ITU

   D. Microsoft

4. A/An _____ requires the use of an external port on the user's workstation.

   A. Capture card

   B. Beta cam SP

   C. Parallel camera

   D. Video card

5. Selecting the _____ button can terminate NetMeeting sessions.

   A. Properties

   B. Refresh

   C. Call

   D. End Call

6. The _____ option allows you to browse an ILS server for other NetMeeting users.

   A. Directory

   B. Properties

   C. SpeedDial

   D. Send Mail

7. Formerly known as ULS, this server provides the medium for locating other NetMeeting Users.

   A. IIS

   B. WINS

   C. ILS

   D. DHCP

8. _____ allows for IP addresses to be managed and issued automatically.

    A. WINS

    B. IIS

    C. ILS

    D. DCHP

9. _____ sound cards allow you to transmit and receive audio at the same time.

    A. Half-duplex

    B. Full-duplex

    C. Multiplex

    D. Bi-directional

10. The _____ shows you the current status of your NetMeeting call.

    A. Outlook bar

    B. Channels bar

    C. Status bar

    D. Explorer bar

11. _____ allows you to collaboratively draw pictures and diagrams.

    A. Microsoft Paint

    B. Whiteboard

    C. Chat

    D. File transfer

12. You cannot connect to another NetMeeting user unless you are currently logged into an ILS Server.

    A. True

    B. False

13. If you wanted to see a list of users that you had recently conferenced with, you would select the _____ option.

    A. History

    B. Place a Call

    C. Directory

    D. Refresh

14. A user complains to you that he can no longer be heard by other NetMeeting users. The hardware has all been checked out and is working properly. What is the most likely cause of the problem?

A. Virus

B. Old version of NetMeeting

C. Microphone volume is not adequate

D. Incompatible microphone

15. Three users, user1, user2, and user3, are participating in a NetMeeting conference. User1 wants to transfer a file to user3, but not to user2. User1 can use the file transfer option to do this.

A. True

B. False

16. The application that allows text-based communication is the _____ application.

A. Chat

B. Whiteboard

C. File transfer

D. Notepad

17. A/An _____ defines the format for decompressing and compressing video images.

A. H.323

B. T.127

C. CODEC

D. IGRP

18. You can initiate an Outlook Express session directly from Microsoft NetMeeting itself, to send a message to another NetMeeting user.

A. True

B. False

19. The T.120 standard includes the following NetMeeting functions. (Choose two)

   A. Video CODECS

   B. Whiteboard

   C. E-mail

   D. File transfer

20. If you know that your NetMeeting user list on a particular server is outdated, you can select the _____ button to get an up-to-date list of users.

   A. Properties

   B. Call

   C. F5

   D. Current Call

21. One of the most expensive personal videoconferencing solutions you can buy is the _____.

   A. Parallel camera

   B. Capture card

   C. Video cipher card

   D. Serial camera

22. Another NetMeeting user you are talking with complains that your voice is varying in volume and is becoming annoying. You tell the user that you will correct the problem by adjusting the microphone sensitivity option in NetMeeting. This will solve the problem.

   A. True

   B. False

23. The quality of the video image can be adjusted in the _____ tab.

   A. Advanced

   B. Video

   C. Audio

   D. General

24. The default ILS server for your organization has experienced a difficulty that may take a few days to repair. In the meantime, you have set up another ILS server for your users to use. What is the best solution to ensure that there is no interruption in the users' NetMeeting use in the short and long term?

    A. Have all the users reinstall NetMeeting and select the new server's name as the default.

    B. Have all the users change their default ILS server in the Information tab.

    C. Tell all the users not to use NetMeeting until further notice.

    D. Change the DNS host name entry from the old ILS server to the new one, and start the new server.

25. You cannot prevent the user information from being displayed when a user logs on to an ILS server.

    A. True

    B. False

26. When starting NetMeeting, all of your users are getting an error message that states that the server is not available. The users can browse the Web through Microsoft Internet Explorer. What is the most likely cause of the problem?

    A. The DHCP server is not functioning and is causing problems with the user's TCP/IP configuration.

    B. The version of NetMeeting the users have is too old.

    C. The default ILS server is down.

    D. The users are not logged into the network.

27. A user complains that the video images that he receives from other NetMeeting users are very poor and choppy. Where would you point the user to in the configuration options, in order to alter the video quality?

    A. General tab

    B. Video tab

    C. Audio tab

    D. Advanced options, Video quality settings

28. You notice that when you log into any ILS server, anyone can call you without any intervention from you at all. Where would you go to stop this, and which option would you choose?

A. Video tab/Do not automatically accept incoming calls

B. Advanced options/Disable Automatically accept incoming calls

C. My Information tab/Deselect Automatically accept incoming calls

D. Call Option/Disable Automatically Accept Calls

29. Your PC is configured for a parallel video camera and a video capture card. When trying to use NetMeeting, you find that you cannot send video to any other NetMeeting user. Which option is probably selected wrong?

A. The Send video option is disabled in the Video tab.

B. The Tuning Wizard needs to be run to configure the camera.

C. The default capture device is incorrect in the General tab.

D. The default capture device is incorrect in the Video tab.

30. The Tuning Wizard can be accessed in the _____ tab.

A. Audio

B. Video

C. My Information

D. Advanced Options

31. If your organization has a proxy server, you needn't be concerned with NetMeeting configurations if the browser works.

A. True

B. False

32. Which of the following services will not work if port 522 is disabled on the proxy server?

A. ILS

B. SMS

C. ULS

D. LDAP

33. You can control the size of the image you are sending over the Internet with the _____ tab.

   A. Video

   B. Audio

   C. My Information

   D. Advanced

34. When using NetMeeting, you would use the _____ protocol to communicate with other NetMeeting users.

   A. IPX

   B. OGRP

   C. TCP/IP

   D. NetBEUI

35. The _____ wizard enables you to configure the microphone.

   A. Registry

   B. ILS

   C. Tuning

   D. ActiveMovie Setup

36. Developing a comprehensive security policy is the best defense against unwanted intrusion into your network.

   A. True

   B. False

Critical Thinking Labs

Lab 3.12 *Troubleshooting Microsoft NetMeeting*

You are asked to solve a problem with a user's inability to connect to other NetMeeting users. The user complains that he is unable to connect to other NetMeeting users with the NetMeeting client while other users in the same office are able to do so. What steps would you take to troubleshoot the user's problem?

Hands-On Labs

Lab 3.13 *Tuning your microphone and sound*

1. Launch the tuning wizard.

2. Tune your microphone and speakers.

3. Which settings were you allowed to change and why?

Lab 3.14 *Connecting and browsing an ILS server*

1. Start Microsoft NetMeeting.

2. Select Call, and then select an ILS server from the directory, such as ILS.FOUR11.COM.

3. Find someone who is testing; you can find someone by looking in the Comments column for testing.

4. Double-click on the user's name.

5. Type a message to the person.

Windows Media Player 6

About Chapter 4

In years past, text-based content was the only method to present and enhance Internet sites. Multimedia is now the new frontier on the Internet. Internet Explorer 5 comes complete with the new Windows Media Player 6, allowing Web developers and content providers to bring audio, video, and other multimedia content to the Internet Explorer browser. In this chapter, we will cover the basics of media technologies and then move on to specifics with Windows Media Player 6.

MEDIA TECHNOLOGIES BASICS

Windows Media Player 6 supports several compression formats. Compression allows you to take an audio or video file and make it smaller using industry standard methods to display and present multimedia content. The media player uses CODECs, as does NetMeeting. CODECs allow the video stream to be compressed for faster transmissions across networks and the internet. CODECs also allow the original image size to be made smaller, which conserves disk space. Popular uses for compression are as follows:

- Trailers for movies
- Excerpts of released movies
- Music playback
- Live broadcasts of concerts and video presentations
- Streaming video

Media Player 6 allows you to use a wide variety of different compression formats. Table 4-1 shows the compression formats supported by Media Player 6.

TABLE 4-1 COMPRESSION FORMATS SUPPORTED BY MEDIA PLAYER 6

VENDOR/ORGANIZATION	FILE FORMAT
Microsoft Windows Media	.avi, .asf, .rmi, .wav, asx
Musical Instrument Digital Interface (MIDI)	.mid, .rmi
Apple Quicktime, Macintosh	.qt, .aif, .aiff, .mov, .aifc
Moving Pictures Experts Group (MPEG)	.mpg, .mpeg, .m1v, .mp2, .mpa, .mpe
Unix Formats	.au, .snd

Media Player 6 allows you to work with a variety of multimedia-based presentation formats, technologies, and scenarios. Some of the possible uses follow.

- Downloading and playing a favorite song.
- Watching Internet-based news, such as streaming video on `http://www.msnbc.com`.
- Viewing internal meetings and speeches via Microsoft NetShow Server.

- Viewing local files on your workstation, such as a `.mov` file or `.mpeg` file.
- Listening to radio broadcasts on Web-based radio sites, such as `http://webevents.microsoft.com/radio/radio.asp`.

There are a lot of reasons to multimedia-enable your user's desktops and your Web site. You can provide this functionality and these features using Microsoft Media Technologies and Microsoft BackOffice. This section discusses the background of Microsoft Media Technologies, and the software components that constitute this technology.

SERVER–BASED STREAMING TECHNOLOGIES

Every video and audio stream has a beginning point or an *origination*. This origination allows the content provider to package an audio/video stream and present this content to the end user.

A server is required to deliver streaming audio/video to the desktop. The server software that is provided by Microsoft for streaming video delivery is called Microsoft NetShow. Microsoft Windows NT Server provides the means to host the NetShow Services for Windows NT. There are four pieces to Microsoft NetShow and NetShow-related services:

- NetShow Server
- NetShow Encoder
- NetShow SDK
- Microsoft Theater Server

Using Microsoft's NetShow

NetShow is similar to a television: you can look at several channels, but you cannot communicate with the broadcaster. Like TV, NetShow can carry live signals, and can display prepared content that has been encoded from a video file, such as an AVI or MPEG.

NetShow delivers content to the desktop from a central point, the NetShow server. The server stores the file (if it is prepared content) and controls the distribution of the signal.

If the content is not prepared, the stream is then considered to be live video. In this case, the NetShow server receives a live feed from a NetShow Encoder workstation. The Encoder's job is to take the analog signal generated by a video camera and convert the signal to digital format, such as an ASF video stream. As the video is being encoded, the stream is sent to the NetShow server for broadcasting. Figure 4-1 shows how NetShow works.

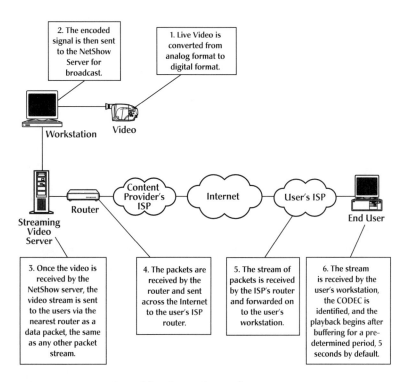

FIGURE 4-1   **Streaming with Microsoft NetShow**

NetShow differs from Microsoft NetMeeting (see Chapter 3) in that NetShow is a one-way service. A NetShow server only sends video and audio; it cannot receive anything. NetShow is also not quite as real time as NetMeeting; NetShow broadcasts are cached locally during reception, creating a small delay in receiving data. Microsoft NetShow Theater Server broadcasts live and on-demand video and audio to NetShow clients, such as Media Player.

NetShow utilizes the multicasting capabilities of TCP/IP. Multicasting allows data to be sent from one object to many objects simultaneously via the TCP and UDP portions of the TCP/IP protocol. NetShow can also utilize the unicasting capability. Unicasting allows a one-to-one broadcast via the UDP (User Datagram Protocol) tool of the TCP/IP protocol suite. UDP is commonly termed as a connectionless protocol; it does not offer the error correction and stability of TCP. UDP is, however, much faster because it offers less overhead. TCP is considered a connection-based protocol because TCP does offer error correction and a more stable format, however, these valuable features do add overhead.

concept link   **For more information on NetShow, check out** `http://www.microsoft.com/ntserver/mediaserv.`

Many different video-based solutions for NetShow are available, and the implementation scenarios are endless. Training seems to be one of the most popular recent uses of NetShow. Corporations can encode VHS-based videotapes and display the taped content directly from their NetShow servers to provide training to their employees on a large scale. The functionality of being able to receive the video on demand enables the user to view the content when it is convenient for him or her.

NetShow Server

NetShow Server is the software that is used to steam video to the user's desktops. NetShow Server is installed on Windows NT Server using the compressed BackOffice file `NSSERVER.EXE`. This file, available on Microsoft's site for free, allows you to install and configure the NetShow services on your Windows NT Server computer. Once installed, this software enables the presentation and distribution of your video and audio.

exam preparation pointer   **The sections about NetShow are meant to give you a 50,000-foot view of NetShow and the components of the software. While it is mentioned on the Internet Explorer exam, all you need to understand for now is the components of the software and what they do. For more detailed information about Microsoft NetShow, check out** `http://backoffice.microsoft.com.`

NetShow encoder

The `NSTOOLS.EXE` file, available on Microsoft's Web site for free, allows you to prepare and create the NetShow streams. NetShow video streams can be created in one of two ways: you can encode video that is currently in MPEG or AVI formats, or you can present live content. The NetShow encoder provides the means to convert the analog live signal or the digital file-based video to a format that can be streamed. Have you ever downloaded an .avi or .mpeg file from the Internet? The files are very large if the video is longer than a few seconds, and can take quite a while to fully download over a modem. In addition, you have to wait for the file to download completely before you can view the video.

Streaming video allows for the file to be compressed and sent bit by bit to enable the signal to be viewed quickly and efficiently. In addition, the video stream does not require a great deal of drive space, as downloading an .avi file does, so, this provides some functionality to users who have drive space considerations. NetShow uses the ASF (Active Streaming) format developed by Microsoft to provide live, or what is called "canned," video stream. "Canned" streams are pre-prepared content that is usually prepared way in advance and can be used in an archive-based scenario, such as training.

When the video is encoded, the video is changed from one video format to another. For example, a video clip that was compiled using the .mov format can be converted to the .asf format by the NetShow Server. The reason that you would want to do this is that .asf format can deliver streaming content, the .mov format cannot.

 tip **NetShow is really not as complicated as it sounds; the software is very easy to install and configure if you know Windows NT fairly well. I suggest that if you have not taken the IIS or TCP/IP exam, you review the documentation on both prior to attempting to implement NetShow. The encoding process is fairly quick and Microsoft provides a variety of templates ready-made for the encoder. The encoder also includes a plug-in for Adobe's Premiere video editing software. If you are planning on embarking on a NetShow implementation that is going to include canned video, I suggest you check this product out; it is very good.**

NetShow Software Development Kit

The NetShow Software Development Kit (SDK) provides some examples and utilities for you to use in developing applications and Web sites that utilize the Managed Webcasting features of Microsoft NetShow. You can develop applications through NetShow using the SDK that will bring live audio and video to your Web applications very quickly and effectively. If you are developing content for NetShow,

I highly recommend that you review the SDK. There are several very good examples, tips and tricks, and some helpful utilities included that can get you to your goal much faster.

concept link

For more information on Microsoft NetShow and the NetShow SDK, check out `http://www.microsoft.com/windows/windowsmedia/en/developers/default.asp`.

The client side of NetShow is the Windows Media Player, which allows the workstation to display the video stream.

MEDIA PLAYER 6

The user's desktop interface to NetShow services is the Windows Media Player. Media Player allows the workstation to display the video stream. Using Web-based scripting languages such as Vbscript and ECMAScript, the developer can embed Media Player within an HTML or ASP page to allow a cleaner look. Media Player displays controls that are similar to that of a VCR, and can be manipulated with other development-based languages.

Figure 4-2 shows the Media Player 6 interface. You can launch Media Player yourself, by navigating to your `start/programs/accessories/entertainment` folder and double clicking on Windows Media Player. You can also launch it via `start/run` and type **mplayer2.exe**.

concept link

This navigation applies to Windows 95/98. The path for Media Player for Windows NT workstation is determined using IEAK, which we will talk about in Chapter 7.

The controls for the Media Player are much like a home VCR. The control features are listed:

- *Play.* Allows you to start viewing a video or audio clip.
- *Stop.* Stops the clip in progress.
- *Pause.* Allows you to temporarily stop the clip; it differs from the Stop button, in that you can restart the clip where you left off.
- *Skip Back.* Allows you to move the clip back a few frames to review.
- *Rewind.* Moves the clip back in an accelerated fashion.

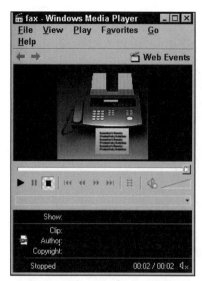

FIGURE 4-2   The Windows Media Player interface

- o *Fast Forward.* Moves the clip forward in a rapid fashion.
- o *Skip Ahead.* Allows you to move the clip ahead a few frames.
- o *Playlist Preview.* In clips that support the playlist function, this feature allows you to view ten seconds of a clip before viewing the entire clip. The preview interval is set programmatically by the developer, and can sometimes be longer than ten seconds.
- o *Mute.* Allows you to temporarily shut off the audio portion of a clip.
- o *Volume.* Controls the volume of a clip.
- o *Elapsed Time.* Allows you to view how much of the clip has already been viewed.
- o *Total Time.* Allows you to see how long the clip is in time length.
- o *Seek Bar.* Allows you to move the clip backwards and forwards using the mouse.

The File Menu

Like most Windows-based applications, the File menu shown in Figure 4.3, has standard application functions, such as Open, Properties, Save As, and so on.

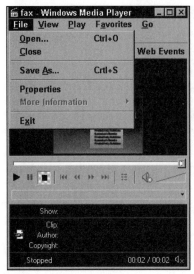

FIGURE 4-3 The File menu

- *Open.* Using the Open option, you can navigate to your local drive to view a multimedia file, such as an MPG or AVI file. You can also type in a known URL to streaming-based content as well. The Open dialog box also has a handy MRU (most recently used) feature that allows you to navigate to previously used multimedia files.

- *Close.* The Close feature allows you to end the multimedia session you are currently viewing without closing the entire Media Player application.

- *Save As.* The Save As feature allows you to save the clip to another file name or location dependent on your personal choice. The Media Player will save the file in the same format in which is was downloaded, `.avi` for example.

- *Properties.* This feature allows you to view a variety of information such as:
  - Author (John Doe)
  - Copyright (Image Copyright 11/2/98)
  - Rating (4)
  - File location (for example, `c:\download\news.mpeg`)
  - File Size (1.7MB 1,652,111 bytes)
  - Clip Length (00:51)
  - Video Size (176 by 112 pixels)
  - Date Created (Monday April 19, 12:00:00 AM)

- Filters used to decompress the image
- Compression algorithms that the image has enabled

The View Menu

The View menu allows you to change the view of your images in Windows Media Player. You have several options available to you, such as standard, compact, and minimal. Let's talk more specifically about the features in the View menu.

The View menu, shown in Figure 4-4, allows you to change various options relating to the view of the clip.

- *Standard.* Allows you to view the clip with all available viewing options, such as the control menus and the clip information window.
- *Compact.* The same as the Standard view, minus the clip information window.
- *Minimal.* The same as Compact, minus the Seek Bar and the Play window.
- *Full Screen.* Blows up the clip to 640×480 (or your workstation resolution). In many cases, video will become very grainy at full screen due to the fact that the image was compiled for a smaller resolution. Reduce the image size for better video if your image is grainy.

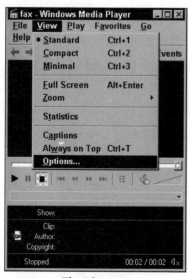

FIGURE 4-4 The View menu

- *Zoom.* Allows you to magnify the clip by up to 200% or shrink it by up to 50%.
- *Statistics.* This option allows you to view the frames per second, lost frames, and other network and video related information.

You may want to get familiar with the Statistics option. This option is a great troubleshooting tool when users complain about choppy or poor quality video. Choppy video can be caused by a congested network or possibly a workstation with an insufficient amount of RAM. Use the Statistics option to narrow down the cause by viewing the networking statistics.

- *Always on Top.* This feature allows the Media Player application to be the primary application displayed on the user's desktop. This allows the user to be working in a word processor, for example, and watching Fox News at the same time.
- *Options.* The Options dialog box allows you to configure a variety of options for the Media Player. Figure 4-5 shows the Options window.

The Options Menu

The Options dialog box, shown in Figure 4-5, includes options for playback, buffering, and file formats, among other things. The following sections discuss the controls in more detail.

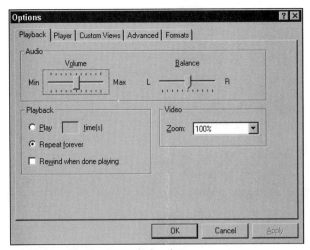

FIGURE 4-5 The Options dialog box

Playback tab

The Playback tab, shown in Figure 4-5, allows you to control the volume of the clip and also the audio balance of the clip. The Playback section allows you to configure defaults for clip playback. You can configure clips to replay a specified amount of times, repeat endlessly, or to rewind the clip to the beginning and wait for further action. The Zoom option allows you to set the default zoom level for the application.

Player tab

The Player tab allows you to set Open options to control how Media Player behaves. Open options enables you to control how many windows are needed when viewing multiple video clips. View allows you to select the default size of the window as Standard, Minimum, or Compact. Always on top and Autozoom player enable you to control the display of the Media Player application. The Show controls in full screen function allows you to see the Control toolbar when Media Player is run in full screen mode. The Player tab is shown in Figure 4-6.

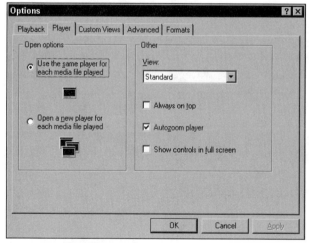

FIGURE 4-6 The Player tab

Custom Views tab

The Custom Views tab, shown in Figure 4-7, allows you to manipulate the options that are displayed when choosing the various player View options, such as Compact and Minimal. You can change various selections, such as allowing the Navigation bar to be displayed in the Compact view if you so choose. The main reasons for making changes in the views is to allow the media player interface to be most effective for your user community.

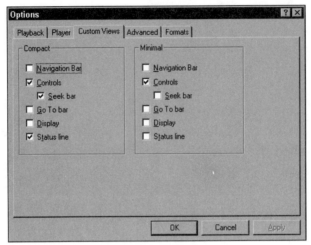

FIGURE 4-7   The Custom Views tab

Advanced tab

The Advanced tab shown in Figure 4-8, is one of the most important configuration options in the entire Media Player application. This feature allows you to change network and buffering information related to the Media Player application.

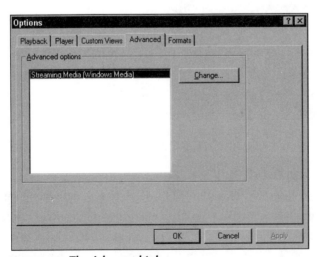

FIGURE 4-8   The Advanced tab

From this option, you can make configuration changes to Windows Media Player and to Real Network's RealVideo player as well. Select the Media Player option and select the Change option to navigate to the Advanced playback settings. Figure 4.9 shows the configuration options available to you.

Buffering allows Media Player to download the first few seconds of the content before displaying the content in the Media Player display. Buffering allows Media Player to get ahead of the stream in the event of a temporary network problem or network latency. In environments where latency is a problem, you may want to consider adding more buffering time to allow Media Player to cache more of the content.

You can also configure Media Player to only allow certain protocols to be used in its operation. These options allow you to exercise more control of the users in your environment.

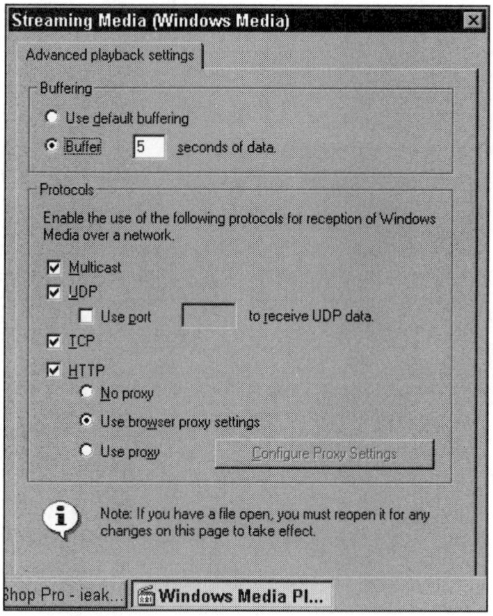

FIGURE 4-9 Advanced playback settings

Probably the most important option here is the proxy configuration. In environments where Proxy Servers exist, Media Player will not be able to display Internet-based content without the proxy settings entered properly. This option allows you to set configurations based on the following:

- *No Proxy.* No proxy server is needed.
- *Use browser proxy settings.* This option uses the Internet Explorer proxy settings for Media Player.
- *Use proxy.* If you want to set proxy settings specific for multimedia content, you can select this option. Figure 4-10 shows the custom proxy settings option.

The Advanced tab is where you would configure specific proxy settings for Media Player. By default, the player uses the browser's proxy settings. In some circumstances, organizations may block streaming video on one proxy server/firewall and not others. Here you can specify a proxy/firewall that is used for streaming video.

FIGURE 4-10 Custom proxy settings option

Formats tab

The Formats tab allows you to configure the audio and video formats that are utilized by the Media Player application. This feature is very useful for enacting some control over the content that your user community is viewing across your network. For example, if your organization has standardized on the ASF (Advanced Streaming Format) for your streaming servers, you could disallow all other formats so that your users are only allowed to view your standard content. Some Web sites have live video content that is inappropriate in the workplace. The Formats tab is shown in Figure 4-11.

The Play Menu

The Play menu is basically a mirror of the controls listed in the Control menu. Here, you can start, stop, forward and otherwise manipulate the media clip through a menu driven interface. If you are like me, I like to use the menu as opposed to the buttons on the Control menu. This is really a matter of personal preference in navigation. The Play menu is shown in Figure 4-12.

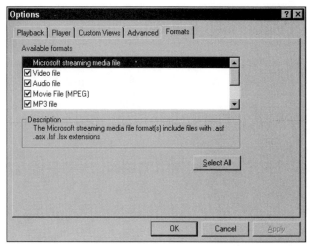

FIGURE 4-11 The Formats tab

FIGURE 4-12 The Play menu

There is an additional option in the menu that is not available on the Control menu. The Language option allows you to change the language that is used on the Control menu.

The Favorites Menu

The Favorites menu, shown in Figure 4-13, allows you to configure popular URLs that contain multimedia content. Using this option, you could add multimedia intranet, extranet, and Internet sites that your users may have interest in.

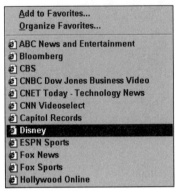

FIGURE 4-13 The Favorites menu

The Go Menu

The Go menu is a built-in feature of Media Player that allows you to navigate to the Microsoft Events Web site located at `http://webevents.microsoft.com`. This site is a nicely organized view of popular multimedia Web sites that are available to you.

   The other option on the Go menu navigates you to the Windows Media Player home page. Here, you can download patches, information, and other related material on Windows Media Player. The Go menu is shown in Figure 4-14.

FIGURE 4-14 The Go menu

The Help Menu

The Help menu is a standard help menu like any other Windows application. You can view Help topics to more familiarize yourself with Media Player by selecting the Help Topics tab as shown in Figure 4-15. There is a large amount of information located in the Help file to assist you in a number of scenarios.

You can also use the Help menu to check the version of your Windows Media Player application to see if a newer version is available. The About Windows Media Player option displays the exact version and build you are currently using.

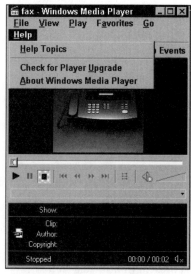

FIGURE 4-15 The Help menu

THE FUTURE OF MP3

MP3 is a way of storing music on your computer so that it takes up relatively little space on your hard drive while still sounding close to what you hear on a CD. Similar to the concept of a turntable, an MP3 player is the software you need to play the music files you download from the Internet.

Any MP3 file works on any MP3 player, and you can get players for both PCs and Macs. The very latest versions of Windows Media Player will also play MP3 files.

You can find MP3 files to download on Web sites such as listen.com. In order to listen to the music files you download, you will need to download a player, such as the Windows Media Player. There are many players to choose from, but for basic music playback, almost any player will do. You can also consider purchasing a MP3 player that will allow you to take your MP3 files on the road with you. These portable MP3 players allow you to play back your MP3 files while you are on the go, much like a portable CD player or cassette player.

The reason that I am taking this time to talk about MP3 is to show you some of the technology that is headed for your desktop. Many people envision MP3 as the future of audio entertainment. Things to think about are not having to purchase CDs from the store anymore, no complex organizers to maintain, and so on. With MP3s, you can download the song or the whole album to your hard drive. From there, you can copy the files to your portable player or take these files to work with you to listen to on your workstation.

KEY POINT SUMMARY

Now that we have covered the features of Windows Media Player 6, let's review the key points of this chapter's discussion.

- Windows Media Player 6 supports several compression formats. Compression allows you to take an audio or video file and make it smaller using industry standard methods to display and present multimedia content.

- Microsoft NetShow is an application for receiving broadcasted audio and video within the context of the user's browser or Windows Media Player. NetShow differs from Microsoft NetMeeting in that NetShow is a one-way service. NetShow only receives video and audio; it cannot send anything back.

- The client side of NetShow is Windows Media Player, which allows the workstation to display the video stream. Using Web-based scripting languages such as Vbscript and ECMAScript, the developer can embed the player within an HTML or ASP page to allow a cleaner look. Media Player displays controls that are similar to that of a VCR, and it can also be manipulated with other development-based languages.

- The Playback tab allows you to control the volume of the clip and also the audio balance of the clip. The Playback section allows you to configure defaults for clip playback. You can configure clips to replay a specified amount of times, repeat endlessly, or to rewind the clip to the beginning and wait for further action.

o The Player tab allows you to set Open options to control how Media Player behaves. Open options allow you to control how many windows are needed when viewing multiple video clips. The view allows you to select the default size of the window: Standard, Minimum, or Compact.

o Buffering allows media player to download the first few seconds of the content before displaying the content in the Media Player display. Buffering allows media Player to get ahead of the stream in the event of a temporary network problem or network latency.

o In environments where Proxy Servers exist, Media Player will not be able to display Internet-based content without the proxy settings entered properly. The Advanced playback settings in the View Menu/Options/Advanced Tab/ Advanced Options allows you to set configurations for buffering, protocols, and proxy settings.

o The Help menu is a standard help menu like any other Windows application. You can view Help topics to more familiarize yourself with Media Player by selecting the Help Topics tab. You can also use the Help menu to check the version of your Windows Media Player application to see if a newer version is available. The About Windows Media Player option displays the exact version and build you are currently using.

Applying What You've Learned

This section is an opportunity to use what you've learned in this chapter. The Instant Assessment questions here will help you practice for the exam.

1. Which of the following is NOT a supported format in Media Player 6?

   A. `.mpeg`

   B. `.avi`

   C. `.doc`

   D. `.qt`

2. Microsoft_____ is an application that runs on Windows NT Server designed to stream video to Media Player clients.

   A. Site Server

   B. Index Server

   C. Internet Locator Server

   D. NetShow

3. Using Media Player configuration options, you can choose to use Internet Explorer's proxy settings or custom settings for Media Player 6.

   A. True

   B. False

4. Unicasting allows _____ broadcasting via the TCP/IP protocol.

   A. Multicast

   B. Unicast

   C. one-to-one

   D. many-to-one

5. One of the NetShow default file types supported by Media Player 6 is the _____ file type.

   A. `.mlv`

   B. `.avi`

   C. `.url`

   D. `.asf`

6. Using the _____ tool, you can compile `.avi` and `.mpg` files into Microsoft NetShow for broadcasting on the Internet.

   A. NetShow Server

   B. NetShow SDK

   C. NetShow encoder

   D. NetShow Theater Server

7. The playlist preview option in Media Player 6 allows you to view a default value of ____ seconds of a clip.

   A. 15

   B. 10

   C. 20

   D. 30

8. A user calls to ask where they can check to see if they are running the most current version of Media Player. Which menu would you point the user to?

   A. The Go menu

   B. The Favorites menu

   C. The Help menu

   D. The Advanced menu

9. Which option would you choose to modify in an environment where network latency is a problem?

   A. Proxy Settings

   B. Fast Forward

   C. Previews

   D. Buffering

10. NetShow can carry live, real-time broadcasts.

    A. True

    B. False

11. Which protocol is faster and why?

    A. TCP-connection oriented protocols are much faster.

    B. UDP-connectionless oriented protocols are much faster.

    C. TCP-connectionless oriented protocols are much faster.

    D. UDP-connection oriented protocols are much faster.

12. Which programming language could you use to control Media Player within an HTML page? Choose the best answer.

A. Assembly

B. C++

C. ECMAScript

D. Cobol

13. Configuration options are accessed through the_____ menu.

A. Favorites

B. Help

C. File

D. View

14. You can change RealVideo player options from within the Media Player application.

A. True

B. False

15. Using NetShow Server and the NetShow player, you can carry on a two-way conversation.

A. True

B. False

16. Media Player 6 supports the following Macintosh file formats (select all that apply):

A. .qt

B. .aif

C. .mpe

D. .mov

17. The ASF streaming format was developed by _____.

A. Real Networks

B. Novell

C. Apple

D. Microsoft

18. NetShow includes a plug-in for the popular _____ video editing software.

    A. Paint Shop

    B. Microsoft PowerPoint

    C. Abode PhotoShop

    D. Adobe Premier

19. The _____ includes examples of streaming content to help get you started.

    A. NetShow starter CD

    B. NetShow SDK

    C. NetShow Encoder

    D. NetShow Steaming Server

20. You can configure Media Player to utilize only certain network protocols.

    A. True

    B. False

The Nuts and Bolts of Internet Explorer

In Part I, you learned about the applications and features supporting the Internet Explorer suite. In Part II, we are going to start out with an in-depth discussion on how the installation of the software works. You will learn about the algorithms used to install the software, migrating from other browsers, and other considerations. You will also learn about event logging, basic troubleshooting, and how to recover a failed installation.

Internet Explorer Setup

About Chapter 5

In Chapter 5, we will discuss the installation process for Internet Explorer 5. There are many aspects of installing Internet Explorer 5 that you will need to know in preparation for Exam 70-080. For example:

- What are the system requirements to install Internet Explorer 5?
- What platforms can Internet Explorer 5 be installed on?
- Are there any coexistence or migration issues to consider?
- What files are created or used while installing Internet Explorer 5?
- What tools are available for troubleshooting an installation?

Reviewing the information in this chapter would also be helpful before creating setup packages using the Internet Explorer 5 Administration Kit.

WINDOWS UPDATE SETUP

Windows Update Setup allows for the quick and efficient installation of Internet Explorer 5 on a variety of platforms. Windows Update Setup intelligently controls the setup process, making the installation and configuration of Internet Explorer 5 more robust, easier to troubleshoot and repair, and overall more cost effective than previous installation methods. If you've used the Internet Explorer 4 Administration Kit, you have already been introduced to much of the technology behind the Windows Update Setup process.

Based on Microsoft's ActiveX engine, Windows Update Setup embodies the best concepts for deploying softwareapplications via an Internet or intranet download. Conventional installation methods using removable media such as floppy diskettes and CD-ROMs are still options; however, the ability to deploy Internet Explorer 5 via the download process is still the browser's strongest feature. The entire Windows Update Setup process is tailor-made for Web-based deployment of software applications.

The concept behind the Windows Update Setup is simple:

- Download a very small executable with minimal support files to collect information from the host machine and evaluate its ability to accept Internet Explorer 5. These can either be downloaded via a browser or copied to the local machine if the machine does not already have a browser installed.

- Collect as much information as possible up front. Determining the required disk space and user information prior to beginning the download process reduces the amount of time you spend connected to a Web site.

- Allow for a variety of installation options and download sites to accommodate a variety of platforms and users.

- Keep log files for every transaction throughout the installation process to aid in troubleshooting and reporting.

- Download only the required components in a compressed format to minimize download time and maximize bandwidth utilization.

- Display relevant installation information during the setup process. By including the estimated time as well as the standard progress meter, a lot of the guesswork can be taken out of how long an installation will take.

- Provide redundant download sites. Errors can occur while downloading information. The ability to change download sites "on-the-fly" and recover where the setup procedure left off minimizes the likelihood of corrupted or lengthy installations.

- Complete the installation by extracting the files from their compressed format and registering all components on the local machine, thus minimizing the amount of time the machine has to be connected to the Internet.

In addition to accomplishing all of these, the Windows Update Setup is highly customizable by using the Internet Explorer 5 Administration Kit. I'll cover how to create custom installation packages using the IEAK in Chapter 10.

Now that we understand the concepts, let's examine in closer detail installing Internet Explorer 5 using the Windows Update Setup.

Preparing to Install Internet Explorer 5

It is always a good idea to check a system for required resources and ensure the system's integrity prior to installing any new software. When installing Internet Explorer 5, a cursory check should be made to see if the machine meets all hardware and software requirements. You should further check to see if the machine has previously had an issue installing a version of Internet Explorer or any other similar software product.

 tip **Internet Explorer 5 can run on a machine with a previous version of Internet Explorer or a competitive browser installed. Web pages designed for other browsers, however, may have to be re-designed to function properly in Internet Explorer 5.**

System Requirements

How many times have you started to install a piece of software only to get the dreaded "Not Enough Disk Space" prompt halfway through the process? Often people forget to check the system requirements before attempting to install software.

Windows Update Setup now includes an upfront disk space-checking to prompt you early in the process should you not have enough disk space. To aid you in your efforts, Table 5-1 illustrates the system requirements for Inte. Explorer 5.

TABLE 5-1 INTERNET EXPLORER 5 HARDWARE REQUIREMENTS				
PLATFORM	*VERSION*	*DISK SPACE REQUIRED*	*MEMORY REQUIRED*	*PROCESSOR REQUIRED*
Windows 95/98	95 OSR1	45MB minimum	16MB	486DX/66
Windows NT 4.0	NT4 w/ Service Pack 3	45MB minimum	32MB	486DX/66
Windows 3.1 for Workgroups	3.1, 3.11	45MB prior to installation	16MB	486DX/66
Windows NT 3.51	3.51	45MB prior to installation	32MB	486DX/66
Macintosh	7.1 and above	45MB	16MB	68030

Note that the English version of Internet Explorer 5 cannot be installed on Hebrew or Arabic versions of Windows 98. Also, if you're using Windows NT 4.0, you must install the Service Pack 3 or later before you install Internet Explorer 5.

 exam preparation pointer **Do yourself a favor and know this table like the back of your hand.**

Previous Installations Using Windows Update Setup

Because the Windows Update Setup logs every action of an installation from start to finish, these log files are a very good way of checking for a previous installation of Internet Explorer 5. The existence of the log file means an application was installed using Windows Update Setup. The log file to look for is named `Active Setup Log.txt` and it resides in the operating system folder of the machine. If there were any issues or problems during the installation, the log file will show it.

The first line of the log file shows the date and time an installation began. Subsequent lines show the events that took place in sequential order from start to finish. The last line even shows the date and time that the last cabinet file (.cab) was successfully downloaded. Errors that occurred will be displayed using HRESULT error codes. Some common errors that may result are as follows:

- o 80100003: Missing file or files from a download folder
- o 800bxxxx: Trust Failure
- o 800Cxxxx: URLmon Failure
- o 8004004: User Initiated Cancel

In addition to the commonly generated errors, use Table 5-2 to identify other possible errors.

TABLE 5-2 HRESULT ERROR CODES

ERROR CODE	PHASE
0	Initialization (creation of temp directories, disk space verification, and so on)
1	Dependencies
2	Download Processes
3	Copy Functions (populating temp directories with download folders)
4	Retrying (attempting to reconnect after a timed-out connection or failed download)
5	Trust Verification
6	Extraction
7	Execution
8	Completion of Installation
9	Completion of Download

Checking the Active Setup Log.txt file is the best way to troubleshoot errors that may have been produced during setup.

 tip **The existence of a file named** Active Setup Log.bak **signifies that multiple installations using Windows Update Setup were attempted (successfully and unsuccessfully) on the machine.**

THE INTERNET EXPLORER SETUP FILE

After verifying the machine has the adequate system resources to install Internet Explorer 5 and that there has not been an unsuccessful attempt to install Internet Explorer 5, the next step is to place a copy of IE5Setup.exe on the local machine.

 tip **If Active Setup parses the** Active Setup Log.txt **and finds that there was an unsuccessful setup attempt, the setup will pick up where it left off on the previous attempt.**

This can be accomplished in a variety of ways. First, it can be downloaded from a known site provided you have a browser such as Internet Explorer 4 already installed on the machine. This site can either be a corporate-sponsored site within your intranet or a site hosted on the Internet. A second way to obtain a copy of the IE5Setup.exe file is to copy it from a network share or removable media device such as a floppy diskette or CD-ROM.

 note **Microsoft tries to ensure that** IE5Setup.exe **is small and compact. While download times vary, even transfers at 28Kbps only take about two minutes.**

IE5Setup.exe collects information from the local machine prior to downloading any files required for installation. This information is then used to determine which components should be installed. In this way, components that are already installed or components that you chose not to install do not have to be downloaded, thus making for a quicker installation with less likelihood of problems.

Running IE5Setup.exe

To get a better idea of what IE5Setup.exe does, let's look at what happens on the machine when you run the executable:

1. Two log files are created in the operating system folder on the local machine. The first is named Active Setup Log.txt. It records the events of the installation. The first line of Active Setup Log.txt will always display the date and time the installation began. The second log file is named RunOnceEx.txt. It logs all actions taken during the Dynamic Link Library (.dll) registration portion of setup. If there are any .dll-related errors during the installation, refer to this log for information. Anyone receiving a .dll error during setup should check this file for troubleshooting the issue.

tip If a log file already exists in the operating system folder, it will be renamed with a `.bak` extension (that is, `Active Setup Log.bak`).

2. Setup files are extracted to a temporary directory on the local machine.

3. The `IESetup.inf` file is checked for the URL location of an `IESites.dat` file.

4. Windows Update Setup then displays to the user the available installation options for download. We'll further discuss the user interface portion later in this chapter.

5. Cabinet files required for the user-selected options are downloaded to the directory specified by the user for installation.

6. The files within the cabinet files are then extracted to their appropriate locations on the local machine.

7. The browser is installed on the machine as well as any custom components you may have included.

concept link For information about including custom components within your Internet Explorer 5 setup package, see Chapter 10.

8. The machine is restarted to configure the desktop environment.

9. A customizable splash screen is displayed welcoming the user to Internet Explorer 5.

Files Used by Windows Update Setup

As you've seen, there are several types of files that are called or used by `IE5Setup.exe` throughout the installation process. Table 5-3 depicts just a few of the many types of files you may encounter while using Windows Update Setup to install Internet Explorer 5 on your machine.

tip Most administrators create and maintain a custom `IESites.dat` file for their enterprise.

TABLE 5-3 INSTALLATION FILE TYPES	
TYPE OF FILE	*DEFINITION OR PURPOSE*
.exe	Executable file. Executable files initiate or manage actions. For example, IE5Setup.exe is the file that controls the setup of Internet Explorer 5.
.cab	Cabinet file. Cabinet files contain structured and compressed files required for installation. Cabinet files are downloaded or copied to a machine, then the files within are extracted. This method enables quicker download times and more efficient installations. This is due to the fact that a compressed .cab is much smaller in size than the files it contains and the files are extracted on the local machine without requiring a persistent Internet connection.
.inf	Information file. Generally cabinet files and executables contain or have available an information file. For example, IESetup.inf is the file that guides the installation process by providing the setup files with the settings and location information they require. IESetup.inf contains information outlining versioning, default component install, destination directories, optional components, locations, and localized string variables. IE5Setup.exe reads IESetup.inf to locate the IESites.dat file.
.dat	Definition file. Definition files are basically text files broken into multiple sections to categorize and store information and variables for use during installation. For example, IESites.dat contains a listing of the available Web sites that can be used for downloading Internet Explorer 5 cabinet files. IE5Setup.exe uses this to provide a list of download sites to choose from during installation.
.ins	Internet settings file. Internet settings files are used by Windows Update Setup to set up the options for the browser and any other associated components. They can be created using the IEAK Profile Manager. I'll cover the IEAK Profile Manager in Chapter 8.
.adm	Administration file. Administration files outline any restrictions and policies as specified in the Internet Explorer 5 Administration Kit.
.cif	Component information file. These files define the ComponentIDs for their associated components. Windows Update Setup verifies whether a component should be installed or replaced with a newer version of the component based on its ComponentID.
.bmp	Windows bitmap file. Windows bitmap is a common graphic files format. Through the Internet Explorer 5 Administration Kit you can include custom bitmaps in place of the standard user interface items. Some of these custom bitmaps could include static or animated logos in place of the IE logo, screen elements on splash screens and setup dialog boxes, and toolbar backgrounds.
.cdf	Channel definition file. Channel definition files list the resources and settings for channels.

The Smart Recovery Feature

One of the greatest items built into `IE5Setup.exe` is the Smart Recovery feature. This feature allows for the most reliable means of downloading the files necessary for installation.

Here's how it works:

1. An error occurs while downloading files.
2. `IE5Setup.exe` detects the error, reads the Active Setup Log to determine where the error occurred.
3. `IE5Setup.exe` then uses the available sites list provided by the `IESites.dat` file to redirect the download process to the next available site picking up where the original setup left off.

This ability to recover instead of crashing or canceling setup is the first step to a trouble-free installation. Unfortunately, the end-user will never truly appreciate this feature because if everything works the way it should, they'll never see it. You as the administrator, however, can check the `Active Setup Log.txt` file on the machine to determine if a retry had to be initiated due to a download error or timed-out connection. Troubleshooting the installation process is especially important in deployment scenarios involving beta or pilot phases. The information you gather during these phases will help you to identify any specific issues that may exist within your organization. The ability to pinpoint possible issues regarding client configurations, server configurations, and bandwidth limitations is critical to any full-scale deployment.

STEPPING THROUGH THE INSTALLATION

Once `IE5Setup.exe` has been placed on the machine, the next step is to actually install Internet Explorer 5. I've shared with you what happens behind the scenes; now let's look at the user interface.

When you launch `IE5Setup.exe`, the first dialog box to appear is the End User License Agreement (EULA). The EULA for Internet Explorer 5 is the same standard agreement we've all come to know and love. Click the "I accept the agreement" option, then the Next button will move things along.

Installation Options

The next dialog box will prompt you for the type of installation for Internet Explorer 5. There are three basic types of installations: Minimal, which installs the bare-bones items; Typical, which installs the most common items; and Full, which is everything but the kitchen sink. The installation options dialog box is shown in Figure 5-1.

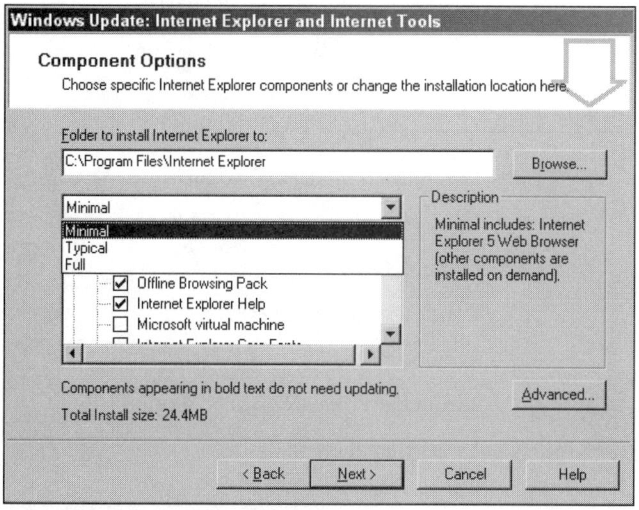

FIGURE 5-1 Installation options

Beyond the three basic installations is the Custom installation, which allows you to pick and chose the components that matter — or don't matter — to you. Table 5-4 is a list of the components installed with each installation type.

Selecting the "Install Now" option will begin the installation using the Typical installation method as discussed earlier. If you prefer use a different installation method, select the Install Minimal or Customize option.

After making the installation type decision, a "Preparing Setup" dialog box appears. It is during this time that the components on the machine are checked to see if they are installed, out-of-date, or current.

TABLE 5-4 COMPONENT INSTALLATION TYPES	
INSTALLATION TYPE	COMPONENTS INSTALLED
Minimal	Internet Explorer 5 Web Browser
	Internet Explorer Help
	Windows Media Player
	Visual Basic Scripting Support
Typical	Internet Explorer 5 Web Browser
	Offline Browsing Pack
	Internet Explorer Help
	Internet Explorer Core Fonts
	Dynamic HTML Data Binding
	Internet Explorer Browsing Enhancements
	Outlook Express
	Windows Media Player
	Windows Media Player Codecs
	Media Player RealNetworks Support
	DirectAnimation
	Vector Graphics Rendering (VML)
	AOL ART Image Format Support
	Visual Basic Scripting Support
	Language Auto-Selection
Full	Internet Explorer 5 Web Browser
	Offline Browsing Pack
	Internet Explorer Help
	Microsoft Virtual Machine
	Internet Explorer Core Fonts
	Dynamic HTML Data Binding
	Internet Explorer Browsing Enhancements
	NetMeeting
	Outlook Express
	Chat 2.5

Continued

TABLE 5-4 *(continued)*	
INSTALLATION TYPE	**COMPONENTS INSTALLED**
Full *(continued)*	Windows Media Player
	Windows Media Player Codecs
	Media Player RealNetworks Support
	DirectAnimation
	Vector Graphics Rendering (VML)
	AOL ART Image Format Support
	FrontPage Express
	Web Publishing Wizard
	Web Folders
	Visual Basic Scripting Support
	Additional Web Fonts
	Wallet
	Language Auto-Selection
Custom	Any combination of components from the other three installations. A Custom installation *must* include all components from the Minimal installation option.

note ▽ **If the versions of all components on the machine are current, a prompt will inform you of this and ask if you would like to exit setup or re-install the components.**

Advanced Installation Options

If you chose a Minimal or Custom installation, a new dialog box will appear allowing you to select from a list of components. On this dialog box is an Advanced button. The Advanced options are shown in Figure 5-2.

Clicking the Advanced button provides three additional options to choose from:

- *Don't Associate File Types.* Internet and Web extensions such as .htm or .asp will not be associated with Internet Explorer 5. This grants you the ability to install Internet Explorer 5 but keeps your files associated with either an earlier version of Internet Explorer or a competitive browser installed on the machine.

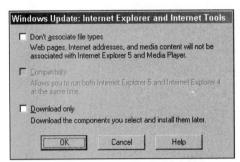

FIGURE 5-2 Advanced installation options

- o *Compatibility.* Denotes whether Internet Explorer 5 and Internet Explorer 4.0 can be installed and run on the same machine.
- o *Download Only.* Downloads the cabinet files for components but does not install the components on the machine. The .cabs can be extracted at any time afterwards to install the components. Doing this enables you to connect to the site, download the required .cab files, and disconnect to run the installation at a later time, thus not requiring a persistent connection.

Download Options

After selecting which components to install, the next step is to choose a download site. Available sites are grouped based on regions. First chose a region, then a site within that region to use for downloading.

concept link   **I cover how to configure download options in Chapter 7.**

While it may seem obvious to select a site that is geographically close to you, the site you choose should be based on the site's reliability, not its location. Choosing one of the high-capacity or high-volume download sites is usually best and will save you time in the long run.

Progress Metering

While all files are being downloaded and installed on the machine, a dialog box displays the progress so you can gauge the ongoing installation.

A new feature to take note of here is the addition of a progress time estimate within the Details section. This estimate is shown in minutes so you are aware of the amount of time remaining in the installation. The progress dialog box also provides information as to which actions are being performed.

Completion

On completion, setup will display an Installation Completed dialog box. Clicking the Finish button here will put into motion the final steps required to complete the Internet Explorer 5 installation. The machine will restart at this time. After restarting, any desktop environment changes or profile settings are applied. Once setup is completed, a splash screen is displayed to welcome you to Internet Explorer 5.

 If at any time during the installation you clicked the Cancel button, the Windows Update Setup would have prompted you to add an icon to your desktop that would allow you to later pick up where the installation left off.

UPGRADING, MIGRATING, AND BROWSER CO-EXISTENCE

More often than not, installing Internet Explorer 5 within your enterprise will involve either upgrading from a previous version of Internet Explorer or migrating from another browser such as Netscape Navigator.

Occasionally, it may be required to have multiple browsers installed on the same machine. Internet Explorer 5 can be installed on machines currently running other browsers without interference. Users can decide for themselves which browser should be the default browser for the machine.

Upgrading from Earlier Versions of Internet Explorer

Windows Update Setup can install Internet Explorer 5 over existing versions of Internet Explorer 3 or Internet Explorer 4. Setup can import items such as cookies, favorites, and proxy settings for you automatically.

Any installed plug-ins and add-ins for Internet Explorer 3 or Internet Explorer 4 will have to be re-installed. The best way to accommodate for this is to include the plug-in or add-in in your custom setup package using the Add Custom Components feature of the Internet Explorer 5 Administration Kit. I discuss this feature in detail in Chapter 7.

 note **Earlier plug-ins or add-ins may not be compliant with Internet Explorer 5. Often the manufacturer of the product will be aware of this and provide (hopefully for free) an upgraded product or a patch for the existing product to make it compliant with Internet Explorer 5.**

Migrating from Netscape Navigator

Windows Update Setup can migrate your browser from Netscape Navigator 3.0 and Netscape Navigator 4.0. Similar to upgrading from a previous version of Internet Explorer, all proxy settings are imported to Internet Explorer 5. In addition, Netscape bookmarks are imported as Internet Explorer favorites, and cookies obtained while running Netscape Navigator are imported to Internet Explorer 5.

Microsoft advises administrators migrating from Netscape Navigator 3.0 and Netscape Navigator 4.0 to obtain the Netscape Switchers Guide. This 27-page Microsoft Word document will outline the steps necessary to successfully migrate to Internet Explorer 5. It includes many checklists that can be used to identify specific information and files to be included in the Internet Explorer 5 Administration Kit to create a custom setup package for migration. The guide can be downloaded free from Microsoft's Web site and is located at `http://www.microsoft.com/windows/ie/business/switchers/default.asp`.

note Any helper applications installed for use with Netscape Navigator will have to be set up to allow Internet Explorer 5 to make calls to them. To do this, add the helper application's Multipurpose Internet Mail Extensions (MIME) and file type extensions to the list of Windows file-type extensions. Don't forget to specify the application to launch when opening the new file types.

Co-existing With Other Browsers

As I stated earlier in this chapter, Internet Explorer 5 can be installed on a machine that already uses another browser. The reasons for setting up Internet Explorer 5 in this configuration will probably be specific to your enterprise. This often stems from previously created Web sites and applications that are by nature incompatible with Internet Explorer 5 in their present state. The cost involved in re-designing these Web sites and applications to be compliant with Internet Explorer 5 can sometimes be greater than the maintenance and support issues involved in running multiple browsers.

When configuring Internet Explorer 5 on a machine running another browser, ensure you take in account the plug-in, add-in, and helper application issues that may present themselves. An easy solution for this is to train your users to access each browser for its intended purpose only, as each one will be configured differently. Unexpected results can be anticipated should there be an attempt made to place a call to an unsupported helper application or to use a plug-in or add-in that is not installed.

KEY POINT SUMMARY

In Chapter 5, we covered all of the concerns and specifics you'll encounter as an administrator installing Internet Explorer 5 using the Windows Update Setup.

- We discussed that the Windows Update Setup embodies the best concepts for deploying software applications via an Internet or intranet download. We also saw that a cursory check of your base platform for adherence to the hardware and software requirements to install Internet Explorer 5 should be your first step.

o We covered the IE5Setup.exe, which demonstrates the lengths to which the setup procedure has been greatly enhanced. Most of the files associated with installing Internet Explorer 5 were covered briefly for familiarity with their purpose and function.

o We went through the installation using Windows Update Setup from start to finish including the Advanced options for installing Internet Explorer 5. Lastly, we focused on the additional considerations you face when migrating to Internet Explorer 5 from other browsers or when attempting co-existence with other browsers.

APPLYING WHAT YOU'VE LEARNED

This section is an opportunity to use what you've learned in this chapter. The Instant Assessment questions here will help you practice for the exam. The labs that follow provide you with important real-world practice using the skills you've learned.

Instant Assessment

1. Windows Update Setup is based on Microsoft's ActiveX engine.

   A. True

   B. False

2. What Microsoft product can you use to customize how the Windows Update Setup installs Internet Explorer 5?

   A. Windows Update Setup Customizer

   B. Setup Administrator

   C. Internet Explorer 5 Administration Kit

   D. Windows Update Setup cannot be customized for installing Internet Explorer 5

3. Internet Explorer 5 can be installed on which of the following platform(s)?

   A. Windows 95, Windows 98, and Windows NT 4.0

   B. Windows for Workgroups

C. Windows 3.1

D. All of the above

4. When installing Internet Explorer 5 on Windows NT, what is the minimum amount of RAM required?

A. 16MB

B. 32MB

C. 64MB

D. 128MB

5. What type of file has an .ins extension?

A. An information file

B. An inclusive file

C. An Internet settings file

D. An Internet negotiation system file

6. Which log file records every action taken by Windows Update Setup while installing Internet Explorer 5?

A. Active Setup Log.txt

B. Windows Update Setup.log

B. Internet Explorer 5 Install.log

D. Log.txt

7. What might a Retry entry in the Active Setup Log.txt file signify?

A. A download error and timed out connection had occurred.

B. Setup had to recreate the log file.

C. The machine did not have enough disk space.

D. Windows Update Setup was called from a CD-ROM.

8. After launching IE5Setup.exe, which is the first dialog box the user sees?

A. Installation Options

B. Establishing a Connection

C. Download Progress

D. End User License Agreement (EULA)

9. What are the four installation types you can chose from?

A. Minimal, Typical, A-Typical, and Advanced

B. Minimal, Typical, Full, and Custom

C. Browser Only, Tools Only, Browser and Tools, and All

D. Custom, Non-Custom, Semi-Custom, Typical

10. During setup you can choose to have Internet Explorer 5 installed but not to associate Internet and Web extensions such as `.htm` or `.asp` with Internet Explorer 5.

A. True

B. False

11. While setup always included a progress bar, what new feature was added to the details section of the progress window?

A. A time estimate in minutes

B. A pie chart

C. News and information about Internet Explorer 5

D. The End User License Agreement (EULA)

12. Internet Explorer 5 cannot be installed and run on a machine that already has a browser installed.

A. True

B. False

13. When migrating to Internet Explorer 5 from Internet Explorer 3 or Internet Explorer 4, all favorites, cookies, and proxy settings are imported to Internet Explorer 5.

A. True

B. False

14. Which items are not imported to Internet Explorer 5 when upgrading from Internet Explorer 3 or Internet Explorer 4?

A. Cookies

B. Favorites

C. Plug-ins

D. Add-ins

15. What document does Microsoft suggest administrators refer to when attempting to migrate to Internet Explorer 5 from Netscape Navigator 3 or Netscape Navigator 4?

    A. Netscape to Internet Explorer in 12 Easy Steps

    B. How to Migrate to Internet Explorer 5 from Netscape

    C. Netscape Switchers Guide

    D. So You Want to Migrate to Internet Explorer 5 from Netscape Guide

Critical Thinking Labs

Lab 5.15 *Configuring Internet Explorer for use with a proxy server*

Your organization is deploying Internet Explorer, and at the same time is deploying an intranet site. The intranet site is behind your proxy server and is destined to become a major part of your organization's business. Which configuration option would you have to specify to enable every employee to start Internet Explorer at the intranet site?

Because your organization has already implemented a proxy server, what are the important considerations regarding proxy server configurations for Internet Explorer?

Lab 5.16 *Configuring Internet Explorer for use on a standard workstation*

Your company has decided to implement Internet Explorer as the standard browser. The organization wants to control access to Web sites that it deems inappropriate. The company also wants to allow unlimited access to its business partners' sites, thus allowing users to do what they please on these sites. Deploying a proxy server is not an option.

Which considerations and configurations would be the best approach for disallowing access to inappropriate sites? Which configurations would you have to change to allow unlimited access to the partner sites?

Lab 5.17 *Configuring advanced options in Internet Explorer*

Your company has recently signed a contract with a benefits manager to handle all of your company's benefit management. The benefits manager has written a Web-based application that handles benefits changes and lets employees review their benefits plan on the Internet. The site uses SSL 3.0 to ensure that the transactions are secure. Benefits plans are changed using several ActiveX controls for which the organization has obtained certificates. Because this is going to save your company several hundred thousand dollars a year, your boss wants you to ensure that Internet Explorer is configured properly for the enterprise to accommodate this application.

What changes would you implement to make the experience more appealing to users? What are some important considerations regarding your browser configuration to ensure that the employees can access and use the site without interruption?

Lab 5.18 *Troubleshooting Internet Explorer content*

You have a user who is complaining that when she visits sites on the Web, the content is outdated. She tells you that when she uses a co-worker's workstation, this does not happen. She also tells you that Internet browsing is extremely slow on her workstation as opposed to other users' workstations. What steps would you take to troubleshoot the problem?

Lab 5.19 *Migrating from Netscape Navigator*

You are in the final stages of the build for your browser configuration and getting ready to deploy one week from today. The CIO of your company walks into your office to express some concerns about your installation that have arisen from other departments. The users are concerned about replacing Netscape Navigator as their browser because they do not want to have to manually re-enter tasks and configuration information. The concerns are as follows:

1. The users do not want to have to re-enter their proxy configurations.

2. The users do not want to have to re-enter bookmarks from their old browser.

3. The users do not want to loose their cookies and plug-ins for Netscape Navigator.

4. The users do not want Netscape Navigator uninstalled until they are sure that Internet Explorer will work for them.

What can you safely tell the CIO about the users' concerns?

Hands-On Labs

Lab 5.20 *Restoring an originally configured home page*

    1. Launch Internet Explorer.

    2. Choose the View menu on the toolbar.

    3. Select Internet Options.

    4. The General tab should be displayed; if not, select the General tab.

    5. Select the Use Default option.

    6. Select Apply and click OK.

    7. Select the Home button on the toolbar. You should see the original home page.

Lab 5.21 *Clearing the Temporary Internet Files folder*

    1. Launch Internet Explorer.

    2. Choose the View menu on the toolbar.

    3. Select Internet Options.

    4. The General tab should be displayed; if not, select the General tab.

    5. Select the Settings button in the Temporary Internet files area.

    6. Choose the View Files option. These files are currently stored in your cache.

    7. Close the dialog box and click OK.

    8. Select Delete Files on the General tab/Temporary Internet files.

    9. When prompted to delete all files in the Temporary Internet files folder, select Yes.

    10. Select Settings again.

    11. Choose View Files. The cache should be empty, with the exception of any cookies you may have (and any files that are open).

Lab 5.22 *Changing, modifying, and testing security changes in Internet Explorer*

    1. Launch Internet Explorer.

    2. Choose the View menu on the toolbar.

    3. Select Internet Options.

    4. Select the Security tab.

    5. Scroll the Zone menu down to Internet zone.

    6. Change the Internet security level to High.

   7. View a few of your favorite Web sites. See the difference?

   8. To correct the settings, select the Security tab again.

   9. Scroll the Zone menu down to Internet zone.

   10. Click Reset.

Lab 5.23 *Changing cookie options*

   1. Launch Internet Explorer.

   2. Choose the View menu on the toolbar.

   3. Select Internet Options.

   4. Select the Advanced tab.

   5. Scroll down to the Cookies option, and change the selection to disable all cookie use.

   6. Browse some of the big commercial Web sites. See how popular cookies are?

   7. To reset back to the default, repeat steps 1 through 5 and select the Always accept cookies option.

Lab 5.24 *Optimizing Internet Explorer*

You can optimize the performance of Internet Explorer using the (Temporary Internet Files) cache settings.

   1. Using these settings located in Tools ⇨ Internet Options ⇨ General, select the Settings button.

   2. Now check the setting for Check for newer version of stored pages on every visit to page.

   3. Close the browser and restart Internet Explorer.

   4. Navigate to one of your favorite pages and then click on one of the links on the page.

   5. Once you are on the next page, return to where you started.

Did you notice the browser running slower than normal? This is because you told the browser to reload the page every time you hit the page, no matter what. This means that every time you navigate to the site, all of the HTML and graphics have to be reloaded.

Managing Internet Explorer Using the Administration Kit

I n Part III, we will talk about the Internet Explorer Administration Kit, the applications that you will learn to use to deploy the Internet Explorer suite. You will learn about licensing the products, how to get them, and what to do with them once you are ready to deploy your browser.

Once we cover the basics, we will walk through all of the configuration options you have for the Wizards and talk in depth about the tool you will use to maintain the browser configuration, the IEAK Profile Manager. You will learn about how to deploy the browser using a variety of methods, ways to maintain your configuration, and other means to manage your browser configurations.

Finally, we will cover the tool you will use to build dial-up configurations for your users, the Connection Manager Administration Kit. Using this tool, you will custom configure proxy settings, phone books, protocols, realms, and other options for your dial-up users.

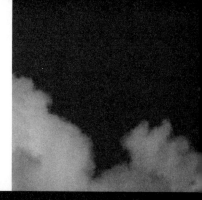

The Internet Explorer Administration Kit

About Chapter 6

In Chapter 6, we are going to cover the basic planning and installation procedures for the Internet Explorer Administration Kit. We will examine the features, tools, and applications used to deploy Internet Explorer effectively in your environment. This examination should leave you with the baseline knowledge that will enable you to continue on with the remaining chapters in the book, where we will look at Internet Explorer in exacting detail. After covering the intricate workings of the browser and its supporting applications, you should be able to confidently configure Internet Explorer, something we will practice in later chapters.

INTRODUCING THE IEAK

The Internet Explorer Administration Kit (IEAK) is used to deploy, administer, and support the Internet Explorer 5 browser and supporting applications. The IEAK is a suite of tools that will allow you to build your configuration of the entire suite of software. Using the IEAK, you will deploy the applications and maintain the software on an ongoing basis in the future. IEAK includes the ability to configure software in the suite, such as:

- Microsoft Outlook Express 5 — E-mail client
- Windows Media Player — Sound and video player
- Microsoft NetMeeting — Videoconferencing software
- Microsoft FrontPage Express — HTML (Hypertext Markup Language) editor
- Microsoft Chat — Online chat client

Depending on your licensing agreement with Microsoft, IEAK allows you to create a custom configuration for your browser that best suits your organization's requirements and the needs of your existing or potential customers. I

If you have not worked with the IEAK before, you are probably wondering why you need to customize your browser. Customization allows you much greater flexibility in deploying Internet Explorer, and you might consider the following:

- Adding customized proxy settings.
- Adding mail settings for your mail servers to Outlook Express.
- Adding links to the browser's bars for intranet and extranet Web sites.
- Customizing the installation without options to lower support costs.
- Managing the browser settings once the browser is deployed.

IEAK is the tool that allows you to make these kinds of changes. Using the IEAK, you can manipulate everything from the browser user interface to the mail server settings of Outlook Express. The tool is designed to give you the maximum amount of flexibility in the browser, without compromising your ability to support your users and to be supported by Microsoft. In the clearest sense, the IEAK is a tool used to customize, deploy, and manage the Internet Explorer 5 suite of applications.

Deployment Methods

The IEAK allows you to deploy the Internet Explorer browser to multiple platforms at the same time. From a single Windows 95/98 workstation, you can create builds for Windows 3.1, Sun Solaris, and Windows NT in a matter of minutes. In addition to multiple platform support, you can also deploy the browser in a variety of different ways. The IEAK supports the following distribution methods:

- *Web download.* Using a single .exe, Internet Explorer is downloaded from an Internet or intranet site.
- *CD-ROM.* Source installation files are located on the CD-ROM; installation is run directly from the CD-ROM.
- *Multiple floppy disks.* The way software was installed in the past, multiple floppies are inserted in the PC one at a time.
- *Single floppy disk.* Uses a single file located on floppy disk to initiate the downloading of the remainder of the Internet Explorer browser setup files.
- *Single-disk branding.* Used to brand an already existing installation of Internet Explorer 5.
- *LAN deployment.* Locating setup files on a local file server to deploy the browser to end-users.
- *E-Mail.* E-mailing the single .exe file to multiple users to deploy the software. This allows a simple, small file to be mailed to users that points to a location containing the balance of the setup files.

In many cases, you will not be able to choose the type of medium to deliver your package. By far, the fastest method will always be the CD-ROM method, as the workstation will have the source data locally. In the event that you do not have the CD-ROM method as an option, then consider the download method or downloading from the LAN. This way, you can more effectively control the downloads, speeds, and any changes that you need to make.

Custom Components

The Internet Explorer 5 suite of applications are not the only options available. You can also install up to ten other applications along with the Internet Explorer browser. These applications are chosen by you, the administrator. For example, I have seen some cases where the administrator installs a copy of Adobe Acrobat along with Internet Explorer to view PDF files. The purpose of this feature is to allow you to add custom applications to your installation that are outside the scope of Microsoft's bundled components.

The IEAK allows you to include `.exe` (executables) or `.cab` (cabinet) files to install other popular applications with your browser package. Cabinet files enable you to bundle lots of files into a single file for unpacking during your installation routine, much like a zip file.

in the real world **If your application does not include a custom installation routine, there are a variety of applications that can assist you in packaging your installation such as Seagate's WINSTALL or InstallShield. These applications can assist you in bundling your options so that you can include them in your Internet Explorer installation.**

Digital Signatures

Microsoft has built protections into Internet Explorer to guard against harmful and malicious applications that users may inadvertently install on their computers when downloading software from the Internet. This protection, called Digital Signatures, allows developers to "sign" their code to ensure that the application is safe for the user to download. The signature process is performed by a standard called Authenticode 2.0.

Authenticode 2.0 support is included with Internet Explorer 5.0. As you know, downloading files from the Internet can be a harrowing experience. You may not know from whom you are receiving files or who created them. This can sometimes cause problems, especially if the applications are unproductive or written in bad code. Authenticode protects the user from harmful ActiveX controls, Java applets, executable files, and cabinet files.

Authenticode 2.0 enables developers to obtain a digital signature for their applications from an organization such as VeriSign. VeriSign is what is commonly called a Certificate Authority, or a trusted organization that ensures that an individual or organization is who they say they are by their own verification process. Verifications include phone calls, articles of incorporation, and other means to ensure that the company or individual obtaining the certificate is safe.

tip **If you would rather create your own Certificate Authority within your organization, Microsoft provides a method to do this called Microsoft Certificate Server. Using Certificate Server, you can set up your own Certificate Authority to verify your own applications. Check out the Certificate Server online seminar at** `http://www.microsoft.com/Seminar/1033/IISSupport/Seminar.htm`.

Once a developer has compressed an application in a `.cab` file for instance, he or she can "sign" the code. Signing the code enables the application to be married with the digital signature, allowing verification that the code is indeed genuine and will not harm the user's workstation. Internet Explorer 5 has built-in security features that use Authenticode to disallow the downloading of unsigned code or to warn the user about the unsigned code before downloading it.

USER INTERACTION

If you have ever worked in a support capacity, you know that the largest number of support calls relate to user error. User errors can be due to a variety of reasons, such as lack of understanding of the application, user experimentation with settings, lack of patience, and so on. As a professional, it is your job to assess the technical ability of your users. In doing so, you can determine the most effective method to deploy software to your end users.

A network engineering firm obviously would require less hand-holding than that of a telemarketing firm. Consider your user base; what do they do most of the day? In the past, which software deployments have been successes and which failures? This information is going to assist you in making decisions about which features of IEAK to deploy. These deployment decisions will, in turn, affect how much interaction the user has with IE when installation occurs. You can choose one of three methods for your installation.

- *Interactive*. The interactive installation allows users to customize components during installation.
- *Hands-Free*. The hands-free installation displays error messages and dialog boxes tracking installation progress, but does not require action on the part of the user.
- *Silent*. The silent installation is hidden from the user completely.

In addition to distribution, your role also determines what you can customize with the IEAK. The following table, Table 6-2, shows the options that are determined by your choice in roles.

TABLE 6-2 ROLE CUSTOMIZATION OPTIONS WITH THE IEAK			
CUSTOMIZATION OPTION	*ISP MODE*	*ICP MODE*	*CORPORATE ADMINISTRATOR*
Corporate disclaimer	No	No	Yes
Silent installation available	No	No	Yes
Choose installation directory	No	No	Yes
Customize desktop	No	No	Yes
Proxy server settings	Static	No	Yes
Internet Sign-up Server	Yes	No	No
Corporate install features	No	No	Yes
Outlook Express customization	Yes	No	Yes
Polices and restrictions	Yes	Yes	Yes
User agent string	Yes	Yes	Yes
Customizing certificates	No	Yes	Yes
Customize security zones	No	No	Yes

exam preparation pointer

Roles also affect the operating system that you can deploy your Internet Explorer package to as well. Rather than giving you yet another table to memorize, just remember that only a Corporate Administrator can use the IEAK to deploy to a UNIX platform. The UNIX operating system is not supported in the ISP and ICP roles.

Downloading the IEAK

The installation files for the IEAK can be downloaded at `http://www.microsoft.com/windows/ieak/en/default.asp`. When you get to the site, I suggest that you decide on how you plan to license the IEAK. The very first information presented on the page, as shown in Figure 6-1, asks you about the IEAK role you choose.

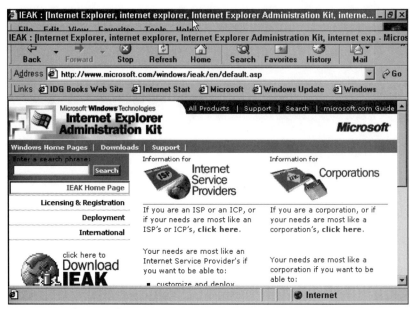

FIGURE 6-1 The IEAK home page

Go ahead and choose to download the IEAK at this time. Downloading the software is the first step in the process. When you choose the download link, you will be taken to the Download home page, as shown in Figure 6-2.

It is important to remember that this is the page in which all versions of the IEAK are downloaded for all versions of Internet Explorer. You might want to think about bookmarking this page for future reference as you may have to come back to download other IEAK options from here. As you page down on the Download home page, you will see the Internet Explorer 5 for Windows 3.*x*, 95, 98, NT 4.0, and UNIX choices, shown in Figure 6-3.

 note   **While you are browsing this page, note that the Macintosh and Intel versions of the IEAK are different downloads; you may see this again on the exam.**

The file that you are going to download is 3.56MB in size. This, in itself, is not that significant from a bandwidth perspective, as you know. What is going to be very significant is when you prepare to download the source files for the entire Internet Explorer 5 suite of applications. I highly recommend that you choose the download option only on an ISDN or better Internet connection.

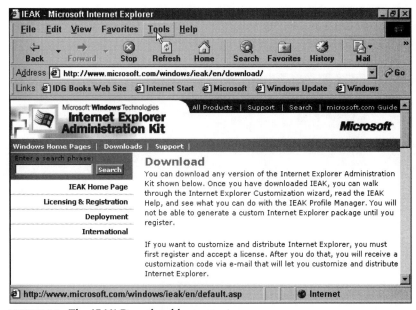

FIGURE 6-2   The IEAK Download home page

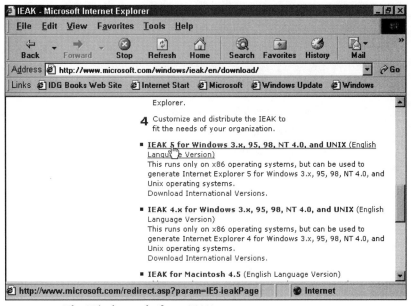

FIGURE 6-3   The Windows platform IEAK

Microsoft gives you estimates of the download times and file sizes for each version of the IEAK, as shown in Figure 6-4.

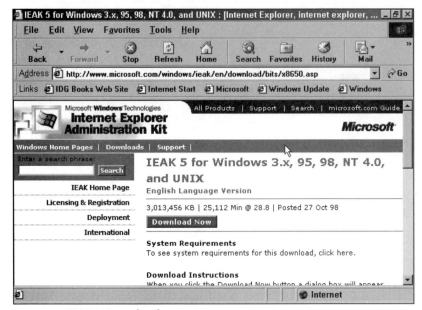

FIGURE 6-4 IEAK 5 Download page

Once you select to download the IEAK, you will be pointed to one of Microsoft's mirror sites around the world for downloads. At this time, you have to choose where you want to download the `ieak5.exe` file on your local drive, as shown in Figure 6-5.

Once you have downloaded the IEAK, you are ready to get an IEAK customization code.

Customization Codes

Remember that your customization code determines your preferred method to deploy the browser. The choices you make determine the ability you have to get your software to the end user. To run the IEAK, you need to register with Microsoft and get an IEAK customization code.

note   **The licensing requirement by Microsoft requires you to obtain an IEAK customization code for every version of Internet Explorer.**

FIGURE 6-5 Downloading the file

To get your code, go to the Licensing and Registration home page from the IEAK home page. The Licensing and Registration home page is shown in Figure 6-6.

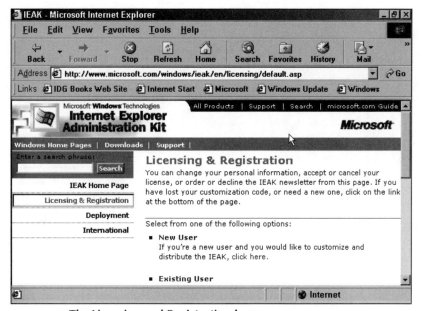

FIGURE 6-6 The Licensing and Registration home page

The process to get a customization code is very simple. You first must choose your role. Once you have done that, you select New User at the Licensing and Registration home page. You must then set up a profile with Microsoft if you have not previously done so. Setting up a profile allows Microsoft to keep track of your licenses and deployments of Microsoft's software.

exam
preparation
pointer

As a part of the license agreement, you must log in once every quarter and report your distributions of Internet Explorer.

Figure 6-7 shows the new profile page — this page consists of your name, address, and contact information that must be provided to Microsoft. The most important information on the page is the e-mail address, as this is how you are going to be provided your customization code.

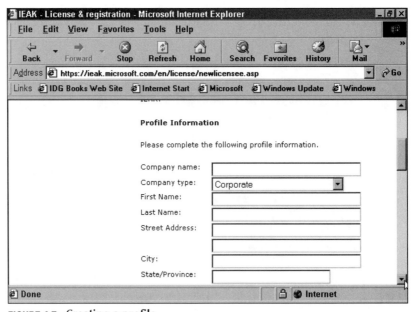

FIGURE 6-7 Creating a profile

On this page, you will also choose your license. When choosing your license, remember that you have to have a license for every version of Internet Explorer that you plan to deploy.

Figure 6-8 is an example of the confirmation mail message you will receive from Microsoft after creating your profile. This message is the original message that I received when I registered for the IEAK 5.

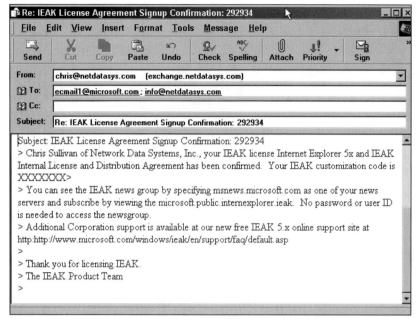

FIGURE 6-8 E-mail confirmation message

note **Remember to keep a copy of this mail message. You will have to use your customization code several times throughout your rollout.**

INSTALLING THE IEAK

Hopefully, you have now negotiated through Microsoft's registration process and downloaded the IEAK. Now, it's time to install the kit on your workstation. Before we get into the installation, let's talk a little bit about the workstation that you are planning to use.

The Build Machine

The build machine is the workstation that you are going to use to create your custom Internet Explorer installation. I recommend you get your hands on a machine that is typical for your user community. If the majority of your users have Pentium II 400s with 128MB of RAM, then plan on using a similar workstation to create your build. It is also important to ensure that your build workstation has all of the applications that your users will typically have installed on their computers. In many cases, this is the Microsoft Office Suite and a few homegrown applications. In very large environments, it may not be practical to install all applications on a single desktop.

The builds that you are going to create are going to reside on this workstation. As you move forward in testing your installation, you are going to be creating multiple versions of your installation as you modify different options. Every time you create a build, the IEAK will automatically assign a version number to it. You will probably want to keep copies of each build on the machine so that you can track the progression of your installation. With this in mind, it is a good idea to design a strategy to back up the data on the build machine on a tape, such as a DDS or DLT media type.

The Test Machine

In an ideal world, you should test your installation on every possible type of workstation that you are going to run into in your enterprise. In many cases, such as an ISP or ICP, you cannot possibly account for every workstation that may get a copy of your installation. In these circumstances, a best guess is your only option.

Internet Explorer makes a substantial number of changes to your computer registry and other important files during the installation. Keep this in mind when testing your installation; uninstalling and reinstalling the browser does not constitute a thorough test of your installation. Once the installation has been run, the existing browser will be upgraded to Internet Explorer 5. While every attempt is made to remove everything upon an uninstall, there frequently are registry changes and files that do not get deleted. The moral of the story is that you should always test once, document the results, and start with a new build or an image of the standard build of your user community.

You may want to consider creating a build that consists of the following software:

- Standard Operating System software
- Service Packs
- Special tweaks to the installation
- Microsoft Office
- Other applications

Once you have created the standard installation on your test machine, consider using cloning software to save a standard configuration to a CD-ROM or a network server.

 There are several very good cloning packages available, such as Symantec's Norton Ghost, and Drive Image from Powerquest. These applications will cut down on your test time dramatically to ensure successful deployment of Internet Explorer 5.

Setting Up the IEAK Software

To install the IEAK, double click the `ieak5.exe` file that you previously downloaded. Remember to do this on your build machine. You will first be prompted to verify that you want to install the IEAK, as shown in Figure 6-9.

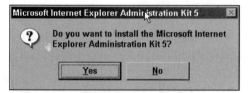

FIGURE 6-9 Installation confirmation

Once you have confirmed the installation, you will be asked to confirm that you have read and understand the IEAK license agreement, as shown in Figure 6-10.

Once you have agreed to the license agreement, you will then be asked for the installation location for the IEAK software. Ninety-nine percent of the time, you should use the default. The only exception to this is if your C: drive is short on space. The installation path is shown in Figure 6-11.

If you have not previously installed the IEAK, you will be prompted to create the IEAK directory, so choose Yes to this option, as shown in Figure 6-12.

 Remember this directory location, you will need to know this for your deployment and the exam.

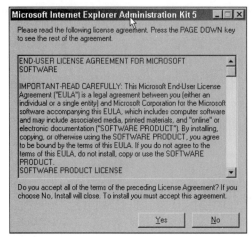

FIGURE 6-10   The IEAK License Agreement

FIGURE 6-11   IEAK installation path

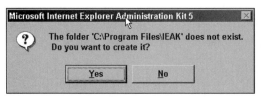

FIGURE 6-12   IEAK directory

After about 20 seconds, the files will be installed and you will be ready to use the IEAK. It is important to remember that at this point, all you have done is download the IEAK tool. This does not include the Internet Explorer source installation files.

concept link

When you run the IEAK for the first time, you will be prompted to synchronize your current source files with the latest files from Microsoft. We will talk more about this feature in Chapter 9.

KEY POINT SUMMARY

In Chapter 5, we talked about how to obtain the IEAK software, basic concepts of the software, and other key points of interest to help you use the IEAK to your advantage.

- The IEAK allows you to deploy the Internet Explorer browser to multiple platforms at the same time.

- IEAK roles allow you to determine the correct licensing method for the IEAK for your organization. These roles enable you to choose the customer base that you are planning on deploying the Internet Explorer suite to, and include features to enhance your ability to effectively deploy the software to your audience.

- You must obtain a customization code from Microsoft before running the IEAK. This code allows you to use specific features of the IEAK. Updates and information on the IEAK can be obtained from `http://ieak.microsoft.com`.

- There are three methods to choose from for your Internet Explorer installation: interactive, hands-free, and silent.

- Internet Explorer builds protection for the end user into the browser to guard against harmful and malicious applications that the user may install on their workstation from the Internet. This technology, called Authenticode, allows developers to sign their code to ensure that the user is aware that the code is from an authentic, verified source.

- The download URL specified during the IEAK build allows you to specify locations where the user can download the Internet Explorer source files.

APPLYING WHAT YOU'VE LEARNED

This section is an opportunity to use what you've learned in this chapter. The Instant Assessment questions here will help you practice for the exam. The labs that follow provide you with important real-world practice using the skills you've learned.

Instant Assessment

1. You can install the IEAK from multiple floppy disks.

   A. True

   B. False

2. To get the IEAK, you can navigate to Microsoft's IEAK site at:

   A. www.microsoft.com/ieak

   B. backoffice.Microsoft.com/ie

   C. ieak.Microsoft.com

   D. internetexplorer.Microsoft.com

3. Which of the following is NOT an IEAK role?

   A. ISP Mode

   B. ICP Mode

   C. Corporate Administrator

   D. Developer Mode

4. Which of the following roles can deploy Internet Explorer via CD-ROM?

   A. ISP Mode

   B. ICP Mode

   C. Corporate Administrator

   D. All of the above

5. Which of the following roles can perform a silent installation?

   A. ISP Mode

   B. ICP Mode

   C. Corporate Administrator

   D. CSP Mode

6. It is a good idea to use a similar workstation for your build machine to that of your user base when building your IEAK configuration.

   A. True

   B. False

7. You have to have a customization code for every role that you plan to deploy Internet Explorer for. For example, if you are an ISP and plan to deploy the software to your customers and to your internal employees, you need two licenses.

   A. True

   B. False

8. The Macintosh IEAK and the Intel/UNIX IEAK are different downloads from Microsoft.

   A. True

   B. False

9. What is the only role where you can use an Internet Sign-up Server with the IEAK?

   A. ICP Mode

   B. ISP Mode

   C. ISP and ICP Mode

   D. None of the above

10. During a hands-free installation, the user may be prompted whether or not to install certain components of the Internet Explorer software suite.

    A. True

    B. False

11. Which of the following technologies helps protect the user from malicious code?

    A. Kerberos

    B. Triple DES

    C. Authenticode

    D. LSA Authorities

12. To obtain a certificate for your Internet Explorer build, you have to buy the certificate from VeriSign.

    A. True

    B. False

13. What is the default installation path of the IEAK?

    A. `C:\ieak`

    B. `C:\Windows\ieak`

    C. `C:\Program Files\ieak`

    D. `C:\Program Files\Internet Explorer\ieak`

14. The compressed file name of the IEAK is _____.

    A. `ieak5setup.exe`

    B. `ieak5.exe`

    C. `ieak5i.exe`

    D. `ieak5inst.exe`

15. Single disk branding is available to which of the following roles?

    A. ICP Mode

    B. ISP Mode

    C. Corporate Administrator

    D. All of the above

16. Which of the following roles can specify proxy settings? (Choose two)

    A. ICP Mode

    B. ISP Mode

    C. Corporate Administrator

    D. All of the above

17. What is unique about running the IEAK with a previous build that you created?

    A. The `.cab` files are updated even if you changed nothing.

    B. You have to reinstall the IEAK.

    C. Your build number gets updated.

    D. You void your license agreement.

18. DSS is a popular backup strategy for servers and workstations.

    A. True

    B. False

19. The Authenticode technology protects users from Macro viruses.

   A. True

   B. False

20. You can specify up to _____ Web locations for your users to download the Internet Explorer source files.

   A. five

   B. twenty

   C. ten

   D. one

Critical Thinking Lab

Lab 6.25 *Identifying roles and licensing*

Open your browser and navigate to `http://www.microsoft.com/Windows/ieak/en/licensing/courtesy/default.asp`. After reading the license agreement for the IEAK, which of the agreements would be applicable to the following scenarios?

1. Major cable modem provider, providing service to the general public.

2. Staff member of the IT department deploying Internet Explorer to the sales department.

3. Web portal providing a customized version of the Internet Explorer browser to their customers.

Running the IEAK

About Chapter 7

The Internet Explorer Administration Kit is an invaluable tool for you, the administrator, to deploy the Internet Explorer suite of software. In Chapter 6, we talked about the deployment and installation basics for the IEAK. In Chapter 7, we are going to walk through the IEAK application, also referred to as the Internet Explorer Customization Wizard, and talk about some of the specific features that you can use to configure and modify Internet Explorer. To adequately prepare yourself for the exam and also to use the application in the real world, pay specific attention to the Exam Preparation Pointers and the tips to use this tool to your best advantage.

THE IEAK BUILD PROCESS

There are five stages to building your Internet Explorer package. The application is broken down into stages that focus on the different configuration options within the browser, the applications, and other features.

- Stage 1: Gathering Information
- Stage 2: Specifying Setup Parameters
- Stage 3: Customizing Setup
- Stage 4: Customizing the Browser
- Stage 5: Customizing Components

Later in the book, we will talk about how to prepare for these stages ahead of time so that you are ready for the questions that the software will prompt you for. The focus of Chapter 6 is to walk through the options as they are presented to give you an understanding of what the features mean and how they may apply to you. Let's jump right in to Stage 1.

STAGE 1: GATHERING INFORMATION

The first stage of the IEAK is the overview of the application. You will see this overview every time you launch the IEAK application. The overview is shown in Figure 7-1.

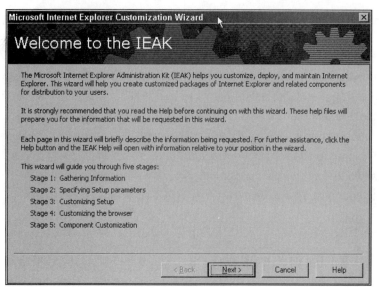

FIGURE 7-1 The IEAK overview

tip **The IEAK Help is available to you at all times by selecting Help. If you get stuck during your build, take a look at the help files to further explain some of the features.**

Gathering Information Overview

The next step is shown in Figure 7-2, introduction to the Gathering Information stage. In the next few screens, you will be prompted for information that is necessary to run the application and to also create your build.

Company Name and Customization Code

In the next step, shown in Figure 7-3, you are going to make some of the most important decisions about your installation routine. Remember that the IEAK has built-in features and restrictions for each role; your functionality and features will be limited or non-existent if you choose the wrong role or violate your license agreement.

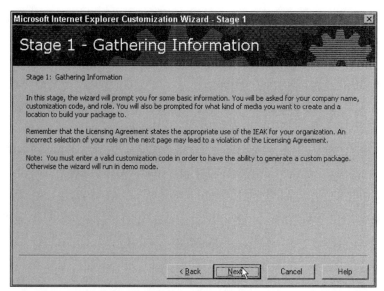

FIGURE 7-2 Gathering Information overview

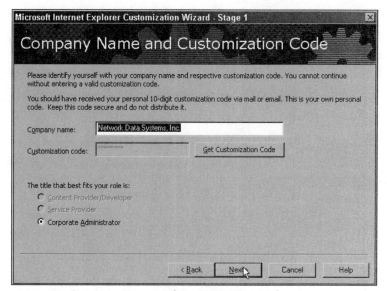

FIGURE 7-3 Company Name and Customization Code

 note In this step, you must have already received your customization code and also be connected to the Internet.

The fields that you provide information for in this phase are as follows.

- *Company name.* Enter your company's name exactly as you registered the IEAK. The name entered here is saved in the registry of the user's workstation, but there is no other way a user can see this name. The option to brand the browser comes later, at which time you can choose another name if you wish.
- *Role selection.* Select the role that fits your organization best by the set of criteria set forth in the license agreement. This option must correspond to the choice you made when you downloaded the IEAK.
- *Get Customization Code.* This option, when selected, will navigate your browser to the following URL to obtain a customization code if you have not already obtained one: `http://www.microsoft.com/windows/ieak/en/licensing/default.asp`.

Once you have selected a role and entered the required information, the code will be e-mailed to you.

 tip   **If you forget your customization code, you can go to** `https://ieak.microsoft.com/en/License/LookupCode.asp` **to have your customization code e-mailed to you again.**

Once you have entered this information, select Next to continue.

Platform Selection

In this step, you will select the operating system platform in which you are creating your Internet Explorer build. As shown in Figure 7-4, you have three choices:

- *Windows 9x/NT 4.0.* This selection is for Windows 95 (all versions), Windows 98, Windows 98 second edition, and Windows NT 4.0 (all service packs).
- *Windows 3.1, 3.11 WFW/NT 3.51.* This option is for 16-bit versions including Windows 3.1, Windows 3.11 (Windows for Workgroups), and Windows NT 3.51.
- *UNIX.* For Sun Solaris 2.51, 2.6, and HP-UX 10.2 and above.

Even though NT 3.51 is a 32-bit operating system, Internet Explorer for 3.51 is a 16-bit application.

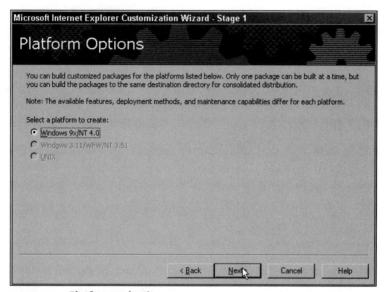

FIGURE 7-4 Platform selection

File Locations

The destination folder, shown in Figure 7-5, is where your build source files will be placed once you complete the IEAK application. You want to ensure that the location has at least enough space to contain all of your files. While this is not on the exam, you should make sure that there is at least 250MB of available space here for your files. Figure on at least 125MB for every build that you are going to create.

 You may want to consider acquiring client backup software that will back up this directory in case something happens to your build machine. If you have a backup copy of your data, recovery of your work is a lot easier. You can accomplish this in a variety of ways, such as removable media, network server, or FTP sites.

A lot of administrators that I talked to suggested creating a descriptive folder structure for your builds. For example, if you are running the build for the first time to test it, create a folder structure that mirrors your project plan:

```
C:\IE Builds\English\Beta 1 120599
```

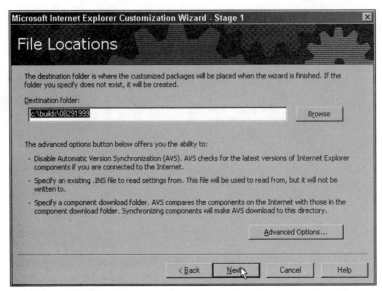

FIGURE 7-5 File Locations

Using syntax similar to this will allow you to easily identify your files based on your stages and the dates that you created them.

The Advanced Options button allows you to make other configuration options, as shown in Figure 7-6.

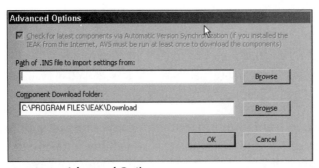

FIGURE 7-6 Advanced Options

o *Disable Automatic Version Synchronization (AVS).* The IEAK uses ActiveX technology to check your source files against the download site you most recently chose. Each component of Internet Explorer on the build machine is checked against the source files at Microsoft to ensure that they are current. You can choose to disable this feature once you have downloaded the components the first time.

 Know that you must download the source files at least once, the first time you run the IEAK.

o *Specify an Existing .INS file.* Throughout the IEAK build, you will be creating a file in the background known as the instruction file (`filename.ins`). This file contains the options that you choose throughout your build. Later, you will use this file to change, modify, and create new installation options for your build. The main reason for specifying the `.ins` file at this stage is to modify an existing build of the Internet Explorer suite.

o *Specify a component download folder.* By default, this folder will be `C:\Program Files\IEAK\Download`. This is the folder in which the AVS feature will place the Internet Explorer source files that you will synchronize with Microsoft. This feature will only update components (if you so choose) that have changed since the last time you synchronized the files.

 Like any other software company, sometimes Microsoft can update a component that can contain a bug in the code. You may want to ensure that you have a backup copy of this folder after you complete your build so that the next time you run the IEAK, you can rollback your source files.

Language Selection

In this phase, you will select the language for the browser package you are putting together. You can create multiple builds for multiple languages if your requirements so dictate.

 At this stage, you must be connected to the Internet to get the language list for the first time.

A subfolder will be created in your build directory for each language that you create a build for. The English source files, for example, are located in the `\EN` subfolder. In order to deploy versions of the browser in different languages, you have to create an installation for each language you choose. For example, if you are planning to deploy your browser in American English, German, and French, you will have to put together three different installations.

Before you deploy a specific language to users, make sure that they have the corresponding language installed on their operating systems. If you are deploying the Mandarin Chinese version of Internet Explorer, the users must have previously installed the Mandarin Chinese version of the Windows platform. The browser will work in most cases, but the Windows Desktop Update (also known as Active Desktop) will not be functional.

The Language Selection dialog box is shown in Figure 7-7.

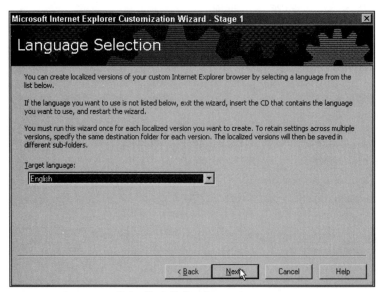

FIGURE 7-7 Language Selection dialog box

Media Selection

In this step, you will select the method or methods that you are going use to distribute your package. Figure 7-8 shows the Media Selection phase.

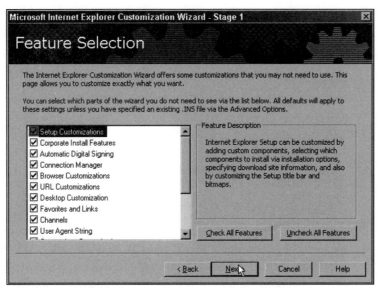

FIGURE 7-9 Feature Selection

- *Browser Customizations*. This allows you to customize the browser to add custom graphics and other related information to your installation package. If you want to create a customized look and feel for your users, select this option.

- *URL Customizations*. This allows you to specify options such as the start page, home page, search page, and other pointer type information.

- *Desktop Customization*. If you opt to install the Windows Desktop Update (also known as the Active Desktop), this feature allows you to create custom toolbars, and desktop-based modifications.

- *Favorites and Links*. This feature allows you to add custom favorites to the user's favorites list. You can also specify the order in which the links and favorites are presented.

- *Channels*. Using your own custom .cdf file (Channel Definition File), you can create new Active Channels to be added to the user's desktop. There are several included by default, such as Microsoft, Disney, and so on, that you can remove, depending on your role.

o *User Agent String.* A User Agent String enables content developers to identify several key factors about a user's workstation by means of HTML code. The user agent identifies the browser type, version, workstation operating system, and a custom string that you can assign with the IEAK.

o *Connections Customization.* Allows you to customize connection-based settings, such as proxy information, proxy bypass settings, and other connectivity related settings.

o *Certificate Customization.* Allows you to customize certificate settings during the installation. You will need to know how to use this if you are planning on using Microsoft Certificate Server.

o *Security Zones and Content Ratings.* Allows you to change the default settings for browser security and content-based ratings. These options protect your users from malicious Web sites and also Web sites that are not appropriate based on the site's content ratings.

o *Programs Customization.* Allows you to specify programs that should be used in your package by default, such as using Internet Explorer as the default program for viewing HTML, Outlook Express as the default mail handler, and so on.

o *Outlook Express Customization.* Allows you to specify settings for electronic mail, such as mail server names, signatures, and other mail-related information.

o *Policies and Restrictions.* Provides you with the ability to configure and restrict options within your package for security, configuration management, and support-related reasons.

A little elaboration on User Agent Strings is necessary here. Because of the many differences in capabilities between Internet Explorer and Netscape, the developer can ID the browser with the user agent and design a single HTML page that runs different code depending on the type of browser. The logic in the HTML code looks for the user agent, and the browser processes the code if the browser is the correct version and type. This scenario prevents developers from having to maintain two separate sites for both types of browsers, which is not uncommon. For example:

o Developers have written sample code for an application that runs on Windows NT and Windows 95/98. Using the User Agent String, the developer can identify the platform the user is running and point the user to the correct download file.

- Intranet developers want to track hits to their intranet site, and they want to be able to differentiate between marketing, sales, and administration. Using the IEAK, you could create a custom User Agent String for each department. The intranet Web server's logs could then track hits by each user agent and correlate statistical information that could be imported into Microsoft Site Server, for example.

- Web server log files can track hits to a Web server using the workstation TCP/IP address and the User Agent String. You can add an environment variable to the User Agent String to track the hits to the Web site using the user's name. In the user agent dialog box in the IEAK, type **%USER-NAME%**. When the user visits the company intranet, for example, the log on the Web server will retain the full user ID, such as John Doe.

Getting tired yet? There is a lot of information in this step. It is important to remember that this section exists to help you speed up your build process. If you don't have the need or requirement to modify some of these settings, then don't. Keep in mind that what you build and deploy, you will also have to support and live with.

STAGE 2: SPECIFYING SETUP PARAMETERS

Figure 7-10 shows the Specifying Setup Parameters overview. This stage allows you to synchronize your source files with Microsoft and to create custom component installation options.

Microsoft Download Site

At this phase, you will select the download site that you are going to download the Internet Explorer source files to. The download location that you have previously specified will be where the files are placed once downloaded. Figure 7-11 shows the download site phase.

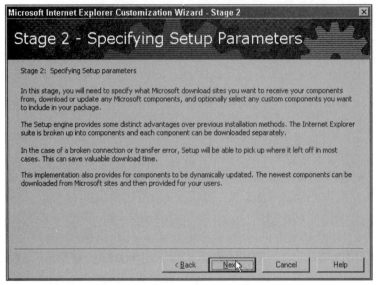

FIGURE 7-10 Specifying Setup Parameters overview

caution   Make sure that the site address you enter here is accurate. If there is an error here, you will have to rebuild your configuration to correct it. You may want to consider going to a DOS prompt at this point and verifying that you have the correct address by using the ping command. You will learn more about Ping in Chapter 13.

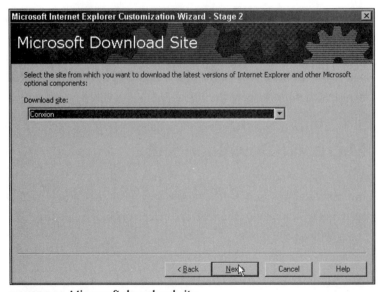

FIGURE 7-11 Microsoft download site

Automatic Version Synchronization

Once you have selected the site, IEAK will contact the site and through the means of an ActiveX control, verify the versions of your files against the files on the Microsoft download site. Once the synchronization is complete, each component will be marked with one of three indicators as shown in Figure 7-12:

- *Red.* The software is not present on your workstation.

- *Yellow.* Your version of the software is outdated.

- *Green.* Your version of this software is current.

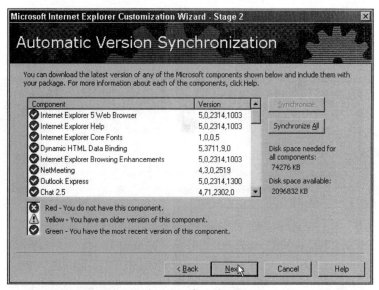

FIGURE 7-12 Automatic Version Synchronization

 note   **If you do not have Internet connectivity when you get to this stage, all of the icons will be yellow.**

At this stage, you have several options to choose from. You can synchronize single pieces of the Internet Explorer suite, or you can synchronize all components by choosing the Synchronize All option. Remember that if the option is red, the software is not present, and you cannot include it later in this build of the IEAK. However, you can add the component later by updating your build with the Profile Manager, another component of the IEAK.

If you don't want to update specific components one at a time, you can choose the Shift and/or Control keys to select multiple or single components, respectively. Once you have selected your options, choose next to download your components. Note that once your options have been selected, you can see the space required versus the amount of space you have left. If you do not have enough space, you can task switch out (Alt + Tab) to clear up enough space to complete the operation.

Add Custom Components

Internet Explorer includes a wealth of applications and add-ons. You can also add on custom applications that can be installed with the Internet Explorer setup. Figure 7-13 shows the Add Custom Components dialog box.

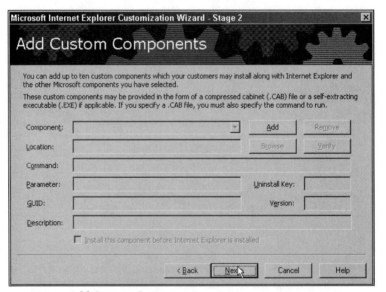

FIGURE 7-13 Add Custom Components

Third-party applications can be installed through the Active Setup process using a variety of methods. Internet Explorer includes an application installation utility called Iexpress, which you can use to install these third-party applications such as Installshield's Installshield application or Seagate's WINSTALL.

In Figure 7-13, you specify the parameters within which your custom application should be installed. The following options control your installation and assist you in deploying your software:

- *Component*. This field is used to name your custom package. The name you choose is the same one your users will see when they choose the options during Active Setup.

- *Location*. This is the path to the installation files on your hard disk.

- *Command*. This is the command used to decompress your cabinet (`.cab`) files during the installation.

- *Parameter*. If your application uses an executable file (`.exe`), enter it here.

- *GUID*. The Globally Unique Identifier is a unique number that you can assign to your application. Select the Generate button to generate your unique ID. If your application already has a GUID, you can enter it here as well. You can use a GUID in a variety of programming languages to determine whether software is installed on a user's workstation, the version information, and so on.

- *Description*. Here you can specify custom terminology that more clearly specifies what it is you are installing. This is informational and has no effect on the installation itself.

- *Version*. You can enter the application's version number here. I suggest that you choose the application's version and then a custom string designated by you. For example, if you were installing a custom component—let's say, Widget Inc.'s software version 2.1—you could add on the date in addition to the 2.1, to make the version number 2.1.121099; 121099 signifies 12/10/99, the date the package was created.

- *Uninstall Key*. If you want your users to have the capability to uninstall your custom component, enter the command line to uninstall the application here. This feature adds a string to the registry on the user's workstation, so when the user chooses to uninstall, the necessary uninstall routine can be executed via the Add/Remove Programs option or through an uninstall desktop icon such as `uninst.exe -f appname.isu file`.

- *Install this component before Internet Explorer is installed*. This allows you to run an executable or a batch file to prepare the workstation prior to launching the Internet Explorer installation. You can also use this to install applications that need to exist prior to the upgrade.

Do yourself a favor and create a database or detailed documentation that holds configuration information for each of your versions. Document any issues or hurdles you had to overcome to get the package or application running. This information will be invaluable to you and your coworkers later on when you have to configure the software again.

caution **If you are installing an application or component using the COTS (Commercial Off the Shelf) installation, do not specify the uninstall key here. Any application that is certified for Windows 95, 98, or NT must include an uninstall option, which is added by the COTS installation. If you add a redundant entry, it will probably be duplicated in the Add/Remove options list.**

Pay close attention to the features that you can use in adding new applications to your deployment. You may be asked on the exam to provide explanations to the purpose of each feature and the reasons to use the feature during the deployment.

STAGE 3: CUSTOMIZING ACTIVE SETUP

In this stage, you will provide the parameters for customizing the browser, such as toolbars, graphics, and the like. You will also specify the download locations for your browser and related information for the browser configuration. Figure 7-14 shows the Customizing Active Setup overview.

CD Autorun Customizations

If you chose to install via CD-ROM, you will be prompted for information to customize the autorun splash screen that is presented to the user when the CD-ROM is inserted into the CD-ROM drive. The CD Autorun Customizations are shown in Figure 7-15.

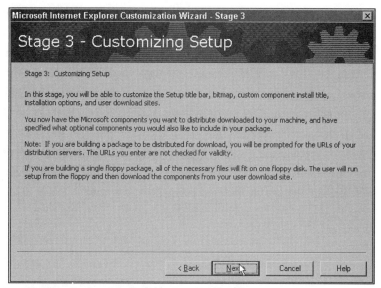

FIGURE 7-14 Customizing Active Setup overview

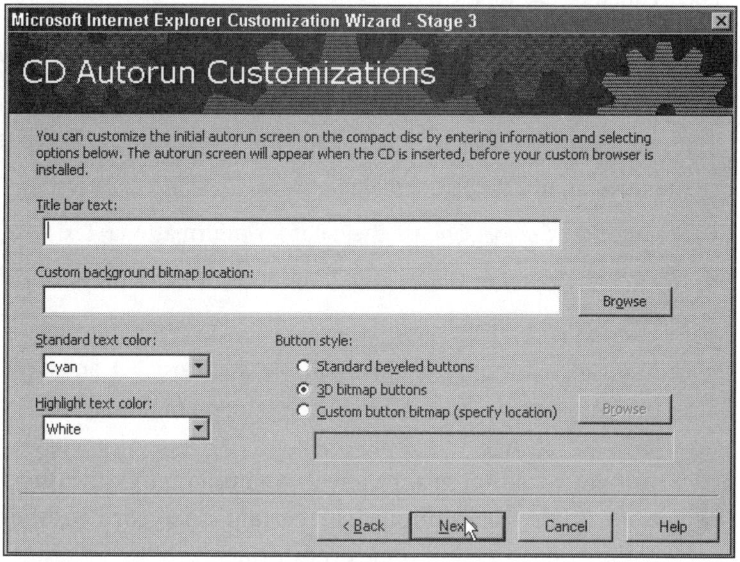

FIGURE 7-15 CD Autorun Customizations

In this step, you can also build and customize the various options associated with the CD-ROM-based installation. Have you ever wondered how CD-ROM-based installations work? Windows 95, 98, and NT include code that scans removable media, such as CD-ROMs for a specific text-based file called an `Autorun.inf`. This search is initiated when the user inserts the media into the drive while he or she is running the various operating systems. It can also be initiated when the drive door is opened and closed. The purpose of the `Autorun.inf` file is to provide instructions to the operating system regarding which executable file needs to be run in order to launch the application, or to launch the installation. The `Autorun.inf` file is a simple text file and looks something like this:

```
[autorun]

open=autorun.exe
icon=autorun.exe, 0
```

When the executable file is launched, the user is prompted with some sort of dialog box. The IEAK enables you to build your own dialog box. Options you can choose include the following:

- *Title bar text*. The title bar can be customized with a string that you choose.
- *Custom background bitmap location*. You can create a custom background for your title bar, such as a logo. Remember that this background is only for the title bar, not the entire dialog box.
- *Standard text color*. Choose the color for informational text.
- *Highlight text color*. Choose the color of text that initiates an action on the screen, such as "Install."
- *Button style*. Three options are available: standard, 3D, and custom bitmap. In the Custom field, type the path to your custom bitmap.

 in the real world **Test your custom graphics with a sampling of your user base hardware. Some workstations with certain video card/resolution combinations may present undesired results.**

More CD Options

In this step, shown in Figure 7-16, you specify the location of the release notes and the kiosk mode start page. Let's touch on these options briefly.

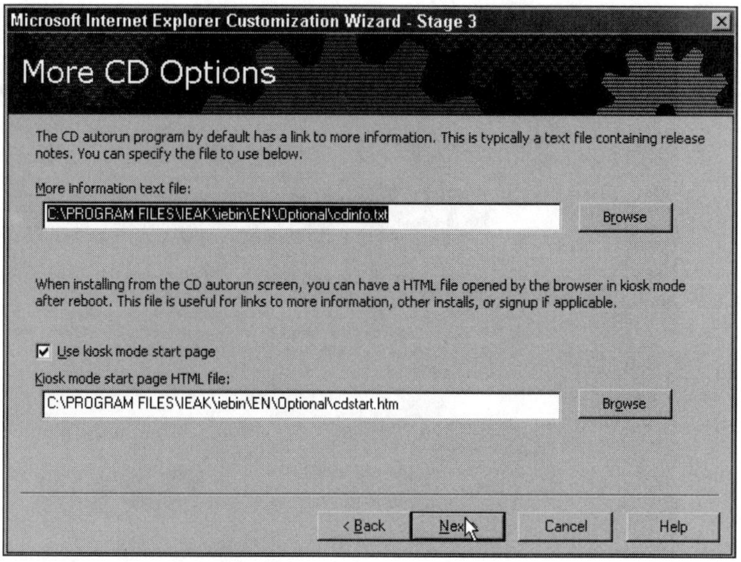

FIGURE 7-16 More CD Options

You can create a text file that contains the latest release notes for your browser information. This option allows you to specify the location of the file itself for your users to view once the installation is launched. For mobile users, for example, you may want to include any documented problems that you have run into and how to resolve them in the event that the user is running the installation at a time when support is not available.

Kiosk mode allows Internet Explorer to be launched full screen, as shown in Figure 7-17. This mode allows for a workstation to be used as a kiosk in public places to display information using web content. You can launch Internet Explorer in kiosk mode by selecting Start ⇨ Run and typing **iexplore -k**.

The kiosk mode start page allows you to specify the location of an .html file that will be displayed in kiosk mode after the first reboot of the workstation. The reasons for doing this are many, such as to force your users to register, update information, or to install other applications via the Web after the upgrade.

Customize Setup

In this step, you will customize the buttons and text displayed during the Internet Explorer setup. Figure 7-18 shows the Customize Setup phase.

FIGURE 7-17 Kiosk mode

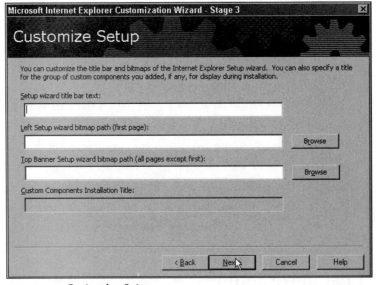

FIGURE 7-18 Customize Setup

- *Setup wizard title bar text*. This is the text that will appear in the installation title bar. This title is displayed during the installation only, such as "Acme Inc's Internet Explorer installation."

- *Left Setup wizard bitmap path*. This shows the path to the bitmap that is displayed on the left-hand side of the wizard.

- *Top Banner Setup wizard bitmap path*. This shows the path to the bitmap that is displayed on top of the wizard.

- *Custom Components Installation Title*. Using this feature, you can group your custom applications with a unique name that your users can identify with, such as "Accounting's custom applications."

Silent Install

In this step, you will choose the installation method that you want to use. You have three choices at this step, as shown in Figure 7-19:

- *Interactive*. The interactive installation allows users to choose customize components during installation.

- *Hands-free*. The hands-free installation displays error messages and dialog boxes tracking installation progress but does not require action on the part of the user.

- *Completely Silent*. The silent installation is hidden from the user completely; any problems or errors will not be displayed to the user.

Installation Options

In this step, you will choose the applications, supplements, and other features of the Internet Explorer suite that you are going to allow your users to install. You can create up to ten installation options for your users.

 In Hands-free and Completely Silent mode, you can only specify one installation option.

The Installation Options phase is shown in Figure 7-20.

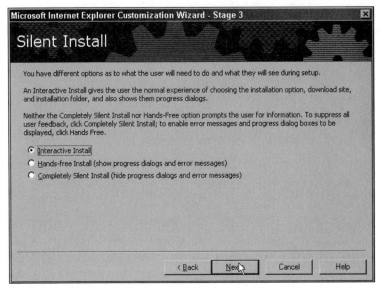

FIGURE 7-19 Silent Install

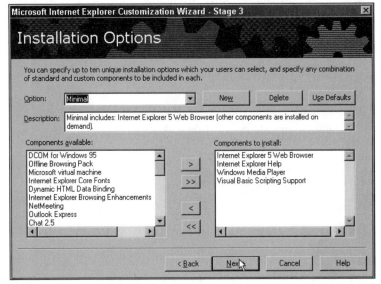

FIGURE 7-20 Installation Options

The installation options are as follows:

AOL ART Image Format
  Support

Arabic Text Display Support

Chat 2.5

Chinese (Simplified) Text
  Display Support

Chinese (Simplified) Text Input
  Support

Chinese (Traditional) Text
  Display Support

Chinese (Traditional) Text Input
  Support

DCOM for Windows 95

DirectAnimation

Dynamic HTML Data Binding

FrontPage Express

Hebrew Text Display Support

Internet Explorer 5 Web
  Browser

Internet Explorer Browsing
  Enhancements

Internet Explorer Core Fonts

Internet Explorer Help

Japanese Text Display Support

Japanese Text Input Support

Korean Text Display Support

Korean Text Inpu

Language Auto-Selection

Macromedia Flash Player

Macromedia Shockwave

Media Player RealNetwork
  Support

Microsoft virtual machine

NetMeeting

Offline Browsing Pack

Outlook Express

Pan-European Text Display
  Support

Thai Text Display Support

Vector Graphics Rendering
  (VML)

VRML 2.0 Viewer

Vietnamese Text Display
  Support

Visual Basic Scripting Support

Wallet

Web Folders

Web Publishing Wizard

Windows Media Player

Windows Media Player CODECs

The many installation options can be confusing. Think of the options here as buckets holding the applications and features you want to install. Each of the ten buckets has a different set of contents. One may contain just IE and NetMeeting; another may have IE, NetMeeting, and Outlook Express; and yet another may offer every application and feature available. Here are the fields described in this phase:

- *Option.* The option name is the unique name you assign to your configuration. You can create up to ten different options with different configurations for each.
- *Description.* Describe your option in language your users will understand. Make the description short, sweet, and concise. This is the text that appears in the Windows Update Setup Wizard.
- *Components available.* This is the list of optional add-ons and applications that you can include in your option. By selecting the component and clicking the > (greater than) button, you then add it to your option. Remember that the "pool" of components listed here is generated by the components downloaded earlier in the IEAK AVS process. If you forgot a component, you can hit the Back button, navigate all the way back to the AVS, and add the component.
- *Components to install.* This field shows you the components that will be installed for this option. When you've selected the options for the install and are ready to configure the next option, select the new button to create another option.

Component Download Sites

If you chose to allow Internet Explorer to be downloaded, Figure 7-21 will be displayed to allow you to specify your download locations.

In this step, you will specify configuration information for the Web sites that will serve up your installation, once completed. Here are your options;

- *Site Name.* Name your site with a unique name that you and your company can easily distinguish.
- *Site URL.* This is the most important option on this page. Here, you select the URL to your IE source file. You can select HTTP or FTP here, and you can use either NetBIOS names or host names for your servers.

- *Site Region.* This is a good place to assign a descriptive organization name or a geographic location to this site. If your organization has multiple sites in the United States, for example, you can organize the sites by location so the users download IE from a site close to them. You don't want the WAN traffic that might be generated by users in Miami downloading files from your Seattle office. Not only is it a waste of bandwidth, it's also slow.

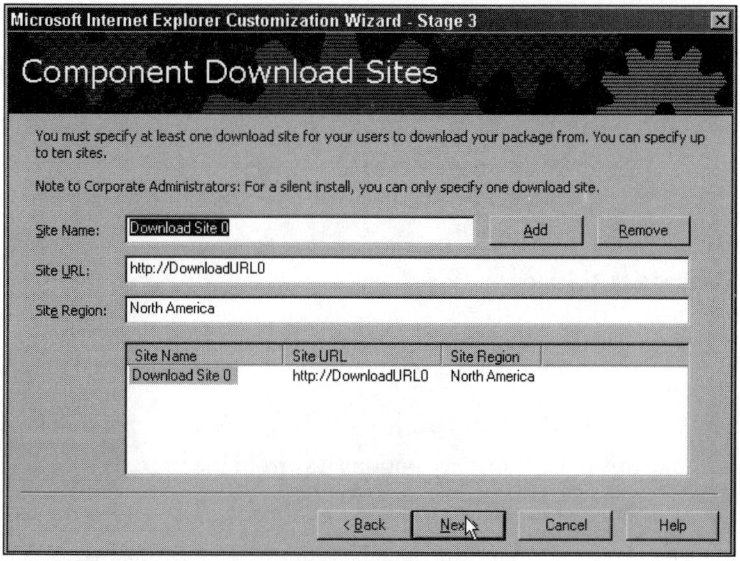

FIGURE 7-21 Component Download Sites

Component Download

This step, shown in Figure 7-22, allows you to select post-installation options for updating the browser. These options can be accessed using Internet Explorer's Tools/Windows Update Feature.

If you choose the Microsoft site, an ActiveX control will run once you have navigated to the site to inventory your workstation for updates. Upon completion of the update, a list of features/updates will be displayed that are not present on your workstation.

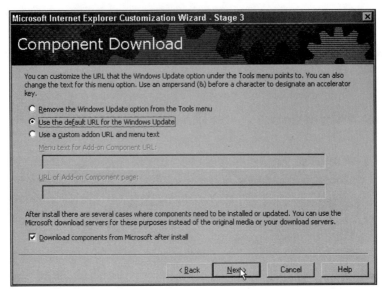

FIGURE 7-22 Component Download

This feature in the IEAK allows you to do one of several things:

- *Remove the Windows Update option from the tools menu.* Allows you to take this most restrictive option away from the user.

- *Use the default URL for the Windows Update.* This allows the user to navigate to Microsoft for the update, as discussed previously.

- *Use a custom addon URL and menu text.* Here, you can specify your own toolbar name for your organization's updates and also a URL to navigate the user to.

Installation Directory

When your custom Internet Explorer 5 package is installed, it needs to be placed in a folder that you select in the window shown in Figure 7-23. You have four options to choose from:

- *Allow the user to choose the installation directory.* Allows the user to pick the location of the installation. This is generally not an option that you will want to use for standardization and configuration management reasons.

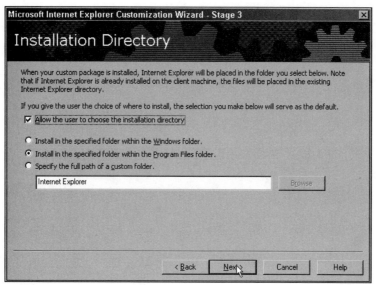

FIGURE 7-23 Installation Directory

- *Install in the specified folder within the Windows folder.* Installs Internet Explorer under the respective Windows directory for the operating system.

- *Install in the specified folder within the Program Files folder.* Installs Internet Explorer to a subfolder in the C:\Program Files folder.

- *Specify the full path of a custom folder.* Enables you to install Internet Explorer in a custom folder.

Remember that regardless of what you enter in this window, Internet Explorer always installs itself in the path to which Internet Explorer was previously installed — if a previous version of Internet Explorer exists on the workstation. If Internet Explorer already exists, the new version is installed to the current path. For example, if Internet Explorer 3 is installed in C:\Internet Explorer3, then Internet Explorer 5 is also installed in the C:\Internet Explorer3 folder.

Corporate Install Options

Corporate Install Options, shown in Figure 7-24, allow you to configure options based on corporate policy and other technical concerns that are generally unique to corporate deployments on Internet Explorer.

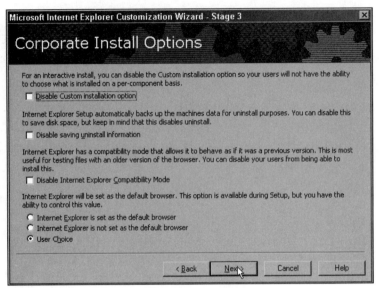

FIGURE 7-24 Corporate Install Options

- *Disable Custom installation option.* Allows you to disable the custom installation option so that your users cannot choose the options to install.

- *Disable saving uninstall information.* This option allows Internet Explorer to not save uninstall information (the previous browser files).

 tip **If drive space is a concern, you may want to think about using this option. Just remember that if you use this feature and there is a problem encountered during the installation, you will not be able to return the user to Internet Explorer 4.**

- *Disable Internet Explorer Compatibility mode.* If enabled, users can run Internet Explorer 4 on the same machine as Internet Explorer 5.

- *Default browser options.* This option allows the user to choose whether Internet Explorer is the default browser.

Advanced Installation Options

Shown in Figure 7-25, the Advanced Installation Options allows you to detect whether certain components are already installed or not. If components already exist, they can be surveyed to ensure compatibility with your Internet Explorer 5 package.

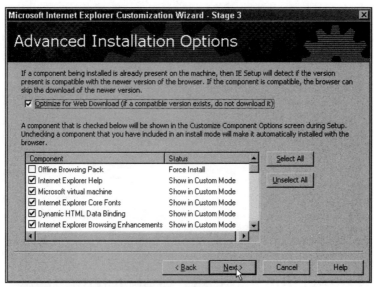

FIGURE 7-25 Advanced Installation Options

You can force the user to install the option if you choose or to hide the installation from the user depending on your requirements. Remember, don't install options that you do not need, it is a waste of space and may cause you headaches down the road.

Components on Media

You can choose to include source files on your media that are not selected for installation. The reason for doing this is to provide the files in the event that these files are needed at a later date. The Components on Media option allows you to select the optional software for inclusion on your media, as shown in Figure 7-26.

This feature complements a new feature in Internet Explorer called Automatic Install. When a user navigates to a page that requires any of the supplemental software, the component is automatically installed. If you choose to include the additional software on the installation media, you can make it quick and easy for your users.

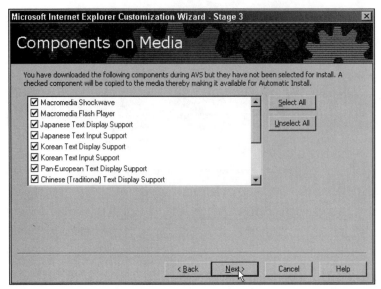

FIGURE 7-26 Components on Media

Connection Manager Customization

As you know, the IEAK can include your Connection Manager Admin Kit (CMAK) profile so that the dial-up configuration is provided with Internet Explorer. The best way to do this is to create your CMAK profile ahead of time with the CMAK software. When you get to this stage, you can be prepared to include your files. The Connection Manager Customization step is shown in Figure 7-27.

concept link

We will cover the Connection Manager Administration Kit in Chapter 9.

Windows Desktop Update

In this step, shown in Figure 7-28, you choose whether or not to install the Windows Desktop Update. Whether you include it or not is a policy decision on the part of your organization. You may want to consider including this update in your pilot to some users and not to others to see your users' reactions.

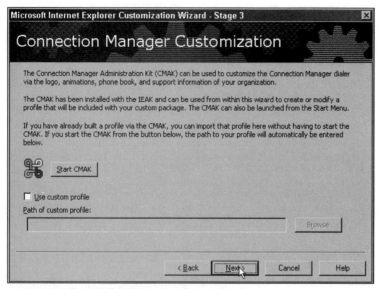

FIGURE 7-27 Connection Manager Customization

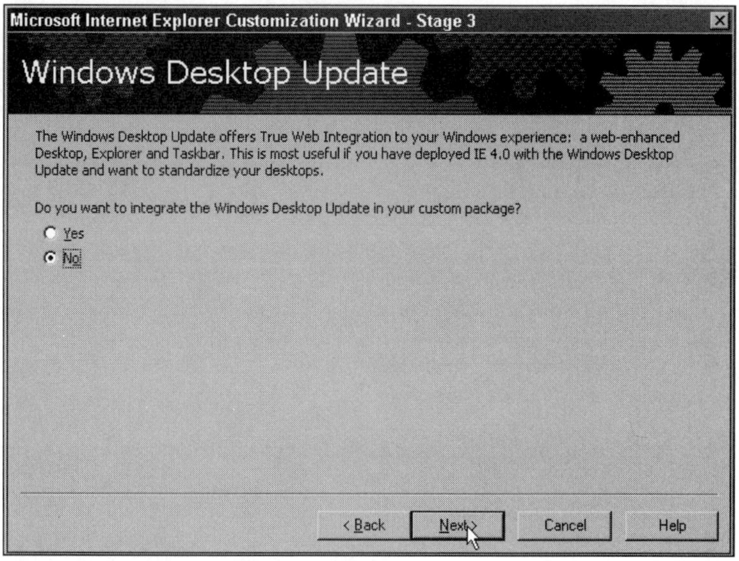

FIGURE 7-28 Windows Desktop Update

Digital Signatures

Using your build machine, you can specify your digital certificates during the IEAK install. The certificates become a part of your installation so that the users will not have to make the decision to accept the certificate when they are presented with it. The digital signatures option is shown in Figure 7-29.

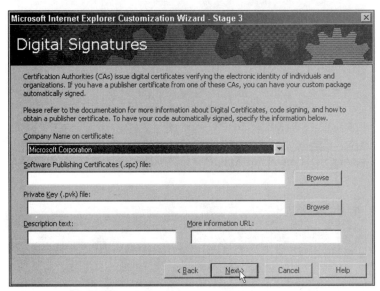

FIGURE 7-29 Digital Signatures

- *Company Name on certificate.* If the Certificate Authority's certificate is on the computer, the name will appear here.

- *Software Publishing Certificate (.spc) file.* Here you should specify the name of the .spc file and the location of the file.

- *Private Key (.pvk) file.* Specify the name of the .pvk file that is a part of the certificate.

- *Description text.* Provide the text that will be shown when the users download programs that are signed with this certificate.

- *More information URL.* This is the Web URL to where the users can obtain more information about the certificate.

STAGE 4: CUSTOMIZING THE BROWSER

In this stage, you will provide information about the browser configuration, such as start pages, titles, home pages, and other information. This stage begins with an overview like the rest, as shown in Figure 7-30.

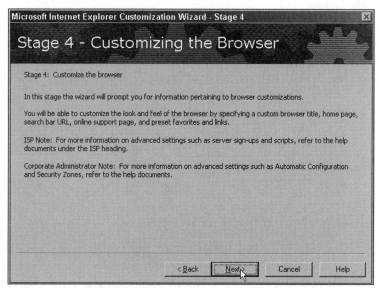

FIGURE 7-30 Customizing the Browser

Browser Title

Also known as "branding" the browser, this feature allows you to provide a name for your browser that is specific to your organization, such as "Internet Explorer provided by Network Data Systems, Inc." The text that you enter in this field, shown in Figure 7-31, allows the browser to obtain your own corporate identity.

You can also provide your own custom bitmap for the toolbar if you so choose by providing the path to the file as shown in Figure 7-31. This is sometimes also referred to as the watermark.

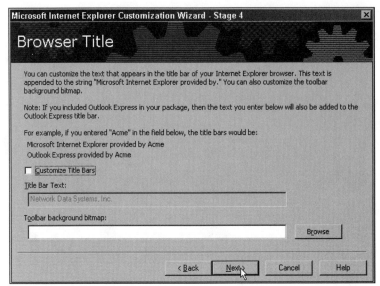

FIGURE 7-31 Browser Title

Browser Toolbar Buttons

You can build your own buttons in Internet Explorer 5 to launch your own custom applications. In Figure 7-32, you can create your own button to be imported into the browser's configuration. For common Web-based applications, this feature allows you to add more of a customized touch to your browser.

Once you have imported the button, you can assign functions to the button as shown in Figure 7-33. Here, you specify the following options:

- *Toolbar caption.* A maximum size of ten characters, this is the label that you should apply to the button. Try to make it brief, descriptive, and similar to the buttons that are already there.

- *Toolbar Action.* Here you specify the script or the executable that is to be launched when the button is pressed.

- *Toolbar color Icon.* This image is used to determine the state of the button, whether or not the button is in use.

- *Toolbar grayscale Icon.* This is the icon that is used for black and white monitors.

This button should be shown on the toolbar by default. This option enables your button to be used by default on the toolbar.

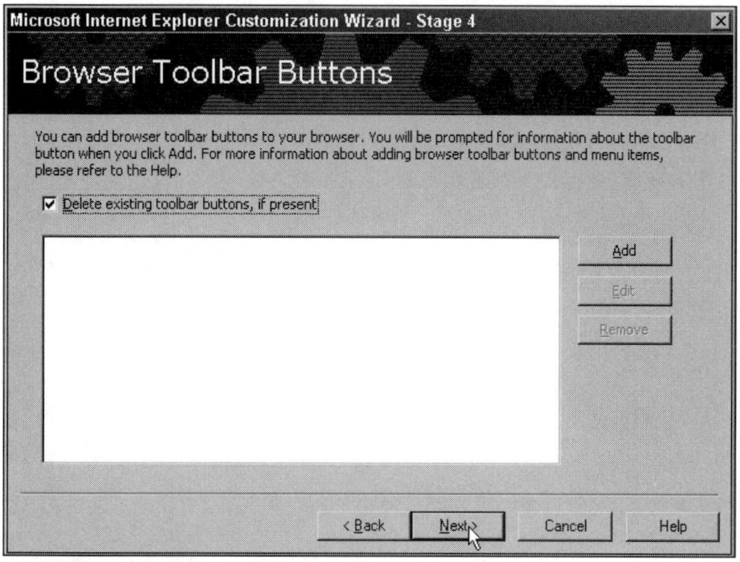

FIGURE 7-32 Browser Toolbar Buttons

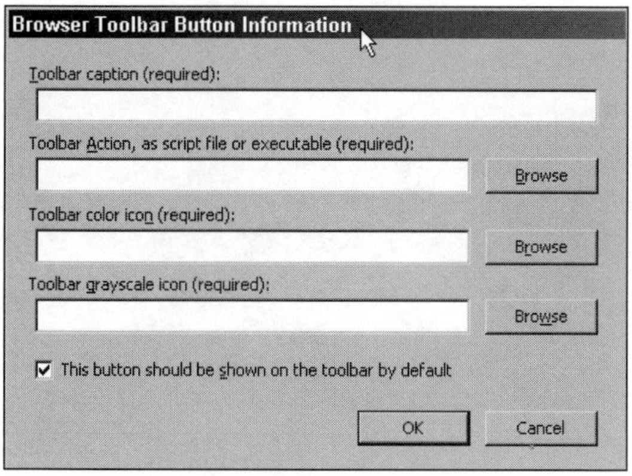

FIGURE 7-33 Specifying button options

Animated Logo

By default, the Windows logo is shown in the upper right hand corner of the browser. You can elect to change this by choosing your own animated bitmap. You should include two files, one for when the browser is performing an action and one for when the browser is idle. Figure 7-34 shows the Animated Logo phase. You can also choose to include a static logo of your choice in your browser package.

Rather than installing an animated logo, you can opt to include a logo of two different sizes, as shown in Figure 7-35.

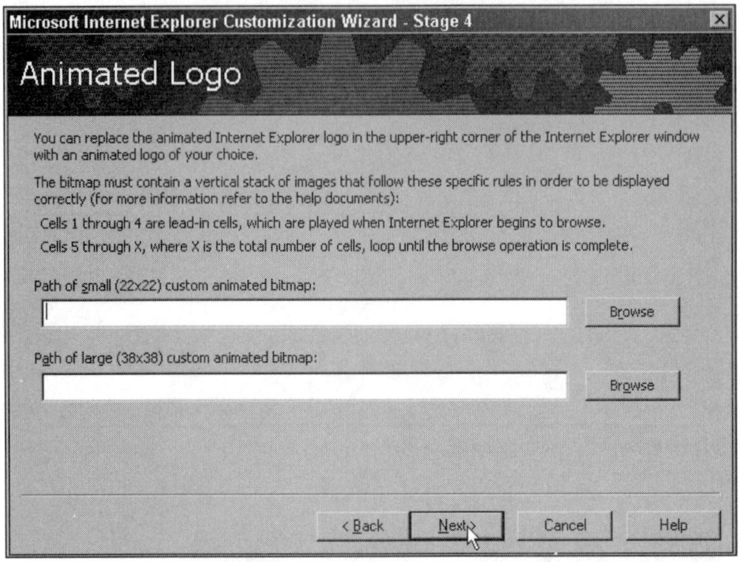

FIGURE 7-34 Animated Logo

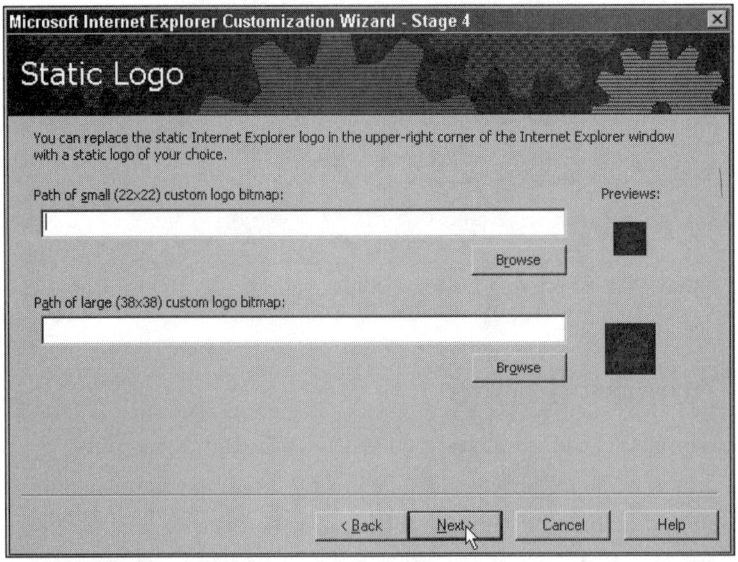

FIGURE 7-35 Static Logo

Important URLs

This phase allows you to specify three important URLs to Internet Explorer.

You can customize your user's start page by entering a URL in the Home page URL option, as shown in Figure 7-36. This is the URL that Internet Explorer is opened to when the browser application is launched. Most organizations use their intranet or Internet home page for this choice.

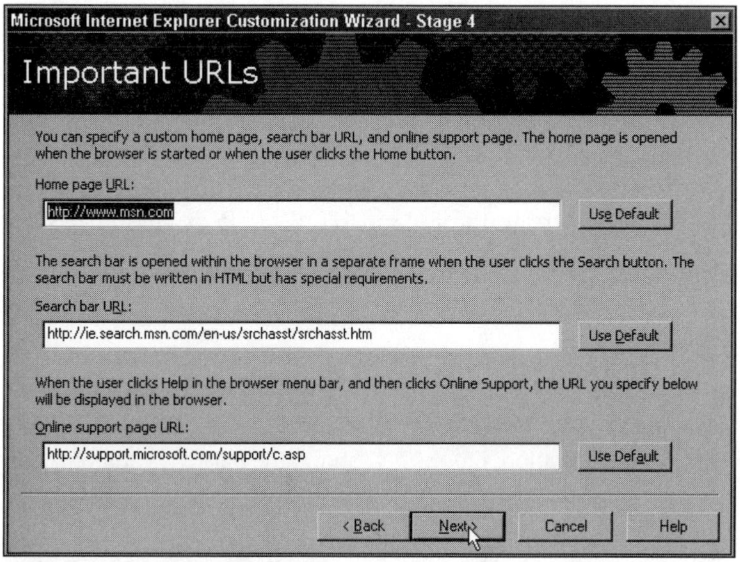

FIGURE 7-36 Important URLs

Remember that if you decide to use your intranet or Internet home page here, every time a user launches Internet Explorer, the browser will navigate first to your site. Make sure you have enough bandwidth and plan for this increased capacity, especially in the morning when most users get to the work site.

Internet searches are a powerful tool for gathering information that can be used in everyday work. Search engines, such as Yahoo, provide a valuable service. However, many of the search engines include advertisements and other distractions that may take employees away from their work. ISPs can use a custom search page to advertise their own products and avoid advertisements from competitors. Providing a custom search page is a good way to give users what they need without distractions. Refer to the Internet Explorer Resource Kit for more information on creating search pages.

Regardless of how much you plan, prepare, and test, you will inevitably receive support calls when you migrate major pieces of software. A handy feature of the IEAK is the capability to create an online support page. Your users can navigate to this page from the Help menu in Internet Explorer, and the page can provide any information you feel is necessary.

Some information you may want to post includes:

o Frequently asked questions

o Support hours of operation

o Support contact phone numbers

o Configuration information

o Rollout schedules

You can create the page in HTML, ASP, or any other supported Internet Explorer format.

Favorites and Links

You can set up pre-elected favorites and links to other sites with your Internet Explorer installation. Figure 7-37 shows the Favorites and Links phase.

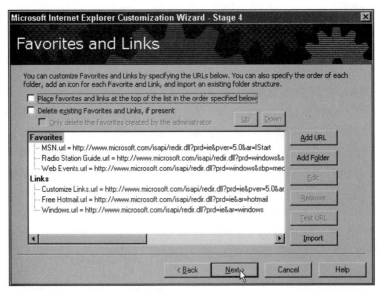

FIGURE 7-37 Favorites and Links

To add your links, enter the URL to selected sites in the URL field. You can assign your link a descriptive name in the Name field to make it easier for your users to understand the purpose of the link. Try to make the list short and concise; the more links that are listed, the more this will confuse the users and possibly cause them to ignore the entire list.

Even though you are adding URLs to the user's configuration here, the URLs imported from Netscape and previous versions of Internet Explorer will also be imported automatically.

To organize the Links option further, you can create folders that contain links to specific research information, search engines, and the like. When you pilot your browser configuration with a small number of users, it's a good idea to get feedback from the people who will be using the browser. Do yourself a favor and test your links with the Test URL option. Once the browser is deployed, correcting a bad link wastes a lot of time; you can avoid this problem by testing the link beforehand. You can also import links from the IEAK workstation by selecting the Import option.

tip **A new feature of the IEAK 5 is to delete existing links and favorites. Using this tool, you may want to consider deleting links that your users no longer need. A survey provided to the users during your pilot phase can help you gather this information.**

Channels

One of the best features of the IEAK is the capability to import custom channel settings into the IEAK custom build. On the build workstation on which you're running the IEAK, you can set up a custom Active Channel for your organization and then import the configuration into your build. Once you complete the development of your channel, you can import the configuration into the IEAK, as shown in Figure 7-38.

Welcome Page

The IEAK allows you to configure the user's welcome page. This page is usually located on a Web server that you can specify. Here, you may want to specify a welcome message, followed by some how-to hints and support information. As shown in Figure 7-39, you can choose the default page or you can choose to have no welcome page at all.

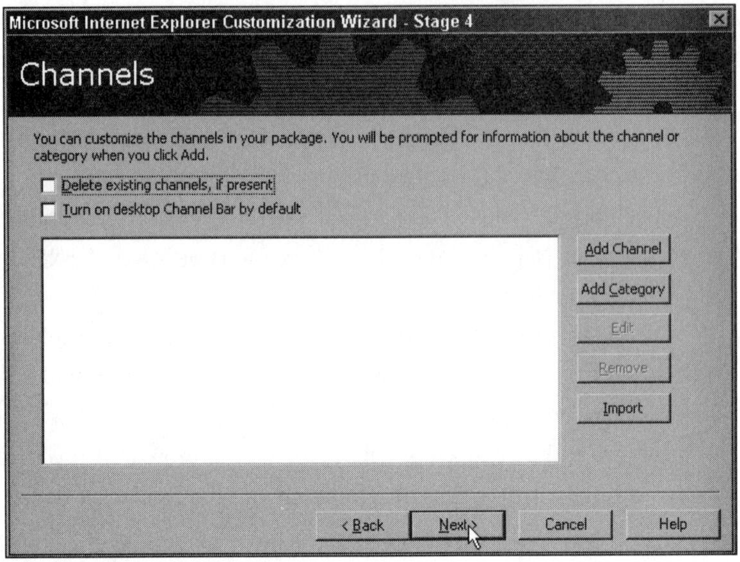

FIGURE 7-38 Channels

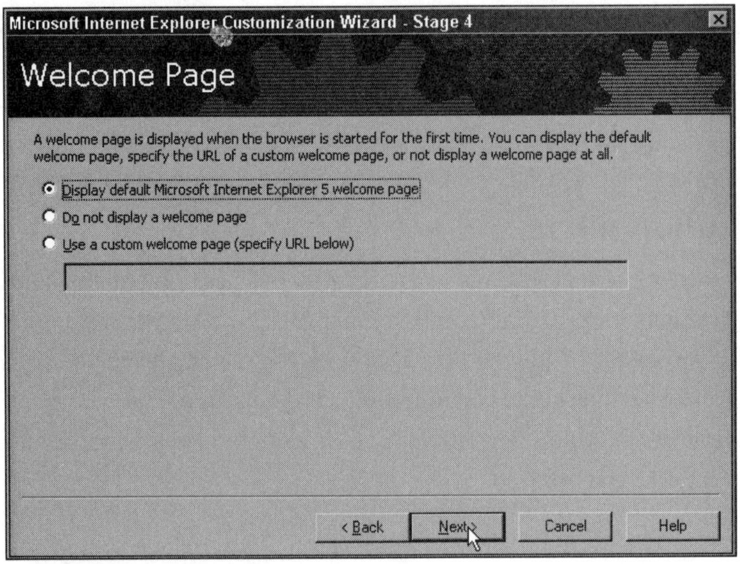

FIGURE 7-39 Welcome Page

User Agent String

In this phase, shown in Figure 7-40, you specify the User Agent String. As you may remember, a User Agent String enables content developers to identify several key factors about a user's workstation by means of HTML code. The user agent identifies the browser type, version, workstation operating system, and a custom string that you can assign with the IEAK.

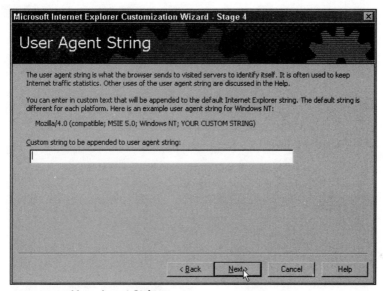

FIGURE 7-40 User Agent String

Connection Settings

You can specify settings for connectivity for Internet Explorer 5, as shown in Figure 7-41. In addition, you can set up all of the connection profiles ahead of time on the build machine and import these settings into the IEAK during the build. You can specify configuration options for each connection if you so choose as shown in Figure 7-42.

You can specify settings for each individual connection, such as proxy settings, user names, passwords, and other configuration information. These settings are discussed later in this chapter.

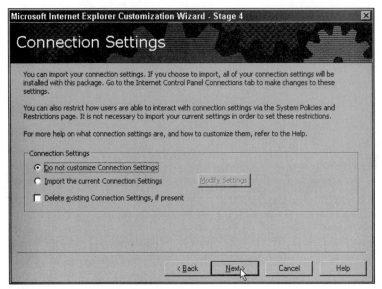

FIGURE 7-41 Connection Settings

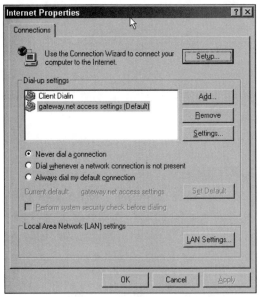

FIGURE 7-42 Individual Connection Settings

Automatic Configuration

The IEAK allows you to specify a location where the IEAK instruction file (.ins)
file is located. The URL to the .ins file is specified in the IEAK, or within Internet
Explorer itself, in the Tools ⇨ Internet Options ⇨ Connections ⇨ Settings page. In
this field, you specify the URL to your .ins file on your Web server. The automatic
configuration is shown in Figure 7-43.

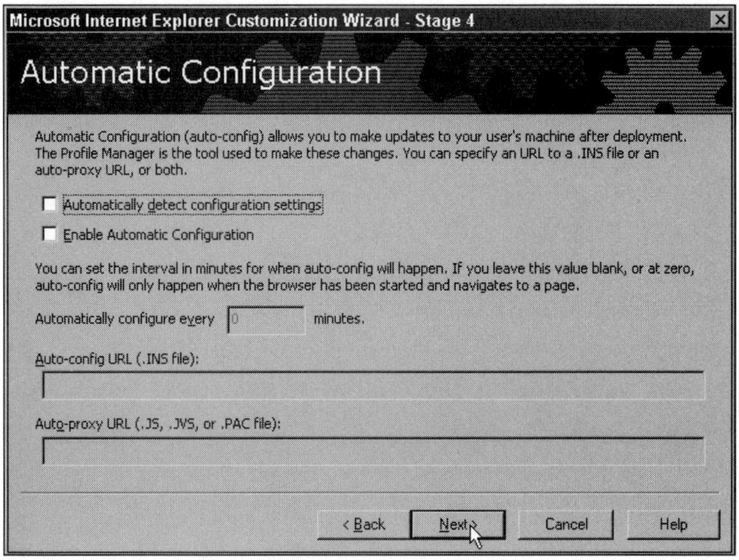

FIGURE 7-43 Automatic Configuration

Internet Explorer checks this URL at a preset interval for changes to the
browser configuration. If Internet Explorer detects any changes, it makes the necessary changes to the browser's configuration.

If you have already deployed Internet Explorer, you can update the automatic
configuration programmatically with a login script or other tool. A string value
called AutoConfigURL should be added with a value of your automatic configuration URL, such as http://www.netdatasys/ie/netdata.ins. You can build
your own .reg file to do this; it would look something like this:

```
REGEDIT4
[HKEY_CURRENT_USER\Software\Microsoft\Windows\CurrentVersion\
Internet Settings]
"AutoConfigURL"="http://www.netdatasys.com/ie"
```

The next option you have is to set the time intervals at which Internet Explorer checks for updates to the `.ins` file. Updates are set in minute increments from 0 (only on Restart) to an interval you choose, such as 240 (that is, every four hours).

The auto-proxy URL enables you to configure your users' proxy settings remotely using a `.jvs`, `.js`, or `.pac` file. The `.jvs` and `.js` files are JavaScript (ECMAScript) files that normally can be used for Netscape and Internet Explorer. A `.pac` file is geared toward Internet Explorer and produces the same results. Using proxy servers and associated automatic proxy configurations is a misunderstood technology in today's environment. Proxy servers and browser configurations can be deployed in several ways to allow both fault tolerance within the proxy environment and ease of administration.

Clustering and arrays enable you to create an acceptable level of fault tolerance within your proxy configuration, so if one of your proxy servers fails for some reason, another proxy can pick up where the failed proxy server left off. An easier way to correct the problem temporarily would be to add a CNAME (canonical name) record to the DNS server for Proxy 1 to point to Proxy 2. Prior to this, both servers would have an IP address and a separate host name. When the CNAME record is added for Proxy 1, Proxy 1 and Proxy 2 point to the same IP address. With this quick change, you can move all of the traffic to Proxy 2 with much less confusion.

You may be wondering what the point of having the auto-configuration is. The point is to make sure that you are adding features to your configuration for the right reasons. If you don't need the feature or function, then don't add it. The more you add, the more you will have to administer and support.

Proxy Settings

As you can see in Figure 7-44, there is one proxy server for my location. This proxy server is the same for all protocols. In the Proxy Settings dialog box shown in Figure 7-44, you specify the proxy settings for your custom browser. In most cases, it's a good idea to use host names for the proxy server wherever possible. If you use a host name rather than a static IP address, it is simpler to make changes in the event of an emergency. In the dialog box, you can specify a single proxy server or multiple proxy servers on multiple ports. Most organizations use a single server and a single port (port 80 for their proxy configurations).

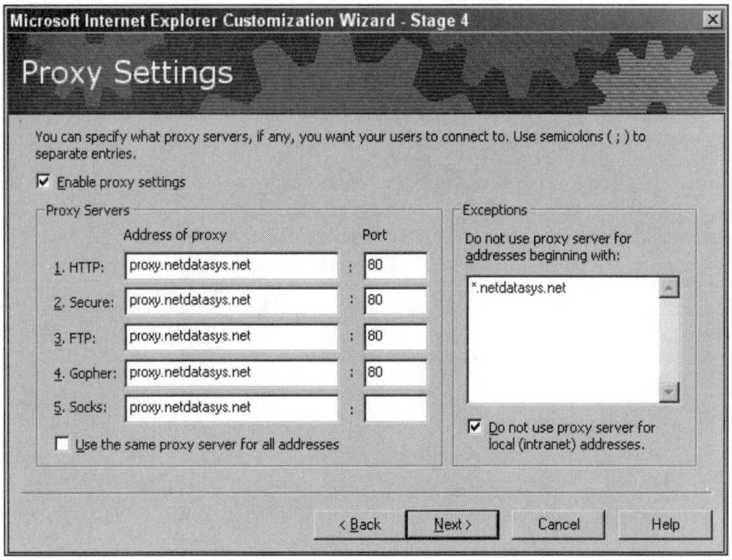

FIGURE 7-44 Proxy Settings

In the Exceptions box, you can specify servers or protocols for which you don't want to use the proxy server. In most cases, the exceptions list is for internal servers within your organization. A well-built firewall will prevent these servers from being accessed from outside your organization, in order to protect the users. If people from outside the organization can gain access to these servers, then they most likely can gain access to you.

You can also exclude protocols in the exceptions list — for protocols that cannot be used through the proxy, for instance. An example of this type of entry would be `https://www.idgbooks.com`.

If you are an avid Netscape user, remember that semicolons and not commas separate the exceptions list in Internet Explorer. Internet Explorer Active Setup will import the old Netscape exceptions and parse the entries, but this is something to remember when manually adding entries. This is also something to mention in any training you may provide, as it may save you some phone calls.

Security

Security is always something you should be aware of. Internet Explorer has built-in security features to allow you to protect your users from harm. Shown in

Figure 7-45, the IEAK allows you to configure the certificate and Authenticode security for Internet Explorer.

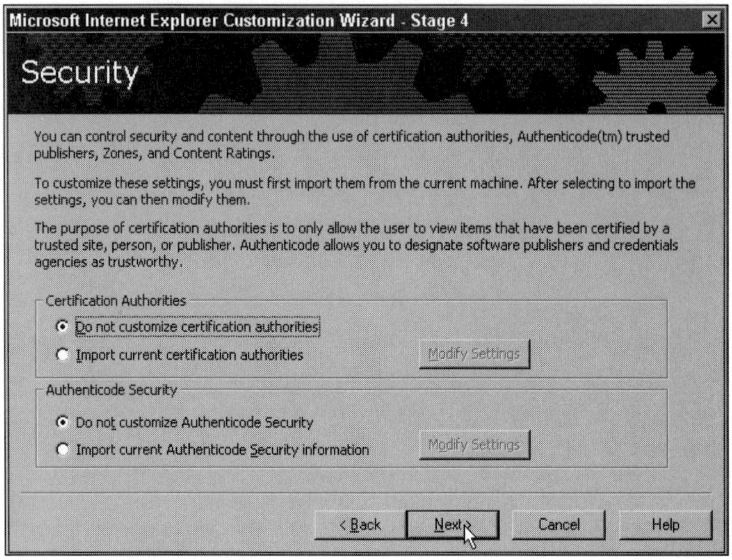

FIGURE 7-45 Security

In the Certificate Authorities window, you can also specify trusted publishers of software, applets, and scripts.

Authenticode enables you to authorize vendors for your users; you can use this dialog box to choose the vendors for your users, one by one. The simplest method for this is to navigate the browser on the IEAK workstation to commonly accessed URLs. If you are presented with any certificates, accept them. Once this process is complete, you can import these certifications and authorizations into the IEAK from your IEAK workstation. Preinstalling certificates for the sites your users visit the most is a good idea. If you go ahead and do this for your user community, you can make decisions for the user base as a whole and avoid support calls for this type of question.

Security Settings

Using the security settings feature, you can modify and import the security zone configurations, as well as the content ratings configuration. The Security tab in

Internet Explorer includes configuration options for four security zones. The zones are as follows:

- *Internet zone.* Any Web server that is not on your local network or is accessed through a proxy server.

- *Local Intranet zone.* Any server that is accessed by bypassing a proxy server, is not included in any other zone, or is accessed by a UNC (Universal Naming Convention). An example of an UNC is \\IIS4SVR\INETPUB.

- *Trusted Sites zones.* Trusted sites are sites you know are safe, such as an extranet you have access to.

- *Restricted Sites zones.* These are the sites you know cause problems.

Technically, there is one more zone, although it is not included in the Security options. The Local Machine zone is also a part of the zone configuration, and it has virtually no special settings; all is fair in this zone. The Security Settings phase is shown in Figure 7-46.

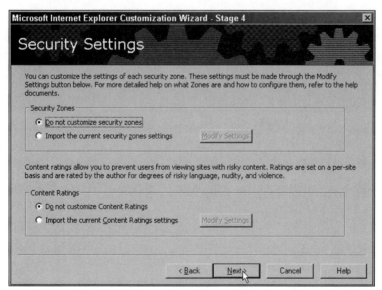

FIGURE 7-46 Security Settings

STAGE 5: CUSTOMIZING COMPONENTS

Stage 5 is focused on configuring the Outlook Express application and configuring policies and restrictions. As you may recall, Outlook Express is the POP/SMTP mail client included in Internet Explorer 5. The Customizing Components overview is shown in Figure 7-47.

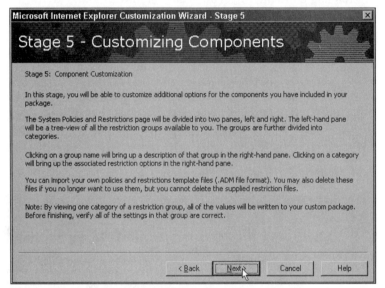

FIGURE 7-47 Customizing Components Overview

Programs

Program settings allow you to modify the default application for handling certain events. For example, you can specify that Outlook Express is the default application for handling e-mail. The Programs step is shown in Figure 7-48. You can import settings from the current build machine by selecting Import the current Program Settings.

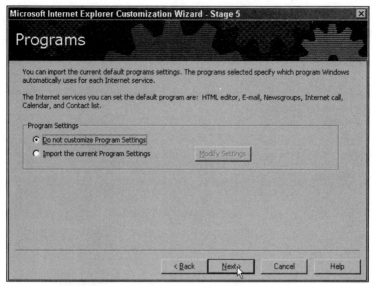

FIGURE 7-48 Programs

Outlook Express Accounts

You must first specify the type of incoming mail server you will use. The choices as shown in Figure 7-49 are as follows:

- *Incoming mail _____ server.* In the server type field, you should specify whether the incoming mail server is a POP3 or IMAP4 server. In the second field, you should specify the server's host name or NetBIOS name.

- *Outgoing mail (SMTP) server.* Specify the name of your outbound SMTP mail server.

- *Internet news (NNTP) server.* If you are providing news services to your users, specify the NNTP server name here, such as news.idgbooks.com.

Note that for each option, logon using Secure Password Authentication (SPA) can be selected. SPA allows the user's mail passwords to be transmitted in an encrypted format so the passwords cannot be intercepted with packet sniffing hardware or software over the Internet.

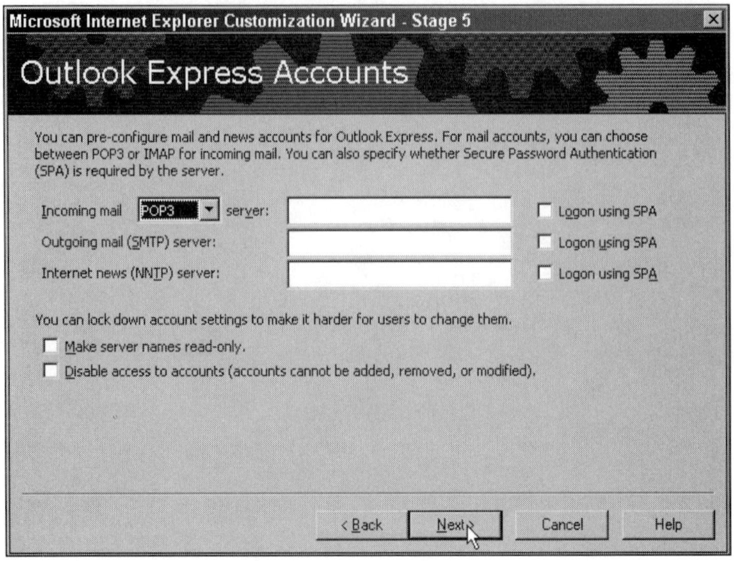

FIGURE 7-49 Outlook Express Accounts

You can also make the accounts read-only if you choose so that the users do not attempt to add or delete accounts in this window. You can also lock the users out from changing the server name as well.

Outlook Express Custom Content

Outlook Express includes a feature called the infopane. The infopane can be customized using HTML and deployed with the IEAK. Here, in this phase, you can add your custom infopane to the Outlook Express configuration.

You can also provide a welcome mail message in this phase to welcome your users to Outlook Express and Internet Explorer 5. You can specify the reply to and the originating address, if you so choose. These options are shown in Figure 7-50.

Outlook Express Custom Settings

In this phase, shown in Figure 7-51, you can specify additional settings for Outlook Express, such as newsgroups and junk mail.

o *Make Outlook Express the default program for*. Allows you to specify that Outlook Express is the default application for mail and news.

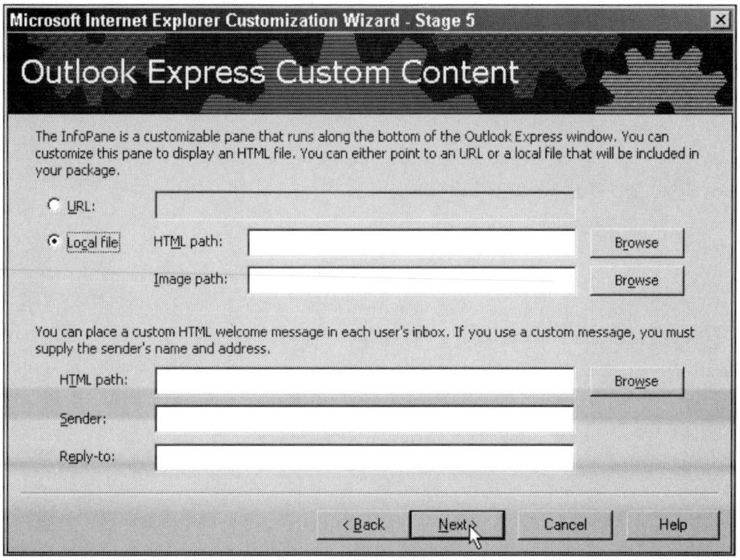

FIGURE 7-50 Outlook Express Custom Content

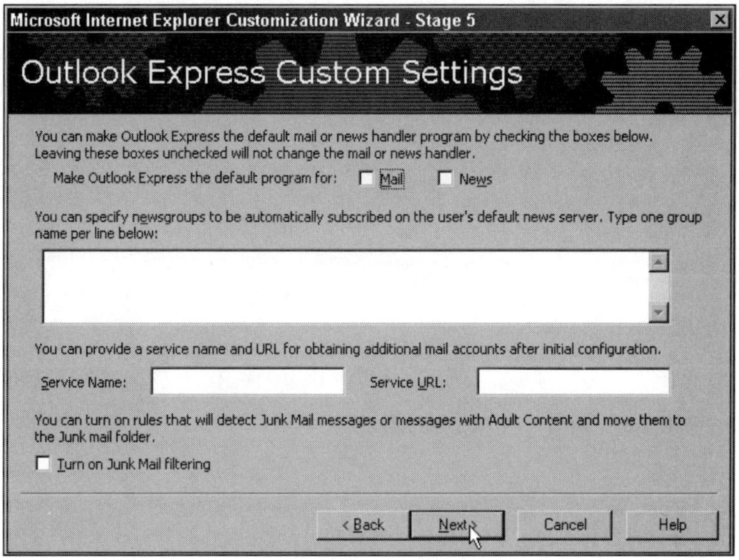

FIGURE 7-51 Outlook Express Custom Settings

- o *Newsgroups.* Allows you to pre-add popular newsgroups to the user's configuration

- o *Service Name/Service URL.* Allows you to specify news servers for your users

- o *Junk mail filtering.* Allows you to turn on the feature to block mail from known spam mailers.

Outlook Express View Settings

This phase, shown in Figure 7-52, allows you to configure the default views for Outlook Express. For more information on these features, refer to Chapter 2.

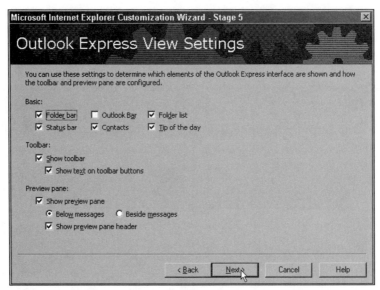

FIGURE 7-52 Outlook Express View Settings

Outlook Express Compose Settings

Figure 7-53 shows the Outlook Express Compose Settings phase. Corporations frequently use signatures as a legal disclaimer to prevent litigation resulting from users sending mail that may not represent the true beliefs or opinions of the organization.

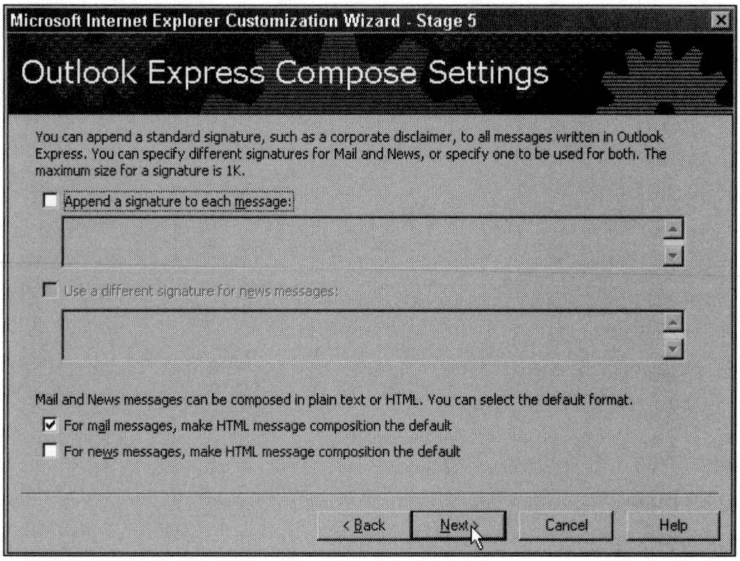

FIGURE 7-53 Outlook Express Compose Settings

Normally, the company has these disclaimers drawn up by the company's legal counsel, and you should enter the verbiage in these two fields. You can enter signatures for both e-mail and news postings or you can specify them separately. You can also choose whether or not to post the signature in HTML format

Address Book Directory Service

The Address Book Directory Service allows you to configure the LDAP server settings for Outlook Express. As you may recall from Chapter 2, the LDAP server allows you to look up users in a database that is compatible with many different operating systems. Figure 7-54 shows the Address Book Directory Service.

System Policies and Restrictions

Figure 7-55 shows the System Policies and Restrictions phase. At this point, we are going to stop and take a break. This phase of the IEAK leads into the IEAK Profile Manager, which we are going to talk about in depth in Chapter 11.

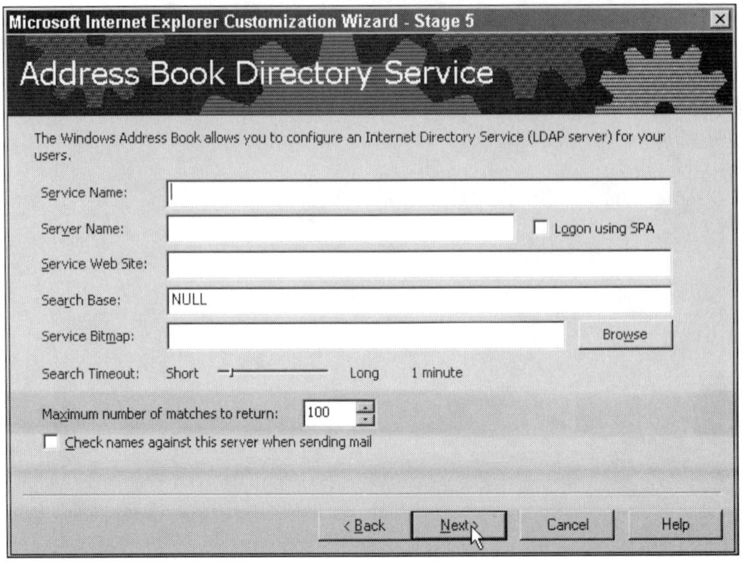

FIGURE 7-54 Address Book Directory Service

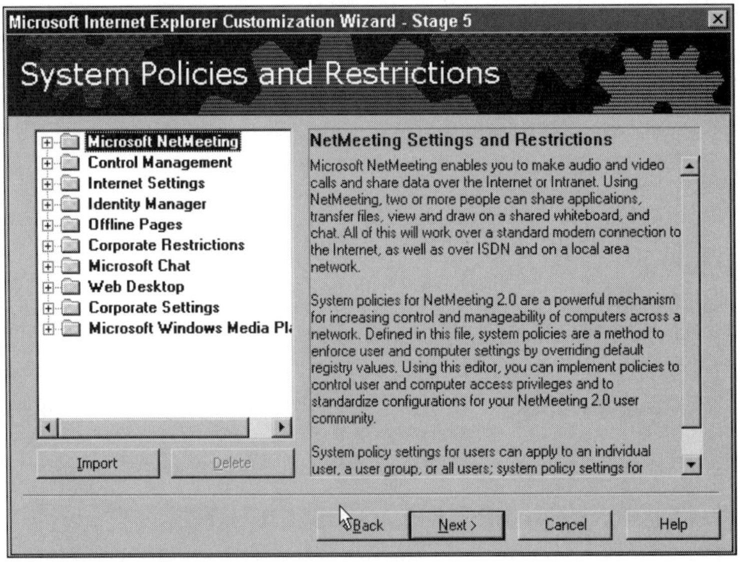

FIGURE 7-55 System Policies and Restrictions

Be sure to understand the options for custom configurations that you have available. The exam objectives touch on the abilities to customize the various applications using these important features.

Key Point Summary

In this chapter, we covered the IEAK in great detail, talking about all of the configuration options available to the IEAK.

- Three roles affect your licensing of Internet Explorer 5 and the IEAK. The corporate administrator has the most options in deploying Internet Explorer within an enterprise. Internet service providers have the capability to brand the browser, and have a custom distribution method available only to the ISP mode: the single floppy disk. Internet content providers are organizations that provide Internet-based content and services to Internet users.

- Silent installation enables setup to be run without user intervention for installation options within the Internet Explorer installation. Silent installation is a good choice if you plan to deploy only a single configuration of Internet Explorer to your users, and do not want to allow the users any choice in the installation.

- You can select up to ten installation options for your users to choose from. The installation options are commonly misunderstood. The option name is the unique name you assign to your configuration.

- The IEAK uses ActiveX technology to check your source files existing on your workstation against the most current source files on the Microsoft download site. Each component of Internet Explorer is checked against the source and is indicated by three icons.

- Third-party applications can be installed with the setup process using a variety of methods. Internet Explorer includes an application installation utility called Iexpress, which you can use to install these third-party applications.

- You can customize your user's start page by entering a URL in the Home page URL option. This is the URL that Internet Explorer is opened to when the browser application is launched. Most organizations use their intranet or Internet home page for this choice. Another feature of the IEAK is the capability to create an online support page. Your users can navigate to this page from the Help menu in Internet Explorer.

- You can set up preselected favorites and links to other sites with your Internet Explorer installation. You can assign your link a descriptive name in the Name field to make it easier for your users to understand the purpose of the link.

○ On the workstation where you are running the IEAK, you can set up a custom Active Channel for your organization, and then import the configuration into your build for your organization once you complete the development of your channel.

○ A User Agent String enables content developers to identify several key factors about a user's workstation by means of HTML code. The user agent identifies the browser type, version, workstation operating system, and a custom string that you can assign with the IEAK.

○ The IEAK allows you to specify a location where the IEAK instruction file (.ins) file is located. The URL to the .ins file is specified in the IEAK, or within Internet Explorer itself, in the Tools ⇨ Internet Options ⇨ Connections ⇨ Settings page.

APPLYING WHAT YOU'VE LEARNED

This section is an opportunity to use what you've learned in this chapter. The Instant Assessment questions here will help you practice for the exam. The labs that follow provide you with important real-world practice using the skills you've learned.

Instant Assessment

1. It is possible to run Internet Explorer 5 in a different language than that of the workstation.

  A. True

  B. False

2. Which of the following installations are available to a corporate administrator?

  A. Multiple-floppy

  B. CD-ROM

  C. Download

  D. Single-floppy

3. An ISP creates an installation using the silent installation option. At the end of the quarter, the ISP reports that it has distributed over 1,000 copies of Internet Explorer. Microsoft sends back a notification to the ISP that the ISP is not complying with the license agreement. What is the problem?

   A. The ISP distributed too many copies of IE.

   B. The ISP reported the distribution too early.

   C. The ISP deleted a competitive channel on the Channel bar.

   D. The silent install is not permitted for an ISP

4. Using the User Agent String, you can identify the OS version (OSR2 vs. OSR1).

   A. True

   B. False

5. You can specify up to _____ sites for downloading Internet Explorer 5 during a regular install.

   A. 8

   B. 5

   C. 1

   D. 10

6. You can specify up to _____ options in configuring your browser.

   A. 8

   B. 5

   C. 1

   D. 10

7. Normally, most organizations set the port settings for their proxy servers for port:

   A. 21

   B. 8181

   C. 80

   D. 1023

8. Automatic browser configuration files are easily identified with a/an _____ extension.

    A. `.jvs`

    B. `.pac`

    C. `.js`

    D. `.ins`

9. `.jvs` and `.js` files use the _____ language to configure proxy settings on the workstation.

    A. ECMAScript (JavaScript), JScript

    B. Java

    C. VBScript

    D. Perl

10. If you are missing a component of Internet Explorer, the icon color will be _____ in AVS.

    A. green

    B. yellow

    C. red

    D. chartreuse

11. The _____ file specifies the executable file that should be run when a CD-ROM is inserted in the CD-ROM drive. The file is located on the CD-ROM itself.

    A. `Layout.inf`

    B. `Control.inf`

    C. `printers.inf`

    D. `autorun.inf`

12. The default folder for customized IE source files is `C:\IEAK\Source`.

    A. True

    B. False

13. You can prompt the user for whether to install the Desktop Update.

    A. True

    B. False

14. Using a single workstation, you can compile configurations for multiple operating system platforms, including UNIX.

A. True

B. False

15. If you create a start page configuration and a welcome page configuration, which page will be seen first when Internet Explorer is first launched?

A. The start page

B. The welcome page

C. The search page

D. The support page

16. When specifying a download site, you can only use HTTP to obtain the source files.

A. True

B. False

17. GUID stands for:

A. Globally Unique Identifier

B. General Unique Identifier

C. Graphical Universal ID

D. General Universal ID

18. Which three options are available for the radio buttons on the CD-ROM splash screen?

A. 3D

B. Standard

C. Custom

D. New Style

19. Which two functions include a signature option for disclaimers in the IEAK?

A. NetMeeting

B. Outlook Express Mail

C. Outlook Express News

D. Internet Explorer Form Postings

20. How many download sites can an ICP select for a silent installation?

    A. 10

    B. 1

    C. 8

    D. None

21. Using the _____ language, you can place a welcome message in the user's inbox in Outlook Express with the IEAK.

    A. Visual Basic

    B. C++

    C. J++

    D. HTML

22. A user has Internet Explorer 3 installed in the `C:\IE3` folder. After running the Internet Explorer 5 setup, where will Internet Explorer 5 be installed if the administrator specified in the IEAK that the installation directory should be in a subdirectory under the Windows folder?

    A. `C:\Program Files\Internet Explorer`

    B. `C:\Windows\Internet Explorer`

    C. `C:\IE4`

    D. `C:\IE3`

23. Which of the following can be identified with the User Agent String?

    A. Browser type

    B. Browser version

    C. Operating system

    D. Custom strings

    E. All of the above

24. You can disable the Welcome dialog box with the IEAK.

    A. True

    B. False

25. Which of the following roles can completely customize the Active Channels?

A. Corporate administrator

B. Internet Content Provider

C. Internet Service Provider

26. Because Windows NT 3.51 is a 32-bit operating system, the 32-bit version of Internet Explorer is the best choice for this platform

A. True

B. False

27. You can enter your customization code after you compile your build to unlock it.

A. True

B. False

28. Which feature allows you to synchronize your files with Microsoft to ensure you have the latest files?

A. AWS

B. AVS

C. VAS

D. SAV

29. In a silent installation, the only thing that will stop the install is an error.

A. True

B. False

30. You can be your own certificate authority if you so choose.

A. True

B. False

31. You can choose specific ports for your browser's proxy settings.

A. True

B. False

Critical Thinking Labs

Lab 7.26 *Troubleshooting the Internet Explorer Customization Wizard*

You are creating your first build with the Internet Explorer Customization Wizard. After walking through Stage 1, you enter Stage 2 and get to the Automatic Version Synchronization page. After reviewing the versions of your components, you notice that all of your components are yellow. After trying to synchronize your files, you get an error stating that the server cannot be found. What do you think would cause this and what would you do to troubleshoot this problem?

Lab 7.27 *Troubleshooting registry and permissions problems*

You are tasked with installing Internet Explorer 5 in your user community that consists of mostly Windows NT Workstation users. What should you consider in deploying the software from a permissions perspective?

Lab 7.28 *Configuring Microsoft NetMeeting*

As a part of your Internet Explorer 5 deployment, you are going to deploy the latest version of Microsoft NetMeeting to allow your users to videoconference with each other. The server team has already set up an ILS server for you to use called ils.widget.com. The company is spread out among several locations across the country and has very fast WAN access to each site with only TCP/IP allowed across the WAN links and routers. Each desktop machine has been outfitted with a microphone and a video camera.

Using the IEAK as a reference, what features would you consider including in your configuration and why? What options do you need to set up based on the information provided?

Hands-On Lab

Lab 7.29 *Working with the IEAK*

Using the IEAK, you will define configurations for the browser based on requirements set forth by the desktop team for your organization. Pay attention to the requirements and design a strategy for each requirement that would be the most effective means to accomplish the task.

1. Provide a means to launch Adobe Acrobat on the user's desktop. All installations of Acrobat are loaded in `C:\Acrobat3\Reader\Acrord32.exe`. Icons have been provided in the same path called `acrobatcolor.ico` and `acobatgrey.ico`.

2. Provide a means for the user to know if the browser is running a task using a graphic. The graphic is 22×22 and located in your `c:\graphics\ie4anim.gif` directory.

3. Add URLs for Support page, Home page, and a search page designed by your Web staff. The URLs are as follows:

   o Search: `http://search.widget.com`

   o Home: `http://intranet.widget.com`

   o Support: `http://ie5support.widget.com`

4. Add default links to the browser using the following URLs:

   o `http://intranet.widget.com/humanresources`

   o `http://intranet.widget.com/parking`

   o `http://intranet.widget.com/security`

   Make sure that no other links are included in the configuration.

5. Ensure that the default Active Channels are not included. Make sure that any existing channels from Internet Explorer 4 are deleted.

6. Add a welcome page to the user's configuration using the following link: `http://intranet.widget.com/ie5/welcome2ie5.htm`.

Using the Profile Manager

About Chapter 8

I n Chapter 8, we are going to talk about the IEAK Profile Manager. IEAK Profile Manager allows you to manage deployed versions of your Internet Explorer package. You can make changes to your browser once it is deployed automatically using a variety of means. In this chapter, we are going to talk about the various system policies and restrictions that you can place on the Internet Explorer suite of software to make supporting the browser an easier task for you and your customers.

OVERVIEW

The IEAK Profile Manager is the tool for managing deployed versions of your package. With the Profile Manager, you can modify the installed versions of your package on your user's desktops without having to visit the user's machine.

 The Profile Manager is only available to the Corporate Administrator role when using the IEAK.

In order to use the Profile Manager, you should have already created a custom package with the IEAK Wizard in Chapter 7. Locate the source files for your package on your hard drive and then launch the Profile Manager. When you first launch the Profile Manager, you will notice that all of the options are grayed out. This is because the Profile Manager is a tool used to modify existing custom builds, and it is necessary to navigate to the build in order to make changes. Figure 8-1 shows the Profile Manager as it appears when it is first launched.

If your organization already has Internet Explorer 5 installed, you can create an .ins file by selecting the File ⇨ New option. The .ins file is the foundation of the entire IEAK. It contains all of the configuration information for the browser and the associated applications. Using the IEAK, you can set a Web-based location for your user's browser to automatically update configurations of the browser.

You don't have to use the IEAK to use .ins files if you have already deployed Internet Explorer 5. You can add the location of your .ins file by pointing to the location of your .ins file in the Tools/Internet Options/Connections/LAN Settings Tab. Shown in Figure 8-2, you can add the location of your .ins file for previously installed versions of your browser.

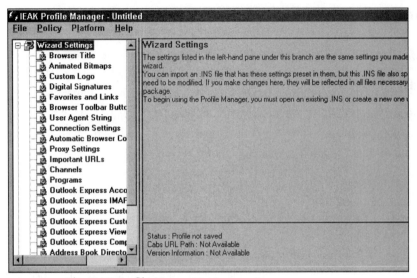

FIGURE 8-1 The IEAK Profile Manager

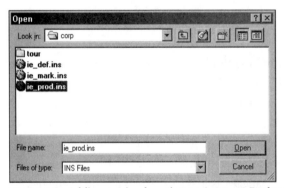

FIGURE 8-2 Adding an .ins location to Internet Explorer 5

Without an .ins file, the Auto Configuration will not work. Let's take a quick look at the contents of an .ins file to get a better understanding of what it is all about.

On the CD-ROM, open the idgbooks.ins with a text editor such as Notepad. The idgbooks.ins file is located in the Chapter 8 directory on the CD-ROM. As you browse through the file, notice that the entries in the .ins file are very similar to those of the IEAK Wizard.

One of the great features of the Profile Manager is that you can work on multiple configurations (.ins files), one after the other and not have to worry about corrupting any of your previous work. Each individual .ins file stands alone in the configuration and does not rely on any other. In addition, you can create a single .ins file using the Profile Manager and use this file as a template to create other .ins files. Using this strategy, you can quickly create templates for organizations within your company.

When you have completed your changes, you can locate .ins files in the same directory on your Web server by choosing different naming conventions for each file. All you have to make sure of is that the file has an .ins extension and is in all lowercase letters.

 For consistency, use lowercase for your file names.

SYSTEM POLICIES

If you have taken the Windows 95 or the Windows NT workstation exam, you should already be familiar with system policies. The System Policies and Restrictions feature in the IEAK uses some of the same technology, but takes the restrictions a step further and incorporates the operating system restrictions with the application restrictions. In the Windows 95, Windows 98, and Windows NT operating systems, you can use the System Policy templates, which are stored with an .adm extension, to develop policy files, which have a .pol extension.

A great feature of the Profile Manager is its ability to import .adm templates into your package. You can import operating system templates and combine these templates with your Internet Explorer settings to create a single solution for enforcing policies on your users' workstations. As you will see, this is a good match.

Do not mix imported templates from one operating system with templates from another. While they are similar in many respects, Windows NT and Windows 95/98 differ considerably in the features they offer in the system policies. The rule of thumb is to create separate directories for each operating system when you distribute Internet Explorer with the IEAK. Now that we have covered the basics, let's jump right into the IEAK Profile Manager.

WIZARD SETTINGS

The Wizard settings are almost identical to that of the IEAK Wizard. The main difference between the IEAK Wizard and the Wizard settings in Profile Manager is that you cannot make any installation modifications with the Wizard settings. Features such as the CD-ROM splash screen, installation options, and installation-related features are not available with the Wizard settings option. To make changes to these configurations, you must rerun the IEAK Wizard and create a new version of the installation.

Because we talk about the features and functions of the Internet Explorer Customization Wizard in Chapter 7, I am not going to cover the Wizard settings here. Take a few minutes to review these settings to refresh your memory from Chapter 7 so that you are familiar with the reasons for making changes to these settings. Table 8-1 shows the functions for each feature as a review of Chapter 7.

TABLE 8-1 WIZARD SETTINGS AVAILABLE IN THE PROFILE MANAGER	
OPTION	*USAGE*
Browser Title	Change "Internet Explorer Provided by organization name."
Animated Bitmaps	Here, you can replace the location of the animated bitmap used in the upper right-hand corner of the browser. This bitmap is used when the browser is performing an action, such as browsing.
Custom Logo	When the browser is idle, you can add a logo for that state as well. Here you add the path to your idle logo.
Digital Signatures	Certificate Authorities can be added here to your configuration for commonly used digital certificates.
Favorites and Links	Here, you can add additional Web links to Web sites and Web applications.
Browser Toolbar Buttons	Here, you can add additional buttons to your browser's toolbar for other functions and applications.
User Agent String	Modifies the User Agent String.

OPTION	USAGE
Connection Settings	Modifies the connection settings for your browser, such as proxy server settings, exception lists, and other proxy and dial-up configurations.
Automatic Browser Configuration	Here, you can change the path and file name of your automatic configuration file, the .INS file.
Proxy Settings	Here, you can make changes to the proxy settings only.
Important URLs	Here, you can change the start page, search page, and online support.
Channels	Add/Delete Active Channels.
Programs	Here, you can change the default programs to be launched for e-mail, calendar, newsgroups, Internet calls, contacts, and the default HTML editor.
Outlook Express Accounts	Here, you can change the server settings for Outlook Express, such as the SMTP, POP, and NNTP Server names.
Outlook Express IMAP Settings	Here, you can specify options for your IMAP users, such as the path to the root folder and other options.
Outlook Express Custom Content	This is used to customize the info pane in Outlook Express and also the Outlook welcome message.
Outlook Express Custom Settings	You can add subscribed newsgroups to Outlook Express, as well as make Outlook Express the default program for mail and news. You can also specify a URL for adding mail accounts and turn on junk mail filtering.
Outlook Express View Settings	This is where you can configure the Outlook Bar to customize your Outlook Express. You can change things like whether or not certain toolbars are displayed.
Outlook Express Compose Settings	Here is where you would add a disclaimer to mail messages sent by your users. You can use this for newsgroups as well. Note that you specify the default stationery here as well, such as HTML.

Continued

TABLE 8-1 WIZARD SETTINGS AVAILABLE IN THE PROFILE MANAGER *(continued)*	
OPTION	USAGE
Address Book Directory	This will enable your users to do LDAP-based lookups on a Web-based LDAP service.
Folder Webviews	You can also change the look of the My Computer and Control Panel applets using `.htt` (HTML templates). This is where you specify the path to the template file.
Security Zones and Content Ratings	Here, you can change the browser security settings from the defaults to best suit your organization. You can also specify the content ratings that you are going to allow for your organization.
Certificate Settings	This is the area where you can import Certificate Authorities, like Verisign and GTE.

SYSTEM POLICIES AND RESTRICTIONS

Here is where we get into the meat of the application, System Policies and Restrictions. This year, one of the hottest buzzwords in the computer industry was TCO (Total Cost of Ownership). While sometimes used as a sales tactic, TCO has a real and important impact on us, as the professionals who make it happen. You know that giving the users flexibility brings more support calls, plain and simple. In order to control the amount of flexibility that the users have, you need a tool to manage and control the available configuration options within the application. In the Internet Explorer suite, that application is the Profile Manager. Let's jump right in and get going.

Microsoft NetMeeting

If you are planning on deploying NetMeeting, you should consider putting some controls on how your users can use the application. The application itself is very powerful, but as you know, video and audio over a network can eat up all of your available bandwidth if you are not careful. Let's talk a little about NetMeeting settings, as shown in Figure 8-3.

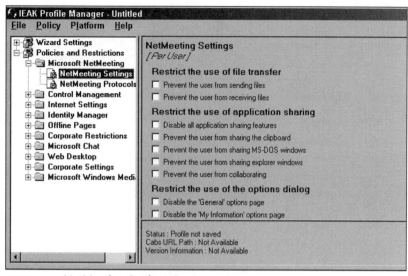

FIGURE 8-3 NetMeeting Settings Part 1

The following options enable you to restrict the file transfer capabilities within NetMeeting:

o *Prevent the user from sending files*. Prevents the user from sending files using the file transfer function within the NetMeeting application.

o *Prevent the user from receiving files*. Prevents the user from receiving files using the file transfer function within the NetMeeting application.

Application sharing can be configured in the Profile Manager to allow the administrator to have better control over the users' capabilities within the NetMeeting application. These features can assist in reducing support costs by not allowing the user too much flexibility with the configuration of the user's individual workstation.

o *Disable all application sharing features.* Prevents the user from using the application sharing function at all.

o *Prevent the user from sharing the clipboard*. Prevents the user from sharing the contents of the clipboard, such as a cut and paste, with another user in a meeting.

o *Prevent the user from sharing MS-DOS windows*. Prevents the user from being able to shell to DOS and share the DOS session with others. If the window is being shared, there is a possibility that an individual could damage or delete important files in DOS.

o *Prevent the user from sharing explorer windows.* Prevents the user from sharing Windows Explorer. The potential for unauthorized activity here is fairly obvious.

o *Prevent the user from collaborating.* Prevents the user from using the collaborative features of NetMeeting altogether.

concept link

As you may recall from Chapter 3, the Tools ⇨ Options dialog box in NetMeeting enables you to make configuration changes to the NetMeeting application. The following options enable you to restrict access to the NetMeeting configuration:

o *Disable the 'General' options page.*

o *Disable the 'My Information' options page.*

Let's page down as shown in Figure 8-4 for Part two of the options.

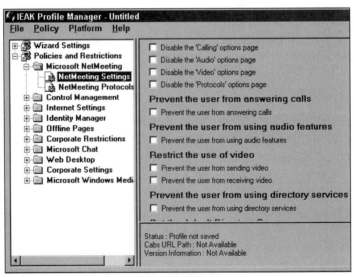

FIGURE 8-4 NetMeeting Settings Part 2

o *Disable the 'Calling' options page.*

o *Disable the 'Audio' options page.*

o *Disable the 'Video' options page.*

- *Disable the 'Protocols' options page.*

- *Prevent the user from answering calls.* Prevents the user from being able to acknowledge a NetMeeting session initiated by another user.

- *Prevent the user from using audio features.* Prevents the user from being able to receive or send audio.

You may want to restrict video altogether for several reasons—the most important reason being its need for bandwidth. The majority of the bandwidth consumed by NetMeeting is for video transmissions.

- *Prevent the user from sending video.* Disables the transmission of video from the user's workstation.

- *Prevent the user from receiving video.* Prevents the user from receiving video from another party in NetMeeting.

- *Prevent the user from using directory services.* Disables the user's ability to use ILS and ULS servers.

Lets page down for Part 3, as shown in Figure 8-5.

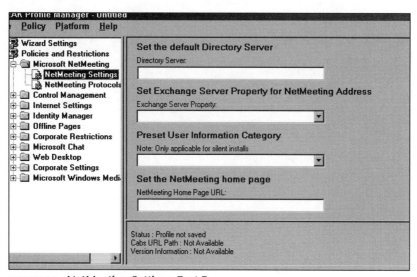

FIGURE 8-5   NetMeeting Settings Part 3

The Directory Server option enables you to specify the default Internet Locator Server in your NetMeeting configuration.

- *Directory Server.* Enter the name of the default ILS server here.

 You can create your own ILS server with Windows NT Server if you would like to allow NetMeeting connectivity within your own network. Check out `http://backoffice.microsoft.com` **for more details.**

- *Set Exchange Server Property for NetMeeting Address.* Sets the extension attribute for Exchange/NetMeeting related functions.

- *Preset User Information Category.* Enables you to preset the category for the user. Options are personal, business, and adult.

- *Set the NetMeeting home page.* Enables you to enter a URL for the NetMeeting home page.

Let's page down for Part 4, as shown in Figure 8-6.

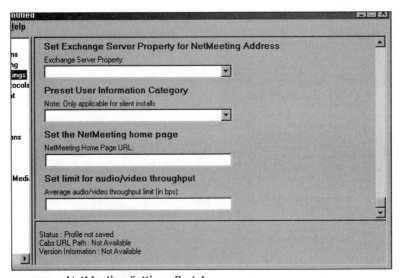

FIGURE 8-6 NetMeeting Settings Part 4

- *Set limit for audio/video throughput.* Enables you to throttle the bandwidth consumed by NetMeeting in bits per second.

You can also control the protocols that NetMeeting will use to connect to other users and the ILS server. The protocol configurations for NetMeeting are shown in Figure 8-7.

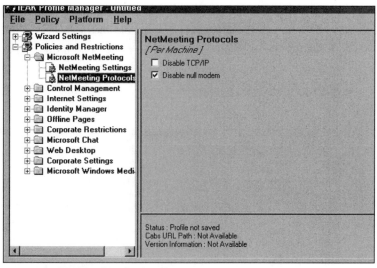

FIGURE 8-7 NetMeeting Protocols

- *Disable TCP/IP.* Disables the use of the TCP/IP network protocol.
- *Disable null modem.* Disables the use of a null modem connection.

Control Management

Control management is not currently covered on your exam, but you should still have a general knowledge of its functions. With the Profile Manager, you can control the browser's installed ActiveX components and other development related data binding tools. With this tool, you can specify the controls that your users have access to and restrict the remainder if you so choose. Control management is shown in Figure 8-8.

You can also restrict use of ActiveX controls by the Internet Explorer Zone, such as Intranet Zone, Internet Zone, and so on. As a part of your organization's overall information security policy, you should consider taking a look at this and developing a plan to protect your users from hostile or undesired ActiveX behavior.

ActiveX controls are basically a bucket of programming code for developers to use in creating applications. The bucket allows for certain actions to be called upon when the developer wants certain actions to take place. The reason to use ActiveX controls for the developer is to more rapidly develop applications so that repetitive code does not have to be written to accomplish the same task. As ActiveX controls are basically programming code, these features have been used to create viruses as well. The malicious code is created in the form of an ActiveX control that does damage to the end user's machine. As most of these controls are downloaded from the Internet, this is the main reason you may want to develop a proactive strategy for reducing your exposure to harmful controls.

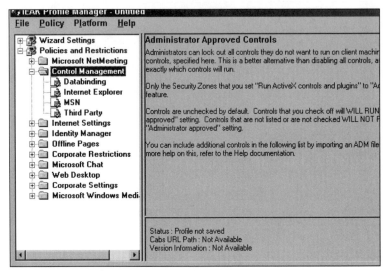

FIGURE 8-8 Control Management

Internet Settings

The Internet Settings feature enables you to modify the layout of various features within the browser. You can change and control the viewing of text, colors, fonts, and many other browser-related options. The Internet Settings and AutoComplete features are shown in Figure 8-9.

AutoComplete

There are two types of AutoComplete in Internet Explorer. You can allow Internet Explorer to display a dialog box of letters you have typed previously with normal AutoComplete or you can choose to automatically complete your typing with Inline AutoComplete. Each of these options can be enabled and disabled with the Profile Manager application.

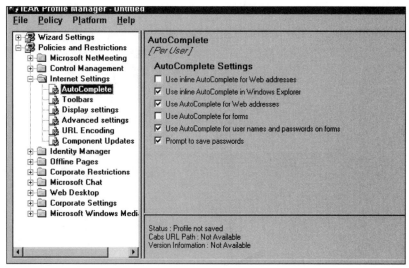

FIGURE 8-9 Internet Settings/AutoComplete

- *Use inline AutoComplete for Web addresses*. Uses Inline AutoComplete for typing URLs.

- *Use inline AutoComplete in Windows Explorer*. Uses Inline AutoComplete for typing paths and file names.

- *Use AutoComplete for Web Addresses*. Uses the dialog box to show previously typed URLs in Internet Explorer.

- *Use AutoComplete for forms*. Uses the dialog box to show previously typed letters in Web forms.

- *Use AutoComplete for user names and passwords on forms*. Allows Internet Explorer to cache user names and passwords for Web locations.

- *Prompt to save passwords*. Prompts the user to save their password locally.

Toolbars

The following options, shown in Figure 8-10, enable you to customize the toolbars in Explorer by activating or deactivating buttons that are available. The following button choices are available to you.

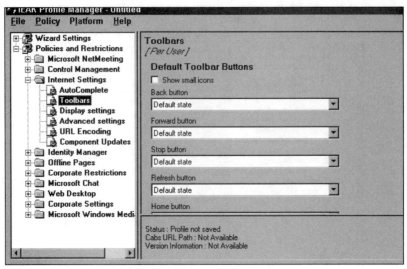

FIGURE 8-10 Internet Settings/Toolbars

- *Back button.* Allows you to go back to the last page you visited.
- *Forward button.* After using the back button, this button allows you to move forward in the page views.
- *Stop button.* Stops navigation requests made by the browser.
- *Refresh button.* Reloads the displayed page on the browser.
- *Home button.* Navigates the user to the home page defined in Internet Options.
- *Search button.* Allows the user to use the Search window in Internet Explorer.
- *History button.* Allows the user to bring up the user's navigation history by day and week.
- *Favorites button.* This allows the user to view his or her favorite Web sites.
- *Folders button.* This allows the user to view his or her directories, or folders as they are sometimes referred to.
- *Fullscreen button.* Changes the browser into Kiosk mode or full screen; the toolbars and menu options are removed.
- *Tools button.* Allows the user to display the Tools option menu.
- *Mail button.* Allows the user to send an e-mail message.
- *Font Size button.* Allows the user to change default fonts.

- *Print button.* Allows the user to print a page that is being viewed.

- *Edit button.* Used to launch the HTML editor, such as FrontPage or FrontPage Express.

- *Discussions button.* Allows the user to join online discussions and collaboration functions for Microsoft Office applications.

- *Cut button.* Used to cut text from one file or document to another.

- *Copy button.* Used to copy text from one file or document to another.

- *Paste button.* Used to paste text from one file or document to another.

- *Encoding button.* Used to encode data, such as encryption.

Display settings

Figures 8-11 and 8-12 show the display settings within the Profile Manager. You may want to consider controlling some of these settings with the following configurable options:

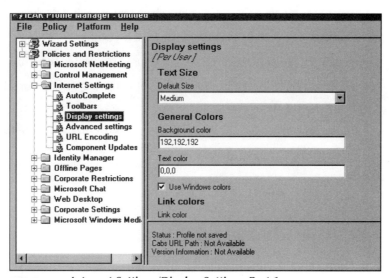

FIGURE 8-11 Internet Settings/Display Settings Part 1

- *Text Size.* Controls the size of the text.

- *Background color.* Specifies the standard background colors for the workstation.

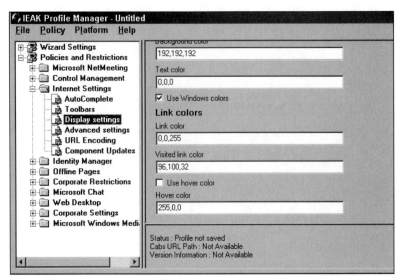

FIGURE 8-12 Internet Settings/Display Settings Part 2

- *Text color.* Specifies the standard text color for the workstation. You can also use the default windows color scheme by checking the box.

- *Link color.* Specifies the color to use for a hyperlink.

- *Visited link color.* Specifies the color to use for a visited hyperlink.

- *Use hover color.* Specifies whether or not to use a specific color when hovering in a Web-based document.

- *Hover color.* Specifies the color to use when hovering in a Web-based document.

Advanced settings

As shown in Figures 8-13, 8-14, 8-15, and 8-16, the following are the available Advanced settings for Internet Explorer 5.

- *Enable Autodialing.* Autodialing allows applications, such as Outlook Express, to dial up the ISP and log in to send and receive mail.

- *Disable Script debugging.* Script debugging is an optional tool available on the Site Builder Network on Microsoft's home page. The Script Debugger enables developers to test their content with Internet Explorer and track down errors quickly.

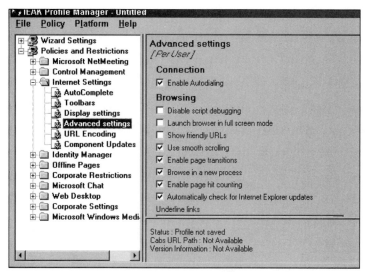

FIGURE 8-13 Internet Settings/Advanced Settings Part 1

o *Launch browser in full screen mode.* Explorer is started in full screen mode when this option is chosen.

o *Show friendly URLs.* Displays the fully qualified URL or path in the status window located at the bottom left corner of the browser.

o *Use smooth scrolling.* Enables you to move the cursor up, down, and across with a consistent speed and transition. This feature makes browsing much easier.

o *Enable page transitions.* This is a really nice feature of both Internet Explorer and Microsoft FrontPage. Page transitions enables you to develop Web pages that provide the user with smooth transitions from one Web page to another without an abrupt change. As a good Web developer and professional, you will learn that the goal of any Web page is to keep the users' interest in the content, not in what is happening with their browser.

o *Browse in a new process.* If Internet Explorer is open and an HTML document is selected, the HTML page is displayed within the context of the open browser session. When this option is enabled, a new session is started when browsing outside the context of Explorer.

o *Enable page hit counting.* Enables tracking of Web page access. This is a good tool for tracking very simple information on page usage.

- *Automatically check for Internet Explorer updates*. This feature checks Microsoft's site or a site you specify for updates to the browser's source files. This is an easy way to ensure that your user's browsers are up-to-date all the time.

caution **This feature helps keep things up-to-date; however, some updates to the browser may not be compatible with custom-developed configurations or applications that you may have developed. If you are thinking about using this feature, consider controlling the update process for your users to save you some headaches.**

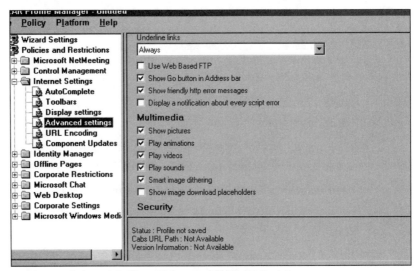

FIGURE 8-14 Internet Settings/Advanced Settings Part 2

- *Underline links*. Internet Explorer can display hyperlinks on Web pages with an underline to enable the user to navigate easily. Selecting Always turns this feature on. Selecting Never disables the feature completely.
- *Use Web Based FTP*. This allows your users a GUI interface to an FTP session to make the FTP experience seem similar to using Windows Explorer.
- *Show Go button in Address Bar*. The Go button is similar to the Return key on the keyboard; it initiates action on the part of the application.

- *Show friendly http error messages*. One of the nice features of Internet Explorer 5 is its ability to display more descriptive error messages to the user. This feature will help cut down on the support calls.

- *Display a notification about every script error*. This feature lets the user know that there were VB scripting errors, ASP, or JavaScript errors in the code of the page they are viewing. This helps the user know that the page may not work as expected.

- *Show pictures*. This option enables downloading of graphics embedded in Web pages.

- *Play animations*. Disables use of animation on Web pages.

- *Play videos*. Disables the display of `.avi`, `.mpeg`, and other related files that are embedded in Web pages. These types of files are played within the context of the browser with Microsoft Active Movie.

- *Play sounds*. Disables Explorer's ability to play `.wav` and other related sound files embedded within Web pages. This does not, however, disable audio that is run within the context of another application. Plug-ins are a good example.

- *Smart image dithering*. Dithering enables you to view sharper images when loading graphics from Web sites, as some images are created in screen resolutions that do not match the user's resolution.

- *Show image download placeholders*. Shows the location of the image for downloading.

- *Enable Profile Assistant*. As discussed in Chapter 1, the Profile Assistant enables users to enter information about themselves into Internet Explorer. Some Web sites track this information for geographic and statistical reasons.

- *Delete saved pages when browser closed*. This option clears the Temporary Internet files folder upon exiting Internet Explorer.

- *Do not save encrypted pages to disk*. Prevents Internet Explorer from saving SSL or any other encrypted pages to disk.

- *Warn if forms submit is being redirected*. Online forms pages are usually logged to a file, HTML page, database, or other related tool. This feature warns the user if the posted data is being sent to a URL other than the original location.

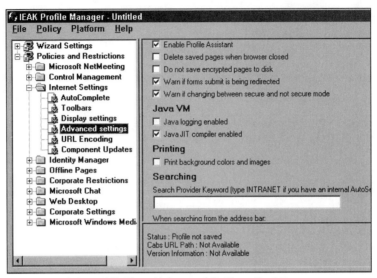

FIGURE 8-15 Internet Settings/Advanced Settings Part 3

o *Warn if changing between secure and insecure mode.* Displays a dialog box when navigating from a secure page to a non-secure page, such as HTTPS:// to HTTP://.

o *Java logging enabled.* Java logging allows the browser to log activity related to the Java Virtual Machine. This is mainly used for Java debugging.

o *Java JIT compiler enabled.* This allows the JIT compiler to function and compile Java applets quickly.

o *Print background colors and images.* By default, Explorer does not print all of the graphics and background colors on Web pages. This is an option to consider if you have a color printer and want the whole effect printed. However, printing a page with a background can sometimes obscure the information on the page.

o *Search Provider Keyword.* Allows you to set up a keyword in Internet Explorer to navigate the user to a pre-defined search server.

o *When searching from the address bar.* Allows you to control the action taken after a search result.

o *Use HTTP 1.1.* Enables the use of the faster, more efficient HTTP protocol.

o *Use HTTP 1.1 through proxy connections.* Enables the use of HTTP 1.1 through a proxy server.

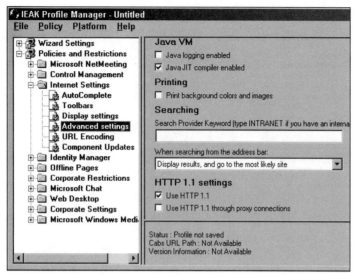

FIGURE 8-16 Internet Settings/Advanced Settings Part 4

Identity Management

The Windows Identity Manager allows you to create multiple user profiles within a single logon on the local machine for such services as MSN, Chat, Outlook Express, and many others. The Identity Manager allows the user to use the same logon for different purposes, such as general mailboxes or anonymous chatting. Figure 8-17 shows the configuration options available for the Identity Manager in the Profile Manager application.

○ *Prevent users from configuring or using Identities.* Allows you to restrict the use of this function.

Offline Pages

As shown in Figures 8-18, 8-19, and 8-20, you can configure Internet Explorer's actions in regard to Active Channels. This feature has an impact in bandwidth sensitive environments; you should take a close look at this feature if conserving bandwidth is something that your organization is sensitive to.

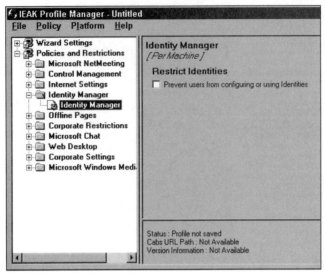

FIGURE 8-17 Windows Identity Manager settings

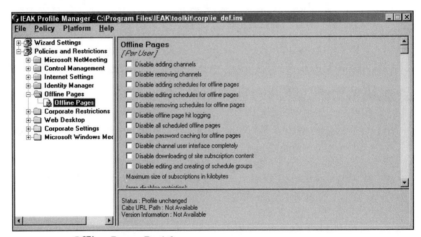

FIGURE 8-18 Offline Pages Part 1

○ *Disables adding channels.* Disables the ability to add channels to the browser.

○ *Disables removing channels.* Disables the ability to remove channels not configured with the IEAK.

○ *Disable adding schedules for offline pages.* Stops the user from adding any non-standardized update schedules for channels.

- *Disable editing schedules for offline pages.* Stops the user from changing any standardized update schedules for channels.

- *Disable removing schedules for offline pages.* Stops the user from removing any standardized update schedules for channels.

- *Disable offline page hit logging.* Disables the page's ability to log additional page hits when the page is viewed offline.

- *Disable all scheduled offline pages.* Stops the browser from performing any scheduled updates.

- *Disable password caching for offline pages.* Prevents passwords from being stored for pages that are viewed offline.

- *Disable Channel user Interface.* Disables the Active Channels Interface.

- *Disable downloading of channel subscription content.* Change notification will still work. Prevents channel subscription content from being downloaded, but the red gleam icon indicating changes will still function.

- *Disable editing and creating of schedule groups.* Prevents the users from changing or creating schedule groupings of channels.

- *Maximum size of subscriptions in kilobytes.* Sets a limit (in kilobytes) to the number of files downloaded in a site subscription.

- *Maximum number of offline pages.* Sets a limit on the number of documents that can be downloaded.

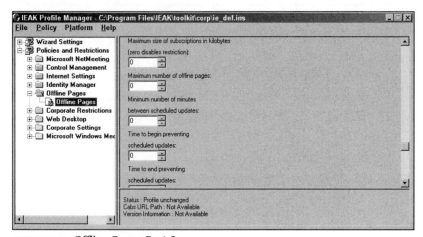

FIGURE 8-19 Offline Pages Part 2

- o *Minimum number of minutes.* The minimum time between subscription updates.

- o *Time to begin preventing scheduled updates.* This selects the time during which updates should not be allowed, so the users are not hindered during their work by a download of subscribed content by the browser.

- o *Time to end preventing scheduled updates.* The time in which updates should not be allowed to end, this is the end time.

- o *Maximum offline page crawl depth.* This is the limit to the depth of the crawl, the number of pages that the browser can access deep into subdirectories on a site for a subscription.

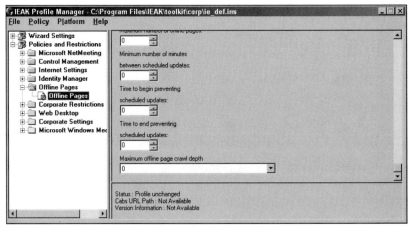

FIGURE 8-20 Offline Pages Part 3

Corporate Restrictions

These features are only used in the Corporate Administrator role and apply to securing the browser in an internal organization. A lot of companies are moving to restrict the configuration options on corporate-owned hardware; take a look at the options available in Figure 8-21.

Most of the settings on the Internet Property page are self explanatory; let's look at the options that you can choose from.

- o *Disable viewing the General Page.*
- o *Disable viewing the Security Page.*

- *Disable viewing the Content Page.*

- *Disable viewing the Connection Page.*

- *Disable viewing the Programs Page.*

- *Disable viewing the Advanced Page.*

- *Disable changing any settings on the Advanced Page.*

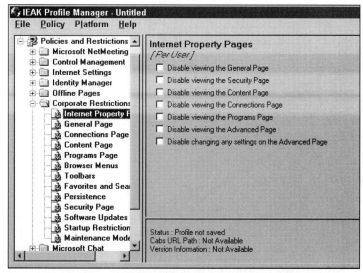

FIGURE 8-21 Corporate Restrictions/Internet Property Pages

General Page

Figure 8-22 shows the General Page settings options. Here you can choose to disable configuration options on the General Page itself. Here are the options that are available to you.

- *Disable changing home page settings.*

- *Disable changing Temporary Internet files settings.*

- *Disable changing history settings.*

- *Disable changing color settings.*

- *Disable changing link color settings.*

- *Disable changing font settings.*

- *Disable changing language settings.*

- *Disable changing accessibility settings.*

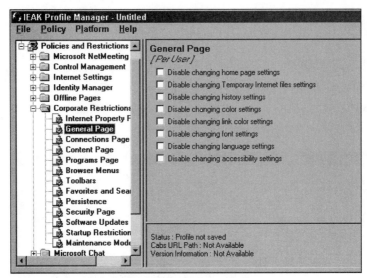

FIGURE 8-22 Corporate Restrictions/General Page

Connections Page

In Figure 8-23, you can make changes to the Connections Page's options as well; here is what you can change if you so choose:

o *Disable Internet Connection Wizard.*

o *Disable changing connection settings.*

o *Disable changing proxy settings.*

o *Disable changing Automatic Configuration settings.*

Content Page

In Figure 8-24, you can also make changes to the Content Page's options; here is what you can change if you so choose:

o *Disable changing ratings settings.*

o *Disable changing certificate settings.*

o *Disable changing Profile Assistant settings.*

o *Disable AutoComplete for forms and saving of submitted strings.*

o *Do not allow users to save passwords in AutoComplete for forms.*

tip For secure environments, you should seriously consider preventing users from saving passwords.

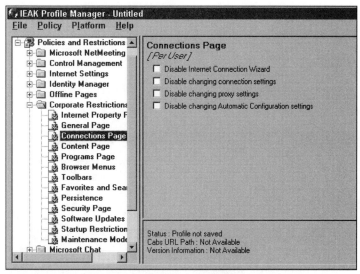

FIGURE 8-23 Corporate Restrictions/Connections Page

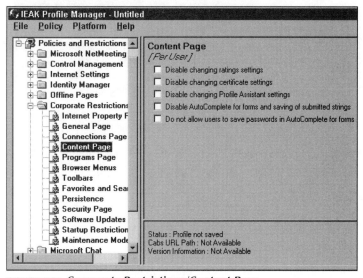

FIGURE 8-24 Corporate Restrictions/Content Page

Programs Page

In Figure 8-25, you can make changes to the Program Page's options; here is what you can change if you so choose:

o *Disable changing Messaging settings.*

o *Disable changing Calendar and Contact settings.*

o *Disable the Reset Web Settings feature.*

o *Disable changing checking if Internet Explorer is the default browser.*

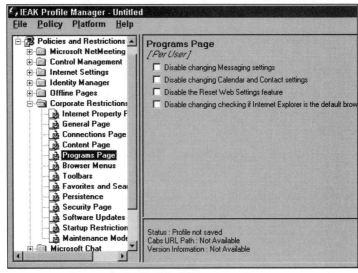

FIGURE 8-25 Corporate Restrictions/Programs Page

Browser Menus

With the Profile Manager, you can also customize the menus. You can remove the default options within the menus as shown in Figures 8-26 and 8-27.

o *Disable Save As... menu option.*

o *Disable New menu option.*

o *Disable Open menu option.*

o *Disable Save As Web Page Complete format*

o *Disable closing of the browser.*

o *Disable Source menu option.*

- *Disable Fullscreen menu option.*

- *Hide Favorites Menu.*

- *Disable Internet Options... menu option.*

- *Remove 'Tip of the Day' menu option.*

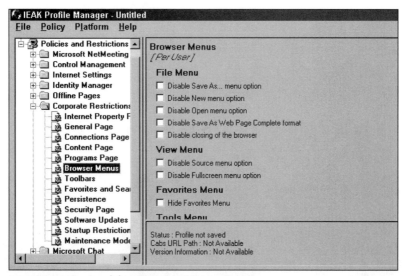

FIGURE 8-26 Customizing Browser Menus Part 1

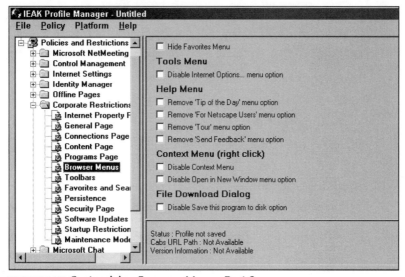

FIGURE 8-27 Customizing Browser Menus Part 2

o *Remove 'For Netscape Users' menu option.*

o *Remove 'Tour' menu option.*

o *Remove 'Send Feedback' menu option.*

o *Disable Context Menu.*

o *Disable Open in New Window menu option.*

o *Disable Save this program to disk option.*

Toolbars

The toolbar restrictions are shown in Figure 8-28.

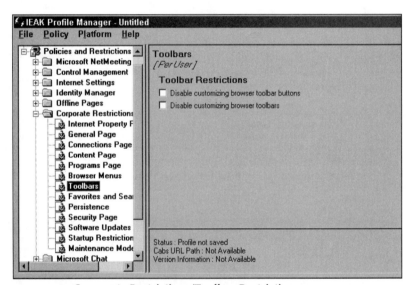

FIGURE 8-28 Corporate Restrictions/Toolbar Restrictions

o *Disable customizing browser toolbar buttons.*

o *Disable customizing browser toolbars.*

Favorites and Search

Favorites and Search options are shown in Figure 8-29.

o *Disable importing and exporting of favorites.*

o *Disable Search Customization.*

o *Disable Find Files via F3 within the browser.*

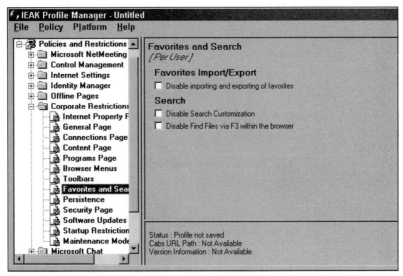

FIGURE 8-29 Corporate Restrictions/Favorites and Search

Persistence

Here is where the Profile Manager gets a little trickier. The Persistence configuration allows you to restrict the aggregated downloads for any particular user. You can restrict the user to certain sizes of downloads based on domains, documents, and security zones. This feature allows you to execute a global strategy to reduce the number of downloads in your organization. This will conserve valuable bandwidth, if this is a consideration in your organization. There are several ways to restrict the sizes, as shown in Figure 8-30.

o *Local Machine Per Domain (in kilobytes)*

o *Local Machine Per Document (in kilobytes)*

o *Intranet Zone Per Domain (in kilobytes)*

o *Intranet Zone Per Document (in kilobytes)*

o *Internet Zone Per Domain (in kilobytes)*

o *Internet Zone Per Document (in kilobytes)*

o *Restricted Sites Zone Per Domain (in kilobytes)*

o *Restricted Sites Per Document (in kilobytes)*

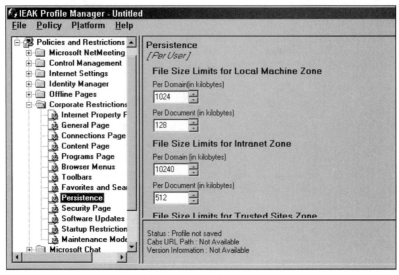

FIGURE 8-30 Corporate Restrictions/Persistence

Security Page

One of the most important configurations is shown in Figure 8-31. The Security configuration enables you to control the user's ability to make changes to the security zone configuration within Internet Explorer 5.

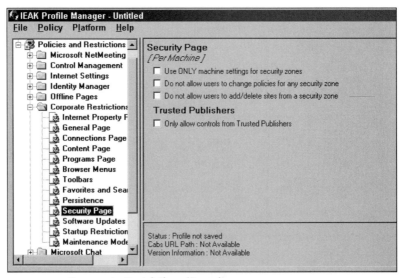

FIGURE 8-31 Corporate Restrictions/Security

- *Use ONLY machine settings for security zones.* Use the workstation's security settings for zone access.

- *Do not allow users to change policies for any security zone.* Prevents the user from making any changes to the security zone configuration.

- *Do not allow users to add/delete sites from a security zone.* Prevents the user from adding or deleting sites to or from the various security zones.

- *Only allow controls from Trusted Publishers.* This allows controls to be only used if signed and authorized by a Trusted Publisher, like Microsoft or Macromedia, for example.

Software Updates

The Software Updates configuration options are shown in Figure 8-32.

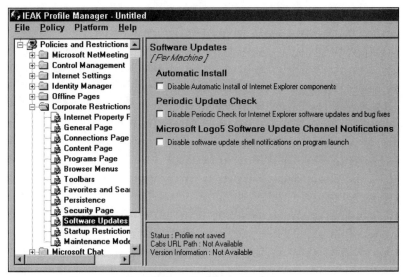

FIGURE 8-32 Corporate Restrictions/Software Updates

- *Disable Automatic Install of Internet Explorer components.* As components are needed for a particular application, they can be downloaded and automatically installed. This feature disables this ability.

- *Disable Periodic Check for Internet Explorer software updates and bug fixes.* This disallows the browser to update itself.

- *Disable software update shell notifications on program launch.* Shuts off the dialog box that notifies you when updates are available.

Startup Restrictions

The Startup Restrictions configuration options are shown in Figure 8-33.

o *Disable showing the splash screen.* Shuts off the Internet Explorer splash screen.

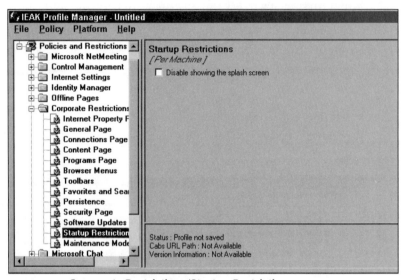

FIGURE 8-33 Corporate Restrictions/Startup Restrictions

Maintenance Mode Settings

The Maintenance Mode Settings configuration options are shown in Figure 8-34.

o *Disable adding Internet Explorer Components via Add/Remove Programs.* Stops the user from adding components via the Control Panel.

o *Disable uninstalling Internet Explorer 5 and Internet Tools.* Stops the user from removing the application.

o *Disable the Internet Explorer 5 Repair utility.* This disables the utility used to make repairs to a damaged, installed version of Internet Explorer 5.

Microsoft Chat

You can also specify settings for the Microsoft Chat application in the Profile Manager. Figures 8-35 and 8-36 show the configuration options available.

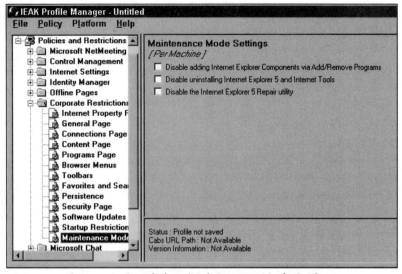

FIGURE 8-34 Corporate Restrictions/Maintenance Mode Settings

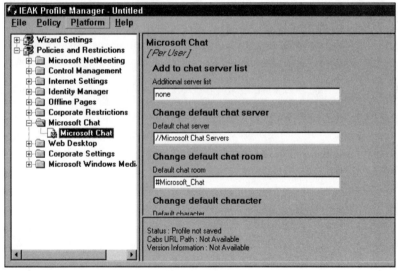

FIGURE 8-35 Microsoft Chat Part 1

- *Add to chat server list.* Used to add chat servers that should be used with Microsoft Chat.

- *Change default chat server.* Used to specify the default chat server.

- *Change default chat room.* Used to specify the starting room in which the user should be chatting.

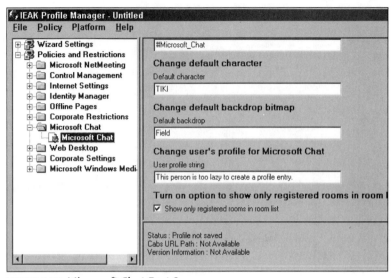

FIGURE 8-36 Microsoft Chat Part 2

- *Change default character.* Used to change the font type that is used for the text collaboration.

- *Change default backdrop bitmap.* Used to alter the background graphic of the chat application itself.

- *Change user's profile for Microsoft Chat.* Enables you to change the text-based profile that is used to describe the user's interests.

- *Turn on option to show only registered names in room list.* Allows the user a safer chat experience by enforcing registration in chat.

Web Desktop

One of the best features of the last version of Internet Explorer was the Web Desktop. If you did not use this feature in Internet Explorer 4, this new feature brings the Internet to the user's desktop and provides the platform for next-generation computing.

The Web Desktop enables the user to make a substantial number of changes to the interface of Windows NT and Windows 95. As in most IT organizations, you will probably want to standardize your desktop both to provide a common look and feel, and to allow desktop configuration consistency to lower support costs. The

IEAK Profile Manager enables you to lock down the Web Desktop with your desired configuration and to prevent users from making alterations and changes. The following options provide you with the ability to configure the Web Desktop.

Desktop

The following are configuration options for the desktop as shown in Figures 8-37 and 8-38.

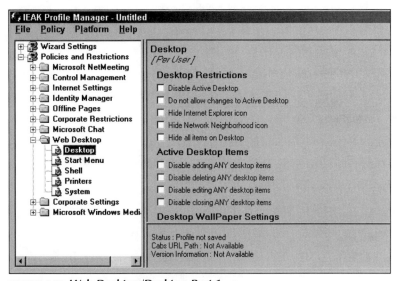

FIGURE 8-37 Web Desktop/Desktop Part 1

- *Disable Active Desktop.* Shuts off the user's ability to use Active Desktop.

- *Do not allow changes to Active Desktop.* Prevents the user from making configuration changes to the Active Desktop.

- *Hide Internet Explorer icon.* Removes the Internet Explorer icon from the desktop.

- *Hide Network Neighborhood icon.* Removes the Network Neighborhood icon from the desktop so the user cannot browse the network.

- *Hide all items on Desktop.* Removes all icons and applications from the desktop, such as Recycle Bin, Network Neighborhood, and so on.

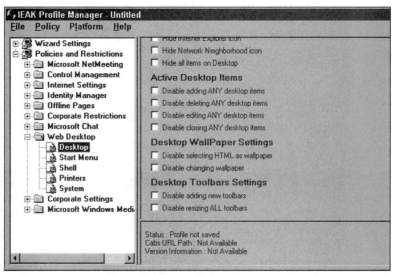

FIGURE 8-38 Web Desktop/Desktop Part 2

- *Disable adding ANY desktop items.* Disallows the addition of any Active Desktop item, such as an Iframe.

- *Disable deleting ANY desktop items.* Disallows the deletion of any Active Desktop item.

- *Disable editing ANY desktop items.* Disallows changes to Active Desktop items.

- *Disable closing ANY desktop items.* Prevents the user from closing any open Active Desktop items.

- *Disable selecting HTML as wallpaper.* Prevents the user from using a Web site or other HTML-related items as the wallpaper.

- *Disable changing wallpaper.* Prevents the use of any wallpaper that may change programmatically through the Web or any other means.

- *Disable adding new toolbars.* Prevents the user from adding any new toolbar configuration other than that of the default installation.

- *Disable resizing ALL toolbars.* Prevents the user from resizing the toolbar.

Start Menu

The Start Menu options that are available for configuration are shown in **Figures 8-39** and **8-40**.

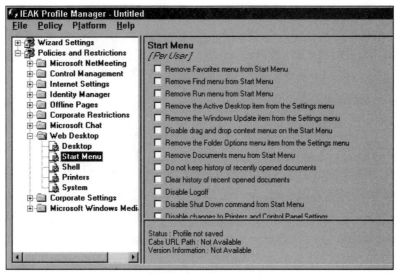

FIGURE 8-39 Web Desktop/Start Menu Part 1

- *Remove Favorites menu from Start Menu.* Enables you to remove the Favorites folder from the Start menu for the user. This option only removes the selection for Favorites in the Start ⇨ Favorites dialog box; the Favorites in Internet Explorer and on the toolbar are not affected.

- *Remove Find menu from Start Menu.* Removes the Find LDAP-based search tool from the Start menu.

- *Remove Run menu from Start Menu.* Removes the Run command from the Start menu. With the Run command enabled, the user could type **command** to get to a DOS window or type **explorer** to launch the Windows Explorer application.

- *Remove the Active Desktop item from the Settings menu.* Removes the Active Desktop settings from the Start Button ⇨ Settings ⇨ Active Desktop dialog box.

- *Remove the Windows Update item from the Settings menu.* Prevents a Windows 98 user from accessing the product updates page on Microsoft's Web site. This site is used to update system files and perform software upgrades.

- *Disable drag and drop context menus on the Start Menu.* Prevents the user from being able to drag applications or objects onto the Start menu. These objects appear at the top of the Start menu when accessed.

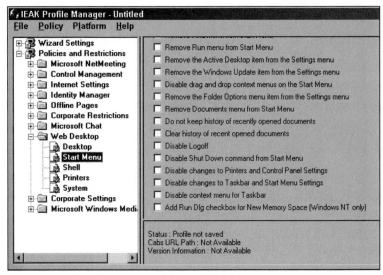

FIGURE 8-40 Web Desktop/Start Menu Part 2

- *Remove the Folder Options menu item from the Settings menu.* Disables the Folder Options from the Settings menu for such configurations as Web style, classic style, and custom style.

- *Remove Documents menu from Start Menu.* Removes the Documents folder from the Start menu. This folder keeps track of recently accessed files and documents.

- *Do not keep history of recently opened documents.* This function disables the tracking of files and documents within the Documents folder.

- *Clear history of recent opened documents.* Clears the Document folder history on shutdown.

- *Disable logoff.* Prevents the user from logging off. This feature is typically disabled in a public kiosk, for example.

- *Disable Shut Down command from Start Menu.* Prevents the user from shutting down the workstation.

- *Disable changes to the Printers and Control Panel Settings.* Prevents the user from being able to make changes to the system Control Panel and printer configurations.

- *Disable changes to Taskbar and Start Menu Settings.* Prevents the user from being able to change, alter, or modify anything on the Taskbar or Start menu.

- *Disable context menu for Taskbar.* Disables the right click on the Taskbar.

- *Add Run Dlg box for New Memory Space (Windows NT only).* Allows you to run Internet Explorer in a separate memory space on Windows NT Server and Windows NT Workstation.

Shell

The Profile Manager enables you to customize the users' ability to modify the updated Windows shell. The following options (shown in Figure 8-41) enable you to secure the Windows configuration.

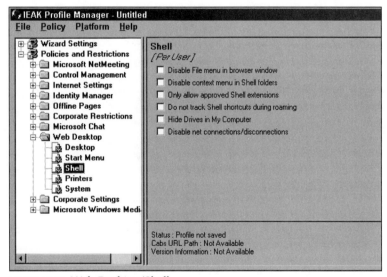

FIGURE 8-41 Web Desktop/Shell

- *Disable File menu in browser window.* This option disables the File menu so the user cannot create a folder, for example.

- *Disable context menu in Shell folders.* Disables the Context menu in a folder.

- *Only allow approved Shell extensions.* Allows only approved extensions for the operating system chosen.

- *Do not track Shell shortcuts during roaming.* Prevents roaming profiles from including Shell shortcuts.

- *Hide Drives in My Computer.* Prevents the user from accessing a drive in the My Computer view.

- *Disable net connections/disconnections.* Prevents the user from changing the login/logoff status.

Printers

Printers can be controlled through the use of the Profile Manager. You have three available features that you can use to control printer configurations with in the Profile Manager. See Figure 8-42.

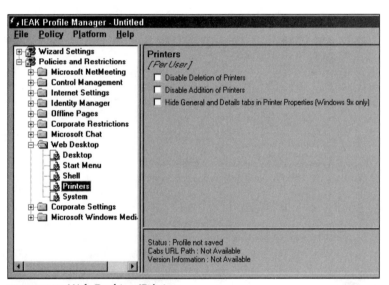

FIGURE 8-42 Web Desktop/Printers

- *Disable Deletion of Printers.* Prevents the user from deleting a configured printer.

- *Disable Addition of Printers.* Prevents the user from adding a printer to the desktop configuration.

- *Hide General and Details tabs in Printer Properties [Windows 9x only].* This option removes the General tab and Details tab for configured printers.

System

Figure 8-43 shows the system restrictions within the Profile Manager used to prevent the user from changing the Windows configuration and to secure the desktop.

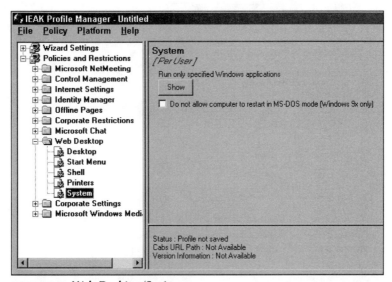

FIGURE 8-43 Web Desktop/System

- *Run only specified Windows applications.* Enables you to create a list of applications that are allowed on the user's workstation. This means that the user can run only the applications that you select.
- *Do not allow computer to restart in MS-DOS mode.* Prevents the workstation from being restarted in DOS to avoid the system policies restrictions.

Corporate Settings

Corporate settings allow you to make changes to settings such as temporary Internet files, ActiveX settings, and others.

Dial-up Settings

The Dial-Up Settings are shown in Figure 8-44.

o *Use Automatic Discovery for Dial-Up connections.* Allows the browser to use Web Proxy AutoDiscovery for automatic configuration of the browser.

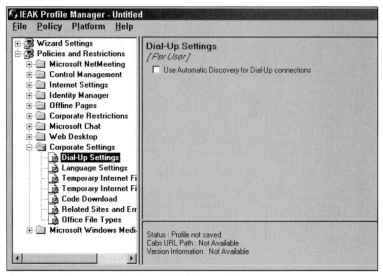

FIGURE 8-44 Corporate Settings/Dial-Up Settings

in the real world

Web Proxy AutoDiscovery allows the browser to automatically configure itself based on DNS and DHCP settings so that the administrator does not have to get involved in setting up the browser's proxy configuration. This technology is supported in Windows 2000, coming to a server near you.

Language Settings

Figure 8-45 shows the configuration options for the Language Settings.

o *Default Language for menus and dialogs.* The default language or character set used by the browser.

Temporary Internet Files (User)

Figure 8-46 shows the configuration options for the user Temporary Internet Files options.

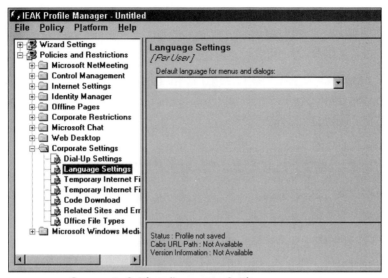

FIGURE 8-45 Corporate Settings/Language Settings

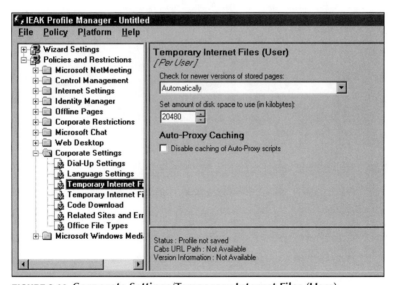

FIGURE 8-46 Corporate Settings/Temporary Internet Files (User)

- *Check for newer versions of stored pages.* Sets the brower's action to be taken when a cached page of a site is available.
- *Set amount of disk space to use (in kilobytes).* Sets the file cache size for the browser.

- *Disable caching of Auto-Proxy scripts.* Allows you to disable caching of Auto-Proxy scripts such as .js server-based proxy scripts.

Temporary Internet Files (Machine)

Figure 8-47 shows the configuration options for the machine Temporary Internet Files options.

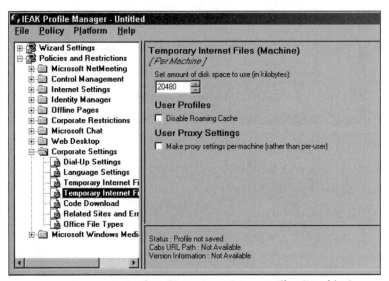

FIGURE 8-47 Corporate Settings/Temporary Internet Files (Machine)

- *Set amount of disk space to use (in kilobytes).* Sets the file cache size for the browser for a global machine setting rather than user-based.
- *Disable Roaming Cache.* This prevents the user from using their cache stored on a server when going from workstation to workstation. The cache is stored on a personal share on the server itself.
- *Make proxy settings per-machine (rather than per-user).* Allows you to set a global machine setting for proxy settings.

Code Download

Figure 8-48 shows the configuration options for the Code Download options.

- *Path.* Sets the path to Microsoft to search for needed ActiveX controls for a Web application.

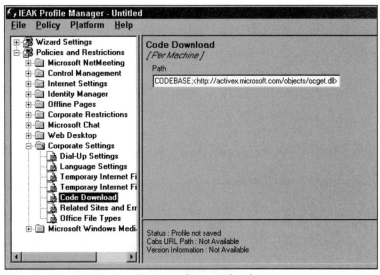

FIGURE 8-48 Corporate Settings/Code Download

Related Sites and Errors

Figure 8-49 shows the configuration options for the Related Sites and Errors options.

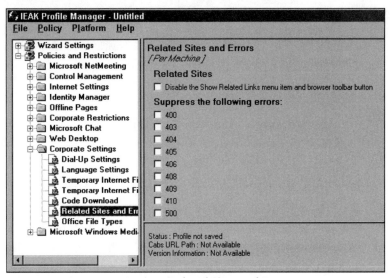

FIGURE 8-49 Corporate Settings/Related Sites and Errors

- *Disable the Show Related Links menu item and browser toolbar button.* Disables the feature to find related links from the browser.

- *Suppress the following errors.* Allows you to hide Web server error codes, such as error 404, file not found.

Office File Types

Figure 8-50 shows the configuration options for Office File Types options.

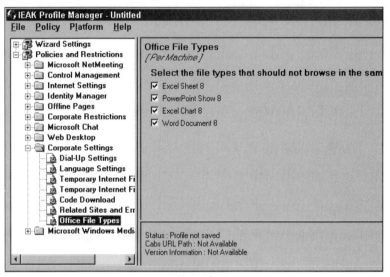

FIGURE 8-50 Corporate Settings/Office File Types

- *Select the file types that should not browse in the same window.* Allows you to disable the use of Office viewers by application in Internet Explorer.

Microsoft Windows Media Player

The Microsoft Windows Media Player section allows you to make tweaks and settings for the Media Player application. If you know that your users are going to use this application, you should pay attention to the settings for Media Player; this application can use a lot of your available bandwidth if you allow your users to experiment with this application.

Customizations

Figures 8-51 and 8-52 show the Media Player Customizations options.

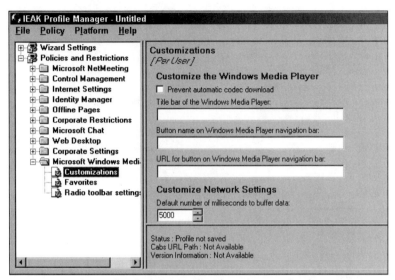

FIGURE 8-51 Microsoft Windows Media Player/Customizations Part 1

- *Prevent automatic codec download.* Stops Media Player from downloading new compression/decompression add-ins.
- *Title bar of the Windows Media Player.* Customization of the title bar as defined by you.
- *Button name on Windows Media Player navigation bar.* Custom name you can apply to the button name.
- *URL for button on Windows Media Player navigation bar.* Custom URL you can specify for navigation.
- *Default number of milliseconds to buffer data.* This allows data to be cached for a specified interval to ensure a crisp, clear video transmission.
- *Enable HTTP protocol.* Allows use of the Hypertext Transfer protocol.
- *Enable Multicast.* Allows Media Player to use TCP/IP multicast transmissions.
- *Enable TCP protocol.* Allows Media Player to use the Transmission Control Protocol.

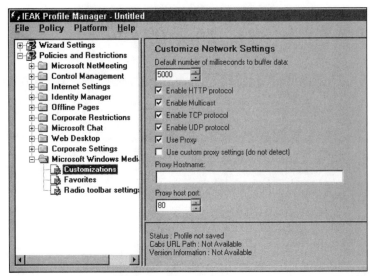

FIGURE 8-52 Microsoft Windows Media Player/Customizations Part 2

- *Enable UDP protocol.* Allows Media Player to use the Uniform Datagram Protocol.

- *Use Proxy.* Allows Media Player to use a Proxy Server.

- *Use custom proxy settings (do not detect).* Allows you to specify a custom proxy setting for the Media Player application.

- *Proxy Hostname.* Allows you to specify a host name for your Media Player proxy, such as `streaming.idgbooks.com`.

- *Proxy host port.* Specifies the TCP/IP port that your proxy server is listening on, such as port 80.

Favorites

Figure 8-53 shows the configuration options for Favorites options.

- *Do not install the default Windows Media Player Favorites in Media folder.* Allows you to not install the default favorites that come with Windows Media Player.

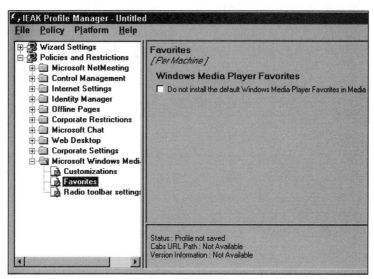

FIGURE 8-53 Microsoft Windows Media Player/Favorites

Radio toolbar settings

Figure 8-54 shows the configuration options for Radio toolbar settings options.

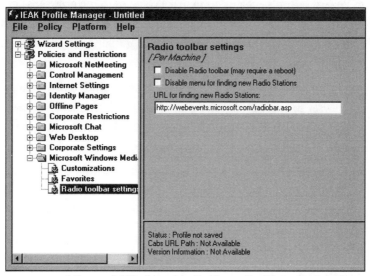

FIGURE 8-54 Microsoft Windows Media Player/Radio toolbar settings

- *Disable Radio toolbar (may require a reboot).* Disallows the toolbar from being used by your users.
- *Disable menu for finding new Radio Stations.* Prevents your users from finding new radio stations.
- *URL for finding new Radio Stations.* Allows you to specify the URL for finding new radio stations.

KEY POINT SUMMARY

In Chapter 10, we talked about bringing everything together with the IEAK Profile Manager.

- The .ins file is the foundation for the entire IEAK. This file contains all of the configuration information for the browser and the associated applications. Without an .ins file, the AutoConfiguration will not work. If your organization already has Internet Explorer 5 installed, you can create an .ins file by selecting the File/New option.
- Wizard settings enable you to make changes to the browser's configuration settings, such as proxy settings, title bars, User Agent, and other software configurations. These changes are made initially with the IEAK build, which is discussed in Chapter 7.
- System policies and restrictions enable you to lock down settings within the browser so users cannot make changes to the browser and other Internet Explorer-related applications. These restrictions help lower the TCO (Total Cost of Ownership) for your organization.
- The System Policies and Restrictions feature within the IEAK uses some of the same technology, but takes the restrictions a step further and incorporates the operating system restrictions with the application restrictions.

APPLYING WHAT YOU'VE LEARNED

This section is an opportunity to use what you've learned in this chapter. The Instant Assessment questions here will help you practice for the exam. The labs that follow provide you with important real-world practice using the skills you've learned.

Instant Assessment

1. You can use the Profile Manager to add applications to the user's desktop using the Wizard settings.

    A. True

    B. False

2. What pages of the NetMeeting configuration options can you disable?

    A. Video

    B. Audio

    C. My Information

    D. All of the above

3. Using the Profile Manager, what is the maximum crawl depth you can specify for site subscriptions?

    A. 1

    B. 2

    C. 3

    D. As many as you want

4. With the Profile Manager, which one of the following options can you not remove?

    A. Favorites menu within Internet Explorer

    B. Active Desktop settings menu

    C. Network Neighborhood

    D. My Computer icon

5. You can disable the Active Desktop with the Profile Manager.

    A. True

    B. False

6. You are getting ready to roll out Internet Explorer to your users. The one problem you face is that your file servers are running low on space, and you want to keep space used on the file servers to a minimum. Which option would provide you with some space relief?

A. Disable Roaming Cache

B. Disable file transfers

C. Disable video transmission in NetMeeting

D. Disable printing changes

7. Using the Profile Manager, you can specify the _____ ILS server for your NetMeeting users.

A. primary

B. secondary

C. default

D. proxy

8. With the Profile Manager, you can limit the throughput for NetMeeting in increments of _____.

A. KB

B. Kbps

C. bps

D. MB

9. A user complains that since your custom version of Internet Explorer was installed, the user's desktop icons have disappeared. What is the most likely cause of the problem?

A. The registry was corrupted.

B. The shell32.dll is the wrong language.

C. Your package had a virus.

D. You restricted the desktop in the Profile Manager's desktop section.

10. The only way to change the Internet Explorer Proxy settings is to configure an AutoProxy or to set the browser manually.

A. True

B. False

11. Your organization has set up subscriptions to provide information to the user base about current events and human resources information. Using the Profile Manager, you can restrict the users from being able to change, edit, or delete an Active Desktop item.

A. True

B. False

12. Soon after deploying Internet Explorer with the IEAK, you realize that you made a typo in the title bar. What part of the Profile Manager would you use to correct the title?

A. Wizard Settings/Browser Title

B. Internet Restrictions/Browser Title

C. Wizard Settings/Internet Explorer Title Bar

D. Internet Restrictions/Title Bar

13. Using the Profile Manager, you can make changes to the size of the Temporary Internet files.

A. True

B. False

14. You can modify the security zones with the Profile Manager.

A. True

B. False

15. The Profile Manager enables you to create a list of applications that are the only applications the user can run.

A. True

B. False

16. Your organization decides to add a second SMTP server to your enterprise. You can use the Profile Manager to update the Outlook Express configuration to reflect the changes.

A. True

B. False

17. Disabling the JIT compiler in the Profile Manager will enable your users to run Java-based applications more quickly, but with less security.

    A. True

    B. False

18. One of your fellow administrators uses the Profile Manager to disable the Windows 95 boot menu. After realizing that some users need this function, what do you recommend to resolve the problem?

    A. Reinstall Internet Explorer.

    B. Correct the entry in the Internet Restrictions option.

    C. Create a `.reg` file to correct it.

    D. None of the above.

19. Of the choices below, what is the best reason for disabling the DOS window within NetMeeting application sharing?

    A. Virus protection

    B. Intentional or unintentional damage through a DOS window by another user

    C. Memory limitations

    D. Bandwidth considerations

20. You can restrict the use of certificates and Certificate Authorities in the Profile Manager.

    A. True

    B. False

21. You can disable options in NetMeeting by the configuration tabs themselves and the individual items within the tabs.

    A. True

    B. False

22. AutoComplete allows your browser to be automatically configured using the Web Proxy.

    A. True

    B. False

23. You can restrict the configuration of printers with the Profile Manager.

   A. True

   B. False

24. The Profile Manager accommodates a configuration where the media streaming is on a separate proxy than that of the HTTP traffic for the browser. In other words, this configuration can be separate and distinct to that of the browser.

   A. True

   B. False

Critical Thinking Labs

Lab 8.30 *Importing system policies*

You are charged with creating and implementing system policies with your IEAK deployment. After a careful review of the policy settings, the organization feels that the policy file included in the IEAK called `inetcorp.adm` will be the best solution for your organization.

You have already configured the location and configuration script for your enterprise on your local intranet server. How would you go about creating the new `.ins` file and deploying the file for your already deployed browsers?

Lab 8.31 *Managing your browser configuration*

You plan to manage your users' browser configurations using the IEAK Profile Manager. The person who had your job before you deployed the browser using the IEAK. The location for the `.ins` file was `http://intranet.widget.com/explorer/widget.ins`. If you wanted to change the file name, what options would you use to do this? If you changed the contents of the file, such as a configuration change, where would you make the change and how would you do it? Why do you think that using an auto-configuration script is prudent in large organizations rather than asking the users to make changes manually, by e-mail for example?

The Connection Manager
Administration Kit

About Chapter 9

Up until now, we've talked a lot about the tools that your users can employ once they are connected to your network or to the Internet. Now, let's talk about a tool you can use to get your users connected to the Internet—the Connection Manager Administration Kit (CMAK). The CMAK allows you to create dial-up profiles for your users to assist in connecting your users to your network. It allows you to configure and set up the software that will allow your users to dial into your network or their local ISP. This tool also allows you to set the dial-up options that you will want the users to employ to use Microsoft Dial-Up networking. For example, you can create phone books, change protocols, and employ many other powerful features. Let's jump right into the CMAK. You may also hear the CMAK referred to as the *dialer*.

OVERVIEW

To get your users connected to the Internet or to your network, you need to create what is called a *service profile*. A service profile allows you to create custom dial-up settings for your users to utilize when launching the dial-up manager. Each time you run the CMAK, you can create a new service profile. Depending on the geographical layout of your organization, you may want to roll out multiple profiles to concentrate the dial-in traffic for your users. For example, you would not want your Los Angeles dial-in users to dial up to your New York POP if there were available ports in your Los Angeles office. Let's jump right in and run the CMAK so that you can learn about its features.

THE WIZARD

When you launch the CMAK, you will see the welcome screen as shown in Figure 9-1. This is the first stage in creating your dial-up profiles for your users.

FIGURE 9-1 The CMAK welcome screen

When you select the next button, you are presented with two options.

- *Create a new service profile.* Allows you to create a new dial-up configuration.
- *Edit this existing service profile.* Allows you to edit one of your existing dial-up configurations.

When you are ready to create your first dial-up profile, you should have already made the decisions that you will be presented with during the CMAK build process. Later in this chapter, we will walk through a checklist that you can use before you run the CMAK.

For now, let's go with creating a new service profile as shown in Figure 9-2.

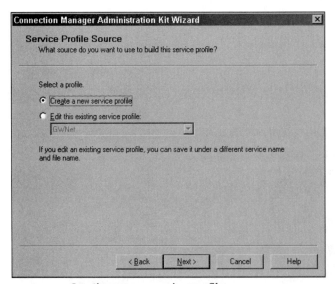

FIGURE 9-2 Creating a new service profile

Service and File Names

When you continue, you are presented with Figure 9-3. Here, you are going to name your service name and your file names.

The service name allows you to brand a name across the top of your dial-in software; this is also called the title bar text. This allows you to create a custom naming scheme to make your users more comfortable with the software and to customize the interface that you are going to use. This is one of the most important naming schemes that you are going to see as this text appears during multiple phases of the build and also when your users work with the dial-up manager software. Other places you will see this text are as follows:

○ In dialog boxes presented while your users are installing the software

○ The desktop icon name

○ On the taskbar as the name of the application running

○ The Tool tip that appears when the mouse is moved over the status area

○ In dial-up networking as a service profile

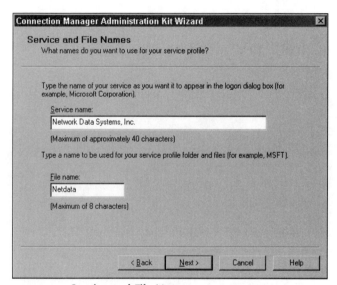

FIGURE 9-3 Service and File Names

exam preparation pointer

Even though your users run your installation software, any other service profiles that are already created on their workstation will still function normally as long as they were created in the same version of the Connection Manager.

An example of branding is shown in Figure 9-4.

File name allows you to create a unique file name for your service profile. This file name can be up to eight characters and cannot contain spaces, or the following characters:

! , ; * = / \ : ? ' " < >

note **You want to make absolutely sure that this name is unique, as duplicate names will cause problems with conflicting application names.**

The file name will be the default file name used in creating the support files for your service profile. For example, if you selected "Netdata" here as the file name, all of your files will be named Netdata with their applicable extensions, as shown in Figure 9-5.

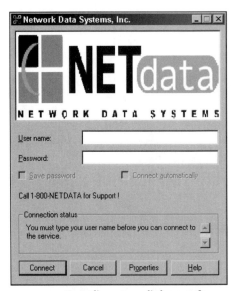

FIGURE 9-4   Branding your dial-up software

Merging Service Profiles

The CMAK also allows you to merge service profiles. The main reason that you would need to do this is to allow your users more flexibility in connecting to your network or to the Internet from multiple locations or dial-in numbers. Other reasons include mergers, consolidations of POPs, or repetitive builds of profiles so that you do not have to re-enter the dial-up information every time you create a new profile. Merging Service Profiles is shown in Figure 9-6.

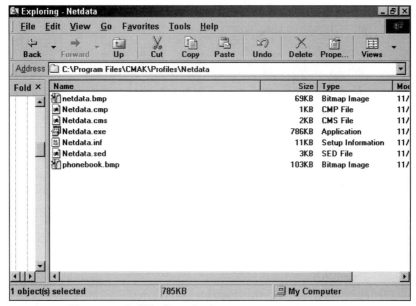

FIGURE 9-5 File names in Windows Explorer

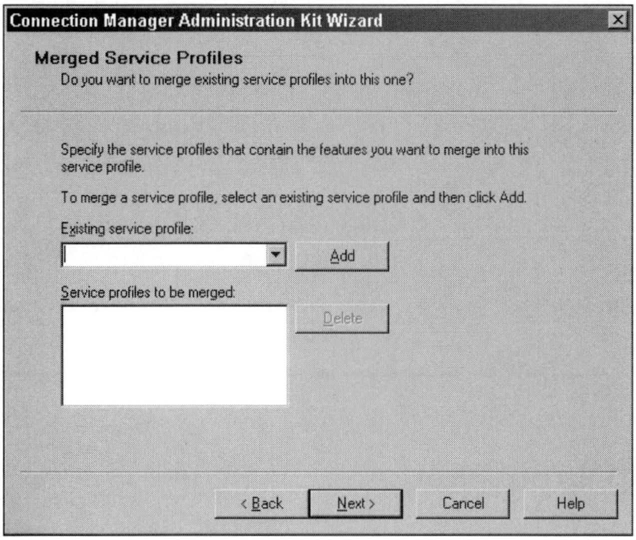

FIGURE 9-6 Merging Service Profiles

Let's say that your networking group is bringing up five new locations that all include dial-in access. You want to add these locations to your user's dial-in profiles, but do not want to have to enter all of this information over again. When you get to this stage of the CMAK, you would reference your old profile, also called the referencing profile, and provide any additional edits later in your build.

Merging a profile brings over a lot of information from your old profile. Table 9-1 shows the information that is brought over.

TABLE 9-1 SETTINGS MERGED WITH THE CMAK

MERGED SETTINGS	DESCRIPTIONS
File Name	This is the file name that you used when you initially created this profile.
Merged Profiles	You can only merge the original profile settings when using the merge function. For example, if you are merging a merged profile of an original profile, only the original profile settings will be brought over.
Realm Name	Realm names are usually domain names, such as @idgbooks.com.
Dial-up Networking entries	These are the dial-up networking names and scripts.
Phone Books	You can only bring over one phone book from a merged profile.
Download Phone Book	You can preset an option that allows your users to download updates to the phone book when they connect using your custom CMAK profile.
URL for downloads	This is the Web URL for downloading updates for the phone book.

Support Information

As shown in Figure 9-7, you can supply telephone support information for your users in the event that they run into dial-up problems.

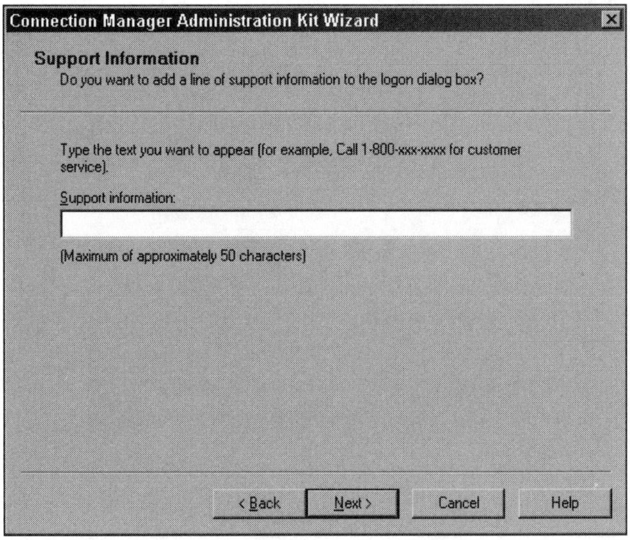

FIGURE 9-7 Support Information

You can provide up to 50 characters here to be displayed on your dial-up software. It's a good idea to include this information every place that you can. For example, here are some locations in which you may want to include this information.

o In the `readme.txt` file that is included in your package.

o In any announcements about the rollout of Internet Explorer 5.

o In any marketing literature that you are providing with your software package.

o In any follow up e-mail messages after the rollout.

o As an Outlook Express signature to your help desk representative's e-mail messages.

Just so you recall what the support information looks like, see the example shown in Figure 9-4.

Realm Name

In Figure 9-8, you supply the realm name for your profile. A realm name allows for your users to be authenticated when they dial-up to an Internet POP or to your dial-up servers. The realm name, `@idgbooks.com` for example, is read by the dial-up server when the user gets the dial-in handshake.

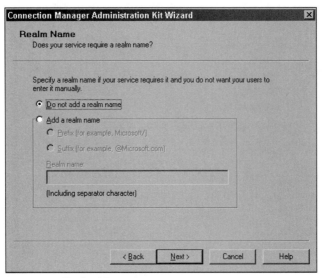

FIGURE 9-8   Realm Name

 tip   **The handshake is that really annoying screeching sound you hear when your modem connects to another modem.**

After the handshake, your realm name is presented to the local authentication server and forwarded to the proper server based on your realm name. For example, if you are dialing into an ISP, but are using your own realm for authentication, your ISP must allow your realm to be used for authentication and your servers must be capable of authenticating you as well.

Dial-Up Networking Entries

You can supply custom networking configurations for your dial-up networking functions as shown in Figure 9-9. Here, you can specify DNS and WINS servers to specific dial-up networking entries in your phone book.

To change the settings for your dial-up networking entries, select the entry and click Edit. Figure 9-10 shows how you would go about changing your dial-up settings for DNS and WINS. You can also specify scripts that are to be run when your users log in as well, using the scripts function.

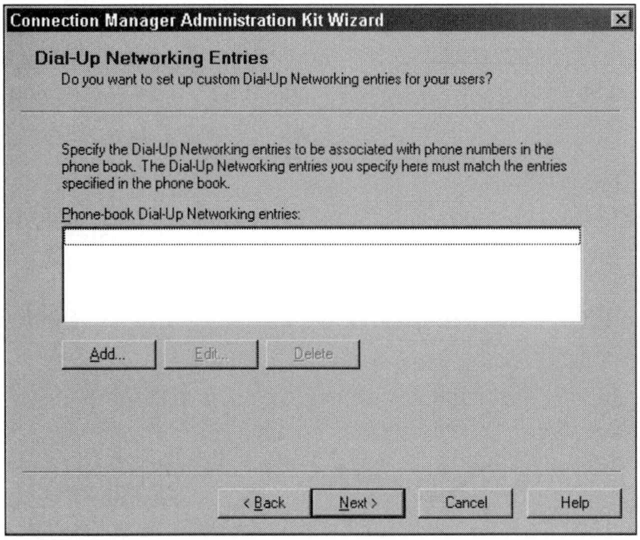

FIGURE 9-9 Dial-up Networking Entries

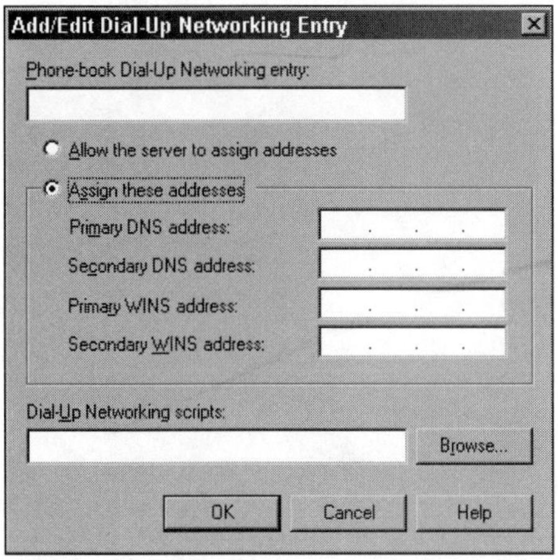

FIGURE 9-10 Editing entries in dial-up networking

VPN Support

The CMAK also includes support for Virtual Private Networking (VPN). VPNs allow you to connect to a network from another network using a secure, encrypted connection also called a tunnel. Generally, most organizations that have deployed VPN technology allow VPN access to their network from the Internet. The user dials in to their ISP with the CMAK client or a custom VPN client and opens a tunnel to their network. What differentiates tunneling from Web access is that VPNs allow access to services such as file and print, intranets, and other data not usually allowed to be accessed via the Web.

The CMAK includes support for VPN technology for Microsoft's current VPN protocol, PPTP (Point to Point Tunneling Protocol).

tip

Windows 2000 greatly expands the Windows VPN abilities.
Check out `http://www.microsoft.com/windows/server/`
`Technical/networking/vpnoverview.asp` **for more information.**

As shown in Figure 9-11, you can enable VPN support in your service profile if you so choose.

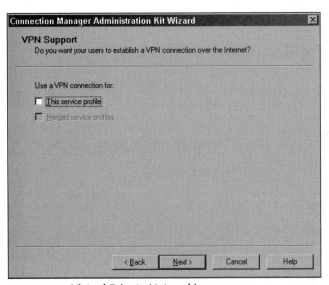

FIGURE 9-11 Virtual Private Networking

Connect Actions

Using the CMAK, you can specify certain actions for the software based on the stage of the connection. The actions you have available are as follows;

o *Pre-Connect Actions.* This is an application or file that you can launch when your users click on the Connect button.

- *Pre-Tunnel Actions (for VPN connections).* This allows you to create actions that take place after the initial dial-in but before the VPN tunnel is opened. This is the function that you want to use for applications that need information before the tunnel is established and when these resources may no longer be accessible due to security or firewall concerns.

- *Post-Connect Actions.* These actions take place after the dial-up session is opened. Here you can add a lot of neat features, such as welcome banners or warning messages.

- *Disconnect Actions.* These are the actions that you want to perform before the connection is terminated. When a user disconnects from their session, this application will run first.

The interfaces for configuring each action are the same. The differences for the actions are chosen according to when the action is to be performed. You can also choose the actions that you wish to use, as shown in Figure 9-12.

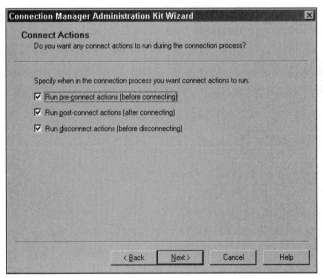

FIGURE 9-12   Connect Actions

The dialog box that is presented when you want to add an action is shown in Figure 9-13.

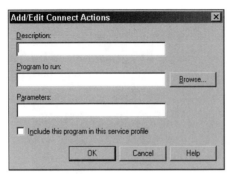

FIGURE 9-13 Adding connection actions

- *Description.* Provide a brief description of what this action's purpose is.
- *Program to run.* This tells the CMAK software the name of the application to run.
- *Parameters.* This is a switch or parameter you can use at the end of your application.
- *Include this program in this service profile.* This allows your application to be bundled with the profile that you are creating.

 note On post-connect actions, you can also specify whether or not to download phone book updates.

Auto-Applications

You can also select applications that will run when the user establishes a dial-up connection. The difference between this and a post-connect action is that the former allows for the dial-up software to monitor the application. For example, if you wanted your user's e-mail application to launch automatically upon login and close automatically on logout, this is where you would set that up. The auto-application settings are shown in Figure 9-14.

Logon Bitmap

You can create your own bitmap to be used on the splash screen of your dial-up software. This image should be 330 pixels by 144 pixels and in bitmap format. You can then import your bitmap into your profile at the stage shown in Figure 9-15.

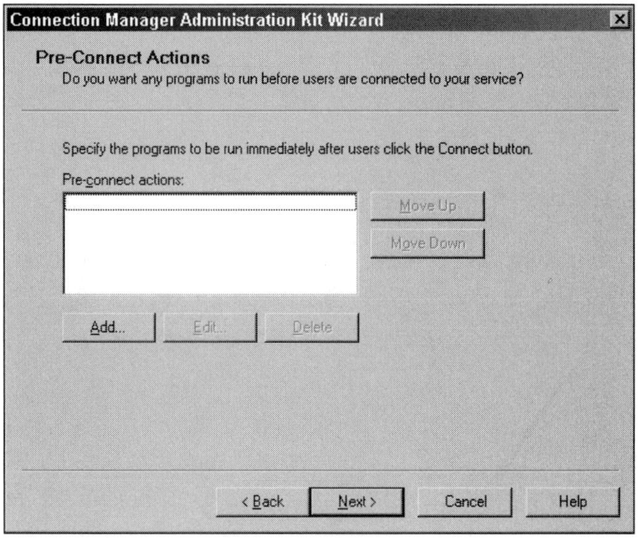

FIGURE 9-14 Auto-application settings

tip A good application to use as an auto-application is a stock ticker, news ticker, or a banner advertising application.

FIGURE 9-15 Adding logon bitmaps

Once your bitmap is imported, it will look at a lot like the bitmap shown in Figure 9-4. Again, this is a great way to make your users feel more at home and also at ease with the new software.

Phonebook Bitmap

You can also specify a 114 pixel by 304 pixel bitmap for your phone book as well. In Figure 9-16, this bitmap is imported into your profile and distributed as the default bitmap for your phone book.

Phone Book

Phone books are files stored with a .pbk extension. Phone books are created with the Phone Book Administrator application, which is included in the Windows NT 4.0 Option Pack. The Phone Book Administrator is a part of an overall suite of applications known as Microsoft Connection Point Services (CPS).

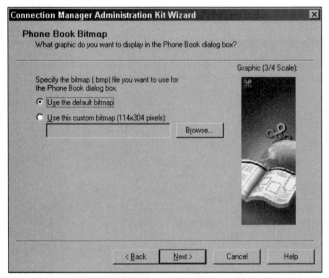

FIGURE 9-16 Phone Book Bitmap

Once your phone book is created, you can import it into your service profile as shown in Figure 9-17.

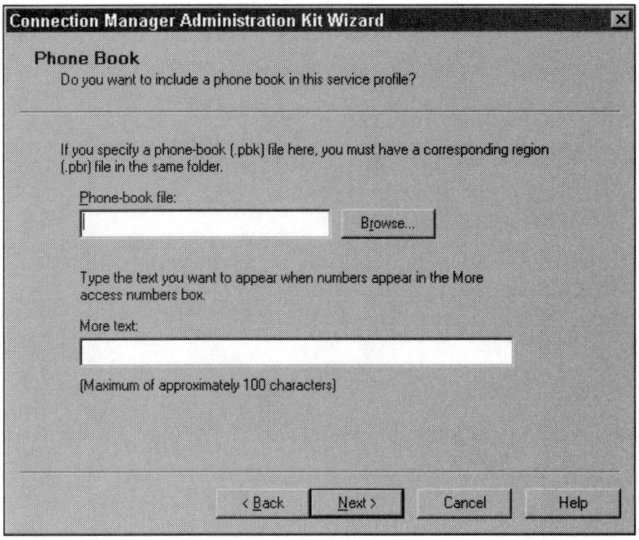

Connection Manager Administration Kit Wizard   ☒

Phone Book
    Do you want to include a phone book in this service profile?

    If you specify a phone-book (.pbk) file here, you must have a corresponding region
    (.pbr) file in the same folder.

    Phone-book file:

    [   ]   [B̲rowse...]

    Type the text you want to appear when numbers appear in the More
    access numbers box.

    More text:

    [   ]

    (Maximum of approximately 100 characters)

                    [< B̲ack]   [N̲ext >]   [Cancel]   [Help]

FIGURE 9-17 Phone Book

You can also specify your own custom text to be displayed for the additional phone book entries.

Phone Book Updates

As you have learned, you can specify that phone books be updated when the user logs in. In Figure 9-18, you specify the location for the phone book server by specifying the HTTP address (URL) for the server.

Icons

In Figure 9-19, you can specify your own icons for your dial-up application. If you do not specify an icon to use for any of the selections, the default icon will be used.

concept link

You might want to try a popular icon creation package called Icon Extractor to create your own icons. For more information, go to `http://www.siliconprairiesc.com/`.

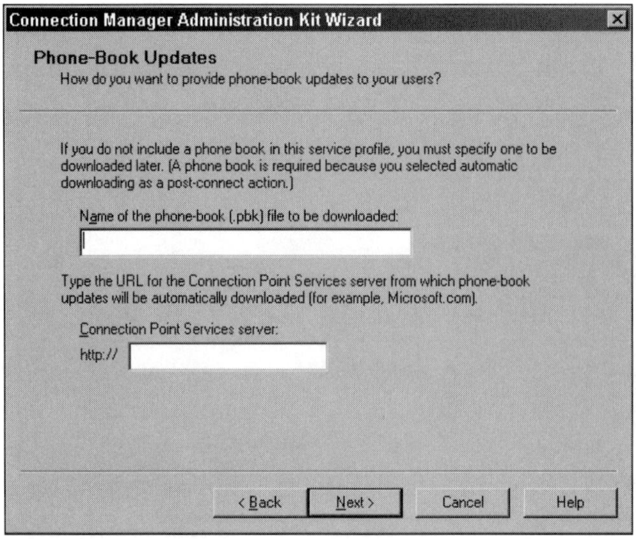

FIGURE 9-18   Phone Book Updates

Status Area Icon Menu

You can also customize the menu that is displayed when your users right-click on the dial-up software in the system tray. In Figure 9-20, you can insert programs and functions to use when you want to add more functionality to the menu.

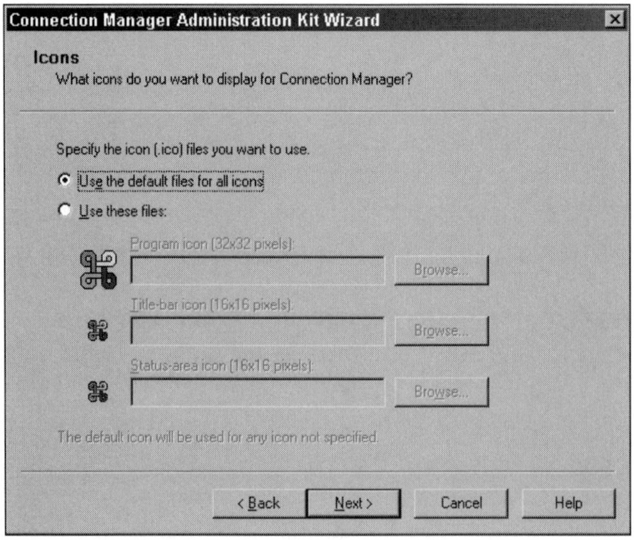

FIGURE 9-19   Adding icons

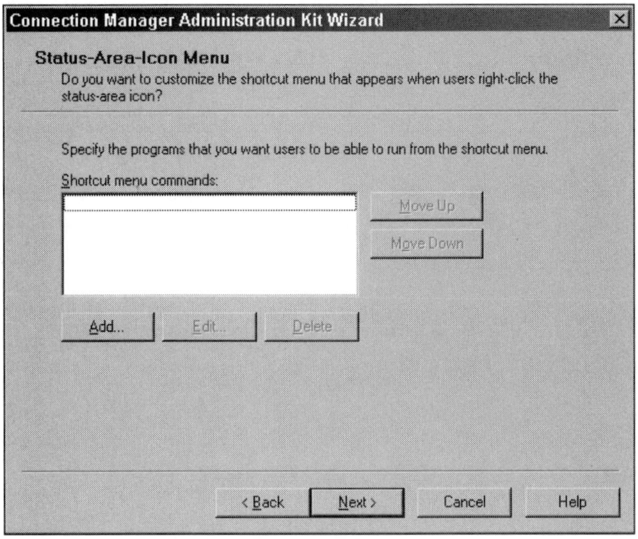

FIGURE 9-20 Status–Area–Icon Menu

There are several options to choose from when you select Add, as shown in Figure 9-21.

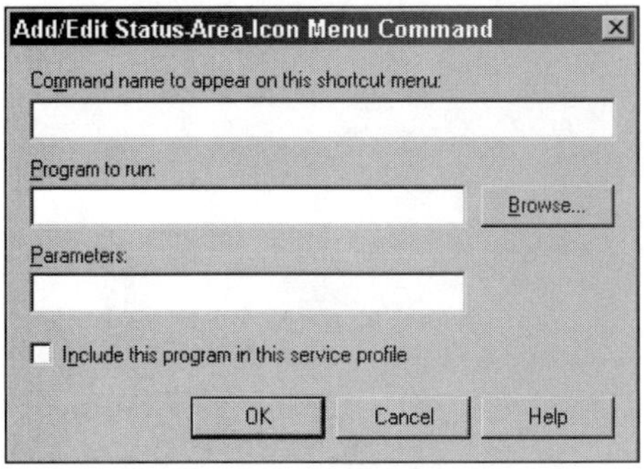

FIGURE 9-21 Adding a menu item

- *Command name to appear on this shortcut menu.* Provide a brief name to describe what this action's purpose is.

- *Program to run.* This tells the CMAK software the name of the application to run.

- *Parameters.* This is a switch or parameter you can use at the end of your application.

- *Include this program in this service profile.* This allows your application to be bundled with the profile that you are creating.

Help File

You can also create your own help file for your dial-up software if you so choose. In Figure 9-22, you specify the location of your .hlp file for your users.

 concept link **One of the more popular help file creation software packages is RoboHelp. Check it out at** http://www.blue-sky.com.

Connection Manager Software

Your users must have the Connection Manager 1.2 software installed on their workstation to use your software once you build the package. You can choose to install the software if it does not already exist by choosing this option in Figure 9-23.

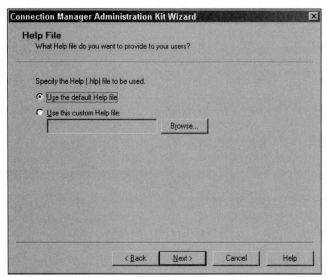

FIGURE 9-22 Help File

If for any reason your users have the older version of the Connection Manager, selecting this option will automatically upgrade the Connection Manager on the workstation to the 1.2 version.

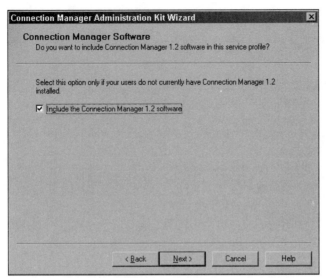

FIGURE 9-23 Connection Manager Software

 The installer will upgrade the client to the latest version of Dial-Up Networking. If the client is already at version 1.2, only the profile will be configured.

License Agreement

If you want your users to agree to a license agreement during the installation, you would specify the location of the agreement in Figure 9-24.

The agreement that you create should be in a text file. You may want to consider formatting the agreement in Notepad at a screen resolution of 640×480 to ensure that everyone can read the agreement in Notepad's default state.

 Make sure that you do not use a hard return when going to the next line. Text will wrap automatically during the build of your package. This way, you will not have to edit the agreement for every platform.

Additional Files

In Figure 9-25, you can specify any additional files that you want to be copied to your user's workstations. This is a good place to put any utilities or other software that you think your users may need.

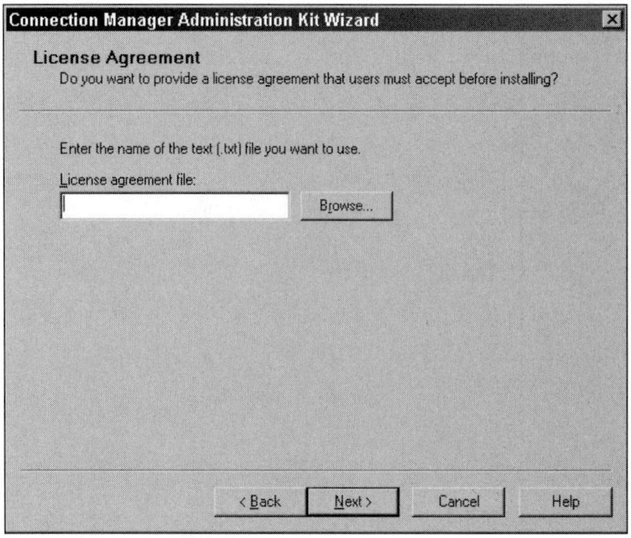

Connection Manager Administration Kit Wizard   ☒

License Agreement
Do you want to provide a license agreement that users must accept before installing?

Enter the name of the text (.txt) file you want to use.

License agreement file:
[   ]   Browse...

< Back   Next >   Cancel   Help

FIGURE 9-24 License Agreement

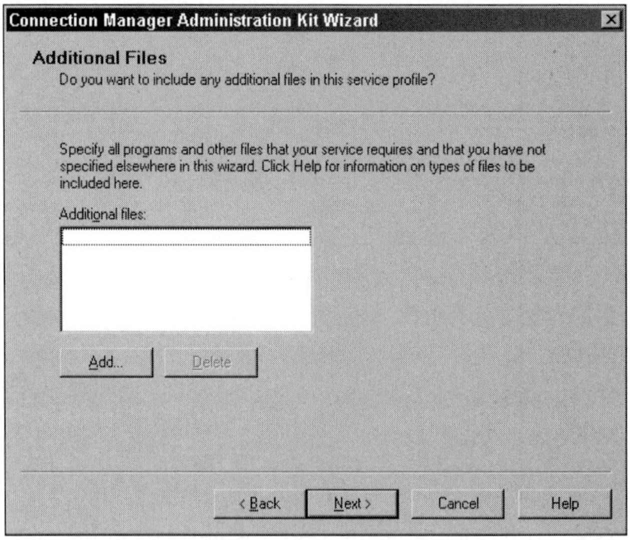

Connection Manager Administration Kit Wizard   ☒

Additional Files
Do you want to include any additional files in this service profile?

Specify all programs and other files that your service requires and that you have not specified elsewhere in this wizard. Click Help for information on types of files to be included here.

Additional files:
[   ]

Add...   Delete

< Back   Next >   Cancel   Help

FIGURE 9-25 Specifying additional files

When you click Add, you will be asked for the location of the files you wish to add to your package.

exam
preparation
pointer

If you are intending to include any applications or scripts to be utilized for auto-applications or connect actions, you must specify them here.

Ready to Build!

That's it! You are ready to build your package in Figure 9-26. Upon selecting Next, your workstation will open a DOS window that launches the cabinet file maker that will compile your application and bundle all of your components. As you will learn in Chapter 10, you will need these files to further bundle your package with your browser build using the IEAK.

 tip **On a Windows-based workstation, these files will be located in the** `C:\Program Files\CMAK\Profiles\`*Service Name* `directory.`

FIGURE 9-26 Ready to Build!

KEY POINT SUMMARY

This chapter discussed the Connection Manager Administration Kit, which you can use to get your users connected to the Internet.

- A service profile allows you to create custom dial-up settings for your users to utilize when launching the dial-up manager. Each time you run the CMAK, you can create a new service profile.

○ The service name allows you to brand the name across the top of your dial-in software; this is also called the title bar text. This allows you to create a custom naming scheme to make your users more comfortable with the software and to customize the interface that you are going to use.

○ The CMAK also allows you to merge service profiles. The main reason that you would need to do this is to allow your users more flexibility in connecting your network or to the Internet from multiple locations or dial-in numbers.

○ You can provide up to 50 characters to provide a support number to be contacted by your users when they have problems. It's a good idea to include this information every place that you can.

○ A realm name allows for your users to be authenticated when they dial-up to an Internet POP or to your dial-up servers.

○ VPNs allow you to connect to a network from another network using a secure, encrypted connection also called a tunnel. Generally, most organizations that have deployed VPN technology allow VPN access to their network from the Internet.

APPLYING WHAT YOU'VE LEARNED

This section is an opportunity to use what you've learned in this chapter. The Instant Assessment questions here will help you practice for the exam. The labs that follow provide you with important real-world practice using the skills you've learned.

Instant Assessment

1. You do not have to install any other software other than your service profile, no matter what.

A. True

B. False

2. VPNs allow you to create an encrypted tunnel to connect to your own internal network to communicate with your organization.

A. True

B. False

3. You can allow your users to download phone book updates from an FTP server.

   A. True

   B. False

4. You cannot create actions based on a VPN connection in the CMAK.

   A. True

   B. False

5. You cannot specify DNS and WINS entries for dial-up networking connections. These must come from the DHCP server that assigns connection and addressing information.

   A. True

   B. False

6. A user calls and states that their ISP has installed the Connection Manager software on their workstation to connect to their network for Internet access. The user is concerned that by installing your package, their connection to their ISP may be affected. You should tell them that their service profile will not be affected by your installation.

   A. True

   B. False

7. You create phone books with the CMAK software.

   A. True

   B. False

8. Auto-Applications allow you to run specified applications before, after, and during your dial-up session.

   A. True

   B. False

9. You can create your own help file with your service profile.

   A. True

   B. False

10. A realm name allows you to specify a host name for your users.

   A. True

   B. False

11. How many phone books can you bring over in a profile merge?

   A. 2

   B. 3

   C. 4

   D. 1

12. You can migrate a phone book location during a profile merge.

   A. True

   B. False

13. Which of the following characters is a legal character to use in a service profile?

   A. *

   B. <>

   C. @

   D. .

14. A pre-connect action actually takes place during the handshake.

   A. True

   B. False

15. Your bitmaps can be any size that you want in creating backgrounds for your application.

   A. True

   B. False

Critical Thinking Labs

Lab 9.32 *Troubleshooting dial-up*

A user contacts you and states that he is having problems connecting to the dial-up server. You know after checking on the server that the server is fine and the user has a good dial-up account. What basic troubleshooting steps could you use to assist the user in troubleshooting his dial-up configuration?

Lab 9.33 *Troubleshooting VPN connections*

Late one afternoon, you get several phone calls from your remote users saying that they are unable to connect to the network over the Internet through their VPN connections. The error message that they are receiving states that they are unable to log in. With your knowledge of the basics of VPN, what would you logically consider checking before calling the VPN administrator?

Lab 9.34 *Deploying PPTP/VPN solutions*

Your organization is deploying a VPN solution using Microsoft technology. You are tasked with providing the browser and connection software to connect the users to the VPN using the IEAK and CMAK. Your organization has its own internal DNS servers that are not propagated on the Internet and are only internal addresses protected by a firewall. In addition, you need to be able to provide WINS access to your protected network to allow the users to connect to server resources inside the network.

Which software component would you use to provide this configuration? What considerations should you keep in mind when configuring the software? Using the software you have, can you accomplish the requirements as set forth to you? Look through the IEAK and CMAK software for solutions before you answer the question.

Lab 9.35 *Deploying dial-up networking*

Your organization is deploying a dial-up solution using Microsoft technology. You are tasked with providing the browser and connection software to connect the users to the dial-up RAS server using the IEAK and CMAK. Your organization has its own internal DNS servers that are not propagated on the Internet and are only internal addresses protected by a firewall. In addition, you need to be able to provide WINS access to your protected network to allow the users to connect to server resources inside the network.

Which software component would you use to provide this configuration? What considerations should you keep in mind when configuring the software? Using the software you have, can you accomplish the requirements as set forth to you? Look through the IEAK and CMAK software for solutions before you answer the question.

Internet Explorer Maintenance

About Chapter 10

In this chapter, we will examine the requirements to maintain user and browser settings in Internet Explorer 5 once it is deployed within your enterprise. The IEAK Profile Manager plays a very important role not only in establishing required user settings, browser settings, and restrictions, but also in modifying those settings once your organization is using Internet Explorer 5.

OVERVIEW

If you've ever installed an application within an enterprise environment, you know that the work doesn't stop just because the application is deployed. There are several maintenance and support issues that need to be addressed. The sooner you plan for these issues, the further ahead of the game you'll be. Internet Explorer 5 includes features that allow you to update browser and user settings after it has been installed throughout an enterprise.

UPDATING CONFIGURATIONS

After the exhaustive process of building and distributing your setup package for Internet Explorer 5, you'll discover there are settings that need to be updated periodically. These settings can apply to user restrictions, browser upgrades, or connection settings. Building your setup package involved gathering a lot of information about how you anticipated your users will connect to and use Internet Explorer 5. Many of these settings are bound to change as your environment changes or grows.

Some of the settings that made sense when you first began your deployment plan may need to be adjusted once Internet Explorer 5 is running throughout your enterprise. A portion of your user base may need additional components that were not installed during the initial deployment. The installation of these components and upgrades to any of the existing components means you'll need a way to continue supporting Internet Explorer 5.

The IEAK Profile Manager

The same tools you used to configure user settings, restrictions, and browser settings for the installation of Internet Explorer 5 can be used to keep your enterprise current with modifications and additions. When you created the auto-configuration file with the IEAK Profile Manager while using the Internet Explorer 5 Administration Kit, you also created the first set of configuration settings. These settings can be modified later by editing the `.ins` file using the IEAK Profile Manager again. Likewise, if you did not enable Automatic Browser Configuration during your initial setup, the IEAK Profile Manager provides the opportunity to do so post-deployment.

The IEAK Profile Manager can open any auto-configuration file that you've created. By editing the file and replacing the `.ins` file and any associated `.cabs` in the automatic configuration directory, you can update all of the settings within your organization without having to revisit every machine.

As I discussed previously, the IEAK Profile Manager creates a number of files for the configuration of Internet Explorer 5. These files are important for establishing the configuration standards for your organization. The files are listed here again as they apply to the IEAK Profile Manager:

- `.cab` *cabinet file.* Cabinet files contain structured and compressed files required for installation. Cabinet files are downloaded or copied to a machine, then the files within are extracted. Remember that you must digitally sign any cabinet files you create for additional components.

- `.inf` *information file.* Generally, cabinet files and executables contain or have available an information file to provide it information. Information files are created by the IEAK Profile Manager to provide specific configuration information for the setting of System Policies and Restrictions.

- `.ins` *Internet settings file.* Internet settings files are created by the IEAK Profile Manager to configure user and browser settings as well as any component settings that apply to your installation. Every `.ins` file created by the IEAK Profile Manager is given a version number as well. This version number shows the date of any modifications to the file and the number of times the file has been revised.

Deploying Updates

A critical step in modifying settings for the user, browser, or restrictions is to thoroughly test new auto-configuration files before moving them to the production environment. To do this, copy the auto-configuration file and any associated cabinet files created by the IEAK Profile Manager to a separate directory and test the configuration for any possible problems or issues that may result. Only once your evaluation of the modified configuration is completed and you've made any necessary changes should you copy the files to the production server.

Auto Detect

Auto Detect is based on Web Proxy Auto Discovery (WPAD) and is supported by both Dynamic Host Configuration Protocol (DHCP) and Domain Name System (DNS). If properly configured, DHCP and DNS can assist your maintenance efforts by automatically detecting existing browser settings and reconfiguring them when necessary. To enable Auto Detect you should check the "Automatically Detect Settings" checkbox while building your setup package with the Internet Explorer 5 Administration Kit.

While setting up Auto Detect, you are also provided the opportunity to select a time interval for automatic configuration. To do this, you would specify an interval in the "Automatically configure every *xx* minutes" box, as shown in Figure 10-1. If you would like the automatic configuration to only happen when a machine is restarted, set the interval to zero.

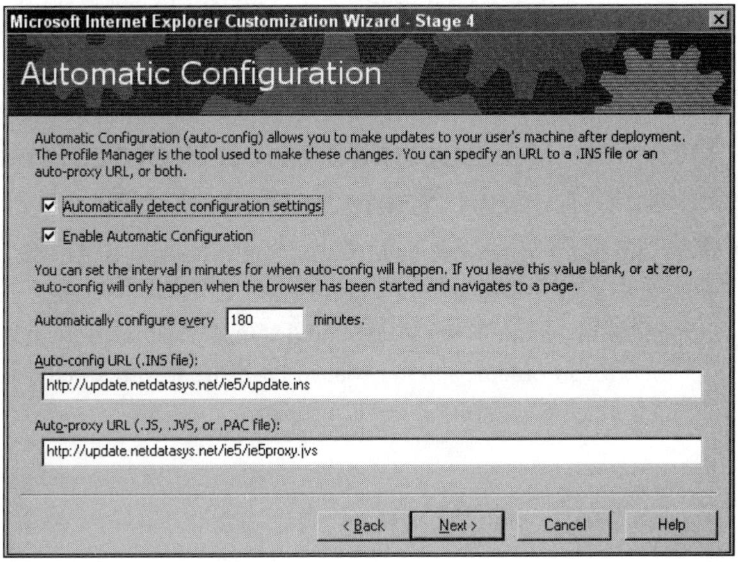

FIGURE 10-1 Auto Detect

The settings for Auto Detect and Automatic Configuration are in the [URL] section of the configuration file (.ins). Below is an example of the entries:

```
[URL]
AutoDetect=1
AutoConfig=1
```

```
AutoConfigTime=0
AutoConfigURL=http://www.netdatasys.com/software/microsoft/IE5
/AutoConfig/Custom.ins
```

The first line specifies to use the Auto Detect feature. The second line enables Automatic Configuration. The third line denotes the interval for Automatic Configuration and the last line specifies the URL to use for Automatic Configuration.

A typical DHCP server allows administrators the means for designating global and subnet-specific TCP/IP parameters centrally. It also provides the ability to define client parameters by using reserved addresses. When using Dynamic Host Configuration Protocol (DHCP) for Auto Detect in Internet Explorer 5, the DHCP server must support DHCPInfoForm messages.

DNS is a set of services and protocols that can be used on networks running the TCP/IP protocol. It is used to allow hierarchical searches of the network by user-friendly text entries known as *host names* instead of the numeric IP addresses assigned to machines. Host names do not replace IP addresses; they just provide an easier way to browse for machines on the network.

Dynamic Host Configuration Protocol (DHCP) versus Domain Name System (DNS)

If you are in a LAN environment, you'll find it best to use DHCP in conjunction with Auto Detect because of its faster LAN access and inherent flexibility when working with configuration files. Should your environment include dial-up users, however, DNS would be a better solution because it works well detecting settings through a dialup connection and can support your LAN-based users as well.

Auto Detect on DHCP

Auto Detect can be configured on a DHCP server by creating a new option type. Create the option type with a code number of 252. The following example shows how to configure a new option type for Auto Detect on Microsoft's DHCP Manager running under Windows NT:

1. With the DHCP Manager open select DHCP Options from the menu bar.

2. Select Defaults from the menu.

3. Click the class for your new option type. Then click the New button.

4. Type a name for the new option.

5. Select the String Data Type in the Data Type list.

6. Type the URL that contains your configuration file.

7. Type the code number 252 in the Identifier box.

8. Type a description in the Comment box.

Auto Detect on DNS

DNS allows for the use of hierarchical user names, known as host names, instead of numeric IP addresses. DNS uses a database file to associate host names with specific IP addresses. Enabling Auto Detect on DNS involves one of two methods. The first is to create a host record. The second is to create a CNAME "alias" record. After using either method, the resulting record would then be added to the DNS database file to resolve the location of the automatic configuration file.

To add a host record

Host records are used to associate host names to specific IP addresses. They are commonly used for static mapping for servers. The syntax is:

```
<host name> IN A <ip address of host>
```

To set up a host record, create a record "wpad" in the DNS database file and ensure that it points to the IP address of the server that contains the automatic configuration file.

Example of a host record for auto configuration:

```
Host Name      IN      A      Host IP Address
WPAD           IN      A      192.55.200.2
```

To add a CNAME record

Often called "aliases," a CNAME (or "Canonical Name") allows for a single host to have many names. The most common use for this is for organizations that use the same machine as both a Web server and an FTP server.

To set up a CNAME entry, enter a CNAME alias named "wpad" in the DNS database file. Ensure the entry points to the resolved host name that contains your configuration file (not the IP address, as was done for a host record).

Once you've properly configured a host record or a CNAME alias record, it will be added to the DNS database file. To test the record, attempt resolving wpad.*domain*.com. **It should resolve to the same computer name as the server that contains your** .pac, .jvs, .js, **or** .ins **automatic configuration file.**

AUTO CONFIGURATION AND AUTO PROXY

Auto Configuration and Auto Proxy provide you with the ability to modify settings post-installation. To do this, a pointer is set to a configuration on a server within your enterprise. Auto Configuration and Auto Proxy will look to this server for configuration information when the user connects to the network and runs Internet Explorer 5.

The location to the server hosting the configuration file was established while using the IEAK Profile Manager to create the initial configuration file. When Internet Explorer 5 discovers a newer version of the configuration file on the server, it will apply the new configuration settings automatically.

To reconfigure proxy settings, you follow the same steps as to modify any other configuration. The IEAK Profile Manager is used to update the .ins auto configuration file with the new proxy settings. Upon next startup of Internet Explorer 5, the proxy server settings will be reconfigured.

The proxy settings for your installation are held in the [Proxy] section of the configuration file (.ins), with entries looking similar to those shown below:

```
[Proxy]
HTTP_Proxy_Server=Proxy.NDS:80
FTP_Proxy_Server=Proxy.NDS:80
Gopher_Proxy_Server=Proxy.NDS:80
Secure_Proxy_Server=Proxy.NDS:80
Socks_Proxy_Server=Proxy.NDS:80
Use_Same_Proxy=1
Proxy_Enable=1
Proxy_Override="10.*;<local>"
```

You can use the IEAK Profile Manager to set a restriction that does not allow users to change their proxy settings.

If your organization uses scripts for proxy settings such as .pac files, JScripts (.js), or JavaScripts (.jvs), the IEAK Profile Manager includes a feature to import these, as discussed in Chapter 8. It's also worth noting here that the use of a proxy bypass may make JScripts and JavaScripts unnecessary and is easier to update and maintain.

 A good rule of thumb when using multiple proxy servers is to populate proxy settings in Internet Explorer 5 for each protocol to take advantage of the multiple servers, thus eliminating the possibility of overloading any one server.

ADDITIONAL COMPONENTS AFTER INSTALLATION

After installation, some or all of your users may require additional components. You can provide these components to your users from a central site for download. Doing this requires an Add-on Components Web site. The Internet Explorer 5 Administration Kit provides templates that you can modify to create an Add-On Component Web site for your organization. These templates are located in the Toolkit folder and require very little Web page authoring experience. By simply editing the templates using an HTML editor, you can design a site that's easy to access and use to download Add-On Components for Internet Explorer 5.

Once the Web site is designed and posted, you can designate the URL as the Add-On Components Web site when using the Internet Explorer 5 Administration Kit. Whenever a user chooses to add or remove an Internet component, they will be presented with the URL you specified.

The information for Add-On Component Web sites is in the [Branding] section of the automatic configuration file (.ins) and resembles the following example:

```
[Branding]
Add on URL=http://www.netdatasys.com/software/
   microsoft/IE5/addons/addons.htm
UseCustAddon=1
Help_Menu_Text=NETdata IE5 Add-Ons
```

The first line specifies the URL of the Add-On Component Web site. The second specifies whether to use a Custom Add-On site. The last line specifies the text to be used on the menu for selecting Add-ons.

 tip **When using the Internet Explorer 5 Administration Kit to designate an Add-On Component Site, be sure to provide the entire path to the page. (For example,** `http://Server/Share/addon.htm`.**)**

KEY POINT SUMMARY

In Chapter 10, we discussed how settings can be modified even after you've deployed Internet Explorer 5.

- The IEAK Profile Manager plays a very important role not only in establishing required user settings, browser settings, and restrictions, but also in modifying those settings once your organization is using Internet Explorer 5. The IEAK Profile Manager can open any auto-configuration file that you've created.

- By editing the file and replacing the `.ins` file and any associated `.cabs` in the automatic configuration directory, you can update all of the settings within your organization without having to revisit every machine.

- Auto Detect is based on Web Proxy Auto Discovery (WPAD) and is supported by both Dynamic Host Configuration Protocol (DHCP) and Domain Name System (DNS).

- After installation, some or all of your users may require additional components. You can provide these components to your users from a central site for downloading.

APPLYING WHAT YOU'VE LEARNED

This section is an opportunity to use what you've learned in this chapter. The Instant Assessment questions here will help you practice for the exam. The labs that follow provide you with important real-world practice using the skills you've learned.

Instant Assessment

1. Using the IEAK Profile Manager, you can modify user settings after Internet Explorer 5 has been installed.

   A. True

   B. False

2. What types of files are created by the IEAK Profile Manager?

   A. .ins files

   B. .cab files

   C. .inf files

   D. All of the above

3. Auto Detect is based on what?

   A. Web Proxy Auto Discovery (WPAD)

   B. Auto Web Proxy Discovery (AWPD)

   C. Web Auto Proxy Discovery (WAPD)

   D. Discovery Web Proxy Auto (DWPA)

4. Auto Detect is supported by which two protocols/services?

   A. IPX

   B. DHCP

   C. TCP/IP

   D. DNS

5. What happens if you enter zero in the "Automatically Configure Every *xx* Minutes" box in the IEAK Profile Manager?

   A. Nothing, zero isn't an option.

   B. Auto Configuration is disabled.

   C. Auto Configuration will only run when the user's machine is restarted.

   D. Auto Configuration will run at midnight every Sunday.

6. In what section of the `.ins` file are the entries for Auto Detect and Auto Configuration?

   A. [AUTO]

   B. [CONFIG]

   C. [ADAC]

   D. [URL]

7. When using Dynamic Host Configuration Protocol (DHCP) for Auto Detect in Internet Explorer 5, the DHCP server must support what?

   A. TCP/IP

   B. DHCPInfoForm messages

   C. Pre-emptive Multitasking

   D. DHCP does not support Auto Detect

8. Which is better to use for auto configuration in a LAN-only environment?

   A. DHCP

   B. DCHP

   C. DNS

   D. DSN

9. To configure Auto Detect on a DHCP server, you create a new option type with what code number?

   A. 255

   B. 252

   C. 525

   D. 225

10. What are the two ways to add enable Auto Detect on DNS?

   A. Create a host record.

   B. Create a post record.

   C. Create a SNAME record.

   D. Create a CNAME record.

11. What is the syntax to create a host record?

   A. <ip address of host> IN A <host name>

   B. <host name> IN A <ip address of host>

   C. No syntax is needed

   D. A <host> IN <IP>

12. Often called "aliases," CNAME is short for Canonical Name.

   A. True

   B. False

13. What types of scripts can the IEAK Profile Manager import?

   A. `.pac`

   B. `.jvs`

   C. `.jc`

   D. All of the above

14. You cannot add new components to Internet Explorer 5 after it's been installed.

   A. True

   B. False

15. When using the IEAK Profile Manager, you have to provide the full path to the Add-On Component Site.

   A. True

   B. False

Critical Thinking Labs

Lab 10.36 *Adding auto-proxy scripts*

Your firewall administrator has provided you with an auto-proxy script to include in your browser configuration. You are tasked with including this script in your browser deployment. Once you are provided with the script, answer the following questions.

1. In what stage of the IEAK will you provide the location of the script?

2. Once you have included the script, what else needs to be done to utilize the script when your browser is deployed?

Lab 10.37 *Downloading the IEAK*

You are asked to deploy Internet Explorer 5 in your organization. You will deploy the browser to your internal users using the IEAK, the platforms will be Windows 95 and Windows NT. Where would you go to download the IEAK software? Use your browser to locate the exact URL to download the software. Once downloaded, what else do you need to do? What role would you choose that would be compliant with the IEAK license agreement?

Lab 10.38 *Platform deployment considerations*

You are tasked with deploying Internet Explorer 5 in your organization. You will deploy the browser to your internal users using the IEAK; the platforms that you will have to deploy the browser to will include the following:

1. Sales department users running Windows 95.

2. Marketing department users running Windows 98.

3. Engineering department users running Windows NT Workstation 4.

4. Maintenance department users running Windows for Workgroups.

5. IT department users running Sun Solaris and HP UNIX.

Using the IEAK as a reference tool, how many builds will you have to create to deploy your software? If you are deploying the browser via CD-ROM, how many CD-ROMs will you have to create at a minimum?

Lab 10.39 *Selecting languages in Internet Explorer 5*

You are tasked with deploying Internet Explorer 5 in your organization. You will deploy the browser to your internal users using the IEAK. The various departments of your company are spread throughout the world and will require you to deploy the browser in various languages. The platforms that you will have to deploy the browser to will include the following:

1. USA-based Sales department users running Windows 95.

2. USA-based Marketing department users running Windows 98.

3. Japan-based Engineering department users running Windows NT Workstation 4.

4. Korea-based Maintenance department users running Windows for Workgroups.

5. Norway-based Support department users running Sun Solaris and HP UNIX.

Using the IEAK as a reference tool, how many builds will you have to create to deploy your software? If you are deploying the browser via CD-ROM, how many CD-ROMs will you have to create at a minimum?

Lab 10.40 *Using Install on Demand*

You are tasked with deploying Internet Explorer 5 in your organization. You will deploy the browser to your internal users using the IEAK. The various departments of your company are spread throughout the world and some do not have access to the Internet, but have access to the local intranet over your company's WAN. After talking with the desktop support department, you find that disk space on over 50 percent of the computers is at a premium. In addition, the offices throughout the world have very different functions and may need other components of the browser a few months from now.

In this case, would it be prudent to allow Install on Demand? What considerations would you consider in adding Install on Demand and why?

Lab 10.41 *Modifying the browser*

You are charged with modifying the configuration of your company's browsers. System policies have been included in your IEAK deployment. After a careful review of the policy settings, the organization feels that by using a User Agent String, the company can identify the browsing habits of the user community more effectively. In addition, the company would like to use the User Agent String to identify the usage on some of the company's partners' extranet Web sites.

You have already configured the location and configuration script for your enterprise on your local intranet server. How would you go about creating the new .ins file and deploying the file for your already deployed browsers?

Lab 10.42 *Choosing installation types*

Given the following scenario, choose the best method to install the Internet Explorer browser by specifying the type of installation: silent, hands-free, or inter-active.

1. A 250-user community that is receiving their first computers and is not experienced in installing software.

2. A group of network engineers with varying Web requirements.

3. A group of developers who need to have exactly the same browser settings.

Tying It All Together

I n Part IV, we will cover planning your installation in detail and point out things you need to think about when deriving your configuration options. Also covered are lessons learned from engineers who have deployed the software and also taken the exam.

We are going to walk through a sample deployment of Internet Explorer from soup to nuts. Using the tools that you have learned about up to this point, we will go through a sample implementation of Internet Explorer.

We will conclude Part IV with a chapter on troubleshooting the various pieces of the suite and common issues that have come up on deployments for our engineers, and also Microsoft's lessons learned.

Pre-Deployment Planning

About Chapter 11

As an administrator, understanding and effectively using the Internet Explorer Administration Kit is only one of the requirements to successfully deploy Internet Explorer 5. In Chapter 1, we walked through the IEAK application and talked about some of the specific features you could configure and modify along the way. In this chapter, we will spend a little time discussing the planning and preparation process required to get your Internet Explorer 5 package deployed throughout your company, organization, or client base. While the information we'll talk about in this chapter concerns Internet Explorer, most of the concepts can be applied to other software deployments as well.

OVERVIEW

The flexibility of the Internet Explorer Administration Kit allows multiple types of deployment methods. Corporate deployment is the most common deployment method, and is usually chosen based on the ability to manage the browser post-installation. There are two types of Corporate Deployment methods:

o Deploying Internet Explorer 5 utilizing a CD image, network, or Web download.

o Deploying Internet Explorer 5 via Systems Management Server.

Internet Service Providers (ISP)/Internet Content Providers (ICP) is the other deployment method, which you would choose based on the speed of development and reduced support requirements.

For the purpose of this book, we've chosen to discuss a corporate deployment scenario, as this role has the most options available. Just remember, the processes by which ISPs and ICPs deploy Internet Explorer follow the same guidelines. For reference, here are the deployment roles for Internet Explorer 5 again:

o *Corporate administrator.* The most flexible role, the corporate administrator has the most options in deploying Internet Explorer within an enterprise.

o *ISP mode.* Internet service providers can brand the browser and have a custom distribution method available only to the ISP mode: the single floppy disk. In addition to using the single floppy disk, ISPs can choose to distribute Internet Explorer with the capability to sign up users for Internet service provider access with the Internet Sign-up Server (ISS) function of the IEAK. ISS enables the ISP to create an automated sign-up capability to acquire new customers online immediately after the Internet Explorer installation.

o *Internet content provider.* Internet content providers are organizations that provide Internet-based content and services to Internet users. This group includes software and hardware vendors that sell and distribute products and services to the general public.

PRE-DEPLOYMENT PLANNING

There's an old adage that states, "If you fail to plan, you plan to fail." Never has that statement been truer than during a software deployment.

Proper planning is the key to a successful deployment. A well-planned deployment will help you avoid numerous headaches and problems. Realistically, the deployment of your Internet Explorer 5 package has many hurdles that should be anticipated prior to assembling the package using the IEAK. One of the first big hurdles that you are going to have to overcome is getting folks to agree on the features to be included in the browser. In many cases, gathering baseline information on the browser is another hurdle.

After witnessing many small- and large-scale deployments, I have discovered that the ones with the highest success rates incorporated many of the following pre-deployment considerations. These key considerations include getting the right resources, gathering the pertinent deployment data, analyzing the system requirements, building a solid project plan, planning a good pilot program, measuring the results along the way, and documenting throughout the entire project.

ASSEMBLING EFFECTIVE REPRESENTATION

The first step to deploying Internet Explorer 5 is the assurance that the deployment will work in your environment. To determine this, you must collect a lot of data. Sometimes the information is already collected for you and it is easy enough to relate it to your project. Other times, the information can be obtained from individuals within a company with "institutional knowledge." And sometimes you have to be part bloodhound to get everything you need.

There are some obvious questions you should already be asking yourself, such as: How does the company do business? What the company does has an effect on the outcome of your configuration. For example, the company may use a lot of Web-based applications in everyday business. You should consider adding links to these applications on the Links bar to make the navigation more effective. Another example is if the users are mainly mobile, you may want to customize the browser for mobile users by using page subscriptions or a very robust dial-up configuration with the CMAK.

How many different types of users are there in the company? In almost all scenarios, the company's users do different things. The human resources staff, for example, has different needs than the sales staff. You may want to also consider creating multiple configurations to best address the needs of different divisions of the company. The better you can address their needs, the happier your users will be with your package.

How many different types of machines are there? In considering the machines that will host your configuration, you should also think about what configuration will suit the machine the best. For example, a laptop has different requirements to that of a desktop machine. By nature, a laptop is a mobile piece of equipment whereas a desktop is not. You may want to consider linking more Web-based tools, such as Webmail links, on the laptop where bandwidth is more of a consideration.

How is the company's network structured? Considering the network structure is an important part of the browser. Different areas of the company may use different resources, such as firewalls, proxy servers, and other related hardware. In many scenarios, there can be big differences in the way the browser should be configured.

Target Audience Representation

Getting to know and understand the target audience is a crucial part of deploying Internet Explorer 5. Always keep this target audience in mind during every step of the deployment process. A target audience is a collection of users who will access and use your software in a similar way. Determining the different types of users you have can be difficult. Here are a few of the questions you should ask yourself when creating a model of your target audience:

- How many desktop users versus laptop users are there?
- How many users are mobile and work through a dial-up, VPN, or other remote connection?

- How many users are technical personnel?
- How many users are managers or executives?
- How many users are administrative or clerical?

As you see, there are many different user types. Each user will have a different notion of how the software should be deployed and used.

Earlier in the chapter, we talked about the reasons to consider laptops and mobile users. In addition, technical personnel may want to have different options than those of executives and administrative personnel. For example, you may consider using policies on your browser that lock down the configuration so that your chosen options cannot be changed. This may be fine for your administrative and executive personnel, but the technical folks may need to make changes to the configuration for testing and evaluation purposes. At the executive level, being unable to change a desktop configuration for a super user may be something to consider as well.

Deployment Media

Once you've identified the types of users, the next logical step is to decide which types of media are best used to deploy Internet Explorer 5. As first introduced in Chapter 6, Table 11-1 shows the available deployment media types (and the roles that can deploy them):

TABLE 11-1 METHODS OF DISTRIBUTION FOR INTERNET EXPLORER 5 WITH THE IEAK

DISTRIBUTION MEDIA	ISP MODE	ICP MODE	CORPORATE ADMINISTRATOR
CD-ROM	Yes	Yes	Yes
Multiple floppies	Yes	Yes	Yes
Single floppy	Yes	No	No
Up to ten Internet-based distribution sites	Yes	Yes	Yes
Single disk branding	Yes	Yes	Yes
Silent installation via a single site	No	No	Yes

Art

Having already examined the IEAK, you're aware of the options allowing you to use a company logo, color scheme, or other artwork to further customize Internet Explorer. Each of the customizations in the IEAK will require a copy of the artwork you plan to use. When starting to plan the deployment, make sure you have the most current copies of the graphic files. Also keep in mind that not all logos and artwork can be used as they are provided to you, and that they may have to be manipulated or enhanced to achieve the proper results.

The additional efforts devoted to customization can aid in company identification and better help to integrate Internet Explorer into a corporate desktop standard. The IEAK allows you to specify custom artwork for the following items.

- Setup Wizard Top Banner (496 × 96 pixels)
- Setup Wizard Left Bitmap (162 × 312 pixels)
- Large Animated and Static Browser Logos (38 × 38 pixels)
- Small Animated and Static Browser Logos (22 × 22 pixels)
- Browser Toolbar Background Bitmap
- CD Autorun Bitmap (540 × 347 pixels)

 tip **Included in the 'Toolkit' directory of the IEAK are tools for the creation and viewing of animated bitmap images. You do not have to use these tools provided you use an image editor of your choice. As long as you conform to the size specifications shown previously, you will have little or no problems deploying your images.**

You can collect or create the artwork you'll need for deployment at any time throughout the deployment planning stages. Often any scheduled down time, such as holidays, can be put to productive use by saving this task until then. We'll discuss time management in greater detail later in this chapter.

Effective Communication

Along with proper planning, effective communication is paramount to the success of a deployment. From start to finish, there will be a lot of individuals and groups that will work with you to deploy Internet Explorer. Open and timely communication is critical when this many people attempt to collaborate on a project.

During the planning stages, you'll want to speak with as many people as possible to get a better understanding of everyone's wants and needs. This is the first communication effort and can be accomplished in many ways. A poll of companies currently engaged in software deployments revealed how each company uses multiple communication methods to ensure all information is provided and shared in a convenient and timely manner. Some of these methods include the following:

- Face-to-face meetings
- Conference calls
- Video conferencing
- Email
- Status or situation reports
- Discussion groups
- Brown bag luncheons

How communication is conducted is not as important as ensuring that it happens. The project plan will normally dictate the communication methods and frequency. During the course of a project, there may be times when it is important to meet weekly or even daily to ensure all is going as planned.

GATHERING DEPLOYMENT DATA

Once a target audience and open communication channels have been established, you need to begin the process of collecting the data you will need to deploy Internet Explorer. This data consists primarily of a requirements analysis. Other data that will need to be collected include the features of the software package, a comparison of wants versus needs, and any correlation of the data collected.

Requirements Analysis

A requirements analysis allows you to examine the desired outcome of the users' requests and translate them into the software's technical capabilities. Many administrators tend to ignore the analytical side of information gathering because they possess institutional knowledge of the environment. What they may fail to consider is that there will be people working on the project who do not have the same background. Knowing the requirements beforehand will enable everyone involved to focus their efforts on the actual work. Another benefit of requirements analysis is that the information can then be shared with others for approval purposes, thus ensuring everyone a chance to make his or her recommendations. At a minimum, a requirements analysis should answer the following questions:

- What is Internet Explorer going to do for the company?
- What are the benefits Internet Explorer will bring?
- Will it alleviate any current problems, issues, or limitations?
- What are the additional support, training, and maintenance requirements?

Information gathering

The first stage of any software deployment is evaluating the product you'll be deploying. Take note of any enhancements, features, and settings that you'll either want to invoke or disable in your package. We'll assume that you already have a working knowledge of Internet Explorer and the IEAK.

Secondly, you'll want to determine if the product will be of benefit. That's easy if you're an Internet Service Provider (ISP) or Internet Content Provider (ICP), because your client base will need Internet Explorer 5 to use your services; however, it gets a little trickier if the deployment is within a corporate environment. Occasionally, administrators have to don their "salesman" hat when recommending new technology. This is when an evaluation of the benefits of Internet Explorer will pay off. Only through proper research and evaluation can you begin to explain the benefits Internet Explorer will have for a company or organization. Here are just a few of the benefits :

- *The Internet Explorer Administration Kit (obviously).* Through the IEAK, the Customization Wizard, and the Profile Wizard you can customize, deploy, and manage Internet Explorer 5 without having to learn complex programming languages.
- *Policies and Restrictions.* User access to specific features and functions can be granted or denied. You can expand or limit functionality of the browser to hone the application to your user base.

- *Enhanced Security.* Security settings can be pre-populated to protect your users and their environment. With the IEAK, you can pre-configure both Content Ratings and Security Zones to further manage the secure integrity of the work environment.

- *Multiple Platform Capabilities.* Windows 32-bit, Windows 16-bit, Macintosh, and UNIX machines can all take advantage of Internet Explorer's features.

- *Web-based Applications Development.* HTML, Visual Basic, and Dynamic HTML support allow you to use Internet Explorer 5 to assist in the development of your own Web-based applications.

 tip **When explaining the benefits of Internet Explorer, don't forget to mention the overall reduction of a company's Total Cost of Ownership (TCO) and the increase on their Return On Investment (ROI). Using the IEAK to manage the browser on an ongoing basis will reduce support calls and future upgrades.**

The next type of information you should gather would be a complete list of the platforms and corresponding configurations you'll encounter within the company or organization. Another list would be of the specific client/server architecture of the environment. Occasionally, upgrades will have to be made in order to deploy the software package. After compiling these lists, however, a better understanding of the most desirable Internet Explorer components to install should be obtained based on the end users' machines and how they behave in the work enterprise. Any compatibility issues should be plainly visible during this stage of planning.

One of the most important pieces of information to obtain is the list of corporate settings desired by the company or organization. Sometimes a deployment will begin prior to fully understanding and deciding upon the settings for the users and machines. Deployments such as these tend to run over budget and over schedule. Proper information gathering early on in the project will help to alleviate any difficulty brought about by the need to redesign or modify the project plan or deployment package.

Lastly, you'll need to identify any pertinent issues in regard to migration and coexistence. If your users currently use a browser, what is it? Will there be a time at which more than one type of browser will be running within your enterprise?

Another big consideration is any Web-based applications that may exist in your organization. In some cases, these applications may be dependent on the previous browser version for certain features that may not exist in the same fashion as the new version. Pay specific attention to VBScript or JavaScript-based functions that may not perform as expected with your new version of the browser. Be sure to test all of your Web applications thoroughly as the cost and time to remediate these applications is something you need to be aware of in planning your deployment.

Learning the Features

Once the requirements analysis is completed, the next step is to educate yourself on the new features Internet Explorer 5 has to offer. Only when you've studied each of the new features can you make a clear determination as to which components and settings can be applied. You will want to install Internet Explorer 5 on a machine somewhere for the sole purpose of examining the new features available. When looking at the new features, also make note of any changes in the user interface if you are upgrading from a previous version of Internet Explorer. If you are migrating to Internet Explorer from another Internet browser, make note of the differences you see between the two.

 Deployment of Internet Explorer 5 in an environment that does currently have an Internet browser will require a more thorough examination of the features available.

Wants versus Needs

We've all seen the scenario where an executive or IT manager goes to a conference or speaks with someone about the latest and greatest software package. He or she then comes back to work with the grandiose idea of deploying it and begins assigning a project team before even researching the product.

 Many companies publish a new features list on their intranet site for any upcoming software that is scheduled for deployment.

In this scenario, no research was done to determine if the software was even needed at the company. Most of the time, our wants speak before our needs. That's usually the time the justification period begins. As human beings we can justify anything to ourselves. That's why it takes multiple points of view or opinions to hone in on what exactly are the needs of a company.

Some companies will desire to implement Internet Explorer 5 simply because it is the latest piece of software. Others will examine the benefits it has to offer and make their decision based on that. After the decision is made to implement Internet Explorer 5, the process of determining wants versus needs begins again because of the degree of customization present in the IEAK. Like the company that weighs the benefits Internet Explorer 5 has to offer them, administrators should weigh which components, settings, and options to enable or disable in the IEAK based on research and feedback.

Correlating Data

The last step in gathering data for a deployment should be the correlation of the data you've collected. You correlate the data by mapping the wants, needs, and features back to the requirements stipulated in the requirements analysis.

For example, the communications department of your company wants to be able to distribute multimedia presentations to the employees. One of the requirements of Internet Explorer for your company was to provide a browser for Web-based applications and communication. Through the IEAK, you can install the Windows Media Player as a new feature.

In the previous example, a feature that complied with a requirement filled a want. A direct correlation exists between the wants, needs, requirements, and the features list offered. As requirements are analyzed further, you may find the wants and needs of the company are derived more from the features list than anything else.

REQUIREMENTS TRANSLATION

There are many aspects of the requirements analysis process that will require translation to assist the process of creating the project plan. Direct considerations concerning timeframes and political management should be addressed prior to writing a project plan. You must have a good idea as to the roadblocks that you may be presented with along the way from both operational and political sources.

Time Management

The timeframes required to deploy Internet Explorer 5 are not fixed by any means. Each environment introduces its own time requirements. Multiple items can drive timelines for deployments. Some companies may want to aggressively implement the new technology just as soon as it's released. Others may want to give the technology a chance to prove itself first. Still others have internal commitments of their own that drive the deployment schedule. When several administrators were asked what drove their particular deployment schedule, here's what some of them had to say:

- "We were understandably cautious during the Y2K date and chose to delay some of your pilot programs until the first quarter of 2000."
- "Our company has a huge project we go through every year at the same time, so we decided to postpone our deployment until afterwards."
- "We're in a zero-failure situation, so we took an inordinate amount of time to thoroughly plan and test our deployment as to assure no stone was unturned."
- "It was purely political."

Whatever the reason for establishing your specific deployment schedule, be liberal with the amount of time you estimate. It's better to finish early than to finish late. Any additional time can be used to fine-tune the deployment. Here are some items to consider when estimating the deployment schedule:

- Operational commitments or blackout dates
- Funding cycles
- Holidays/vacations
- Existing or potential dependencies
- Impact on the target audience
- Industry deadlines for upgrade releases
- Deployment staff availability

Political Management

Believe it or not, politics plays an important role in the deployment of software in all environments. Think of it this way; if the Chief Information Officer (CIO) of a company isn't particularly impressed with a certain application or has had problems with it in the past, how reluctant will he or she be to assign funds and resources to implementing it? You can be sure that it's not going to be at the top of their list.

Things can get even more complicated if there are to be multiple departments or divisions working together during a deployment. Each division has its own supervisory structure, and the supervisors and subordinates do not always work well with members of other divisions. The task then becomes to overlook the differences in opinion and learn to compromise.

Some decisions made during a deployment that affect the items that are being installed, tasks to be performed, or project milestones and deadlines can be directly related to the desires and compromises made by upper management. In a profit-driven business, the deployment of software may be accredited with an increase in revenue. In that case, management will be more allowing of funds but probably more critical of timeframes. In a deployment scheme that does not affect the bottom line of the company, funds may be the problem while timeframes are flexible.

ASSEMBLING PROJECT PLANS

The cornerstone of any deployment is the project plan. This is the one document that everyone should always refer back to for the goals, timelines, and resources for the project.

Developing project plans can quickly become labor intensive. To ease the burden somewhat, here's a proven process in use by many administrators.

First, solicit as much input/feedback on deploying the software as you can stand. Be sure to involve a broad range of technicians, end users, and managers. Each type of person presents a different point of view that can be very useful in determining the best deployment scenario. Consolidate the feedback you receive into specific categories. These categories will probably consist of goals, timelines, risks, concerns, success and failure factors, and spin-off tasks.

There are many software packages available, such as Microsoft Project, that contain wizards to aid in preparing project plans. A good project plan includes goals, required resources, proposed timeframes, milestone markers, beta phases, pilot phases, contingency plans, end user support/training, and any related task that may either have to be completed prior to deployment or post-deployment.

Before finalizing the project plan, make sure you have it reviewed by everyone involved. A good strategy is to take it back to the initial people who were asked for feedback. This assures them that their concerns are being met, and you'll benefit by having their "buy-in" early in the project.

Setting Goals

The goals of the project will establish the criteria by which the project is judged. Even the milestones and deadlines are not as important as achieving the goals set forth by the project plan. Missed deadlines may be forgotten, but missing the goals and expectations of the target audience will not.

By now the requirements have been determined, the timeline should be taking shape, and the benefits of Internet Explorer are evident. The goals are simply these items tied together and documented as a way to measure success.

Specific goals while deploying Internet Explorer could include the following:

o Deployment by a certain date

o Installation of a custom component

o Enhanced productivity

o Access to previously inaccessible information

o Specific user, machine, or connection settings applied globally

As a rule of thumb, the goals section of the project plan does not have to read like a mission statement. It's more productive if you keep it concise and to the point. It is important that goals of the project are reasonable and driven by the technical abilities and timetables necessary to complete the project effectively. Managing time is one of the most important aspects of large software deployments.

Communication

In effect, the more people you communicate with during the project planning stages, the better. Your project plan should include a section describing the best methods of communication for the parties involved in the deployment. Meeting schedules are commonplace in project plans and should have the following information:

o Chairing body

o Required members

o Optional members

o Location

o Frequency

Your communication efforts become harder the more people that are involved in the deployment and the greater the geographical boundaries. Ensure that any schedule you provide will accommodate conference calling capabilities and multiple time zones. Moreover, every meeting should include follow-up documentation and/or minutes of the meeting to the members.

Resource Planning

You'll need many resources to successfully deploy Internet Explorer. By resources, we mean any person, place, or thing that will be utilized to move Internet Explorer from a consideration to a fully implemented and managed software package. The two major resources a deployment needs are as follows:

- *People.* The personnel to do the job.
- *Materials.* The hardware, software, and reference items for the people.

People (IT professionals)

Let's face it; no one would want to tackle something like this on his or her own. A proven team structure for deploying software should include the following teams:

- *Development and Planning Team.* These people are responsible for the development of the custom Internet Explorer package. They assist the Project Manager in creating a Deployment Plan.
- *Implementation Team.* This team is responsible for the installations of Internet Explorer during beta, pilot, and final deployment phases. They assist the Development Team in evaluating and testing custom packages.
- *Customer Support Team.* This team is responsible for ensuring the users are trained to use the new software and troubleshoot any problems the users may have during and after the installation conducted by the Implementation Team.

 note **The needs of your deployment will drive the exact number of personnel required. Larger deployments may require multiple members for each team listed previously, while smaller scale ones may have people wearing multiple hats (developer AND implementer AND customer support).**

The teams should be headed or chaired by a Project Manager. It is the responsibility of the Project Manager to manage the overall efforts and aspects of the deployment. The Project Manager determines all resource and time requirements. One of the key objectives of the Project Manager is to raise support for the project throughout the organization. By addressing the needs of various departments, the Project Manager can gain more support for the project as a whole.

Materials

Simply put, the personnel listed previously will require certain tools and materials to accomplish their duties. Their material needs fall into three categories: hardware, software, and reference items.

Hardware should include samples of each type of platform run by the company or organization. For best results, an isolated lab environment where the Development Team and the Implementation Team can work together to test packages should be set up.

The software needs will reflect the individual duties of each team member. For example, a project management suite such as Microsoft Project will be required for the Project Manager while a Development Team member may require migration tools.

Assurances should be made that the teams have the most up-to-date information concerning the environment and the software being deployed. This includes, but is in no way limited to: the Deployment Plan, resource kits, white papers, trade publications, and so on.

 caution

When examining hardware, take note that the IEAK and its additional tools/wizards have their own system requirements that are separate from Internet Explorer 5.

PLANNING GOOD PILOTS

Pilot programs are very important because they provide a working model of how the deployment is anticipated to behave. Everything from the distribution media to the user settings are tested and finalized during the pilot phase of the deployment. There are two different ideas on how to conduct pilot phases. The first idea is that testing should be conducted in a controlled lab environment. The second idea is to test the same elements of the pilot, but instead use a small group of willing participants within the corporate environment. The latter idea has the added benefit of not attempting to replicate the target environment, but rather introducing the software into it.

As a minimum, during the pilot phase you should do the following:

- Install Internet Explorer 5 using the package built with the IEAK.
- Ensure you have conducted testing on all corporate standard hardware platforms (if applicable/available).
- Test Internet Explorer 5 and any installed custom components.
- Test all pre-existing software applications on the machines.
- Uninstall Internet Explorer 5 on the machines.
- Re-test the pre-existing software applications on the machine.

 Machines to be used in the pilot phase that have not been scanned for viruses or physical integrity issues may produce invalid results.

Conducting the pilot phase using the steps listed previously will ensure the deployment package works and does not interfere with any pre-existing software applications.

The use of a pilot deployment checklist is highly recommended. The checklist is created in conjunction with the Development Team and the Implementation Team. The checklist should outline the measures necessary to complete the previous steps. It should also include directions for exceptions, reporting problems, and troubleshooting.

 A beta phase is a great way to observe how the software will react within your environment prior to piloting. In a beta phase, you generally do not pre-configure any options or settings. Beta phases are sometimes conducted prior to a full commitment to deploy a product to ensure the software will be a viable solution for a company. If a lab environment can be constructed, this is the best place to conduct a beta phase. If not, a small group of willing users can usually be rounded up.

Marketing

During the pilot phase of the deployment, it is important to have an established marketing strategy. Marketing the deployment of Internet Explorer 5 may not sound like something your company needs, but if done properly, the impact on the company is lessened. This is evident in the reduced amount of helpdesk calls. Methods of marketing the deployment can include a feedback forum, information phone line, intranet site, brochures, brown bag luncheons, FAQ sites, and knowledge bases. By placing information in the hands of the target audience, you also involve them, making them less resistant to the changes the deployment may bring.

Communicating to Users

As we've stated several times in this chapter, open lines of communication are one of your best allies when deploying Internet Explorer. Communicating with the participants of the pilot phase is the best way to finalize the deployment process. If the pilot is being conducted under lab conditions, the communication will flow back and forth between the Development Team and the Implementation Team. If the pilot is being conducted with a group of users, the communications should be freely open between the users and all project teams. Simple forms of communicating with the users could consist of phone calls, e-mails, and customer survey forms. More advanced means of communications could include discussion groups, online survey forms, and conferencing.

Anticipating Problems

No matter how well you plan, many variables are unknown until you enter the pilot phase. There maybe hardware or software compatibility problems that weren't apparent during the planning stages. No one likes to think there will be problems, but you must plan for them. The communication methods mentioned in the previous section will help to inform you should a problem arise. Most problems that arise are easy to solve and are generally just items that were overlooked during planning. Other problems may be more serious, at which point it is usually best to contact Microsoft Premier Support for assistance.

 tip **If you are pilot testing with actual users, the need for a contingency plan is much greater than if you are testing in a lab environment.**

However you resolve the issues, you'll want to establish a knowledge base. When tracking the issues, pay close attention to patterns that may emerge. Very often a recurring issue is based on a deviation from your corporate standards or a traceable configuration difference. Items you may want to track on the knowledge base could include the following:

- Make and manufacturer of machine
- Operating system
- Installed software
- Non-standard configurations
- Location on segment or network

 tip **Many companies use disk replication or cloning utilities to deploy standard hardware and software platforms. If your company does this, it may be of importance to record the date and time the original or parent disk image was created.**

A periodic review of the knowledge base is good practice and can be included as a topic of discussion during deployment-related meetings.

MEASURING RESULTS

When project goals are created, measuring the results of a project becomes clear. The best way to determine if the goals were globally met is by soliciting feedback from the recipients of the Internet Explorer deployment package.

Customer Feedback

No one will know better if the final deployment package works than your internal customers. Their feedback can be solicited in various ways. Just as feedback is used to determine if changes need to be made during a pilot phase, feedback is required after a deployment to ensure that all objectives were met. Most of these objectives can be found in the project plan. Some of the objectives will be expectations that the customers had based on the marketing efforts prior to deployment.

Management Feedback

Feedback from management is just as important as that from the users. The only difference here is that the expectations may be different. Management expectations involve items in the project plan that the end users are not aware of. Some of the additional elements that management will be judging the deployment on include the following:

o Adherence to milestones and deadlines

o Project expenditures

o Impact on the company's work force

o Impact on support, training, and maintenance

 By involving management early on in the project, you set their expectations. Doing this affords you more control over the project's outcome and minimizes negative feedback based on ill-conceived expectations.

Quality Lessons Learned

"Been there, done that." That's what lessons learned are all about. So much of what you'll encounter during the deployment of Internet Explorer can provide valuable insight for deploying other applications within your target environment. A "lessons learned" document is generally a summary report of everything the project teams learned during the deployment. In addition to providing an existing knowledge base for subsequent deployments, the "lessons learned" document might also show discrepancies in the project plan.

DOCUMENTATION

It seems you never get away from paperwork. From the beginning of the project until the end, you'll find that there is more paperwork than people realize. There were documents explaining the benefits for Internet Explorer 5. There were documents covering the enhancements and new features. Some documents were used to gather and report information. Other documentation laid the framework of what would become a project plan. Some documentation was constantly revised, while other documents were used once and discarded. All this documentation gave the project life.

Documenting Projects

One of the biggest favors you will do yourself is to document the project every step of the way. From inception to completion, the documents used for the project can be a ready source of information. No item is too big or too small to document. Project documents are the source for lessons learned. Proper documentation also means that any valuable pieces of information learned along the way are not lost. Project managers often look back to previous projects' documents for insight and guidance.

Creating Support Documentation

Support documentation is any item created specifically to address a problem, issue, exception, concern, or training.

Many projects involve the training of end users. Documents can be purchased or developed that instruct the end users how to use Internet Explorer.

Checklists are a great idea for the Implementation Team. Through the use of a checklist, the Implementation Team can ensure all installations of Internet Explorer 5 were conducted using the same sequence and steps.

Knowledge Bases

Knowledge bases are collections of data relating to the project. Knowledge bases can be used for several reasons. Here are some examples of typical uses for knowledge bases during the deployment of Internet Explorer 5:

- Vendor-supplied known issues or problems
- Pilot program issues, problems, and trouble calls
- Final deployment issues, problems, and trouble calls
- Tips and tricks for users
- Frequently asked questions
- Lessons learned

End User Training

User acceptance is the most important part of the deployment. You have to provide the tools and features that the users want and need to make it a success. With many complicated applications, there is a need to educate the end user on how to use the software effectively.

Training can be provided in a number of ways to your end users. In the end, you should help determine what is the most effective means to communicate this information to the end user. Consider using the following means to educate your users on your product.

- Classroom training provided by an instructor.
- Computer Based Training (CBT). These are generally CD-ROMs that are multimedia-based that you can provide to the users. These products are widely available and can help walk the user though how to use the products more effectively.
- Distance learning. You can provide access to a number of Web-based tutorials provided by a wide variety of vendors. The user can participate in the learning process through collaborative, Web-based training sessions.

KEY POINT SUMMARY

- The first step to deploying Internet Explorer 5 is the assurance that the deployment will work in your environment.
- Getting to know and understand the target audience is a crucial part of deploying Internet Explorer 5. Always keep this fact in mind during every step of the deployment process. A target audience is a collection of users who will access or use the software.
- Along with proper planning, effective communication is paramount to the success of a deployment. From start to finish, there will be a lot of individuals and groups that will work in direct cooperation to deploy Internet Explorer. Open and timely communication is critical when this many people attempt to collaborate on a project.

- Once a target audience and open communication channels have been established, you need to begin the process of collecting the data you will need to deploy Internet Explorer. This data consists primarily of a requirements analysis.

- Knowing the requirements beforehand will enable everyone involved to focus their efforts on the actual work instead of interpreting why the work is being performed. Another benefit of the requirements analysis is that the information can then be shared with others for their approval, thus ensuring everyone is afforded a chance to make his or her recommendations.

- The last step in gathering data for a deployment should be the correlation of the data you've collected. You correlate the data by mapping the wants, needs, and features back to the requirements stipulated in the requirements analysis.

- There are many aspects of the requirements analysis process that will require translation to assist the process of creating the project plan. Direct considerations concerning timeframes and political management should be addressed prior writing a project plan.

- The use of a pilot deployment checklist is highly recommended. The checklist is created in conjunction with the Development Team and the Implementation Team. The checklist should outline the steps necessary to complete the deployment.

- When project goals are created, you can clearly measure the results of a project. The best way to determine if the goals were globally met is by soliciting feedback from the recipients of the Internet Explorer deployment package.

- User acceptance is the most important part of the deployment. You have to provide the tools and features that the users want and need to make it a success. With many complicated applications, there is a need to educate the end user on how to use the software effectively.

APPLYING WHAT YOU'VE LEARNED

This section is an opportunity to use what you've learned in this chapter. The lab here provides you with important real-world practice using the skills you've learned.

Critical Thinking Lab

Lab 11.43 *Choosing deployment solutions*

In the following lab, you will be asked to provide deployment solutions for a variety of scenarios. Pay close attention to the technical requirements of the scenario to arrive at the best answer. Use Chapter 7 to help you make the best selection for the requirement. The goal is to provide the quickest, easiest, and least expensive installation method.

1. A corporation whose employees are almost entirely sales staff. The sales people are always on the move and are equipped with laptop computers with a configuration consisting of dial-up access, and CD-ROM and floppy drives.

2. An ISP that is deploying the browser to its internal employees all over the US. The workstations have fast network access, and CD-ROM and floppy drives.

3. An ICP with Internet Explorer 5 pre-installed on its new workstations. The CIO would like to customize the browser for the organization to enable the browser to be more productive. The workstations have fast network access, CD-ROM and floppy drives.

4. A small office with 40 workstations and very slow Internet access — the browser will be used to view intranet information loaded on the local network. The intranet server hosts several applications that are Web-based and run at 90 percent CPU utilization all day long. The users have separate file servers that are not very busy during the day. The workstations have fast local network access, CD-ROM and floppy drives, but slow Internet access.

5. A major ISP that desires to do a bulk mailing to potential customers. The goal will be to provide new customers with their services along with their customized version of Internet Explorer. Since the customer base varies, the workstation configurations are not known.

6. A small, 20-person printing firm that wants to provide the new browser to eight sales staff using old laptops. The workstations have slow dial-up connections to the Internet, floppy drives only, and no local network access.

Some Real World Scenarios

About Chapter 12

I n this chapter, we are going to walk through a soup-to-nuts implementation of Internet Explorer 5. We are going to cover implementation issues, configuration considerations, and other things to keep in mind when implementing the entire suite of software. We will discuss in detail the processes and configuration data that you are going to need to make technical decisions for configuring the suite. This chapter deals with the business side of the implementation and things to think about when making your key configuration decisions. Just remember, the more information you have on hand about your user community, the better.

THE BEGINNING

Like with anything else, getting started is usually the hardest part. For the purposes of this discussion, I'm assuming that you've already downloaded and installed the IEAK. Starting there is easy; the only decision you have had to make up to this point is to whom you will distribute Internet Explorer. We have talked about the roles of Internet Explorer earlier in the book. Are you distributing it to corporate users, ISP customers, or CSP customers? The audience you are delivering to dramatically affects your licensing and configuration options. The IEAK site will ask you a series of questions about your organization and your intent to distribute Internet Explorer 5.

 caution

If you are obtaining the IEAK for your organization, during the registration you agree to certain terms that apply to your company or organization. Make sure that you have your organization's approval to agree to these terms.

LEARNING THE FEATURES

After studying for this exam and hopefully passing it, you'll be a recognized expert in implementing and supporting Internet Explorer 5. You will have the advantage of knowing which features, modifications, and restrictions you can implement with Internet Explorer 5 and the IEAK. The problem you will most likely encounter is that decision-makers in your organization will not have that same intimate knowledge. With this in mind, you have to act as the evangelist for Internet Explorer and demonstrate the capabilities of both the browser and the IEAK in general.

To develop a list of requirements for your configuration, the decision-makers need to know what Internet Explorer is capable of. It will help if you show the decision-makers what exactly the software is capable of. You can demonstrate the features and possible options that you can include to assist them in making sound, manageable decisions on what to include in your package. You can educate these individuals on the features of the IEAK in several ways:

- Develop a high-level document in layman's terms on the IEAK and Internet Explorer.
- Develop a prototype workstation for the decision-makers to view and give you feedback on.
- Show these individuals success stories from other organizations that have implemented Internet Explorer and the IEAK.

In addition to receiving input from the decision-makers, you should also get some feedback from the end users. As I'm sure you know, the decision-makers don't always think the same way as the end users. These are just examples; obviously some other approaches may be just as effective. Once you have completed this educational process, you can then develop a list of requirements for your implementation.

GATHERING BASELINE INFORMATION

Like any other application, the Internet Explorer suite of applications can operate and behave differently on different workstations depending on various factors, such as the processing power, disk space, and operating system version. In Chapter 1, we learned the minimum requirements for Internet Explorer (see Table 1-1).

Armed with this information, you should take a look at the inventory of your workstations to ensure optimal performance of Internet Explorer in your enterprise. If your organization does not maintain correlated information on hardware, you can use several tools to gather this information. Microsoft's Systems Management Server (SMS) is a fantastic tool that helps you, as the administrator, gather information about your users, such as:

- Processor speed/type
- Workstation RAM
- Free disk space

- Applications currently installed
- TCP/IP information

 If you have HP Openview deployed in your enterprise, you may want to take a look at HP Openview Desktop Administrator (DTA). DTA is an integrated suite of applications that is a competitor of SMS.

SMS provides many other capabilities as well. SMS uses client applications and utilities to gather information about the workstation; this information is then gathered by SMS and correlated in a Microsoft SQL database. Once the data has been gathered, you can query the database to get the answers to questions such as:

- How many users have enough free space for Internet Explorer 5?
- How many users are upgrading from Internet Explorer 4?
- How many users already have Internet Explorer 5?
- How many users have less than 16MB of RAM?
- How many users already have Internet Explorer 5 installed?
- How many users have a Pentium-based computer or above?

This information will tell if you need hardware upgrades before implementing Internet Explorer 5. This list can also give you the information to estimate the cost of the upgrade, including hardware costs.

PRE-CONFIGURATION PLANNING

At this point, you have downloaded the IEAK and gathered your requirements and your hardware baseline. You know which users are capable of running Internet Explorer 5 and which are not. Aside from the actual rollout, the next phase is the most important part of your implementation and affects the future of Internet Explorer 5 in your organization.

I'll start by discussing the implementation structure. As you know, Internet Explorer 5 has several distribution vehicles that can be used to deploy the software. The goal is to determine which method offers the fastest and most efficient way to complete the project. You should also decide at this time whether or not you will use the auto-proxy and auto-configuration options. Let's take a look at the hypothetical implementation scenario I will use throughout this chapter.

In this sample scenario, you are laying all of the groundwork for implementing Internet Explorer 5 on the entire Netdata network. I'll cover the information necessary to plan and implement your customized version of Internet Explorer 5 for all your users. Figure 12-1 shows a hypothetical diagram of the Netdata internal network.

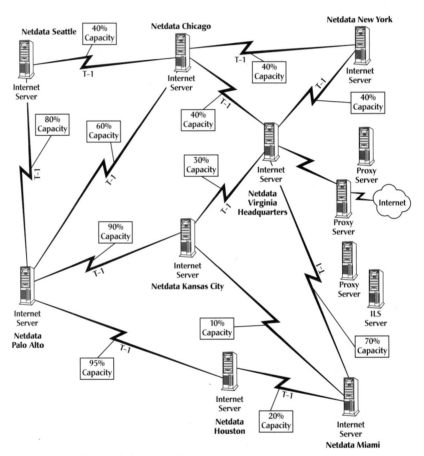

FIGURE 12-1 The Netdata network

The diagram shows the headquarters' location and the seven field offices; each location contains on average about 50-100 users. Each location also maintains a separate intranet server site that is linked by the headquarters' main intranet server. As you can see, the intranet servers are located in each site, with one main server located at the headquarters. Each office is connected to the headquarters location via T-1 circuits, which provide the connectivity to the headquarters and to the other field offices as necessary. Mail, transfers, and intranet/Internet traffic comprise the majority of the traffic on the circuits, so some circuits tend to work harder than others at different periods throughout the day.

Because Netdata has a good IS budget, all workstations are PII400s and above with 128MB of RAM each. The workstations also have at least 1GB of free disk space each. Users are currently running Netscape Navigator, version 4.06. When looking at the diagram of the network, ask yourself the following questions:

- Where should I consider placing my distribution points for my Internet Explorer installation?

- Where should I consider placing my `.js`, `.jvs`, or `.pac` files for my auto-proxy configuration?

- Where should I maintain my auto-configuration files? How difficult is it going to be to maintain these files?

- Where should I place online references, such as support, add-ons, and start pages? Where should I place my search pages?

Simple math will tell you the answer to the first question. A T-1 circuit provides a maximum throughput of 1.544Mbps. A 100BaseT Ethernet provides a maximum throughput of 100Mbps. In looking at the diagram, you can see that some of your WAN circuits are already running at 70–80 percent of capacity with your current traffic. With this information in mind, placing your distribution files on the opposite end of your circuits is probably not a good idea.

Each site has an intranet server, so the most logical choice would be to distribute the files on each intranet server. This also enables each site to control the Internet Explorer 5 distribution. If one of the WAN links fails, the users will still be able to continue with the Internet Explorer installation.

As a second redundancy, you should include a second server from which to download files in case the intranet server fails for some reason. In this instance, you should use the headquarters' intranet server for your files.

Auto-proxy

You know from the diagram that Netdata hosts a proxy server at the headquarters. This proxy server is configured in a proxy array, which provides fault tolerance in case one of the proxy servers fails. Some may argue whether the auto-proxy is needed in this scenario, but you should go ahead with the auto-proxy for hypothetical purposes. You have two options for placing the auto-proxy files:

- Place the files on the headquarters' intranet server.
- Place the files on each intranet server.

The first option provides a single point of failure in case the headquarters' server fails. There's also the argument that if the WAN link fails, the clients will not be able to access the headquarters' intranet server. The answer to this one is simple: if the WAN link fails, the users will not have Internet access anyway, and the auto-proxy is then useless until connectivity is restored.

The other option is to place the auto-proxy files on the users' local 100BaseT network. This configuration does reduce some of the risk involved and provides for less traffic across the WAN. (The network traffic created by the auto-proxy is very low, however.) The negative side to this scenario is that a lot more administration is involved. If a change needs to be made to the auto-proxy file, all eight intranet servers must receive a copy of the new files.

Auto-configuration

Auto-configuration files present questions similar to those of the auto-proxy. The auto-configuration will hinge on the options you choose while using the IEAK Wizard. You may want to consider, for starters, staying consistent with your other files and configurations by deploying the auto-configuration files in the same manner as you did the auto-proxy files. I cover some of the considerations for auto-configuration a little later in this chapter.

Online Features

As you know, you can add online features to your Internet Explorer configuration using the IEAK. Online support, add-ons, and start pages are features you should consider when assembling your package. Let's take a look at your choices.

Online Support

No matter how well you assemble and plan this implementation, you should expect some problems or questions. The IEAK online support feature enables you to add your own URL to a support site you can customize. Each of your eight sites has IS support personnel that will be assisting you in the Internet Explorer deployment. As you know that each field office handles its support internally, it would be prudent to create a site for each field office to reference local personnel for support.

Add-ons

Your package will include the options you want for the organization. You really don't want your users adding anything to their configuration without prior approval. With this in mind, you should still include an `addon95.htm` file for your configuration. If you keep the default page with Internet Explorer, users will be able to access the Microsoft add-on site and add components to their configuration. The add-on page can be simple, stating that no updates are available at this time.

Start Page

Now you are faced with the question, "Where will your users start browsing?" Here's where you select what is commonly called a portal, or gateway, to the Internet. Given the layout of your network, it would make sense to start your users at the site's intranet server. Because each site maintains content specific for the site, the user should always start browsing on the local site. This will also keep the intranet traffic local, until the user chooses to navigate elsewhere.

 tip **If you split up the start pages for each of your locations in separate packages, remember to use an IP host name, like** `intranet.chicago.netdatasys.com`. **Try to avoid using Netbios names or IP addresses, as these do not allow any flexibility in making changes down the road.**

Welcome Page

You can configure a URL to be displayed the first time the user launches Internet Explorer. Because you are trying to keep the files somewhat localized, you will keep the welcome page consistent by developing a welcome page for each site. This page should reside on the local intranet server in the event of link failure. Having the site local also allows the local staff to maintain the page more easily.

Search Sites

Users will need a place (a URL) to search the Internet. Most people prefer certain search engines, such as Yahoo, Excite, WebCrawler, and many others. You want to keep the users focused on business and keep them from being sidetracked with advertisements, horoscopes, and other material that has nothing to do with the business at hand. With the IEAK, you can build your own search page, which can tie together the many different search engines on the Web, or you can leave the default, which enables you to choose the search engine yourself. Let's stick with the default at this point so as not to get too complicated.

OUTLOOK EXPRESS

Each of the sites has its own POP and SMTP server for routing email. You need to gather the list of server host names before your IEAK build. If you want to use IMAP, you can use that as well by specifying the folder and service names.

NETMEETING

You should plan on using NetMeeting in your implementation, with one Internet Locator Server (ILS) server located at headquarters for users to use. The ILS server name will be the same for all your NetMeeting users.

PREPARING FOR THE IEAK WIZARD

You've gathered a lot of information so far; now it's time to start preparing to build your Internet Explorer configuration. Gathering files for the IEAK helps you ensure that preparing to build Internet Explorer will be trouble-free.

The files you will need for the IEAK build, in order of presentation, are as follows:

1. A custom .bmp file for the CD-ROM splash screen (if you are using CDs for distribution)

2. The Active Setup Wizard .bmp file

3. Source files for your custom applications

4. Internet Explorer toolbar .bmp file

5. Favorite links

6. Custom wallpaper file

7. Service .bmp for the LDAP configuration (if applicable)

8. Welcome message for Outlook Express

PREPARING THE WORKSTATION

Remember that the workstation on which you are assembling your Internet Explorer configuration can also act as your model for assembling Active Channels, toolbars, and other components. You can create these features and configurations ahead of time and import these custom features into your IEAK build when the time is right.

Active Channels

You may remember that with the IEAK, you can customize the Active Channel Guide on your desktop. Prior to deployment, you should decide whether to implement Active Channels, such as Microsoft, Disney, MSNBC, and many more. You can also create and build your own channels. Two quick things to remember about Active Channels:

1. The Active Channels configuration is directly affected by the license agreement chosen for the IEAK. Only corporate administrators can completely customize Active Channels.

2. Remember that you can also lock down the channel configuration with system policies and restrictions while using the IEAK Wizard or in the IEAK Profile Manager.

Desktop Update

As with Active Channels and software distribution, you can customize and import Desktop Update items as well. You can import desktop IFRAMES (Web pages displayed on the desktop), Web-based wallpaper, and channel screen savers. These options can be set on the workstation before or during use of the IEAK Wizard. It is usually a good idea to do as much as you can before running the IEAK Wizard. Following are some additional notes regarding the Desktop Update:

Desktop wallpaper

Remember that this content will be displayed in a window that is one-fourth the size of a normal Web page. With this in mind, it is worth testing and evaluating graphic size, fonts, and general appearance for consistency. These factors are dramatically affected by the desktop screen.

Channel screen savers

Channel screen savers enable you to navigate within the screen saver using the mouse without disrupting the screen saver. Sometimes the workstation appears "hung," or completely locked up, when actually the channel is merely being displayed as requested. You may want to ensure your end users are made aware of this through any training materials you prepare.

Overall load

As with all network-based applications, load is always a concern. Channels, as you know, place a load on the network on a scheduled, predetermined basis. These downloads can also be initiated manually at the user's request. Let's say your channel screen saver is set to display the headquarters' intranet site. Let's also say that at 9:00 PST, there will be a human resource teleconference that all 8,000 employees must attend. If you have set your screen savers to initiate after, say, 30 minutes of inactivity, then 30 minutes into this teleconference, chaos will likely break out on your network. All the workstations on your network will be initiating requests to the channel screen saver site at the same time. After taking several antacids, the administrator will realize that planning is the key to a successful implementation and future.

Desktop toolbars

You can customize the taskbar with several features and import these features into your IEAK configuration. Some of the options you can modify and import are:

- The Address bar
- The Quick Launch toolbar
- The Quick Links toolbar
- The Desktop bar

RUNNING THE IEAK WIZARD

Now it is time to assemble your IEAK configuration. For the sake of space, we will not go through every screen in the IEAK Wizard. Instead we'll cover only the topics in the scenarios I have just discussed. Because you have customized your configuration for every site (a total of eight), you have to create eight builds for your Internet Explorer implementation. We'll focus on the build for the Houston, Texas office for the remainder of the chapter.

Now you are ready to run the IEAK and create your first package. You have all of your custom files, URLs, and other information prepared. You also have your customization code handy so that you can be off and running.

TITLE BAR

The first configuration decision you need to make concerns your title bar text, as shown in Figure 12-2. I chose "Netdata" as the title so the employees know that this is a custom version for the organization.

As you can see, I also added the path to the Active Setup Wizard bitmap I created.

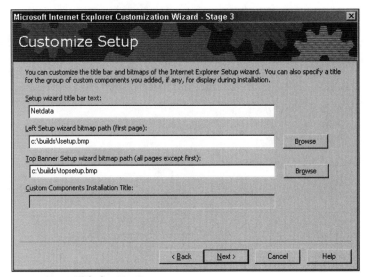

FIGURE 12-2 Title bar text

VERSION NUMBERS FOR ADD-ON COMPONENTS

You need to specify version numbers for your add-on components. Start at one by default, and increase every time your rerun a build for this configuration. You can also create a globally unique identifier for this package, as I did in Figure 12-3, which makes this configuration unique for Houston.

In the version information, you also specify the URL to your add-on component page. As you can see, I specified this for the local intranet server in case you perform a major upgrade to Internet Explorer in the future.

DOWNLOAD URLS

Next, you get to specify your download URLs. As I mentioned earlier, you need to specify that the local intranet site is primary, with the headquarters site being a secondary location in the event that the primary one is down. Figure 12-4 shows the URL configuration. Note that you only need to specify the URL here; `ie5setup.exe` will look at the root for the `ie4sites.dat` file in this configuration.

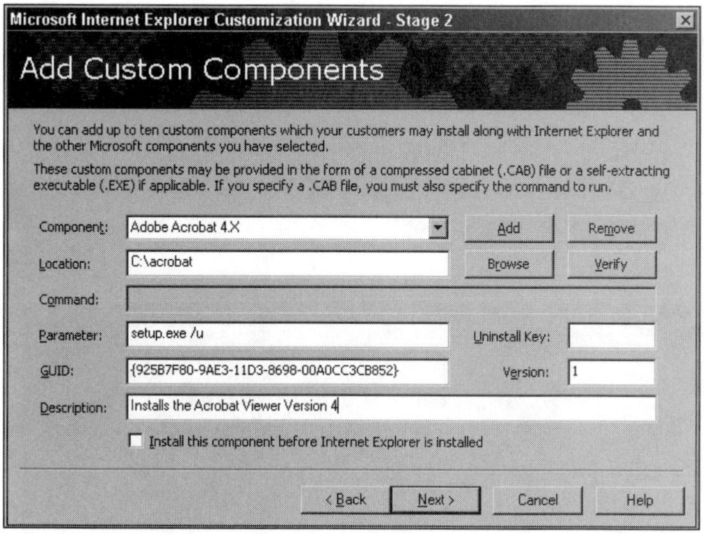

Figure 12-3 Version numbers

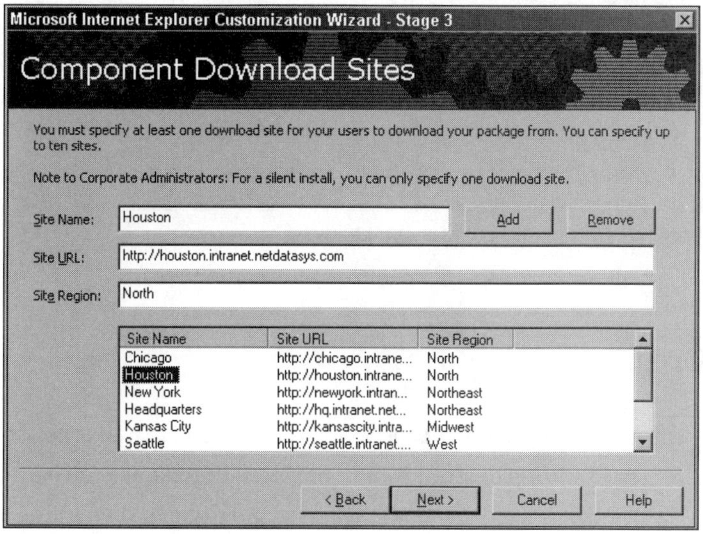

FIGURE 12-4 Download URLs

WINDOW TITLE AND TOOLBAR BACKGROUND

Next, you create the window title bar and specify the background toolbar bitmap. The text I entered in Figure 12-5 will make the window title say, "Microsoft Internet Explorer provided by Netdata." The toolbar bitmap, as you know, enables you to customize the menus.

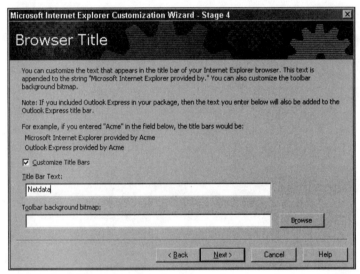

FIGURE 12-5   Title and toolbar background

START, SEARCH, AND SUPPORT

In Chapter 10, I talked about specifying the start and search pages. In Figure 12-6, I did this by localizing the start page to the local intranet. I decided to leave the search page as the default. As you know, each office will have to support the browser rollout for its users. With this in mind, you need to create a support page for each office.

FAVORITES AND LINKS

You don't want to confuse the users with too many favorites, so you should include links to the local intranet and the headquarters' intranet server. The headquarters server's home page provides links to the other sites in case the user wants to see what is going on in other offices. Figure 12-7 shows the Favorites and Links configuration.

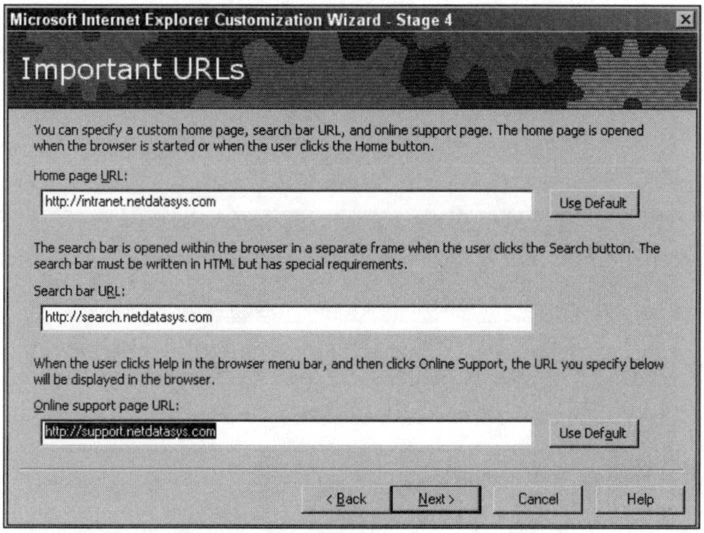

Figure 12-6 **Start and search pages**

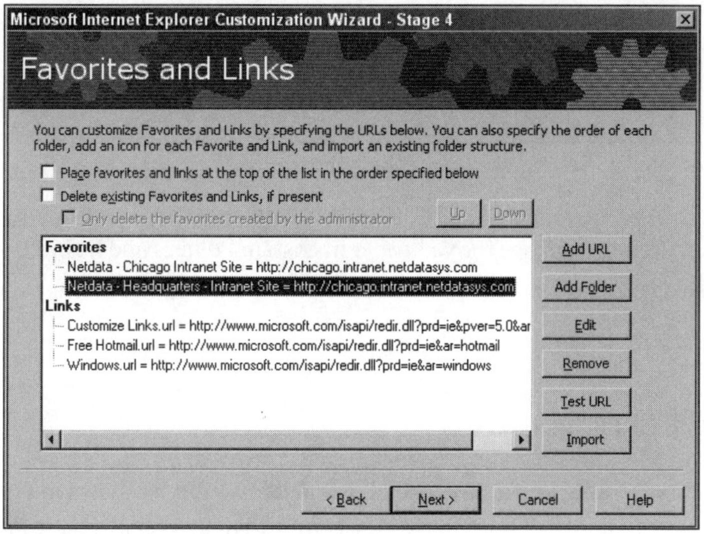

FIGURE 12-7 Favorites and Links

WELCOME MESSAGE

As discussed, you will include a welcome page on the local intranet. The URL is specified as shown in Figure 12-8. You also want to disable the welcome window in Internet Explorer in exchange for the welcome page; there is no need to be redundant. Give the users a little flexibility by not changing the desktop wallpaper at this time.

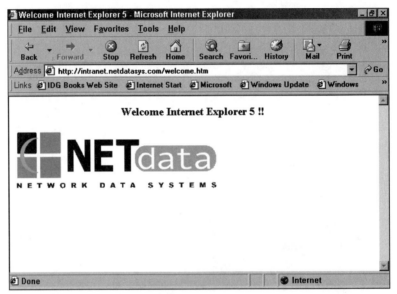

FIGURE 12-8 Setting up the welcome message

You can change the wallpaper in System Policies and Restrictions (the Profile Manager) if you want to force the users to use the same wallpaper.

USER AGENT STRING

Now you will set up a very special User Agent String, as shown in Figure 12-9. User Agent Strings are used by Webmasters to compile statistical information. User Agent Strings can also be used programmatically to specify special content for a specific string. In this case, you just want to see who is hitting which servers and when. The string, as you may notice, is a little cryptic (HOUTXOFC is the Houston Texas Office). I created the name this way intentionally so the string is more anonymous on the Internet. Remember that if you specify your company name in the string, Web servers can track this on the Internet. This may not be a good idea if you don't want your company's name being tracked on a site that your users should not have accessed in the first place.

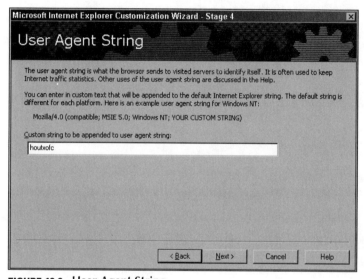

FIGURE 12-9 User Agent String

BROWSER CONFIGURATION

Next, you need to specify two of the most important parts of the IEAK configuration. First, you should specify the `.ins` file URL on the local intranet, and then the `.pac` location. Note that the time specified is every 240 minutes (four hours). This means that if any of the administrators want to make configuration changes, the process will take anywhere from a few minutes for some workstations, and up to four hours for others. Figure 12-10 shows the `.ins` and `.pac` configurations.

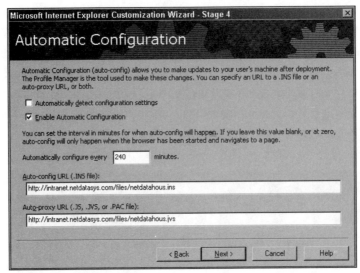

FIGURE 12-10   Configuring auto-proxy and auto-configuration

PROXY SETTINGS

Next, you actually make the proxy settings for the workstation configuration. You will use the same proxy server for all protocols and also bypass the proxy for local intranet addresses. Figure 12-11 shows the proxy configuration.

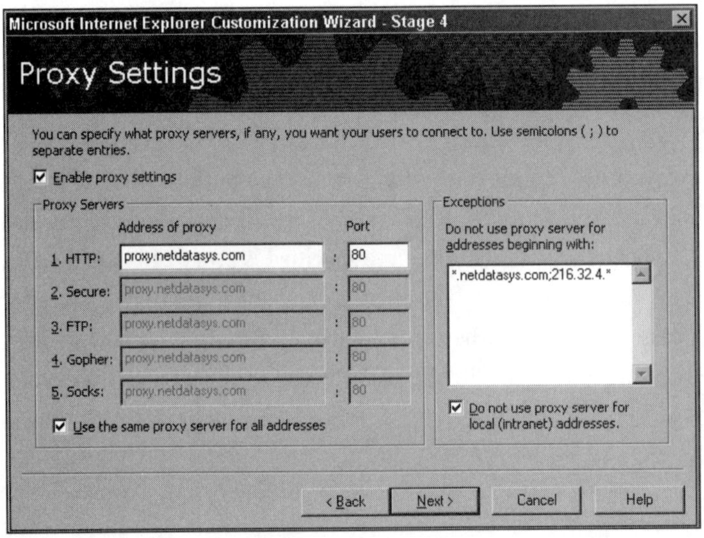

FIGURE 12-11   Proxy settings

You may also want to consider adding all the intranet servers to the local intranet zone list. This can give you some added protection for content located on these servers, and lets Internet Explorer know that these servers are safe.

 tip   **Did you know that you can use wildcards for IP address ranges and host names? For example, if you had an entire class C address range in your organization, such as 216.32.4.0, you could enter this in your proxy exclude list as 216.32.4.* This will exclude all addresses in this range. You can do the same with host names. For example, using the syntax** `*.netdatasys.com` **will exclude all hosts in the Netdatasys.com domain.**

Outlook Express Welcome Message

Just as an added nicety, you'll include a welcome message in each user's Outlook Express mailbox. This file is in HTML format and is copied down with the Internet Explorer installation. You can also specify the mail originator and the "reply to" address, as shown in Figure 12-12. If the user wants to reply, the replies go right to your Webmaster.

FIGURE 12-12 Welcome page

INTERNET MAIL

Now you have to configure Outlook Express. The organization has a POP3 server and an SMTP server for every office. As you planned ahead and gathered these names, this configuration will be a snap. In Figure 12-13, the names of the POP3 server and the SMTP server are specified.

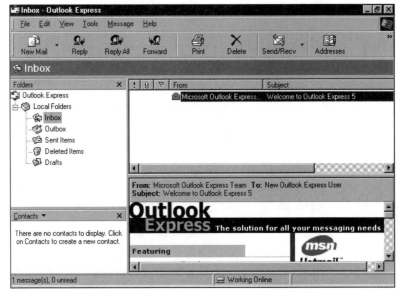

FIGURE 12-13 Internet mail

Note that Outlook Express is also made the default mail client.

You don't want to implement any restrictions at this point, so the package is ready to be compiled. When you select Finish at the end of the IEAK Wizard, your Houston package is complete.

After you have created packages for every site, you are ready to begin copying your files to the intranet servers. Make sure you pay special attention to the URLs at which you are copying files. There are static references to URLs in the custom Internet Explorer package for each server; you don't want any errors during and after the installation.

Well, that's all there is! You're ready to start installing Internet Explorer for this organization. In best-case scenarios, you would pilot the installation in one site before moving ahead to other sites. If you have the time to do this, I highly recommend it — it may uncover problems you didn't think about.

KEY POINT SUMMARY

In Chapter 12, we walked through the process of deploying Internet Explorer 5.

- We began by reviewing the topology of the organization and making decisions as to where we were going to deploy our installation files.

- We reviewed the workstation baseline and made decisions about where and how we were going to localize our version of Internet Explorer 5.

- We walked through configuration options for the browser, the application, and the other features that we were going to include in our browser package.

APPLYING WHAT YOU'VE LEARNED

This section is an opportunity to use what you've learned in this chapter. The labs provide you with important real-world practice using the skills you've learned.

Critical Thinking Labs

Lab 12.44 *Configuring Offline Viewing*

Your boss recently read an article in a popular computer magazine about Offline Viewing. Your boss has asked you to do a review of the organization and develop a plan to implement Offline Viewing for the user community. Following are listed the scenarios in which you could implement Offline Viewing. Describe whether or not you would choose to implement Offine Viewing for these users and why you would or would not. Use Internet Explorer 5 to assist you with your answer.

1. Company employees with very fast, local Internet access.

2. Satellite office employees with WAN access to the Internet that is somewhat slow.

3. Sales staff on the road most of the time with little or no Internet access.

4. Warehouse staff with a local LAN but no connectivity to any other office.

Lab 12.45 *Choosing Security Options*

You are given the task of deploying Internet Explorer 5 in your organization. You will deploy the browser to your internal users using the IEAK; the platform will be Windows 95 and Windows NT. You have been asked to provide a security solution for each scenario that will ensure that the workstation is as secure as possible, but will not impede the user's ability to work. Which features would you consider adding or restricting based on each given scenario?

1. Satellite offices with no Internet access.

2. Corporate offices with fast, reliable Internet access.

3. Corporate kiosks located in the main entrance of every office.

4. Corporate call centers with access to only one Web-based application.

Considering these scenarios, which tool would you use to enforce your security settings? Which features would you consider using to comply with the company's security concerns?

Lab 12.46 *Configuring Outlook Express with the IEAK*

You have been asked to incorporate Outlook Express into your browser configuration. Given the following requirements, describe where these requirements can be accommodated using the IEAK. Name specific locations within the IEAK to configure these options.

1. You will provide your users with access to the company's POP and SMTP mail server using the correct tools and make the server names read-only. You will include a configuration for a company news server and not allow the users to add any additional accounts.

2. You will use the `welcome.html` file provided by your Web developers as the welcome message when the users first install Outlook Express. Specify `ie5help@widget.com` as the sender and reply address.

3. Configure Outlook Express as the default mail and news program. Include a news server named `news2.widget.com` as one of the default news servers.

4. Disable the Tip of the Day from view.

5. Use the following text as a signature for your e-mail users, "This message from a user at Widget.com may not reflect the views or policies of widget.com. For more information, please contact webmaster@widget.com." Also, do not use HTML as the message composition default.

Troubleshooting the Internet Explorer Suite

About Chapter 13

Getting your package out to your users is only half of the job. To deploy, troubleshoot, and resolve issues with Internet Explorer, it is a good idea to know your organization's operating platforms, networks, and other configuration related data that you will need to support the suite of software. The exam will test you on your knowledge in troubleshooting various problems with configuring the software. Pay close attention to the tools used in this chapter, such as Ping, Nslookup, and Tracert.

In Chapter 13, we are going to walk through how to use each troubleshooting tool used with Internet Explorer. We are also going to talk about the resources available to you to troubleshoot and resolve issues with the Internet Explorer 5 suite of software.

UTILITIES YOU CAN USE

Armed with some of the following utilities, you can successfully troubleshoot problems and issues related to connectivity in Internet Explorer 5. Let's talk about troubleshooting utilities in more detail.

Ping

Ping enables you to determine whether your destination host is responding and to troubleshoot your own TCP/IP configuration by "pinging" your workstation with your loop-back address. One of the most popular utilities, Ping sends a series of four ICMP (Internet Control Message Protocol) packets to a destination address. The Ping utility can be used with TCP/IP addresses, host names (such as ftp.idgbooks.com), and NetBIOS names (such as SERVER1). To ping your own workstation, type the following at the command line:

```
Ping 127.0.0.1
```

Ping is also used to troubleshoot connectivity to other hosts. Try to ping the Web server at www.netdatasys.com. You should receive a response that looks something like Figure 13-1.

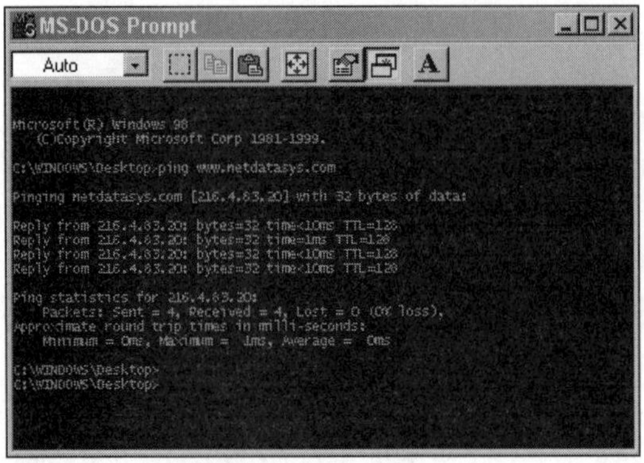

FIGURE 13-1 The Ping command

Ping basically sends a packet to the destination; the packet is then routed directly back to you, the originator. The packet is 32 bytes in size and is sent four times to the destination. If you know the host's TCP/IP address but do not know the host name, you can use the Ping command with the -a switch to get the host name. An example of the -a switch with Ping is shown in Figure 13-2.

FIGURE 13-2 The Ping –a command

Tracert

The Tracert utility is used to determine the path that a packet takes to the destination. Tracert is one of the best utilities to use for TCP/IP-related troubleshooting. Using Tracert, you can identify where in the packet's path connectivity has stopped. To trace a route from your workstation, type the following at the command line:

```
Tracert www.digex.net
```

The message shown in Figure 13-3 is similar to what you should see on your screen.

The way in which you are connected to the Internet determines the results of your trace route. The common denominator in this case should be the IP addresses of an ISP by the name of Digex.

FIGURE 13-3   The Tracert command

Winipcfg

The Windows IP Configuration utility displays the TCP/IP information for your Windows 95/98 workstation. You can use this tool to assist in troubleshooting connectivity issues between the browser and the destination URL. These utilities display important configuration information regarding the TCP/IP configuration of the workstation. For example, you can obtain the unique TCP/IP address of the workstation, the DNS server's addresses, and other TCP/IP-related information. If you have not done so already, familiarize yourself with this information. You will need to know how and when to use these utilities when your users have problems. Figure 13-4 shows the Windows-based Winipcfg utility.

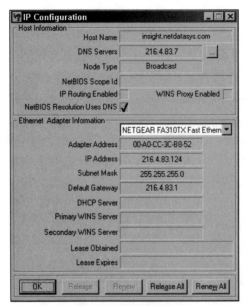

FIGURE 13-4 The Winipcfg utility

Winipcfg displays a variety of information, described in the following list:

- *Host Name*. This is your workstation's TCP/IP fully qualified domain name (FQDN). This can be assigned either manually or by software in a case where the administrator wants to control the naming conventions used on the network. The FQDN is a combination of the TCP/IP host name and the domain name, such as `jeffsmith.idgbooks.com`.

- *DNS Servers*. This is the primary DNS (Domain Name Service) server that has been configured on your workstation. The DNS server translates host names to IP addresses. The DNS server also translates IP addresses to TCP/IP addresses (known as a reverse lookup). The primary DNS server is displayed in the IP Configuration window. You can configure additional servers in the Network Control Panel applet in Windows 95, 98, and NT.

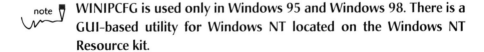

note   **WINIPCFG is used only in Windows 95 and Windows 98. There is a GUI-based utility for Windows NT located on the Windows NT Resource kit.**

- *Node Type*. The Node Type entry displays the NetBIOS broadcast type that the workstation is configured for. NetBIOS can be configured in several different ways with multiple combinations, such as Hybrid, Broadcast, and so on.

- *NetBIOS Scope Id*. The NetBIOS Scope ID relates primarily to WINS servers. WINS (Windows Internet Naming Service) provides a database of NetBIOS names with their related TCP/IP addresses. WINS, much like DNS, translates NetBIOS names to TCP/IP addresses. The NetBIOS Scope ID is basically a wall between networks that an administrator can configure to prohibit NetBIOS broadcasts from one network to another. Each network is assigned a unique NetBIOS Scope ID.

- *IP Routing Enabled*. This feature enables the Windows NT Server and Windows NT Workstation to act as routers. The server or workstation is assigned a TCP/IP address for each network card (or modem) in the machine, and IP routing is enabled.

 in the real world **IP routing does exist in Windows 95/98, but is not supported by Microsoft.**

- *WINS Proxy Enabled*. Some routers cannot forward NetBIOS-based broadcasts and other NetBIOS-based traffic. A WINS proxy agent is installed on the network and is configured to send the NetBIOS traffic to a specific address, usually a WINS server.

- *NetBIOS Resolution Uses DNS*. Microsoft DNS servers can also be configured to perform lookups on a Microsoft WINS server. If a name request cannot be resolved on a DNS server, the request is checked against a WINS server for resolution. If a match is found, the name and address are sent back to the client.

- *Ethernet Adapter Information*. If you have more than one network adapter configured, you can pull down the list box for more adapters.

- *Adapter Address*. Also known as the MAC address, this number is your workstation's unique identity on the network.

- *IP Address*. This is the IP address of your workstation.

- *Subnet Mask*. Subnet masks are 32-bit numbers that enable devices such as servers, workstations, and other hardware to determine which part of a TCP/IP address is the network ID and which part is the host ID.

- *Default Gateway.* When a packet is sent out to the network and is not destined for the local network in TCP/IP, the packet is forwarded to the default gateway. Default gateways are usually routers on the network that store the paths for your packet to reach its destination on your network or on the Internet.

- *DHCP Server*. The DHCP Server entry shows the TCP/IP address of your DHCP server. As explained in Chapter 1, the DHCP server dynamically assigns you a unique TCP/IP address.

- *Primary WINS Server.* This entry displays the TCP/IP address of your first listed WINS (Windows Internet Naming Service) server. The WINS server provides the user with NetBIOS-to-TCP/IP address translation. It also enables you to search for common names on the network, such as "SERVER1."

- *Secondary WINS Server.* This entry displays the TCP/IP address of your second listed WINS (Windows Internet Naming Service) server.

- *Lease Obtained*. This is the date and time that your DHCP lease was obtained. As explained in Chapter 1, the DHCP server dynamically assigns a TCP/IP address to the workstation for a specific period of time called a lease. When a lease has reached 50 percent of its time expiration, the client attempts to renew the lease with the DHCP server. If the DHCP server is unavailable, the client continues to use the address until the expiration of the lease.

- *Lease Expires*. This is the date and time that your DHCP lease expires. Once this time has passed and the lease has not been renewed, the user will be unable to use TCP/IP-related services on their workstation.

IPconfig

The IPconfig utility is used on Windows NT Server and Windows NT Workstation. IPconfig displays various TCP/IP-related information at the command line level. Because IPconfig is a command line utility, it is not as easy to use as Windows 95 Winipcfg. Generally, you use the IPconfig utility with the /ALL switch to get IP information for a Windows NT-based computer. The information provided at the command line is almost identical to that of Winipcfg, except that all adapter information is shown. For example, if you have two adapters installed, IP information for both adapters is displayed.

> note
>
> **Although this is not covered on the exam, the IPconfig utility is also included in Windows 98.**

Here is what the output from the IPconfig utility used on Windows 98 looks like:

```
Windows 98 IP Configuration
Host Name . . . . . . . . . : insight.netdatasys.com
DNS Servers . . . . . . . . : 216.4.83.7
                                    216.4.83.9
Node Type . . . . . . . . . : Broadcast
NetBIOS Scope ID. . . . . . :
IP Routing Enabled. . . . . : No
WINS Proxy Enabled. . . . . : No
NetBIOS Resolution Uses DNS : Yes
0 Ethernet adapter :
Description . . . . . . . . : PPP Adapter.
Physical Address. . . . . . : 44-45-53-54-00-00
DHCP Enabled. . . . . . . . : Yes
IP Address. . . . . . . . . : 0.0.0.0
Subnet Mask . . . . . . . . : 0.0.0.0
Default Gateway . . . . . . :
DHCP Server . . . . . . . . : 255.255.255.255
Primary WINS Server . . . . :
Secondary WINS Server . . . :
Lease Obtained. . . . . . . :
Lease Expires . . . . . . . :
1 Ethernet adapter :
Description . . . . . . . . : AOL Adapter
Physical Address. . . . . . : 44-45-53-54-61-6F
DHCP Enabled. . . . . . . . : Yes
IP Address. . . . . . . . . : 0.0.0.0
Subnet Mask . . . . . . . . : 0.0.0.0
Default Gateway . . . . . . :
DHCP Server . . . . . . . . : 255.255.255.255
```

```
Primary WINS Server . . . . :
Secondary WINS Server . . . :
Lease Obtained. . . . . . . :
Lease Expires . . . . . . . :
2 Ethernet adapter :
Description . . . . . . . . : NETGEAR FA310TX Fast Ethernet
PCI Adapter
Physical Address. . . . . . : 00-A0-CC-3C-B8-52
DHCP Enabled. . . . . . . . : No
IP Address. . . . . . . . . : 216.4.83.124
Subnet Mask . . . . . . . . : 255.255.255.0
Default Gateway . . . . . . : 216.4.83.1
Primary WINS Server . . . . :
Secondary WINS Server . . . :
Lease Obtained. . . . . . . :
Lease Expires . . . . . . . :
```

Netstat

The Netstat utility enables you to view network protocol information at the command line. With a combination of command line switches, this utility has several uses. Some of the command-line switches are:

```
NETSTAT [-a] [-e] [-n] [-s] [-p proto] [-r] [interval]
```

- -a displays all connections and listening ports.
- -e displays Ethernet statistics. This may be combined with the -s option.
- -n displays addresses and port numbers in numerical form.
- -s displays per-protocol statistics. By default, statistics are shown for TCP, UDP, and IP; the -p option may be used to specify a subset of the default.
- -p proto shows connections for the protocol specified by proto; proto may be TCP or UDP. If used with the -s option to display per-protocol statistics, proto may be TCP, UDP, or IP.
- -r displays the routing table.

o `interval` redisplays selected statistics, pausing interval seconds between each display. Press Ctrl+C to stop redisplay in statistics. If interval is omitted, Netstat prints the current configuration information only once.

When troubleshooting complex network problems, you will probably use the Netstat command from time to time. Figure 13-5 shows the Netstat command on one of my workstations. This command was run with the `-a` switch and shows that I am currently logged in to Microsoft's FTP server.

FIGURE 13-5 The Netstat utility

Nbtstat

Nbtstat is a great utility for troubleshooting Windows NT and Windows 95 network problems. With Nbtstat, you can view the NetBIOS name cache of remote servers and workstations and perform other NetBIOS-related troubleshooting tasks. Nbtstat is most widely used to view broadcast services by a Windows NT server. The following are some of the command line options available with Nbtstat:

```
NBTSTAT [-a RemoteName] [-A IP address] [-c] [-n] [-r] [-R]
[-s] [S] [interval] ]
```

o `-a` (adapter status) lists the remote machine's name table when given its name.

o `-A` (Adapter status) lists the remote machine's name table when given its IP address.

- ○ -c (cache) lists the remote name cache, including the IP addresses.

- ○ -n (names) lists local NetBIOS names.

- ○ -r (resolved) lists names resolved by broadcast and by WINS.

- ○ -R (Reload) purges and reloads the remote cache name table.

- ○ -s (sessions) lists sessions table, converting destination IP addresses to host names through the hosts file.

- ○ -S (Sessions) lists sessions table with the destination IP addresses.

- ○ RemoteName is the name of the remote host machine.

- ○ IP address is the dotted decimal representation of the IP address.

- ○ interval redisplays selected statistics, pausing interval seconds between each display. Press Ctrl+C to stop redisplaying statistics.

Figure 13-6 is an example of the Nbtstat command in use.

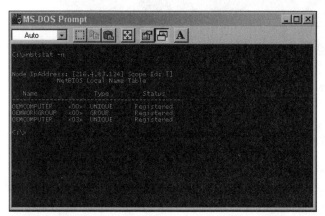

FIGURE 13-6 The Nbtstat utility

Nslookup

NSLOOKUP.EXE is the primary troubleshooting utility for DNS-related issues in Windows NT. Using Nslookup, you can locate host names and IP addresses for devices that have DNS entries. The syntax for Nslookup is very simple:

NSLOOKUP -{option} {host being located} {DNS server}

You can get all the command options by typing Nslookup and then typing help. If you leave off the DNS server name, the currently configured DNS server is used.

Network Monitor

The utility is not quite as comprehensive as its Windows NT counterpart, but it can provide you with some valuable information on the performance of your network and the networking aspects of your workstation. You can use this utility to troubleshoot network-related problems, such as excessive traffic and collisions. You can find this utility in Start ⇨ Programs ⇨ Accessories ⇨ System Utilities. If you do not see it there, you can install it in the Add-Remove Programs option in the Control Panel. The program is located under System Tools.

KNOWN ISSUES

Quite a few known issues and incompatibilities exist with the Internet Explorer suite of software. Let's go over some of the most prevalent.

Internet Explorer Browser

Like any other major application, Internet Explorer cannot account for every possible hardware/software combination, it's just not feasible. Microsoft has done an excellent job of integrating Internet Explorer 5 into the Windows 95, 98, and NT operating systems. For incompatible software that may affect your deployment, check TechNet for the latest information.

Cache and Temporary Internet Files Folder

If you are using roaming profiles, remember that in Windows NT the user must have full control permissions to the Temporary Internet Files folder. If the user does not have sufficient permissions, objects cannot be cached and other strange behavior can occur. Remember that the cache is stored in a subdirectory under <Windir> by default. If you restrict permissions to this folder in Windows NT for the group "Everyone," chances are the computer will not boot.

If a user fills up the home directory with Internet files, the home directory must be cleared for the user to save additional files to the home directory. Internet Explorer itself must clear space in the home directory to store newer cache files. This type of traffic over an already bogged-down network can cause problems. If the network is already congested, the traffic generated from the constant updating of temporary files will cause the browser to be slow or unresponsive. Try using the local driver whenever possible.

Proxy Server Issues

If you have multiple users at a workstation and have not used the Internet Explorer Administration Kit (IEAK) to build your installation of Internet Explorer, each user must configure his or her proxy server settings. In this situation, you have several options available to you.

1. You can use the Single Disk branding option that you learned about in Chapter 7. This will provide proxy configuration information for your users for every existing and new profile that is created.

2. You can use an auto-update script on your Web server. To enable scripting, use the Tools ➪ Internet Options ➪ Connections ➪ Settings to point the users to your script.

3. I have seen many organizations that include a registry update in the login script that updates the registry key for the auto-update scripts. The key is located in `hkey_users\.default\software\microsoft\windows\ current version\internet settings\autoconfigurl`.

Usually, the result of no proxy configuration is the inability to navigate to any site on the Internet or an intranet.

Security Zone Problems

Many reported problems relate to security settings in large enterprise environments. If you decide to modify the default security settings during your IEAK build, you should document the changes that you make in a place that your support organization has access to. Once you have documented your changes, you should provide copies to anyone who may have to support the browser.

Most of the problems that I have seen are caused by developers writing ActiveX controls that they do not sign. When these controls are put out on the Internet, they do not work because the controls are located in the user's Internet security zone, which does not allow unsigned ActiveX controls.

HTTP/1.0 404 Object Not Found Error

Several conditions cause the 404 Object Not Found error, the first being nonexistent files. The two add-on HTML pages, `addon95.htm` and `addonnt.htm`, must exist at the URL you specified in the IEAK. If these pages are not present, the 404 error is displayed. I also encountered a problem when placing these files on a Solaris/UNIX server; some of my clients got the same error. The answer is easy: filenames in UNIX are sometimes case-sensitive. The directories on UNIX servers, especially FTP servers, should be in lowercase. Be sure, however, that the `.cab`, `.cif`, and `.dat` files are in uppercase, or the Internet Explorer download will fail. Remember this when entering URLs that are located on a UNIX-based server.

Even with Microsoft Internet Information Server, a known issue with using different cases in the file extension exists. If you use `xxxx.Ins`, Internet Explorer cannot read the file. Be sure to use consistent case formats, and always use lowercase for `.ins` files.

Active Setup

Troubleshooting setup is fairly easy. When the setup is launched, a log file called `Active Setup Log.txt` is created in the `C:\Windows` (`WINNT` in Windows NT) folder. The purpose of this file is to track the file download process and log the Internet Explorer setup process. If the download fails, Smart Recovery reads this log file to determine where the installation failed. When the installation is initiated again, the download process can pick up where it left off. The Active Setup Log is the first thing to check if your Active Setup fails.

As you will see in the following example, the log details data gathered during the installation phase of Internet Explorer. The log can assist you in troubleshooting failed installation routines that install the Internet Explorer suite. When viewing the file, pay attention to any lines that show the word "failed" or "error." These keywords can be used in searching to find the cause of a failed installation.

Here is an example of the Active Setup Log.

```
****************************************************************
Microsoft Setup Log File Opened 10/31/99 22:12:53
Version number: 3.01.0.1622
Running under Windows NT.
[22:12:53  Start of Pass: 0]
```

```
Command Line: /T ie40nt.stf  /S
C:\WINNT\msdownld.tmp\AS3F4B1A.tmp\ /QT /g "C:\WINNT\IE Setup
Log.Txt"
[22:12:53  Start of Pass: 1]
Floppy mode
Processing the header information of the file:
C:\WINNT\msdownld.tmp\AS3F4B1A.tmp\ie40nt.stf
************************************************************
  Application name: IE4.DLL
  Application version: 5.00.2314.1003(1033)
  Dialog caption base: Internet Explorer 5 and Internet Tools
  Frame caption: Internet Explorer 5 and Internet Tools
  Frame bitmap: ie4.dll, 102
  Modules: Themes, Desktop Theme Selector
  HLP file name: acmsetup.hlp
  INF file name: iebase.inf
  MSApps mode: local
[22:12:54  Start of Pass: 2]
[22:12:54  Start of Pass: 3]
[22:12:54  Start of Pass: 4]
[22:12:54  Start of Pass: 5]
 Object 1 - Setup is replacing an older version of Microsoft
Internet Explorer in the folder: C:\Program
Files\Plus!\Microsoft Internet\.
[22:12:54  Start of Pass: 6]
Phase = camfInitializeObject
Begin Custom Action: LogAndUpdatePhases
  Safe = 1
  CamfFriendlyName for jobexec: Initializing
End Custom Action: LogAndUpdatePhases
[22:12:55  Start of Pass: 7]
Phase = camfCalcDstDir
Begin Custom Action: LogAndUpdatePhases
  Safe = 1
End Custom Action: LogAndUpdatePhases
Phase = camfPropagateDstDir
```

```
Begin Custom Action: LogAndUpdatePhases
  Safe = 1
End Custom Action: LogAndUpdatePhases
Phase = camfGetCost
Begin Custom Action: LogAndUpdatePhases
  Safe = 1
End Custom Action: LogAndUpdatePhases
[22:12:56  Start of Pass: 8]
[22:12:56  Start of Pass: 9]
Phase = camfCheckObjectIBSE
Begin Custom Action: LogAndUpdatePhases
  Safe = 1
End Custom Action: LogAndUpdatePhases
Phase = camfSetModeOfObject
Begin Custom Action: LogAndUpdatePhases
  Safe = 1
End Custom Action: LogAndUpdatePhases
[22:12:57  Start of Pass: 10]
Phase = camfCheckObjectIBSE
Begin Custom Action: LogAndUpdatePhases
  Safe = 1
End Custom Action: LogAndUpdatePhases
Phase = camfCheckObjectIBSE
Begin Custom Action: LogAndUpdatePhases
  Safe = 1
End Custom Action: LogAndUpdatePhases
Phase = camfSetModeOfObject
Begin Custom Action: LogAndUpdatePhases
  Safe = 1
End Custom Action: LogAndUpdatePhases
Phase = camfFinalizeObject
Begin Custom Action: LogAndUpdatePhases
  Safe = 1
End Custom Action: LogAndUpdatePhases
Begin Custom Action: ShortPath
End Custom Action: ShortPath
```

```
Begin Custom Action: IsSP4LevelCryptoInstalled
  Version of C:\WINNT\System32\crypt32.dll: 5.131.1877.4
  SP4 level crypto is  installed.
End Custom Action: IsSP4LevelCryptoInstalled
Begin Custom Action: SaveChannelFolder
  Saved ChannelFolderName to the registry.
  Saved LinkFolderName to the registry.
End Custom Action: SaveChannelFolder
Begin Custom Action: UpdateVersionOnFile
Fileversion :C:\WINNT\System32\iepeers.dll: :0:0
End Custom Action: UpdateVersionOnFile
[22:13:00  Start of Pass: 11]
Phase = camfAddToCopyList
Begin Custom Action: LogAndUpdatePhases
  Safe = 1
  CamfFriendlyName for jobexec: Backing up current
configuration
End Custom Action: LogAndUpdatePhases
Begin Custom Action: FileSave
Date: 10/31/1999 (mm/dd/yyyy)  Time: 22:13:00 (hh:mm:ss)
```

 This is not a complete log file; this is meant to give you some examples of what the log looks like in real life. Open your own Active Setup Log when you have an opportunity.

You can check the `Active Setup Log.txt` for errors by opening the file in a text editor. Once you have located the error, use Table 13-1 to determine where the installation failure occurred.

TABLE 13-1 HRESULT ERROR CODES	
HRESULT **ERROR CODES**	*DOWNLOAD PHASE*
0	Initializing (making a temporary folder and checking disk space)
1	Dependency (checking for all dependencies)

HRESULT ERROR CODES	DOWNLOAD PHASE
2	Downloading (from the server to download folder)
3	Copying (from download folder to temporary installation folder)
4	Retrying (restarting download because of timeout or some other download error)
5	Checking trust
6	Extracting (decompressing files from a .cab file)
7	Running (.inf or .exe files)
8	Finished (installation complete)
9	Download finished (download complete)

The following codes represent other common errors:

- *80100003*. During installation, one or more files are missing from the download folder. (For example, the administrator did not copy all the files necessary for the installation or has assigned improper permissions.)

- *800bxxxx*. Anything starting with 800b is a trust failure (for example, 800b010b indicates that the trust check failed). This usually occurs when a file is corrupted or otherwise damaged during the download process.

- *800Cxxxx*. Anything starting with 800C is a URLmon failure (for example, 800C005 indicates that a file or server was not found, and 800C00B indicates that the connection timed out). This error is usually caused by network congestion or server overloads.

- *8004004*. A user stopped the installation by selecting cancel, Ctrl+Alt+Delete, and so on.

During the last phase of Active Setup, Runonce processes entries such as file replacements, registry entries, and so on, that could not be performed during the initial setup. A log of this activity called RunonceEx Log.txt can give you some assistance in troubleshooting these types of issues. The log file is located in the C:\<WINDIR> folder and can be opened in any text editor. Look in the file for the .dll name that failed, and look at the status to see where the registration failed.

Errors Relating to Digital Signatures

For some browsers to download files, some components of the download may have to be digitally signed from a vendor, such as Verisign. As previous chapters explain, the digital signature provides verification that the content is not harmful to the user's workstation. After you complete your custom Internet Explorer build, the following files should be signed with a digital signature:

- `Branding.cab`
- `Desktop.cab`
- `Ie40cif.cab`
- `IE4setup.exe`
- `Folder<n>.cab`
- `Chl<xxxx>.cab`

Windows NT Workstation Issues

You must be a local administrator to complete the Internet Explorer installation. The easiest way to accomplish this task is to enable the AutoAdminLogon options in Windows NT remotely. This option enables you to script a change to the registry that enables an account to log on to the workstation automatically. This account is an administrator-level account that can complete the Internet Explorer installation. For more information, check out article Q185339 in the Microsoft Knowledge Base.

You can also use the AutoAdminLogon in end-user kiosks. As you know, you cannot boot Windows NT without logging in to the workstation by default. With the AutoAdminLogon, you can enable this feature so that when the workstation is rebooted, the workstation logs in without user intervention.

Failure to Download

In my experience, the most likely cause of a failure to download information about available installation sites is that network congestion or an overloaded server is preventing you from accessing the download server for Internet Explorer. The best workaround is to select another site to download the application. If this happens to your users, you may want to consider immediately adding another server to your download locations to help spread the load of your Internet Explorer downloads.

Invalid Folder Path

The user may see the message "the folder '<path>' is invalid" when trying to install Internet Explorer on a network or virtual drive. The Internet Explorer installation looks for fixed drives on your workstation. If none exist, you may also get the error "Setup could not retrieve the information needed for the installation." Internet Explorer can be installed only to a fixed local drive; network-based configurations (Internet Explorer located on the server) are not supported.

Outlook Express

You can immediately do several things to troubleshoot Outlook Express. After verifying that the TCP/IP configuration of the workstation is valid, the first thing to do is to verify that you are able to connect to the mail server. Verify the problem and attempt to send and receive mail by sending the message to the same account from which the mail originated. If errors occur, try using the mail logging option in the Advanced tab of Outlook Express Tools ⇨ Options. Then attempt to connect to and send mail from the server again. At this point, a log file is created for both POP and SMTP mail in the Program Files ⇨ Outlook Express ⇨ Default User ⇨ Mail directory. Two separate files, `pop3.log` and `smtp.log`, contain error information compiled during the login attempt.

Based on the criteria of the log, you can verify that the mail server is in operation by tracing a route to the mail server with Tracert and attempting to send mail from another user's workstation. If everything is working, check the Tools ⇨ Accounts ⇨ Mail tab. In the Properties ⇨ Servers tab, you can verify the servers that you are attempting to connect, to ensure that the host name is entered correctly. Immediately below, you can also ensure that the password is correct by reentering the password. You may also want to try to send mail from another user's workstation with the problem user's account. You may find that the account is disabled or needs the password changed.

A big consideration with Outlook Express and any other network application is the state of the network itself. If a lot of congestion exists on the network, Outlook Express may have difficulty in connecting to the mail server. The length of time that Outlook Express can wait until the application establishes a connection with the mail server is a configurable option called a timeout. You can configure Outlook Express to timeout anywhere from 30 seconds to five minutes.

tip   **If you have a user that uninstalls Outlook Express 5, but remembers that he or she needs copies of their messages, look in the Program Files\Outlook Express folder. The message files do not get deleted by default.**

IMAP Users

Message Rules allow you to process inbound messages and manipulate them based on a set of criteria that you define. Rules allow you to work with your mail more effectively. Unfortunately, IMAP Users cannot use message rules in Outlook Express.

Slow starts of Outlook Express

Some users have reported problems with Outlook Express starting up very slowly. This behavior has been attributed to a damaged Outlook Express file called imagehlp.dll. This happens frequently when uninstalling the McAfee Virus scan. This can be repaired by extracting a copy of the file from the installation media.

NetMeeting

NetMeeting is a very simple application and normally requires little or no support for the end user once the application is configured and the user is comfortable with NetMeeting navigation. In certain instances, you may run into the problem of microphone sensitivity.

Sometimes, the user modifies the default settings for the microphone in NetMeeting, which makes the application incapable of adjusting the sensitivity of the microphone. You can correct this by adjusting the microphone sensitivity using the audio tuning wizard.

Unless there is a major problem, you should let NetMeeting adjust the sensitivity for you. You can also adjust the speaker volume and auto-tune the microphone by selecting the tuning wizard. Between these two options, you should be able to resolve any audio issues.

Working Offline

Internet Explorer 5 provides a feature in the File menu that enables you to work offline. When this feature is enabled, NetMeeting cannot connect to ILS servers and other NetMeeting users. When the user puts Internet Explorer into offline mode, this creates a known issue that prevents the user from being able to make any NetMeeting connections. The fix is to put Internet Explorer back in online mode by clearing the checkbox in the File menu.

ILS Servers

To browse lists of NetMeeting users, you need to connect to an ILS server to view the LDAP-based services. If you are unable to connect, try pinging the ILS server from DOS. If you are not successful, the server may be having problems, or a larger network problem may exist. Tracing a route to the ILS server can assist you in troubleshooting connectivity within your own network.

Reach Out 5.0

Microsoft NetMeeting 3.0 is not compatible with Reach Out 5.0. Reach Out 5.0 is a popular remote connectivity tool used by many organizations. Reach Out allows your users to connect as if they were local to the PC over a dial-up or VPN connection.

Dual-Homed Workstations

In some cases, problems exist in connecting to a directory service in workstations that have more than one configured network interface card, also known as dual-homed. In some cases, users may have a business need to connect to two local networks via a different network interface card. In the cases that I have seen, these setups tend to generate a lot of support calls. You may want to consider assisting the user in obtaining another solution to meet their needs.

Windows NT

To share applications using the application-sharing features, the NT workstation or server has to be running at least Service Pack 3 for Windows NT. In most cases, the user can tell you what service pack they are running on their workstation by selecting Start⇨Run and typing **WINMSD**. WINMSD is a diagnostic utility included in Windows NT that will show the user the configuration information related to Windows NT. You can also consider using the inventory features of the Systems Management Server if you have this tool available to you.

Sun Solaris

If you have an Ultra 5 or an Ultra 10, you need to apply the video card patch from Sun in order to use Internet Explorer 5. Check out Sunsoft for more details.

You can run Internet Explorer 5 on Solaris 2.5, with patch 103792-09. Check out Sunsoft for this patch and any current updates.

The user agent is different for Unix users. If you parse your Web server logs for usage information, you may see something that looks like this for your Solaris users.

- Sparc 5, Solaris 2.5.1:Mozilla/4.0 (compatible; MSIE 5.0; SunOS 5.5.1 sun4m; X11)

- Any Ultra, Solaris 2.5.1:Mozilla/4.0 (compatible; MSIE 5.0; SunOS 5.5.1 sun4u;X11)

Internet Explorer 5 also includes support for NTLM Challenge Response authentication for Sun Solaris. You can configure your IIS 4.0 Web server for NTLM and allow the same access to Sun users as a Windows 95/98/NT workstation.

 tip **Windows 2000 supports Kerberos encryption, which you will be able to use in Windows 2000 and Sun Solaris.**

NetShow

Supporting Microsoft NetShow is fairly simple, as is supporting Microsoft NetMeeting. Some common issues with NetShow are as follows.

Failure of the NetShow Encoder

The NetShow Encoder requires the presence of DCOM. DCOM is installed by default in Windows 98 and Windows NT, but it is an add-on for Windows 95. Download DCOM for Windows 95 from `http://www.microsoft.com/com`. After the DCOM installation is complete, rerun the Encoder installation and try again.

Failure to receive NetShow broadcasts

One of the most popular manufacturers of PCMCIA cards, Xircom, had problems with early editions of its IIPS model Ethernet card and IP multicasting. Under the original set of drivers issued with the card, IP multicasting was not supported at all. When the issue was discovered, Xircom released a new driver for the IIPS. You can download the driver and use NetShow with IP multicasting by downloading the latest drivers from `http://www.xircom.com`.

Administration Kit

Indisputably, Internet Explorer 5 is a complicated application. The Internet Explorer Administration Kit (IEAK) is a tool that you can use to standardize your Internet Explorer 5 configuration. This standard configuration enables you to support your users more efficiently. Like any other application, there are some common IEAK-related support issues that you should be aware of.

Failure of the INS file

A known configuration concern with `.ins` files is to allow the directory to have read and execute access on the Web server. In addition, the directory must be allowed anonymous access and provide no authentication, such as Microsoft Challenge Response (MS CHAP). If any authentication is provided, the auto-configuration will not work properly.

Branding errors

Check your package for files that you created with long filenames (longer than the standard 8.3 format). If you find any, regenerate the package without the long filenames. Try to maintain the 8.3 naming convention when using the IEAK.

Microsoft Systems Management Server (SMS) has a similar problem with long filenames. If an SMS server distributes your Internet Explorer Administration Kit package to Novell NetWare 3.X servers, errors will be reported and exist with the package source files. The resolution is to eliminate the long filenames created by the administrator and to prepare these files to comply with the 8.3 convention.

 caution

Remember that you must have Internet connectivity the first time you launch the IEAK. If you are not connected to the Internet, the IEAK cannot download the language data from the Internet. Verify that you have connectivity, and restart the IEAK.

A red icon with AVS

Usually, when a red icon appears with Automatic Version Synchronization (AVS), this means Internet Explorer 5 is not installed on the workstation. Your best bet at this point is to download Internet Explorer 5, install the software, and reinstall the IEAK.

Incorrect customization code

After you have verified that you are selecting the correct role, check the taskbar to see whether you already have the IEAK Wizard running. I ran into this problem a few times when I had a lot of applications open and forgot that I had already started the IEAK Wizard. I've learned that this has happened to other administrators as well.

RESOURCES

Many resources are available to you, the Internet Explorer administrator. Do yourself a favor and take advantage of the tools available to you. Some of the best resources that you can use are in this section.

HELP Files

The Internet Explorer Administration Kit includes a lot of valuable information on all topics of Internet Explorer, starting with the `ieakhlp.htm` file that is installed with the IEAK. The HELP files can assist you with issues that you discover as a result of using and supporting Internet Explorer 5 with the IEAK.

The files that make up the IEAK HELP can be copied from the workstation to your intranet. This is definitely something to consider if several members of a team are working on the Internet Explorer implementation.

TechNet

TechNet is an invaluable reference tool that no Microsoft professional should be without. TechNet is a subscription-based service that Microsoft sells to the public. It contains tools, tips, and information related to supporting and implementing Microsoft products. TechNet costs vary by country and type; a U.S. subscription for a single user is currently $399 per year. You can also load TechNet on a server in your enterprise; this costs $699 per year. The media come on CDs in a nice ring-bound CD holder; updates are done monthly. Some of the most valuable items in TechNet are the following:

Knowledge Base

The Knowledge Base is a database that contains over 60,000 documented issues with various Microsoft products. The Knowledge Base is the first stop for resolving most of the problems you experience with Internet Explorer and other Microsoft products. This service is also available on the Web for free at `http://support.microsoft.com`.

Resource Kits

The Resource Kits also provide a lot of information on Microsoft products, such as reference materials, utilities, and other related documentation. The Resource Kits are worth their weight in gold when it comes to implementation resources and other research-related materials.

Technical Information

The Technical Information contains publications, articles, and other information related to Microsoft products. The Technical Information also provides information related to other competitors' products, such as comparisons and evaluations, and it contains white papers and other how-to documentation.

Service Packs

As you know, sometimes software requires updates, corrections, and other problem-resolution fixes. Microsoft provides these for most of its major software in the form of numbered Service Packs. Windows NT Server 4, for example, is currently up to Service Pack 6a as of this writing. TechNet provides the Service Packs for most Microsoft products; they are listed by operating system on a CD-ROM.

Drivers and patches

TechNet also contains a CD-ROM that has drivers and patches for several hardware- and software-related issues for Microsoft products. The CD-ROM contains the updated versions and fixes necessary for a wide variety of products.

Case Studies

Case Studies are a valuable way to gain information on an upcoming software deployment by looking at organizations that have done it before. The case studies show step-by-step information about organizations that have successfully deployed a wide variety of Microsoft products.

Training materials

One of the most difficult aspects of a major upgrade in software is training. Training end users on new versions of software or overall software replacement can be expensive and complex. Microsoft includes valuable training information on the TechNet CD-ROMs that can assist you in developing your training plan for your upgrade.

Microsoft Support

As an IT professional, a time will come when you have to contact Microsoft for help in resolving a major problem. Sometimes, this can be a humbling experience if you have not performed all the testing, research, and documentation necessary to resolve the problem. I have dealt with Microsoft Premier Support for one of my clients on several occasions, and have found the service to be one of the best support-related experiences in the industry.

You have several options for purchasing support directly from Microsoft.

Standard no-charge support

Some end-user products sold by Microsoft include a certain period of free support. This support is provided during business hours and usually focuses on simple problems and resolutions.

Pay-per-incident support

Business products, such as Microsoft BackOffice, are supported on this level. You call into Microsoft's support line and pay an incident charge, which is around $195, and Microsoft assists you in resolving the problem that you are reporting. This is the most expensive (per incident) way to obtain support from Microsoft. It is used when the standard no-charge support has expired or does not exist.

Priority Annual Support

Priority Annual Support provides organizations with a specified number of support incidents per year. The customer signs an agreement for a specified number of trouble calls and is then provided support 24 hours a day, seven days a week.

Priority Plus

Priority Plus is geared toward higher volume Priority Annual Support customers with 100 or more incidents a year. Priority Plus is marketed to individuals like you and me, who support organizations running Microsoft products. This is a "third-tier" support-type vehicle that organizations with a big inventory of Microsoft products obtain.

Priority Consult Line

The Priority Consult Line provides advice and consulting-related services for Microsoft products. These professionals can assist you with code review, planning, architecture, and other issues related to pre-deployment or implementation. This service is available during business hours, and the U.S. cost is about $195 per hour with a one-hour minimum.

Premier Support

With Premier Support, Microsoft assigns you a TAM (Technical Account Manager). This individual provides you with information and issues related to new technologies, events, and other Microsoft news that affects you. This individual acts as a liaison between your organization and Microsoft on support issues. Premier Support provides you with the best of the best at Microsoft. These agreements provide you with a specified number of incidents and can also include other features, such as TechNet and the Microsoft Solution Developer Network CD-ROMs. Premier Support has its own phone numbers and help-desk personnel who provide high-quality, fast turnaround answers. Premier Support subscriptions also give the customer access to secured areas on Microsoft's Web site that are not available to the general public.

Microsoft Internet Explorer Resource Kit

Like any other Microsoft Resource Kit, the Internet Explorer Resource Kit contains the nuts and bolts of the Internet Explorer suite of software. The Resource

Kit provides technical information on all the components of the suite, product deployment tips, and other valuable information. If you are planning to support Internet Explorer, you should have at least one copy of this book.

KEY POINT SUMMARY

In this chapter, you learned how to troubleshoot the Internet Explorer 5 suite of software.

- The Ping utility sends a series of four ICMP (Internet Control Message Protocol) packets to a destination address. Ping can be used with TCP/IP addresses, host names (such as `ftp.idgbooks.com`), and NetBIOS names.

- The Tracert utility is used to determine the path that a packet takes to a destination. Tracert is one of the best utilities to use for TCP/IP-related troubleshooting. Using Tracert, you can identify where in the packet's path connectivity has stopped.

- Windows IP Configuration (WINIPCFG) displays the TCP/IP information for your Windows 95/98 workstation. You can use WINIPCFG by typing **WINIPCFG** at a DOS prompt.

- The Netstat utility enables you to view network protocol-related information at the command line. Netstat can provide you with network troubleshooting clues to solve connectivity problems.

- Nbtstat is a great utility for troubleshooting Windows NT- and Windows 95-related network problems. With Nbtstat, you can view the NetBIOS name cache of remote servers and workstations and perform other NetBIOS-related troubleshooting tasks. Nbtstat is most widely used to view broadcast services by Windows NT Server.

- Nslookup is the primary troubleshooting utility for troubleshooting DNS-related issues in Windows NT. Using Nslookup, you can locate host names and IP addresses for devices that have DNS entries.

- The Internet Explorer Administration Kit (IEAK) includes a lot of valuable information on all topics of Internet Explorer, starting with the `ieakhlp.htm` file that is installed with the IEAK. The help files can assist you with issues that you discover as a result of using and supporting Internet Explorer 5 with the IEAK.

o TechNet is a subscription-based service that Microsoft sells to the public. It contains tools, tips, and information related to supporting and implementing Microsoft products. If you are a support professional for Microsoft products, you should have at least one copy of TechNet.

o The Resource Kit provides technical information on all the components of the Internet Explorer 5 suite, product deployment tips, and other valuable information.

APPLYING WHAT YOU'VE LEARNED

This section is an opportunity to use what you've learned in this chapter. The Instant Assessment questions here will help you practice for the exam. The labs that follow provide you with important real-world practice using the skills you've learned.

Instant Assessment

1. What utility should you use to see whether your company's router is down?

   A. IPCONFIG

   B. WINIPCFG

   C. NSLOOKUP

   D. TRACERT

2. What file should you view to see whether file download problems exist in the Internet Explorer installation?

   A. `IE Setup Log.txt`

   B. `Active Setup Log.txt{correct]`

   C. `Active Setup Log.err`

   D. `Active Setup.inf`

3. You have laptop users that dial into your network using host software called Reach Out 5.0. After installing your Internet Explorer package, the host software is not working. What is the most likely cause of the problem?

   A. Network congestion

   B. Insufficient disk space

   C. Software incompatibility

   D. A virus

4. Where should you first go to research a problem you are having with a Microsoft product?

   A. Premier Support

   B. Technet

   C. `Active Setup Log.txt`

   D. The Outlook Express Resource Kit

5. NetMeeting audio features can be changed only with the IEAK.

   A. True

   B. False

6. Which of the following are not valid `.ins` files for Internet Explorer?

   A. usergroup.Ins

   B. usergroup.INS

   C. usergroup.ins

   D. usergroup.iNs

7. Which of the following utilities can you use to monitor your network performance from your Windows 95 workstation?

   A. Ping

   B. Performance Monitor

   C. WINIPCFG

   D. Network Monitor

8. What are the minimum permissions recommended for Temporary Internet Files for Windows 95?

   A. Read/write

   B. Read

   C. Full control

   D. Does not apply

9. Roaming profiles enable a user to access any application that is on his or her personal workstation from any other workstation in the network.

   A. True

   B. False

10. A user explains to you that he installed Internet Explorer on his home directory in his Windows NT server. The user says that he needs more space to accommodate the Temporary Internet Files. What would your best response to this be?

   A. Give the user the space.

   B. Investigate the issue and clear some of the Internet Explorer installation files from the server.

   C. Do not give him the additional space.

   D. Investigate the issue because this type of installation is not possible.

11. Your friend, an administrator in another group, calls you for advice. He explains that they are having trouble getting the NetShow Encoder to work on their Windows 98 workstation. An associate told them that they need to install DCOM to make the Encoder work.

   A. True

   B. False

12. In which file would you view SMTP-related error messages in Outlook Express?

   A. `Active Setup Log.txt`

   B. `netlog.txt`

   C. `smtp.err`

   D. `smtp.log`

13. What is the correct address to use if you want to ping the workstation that you are currently using?

A. 255.255.255.255

B. 126.1.1.1

C. 121.0.0.1

D. 127.0.1.1

14. Receiving an HTTP/1.0 404 Object Not Found error when accessing a file on a Web server means _____.

A. you do not have permission to see the file

B. the network is congested

C. your workstation has a virus

D. the file or path does not exist

15. The _____ feature in the Windows NT registry enables you to set up Windows NT-based machines that log in automatically.

A. AdminLogon

B. AutoAdminLogon

C. AutoLogon

D. AdminLogon

16. You do not need an Internet connection after you have downloaded and installed both Internet Explorer and the IEAK.

A. True

B. False

17. The maximum timeout you can specify in Outlook Express is _____ minute(s).

A. one

B. two

C. five

D. ten

18. Which of the following files does not need a digital signature?

    A. `branding.cab`

    B. `ie5setup.exe`

    C. `desktop.cab`

    D. `tempfiles.cab`

19. Which of the following commands would produce usable results?

    A. NBTSTAT -A 209.123.34.23

    B. NBTSTAT -a 209.123.34.23

    C. NBTSTAT -a 209.123.34.23 0 -n

    D. NBTSTAT -A SERVER5

20. You can ping an ILS server.

    A. True

    B. False

21. What command would you type to get your TCP/IP address on a Windows 95 workstation?

    A. WINIPCFG

    B. WINIPCONFIG

    C. IPCONFIG

    D. WINIPCFG.COM

22. What command would you type to get your TCP/IP address on a Windows NT workstation?

    A. IPCONFIG

    B. WINIPCONFIG

    C. IPCONFIG /ALL

    D. WINIPCFG.COM

23. No patches are needed to run Internet Explorer 5 on Sun Solaris.

    A. True

    B. False

24. When you are using application sharing under the Windows NT platform, the minimum service pack that must be installed is Service Pack 4.

A. True

B. False

25. To get a Web server's TCP/IP address in Windows 98, type **nslookup**, then a space, then the host name.

A. True

B. False

Critical Thinking Labs

Lab 13.47 *Using the Ping utility*

What is the TCP/IP address of www.microsoft.com? Use the Ping utility to obtain it.

Lab 13.48 *Using the Tracert utility*

Use the Tracert utility to discover how many "hops" you are from www.idgbooks.com.

Lab 13.49 *Using the NSLOOKUP utility*

Use the Nslookup utility from a Windows NT server to find out what the TCP/IP address of www.microsoft.com is.

Lab 13.50 *Using IP configuration utilities*

Using the correct utility, open your IP configuration and note the default gateway. After you have obtained the TCP/IP address, ping the address from a DOS prompt. Which utility did you use, and what happened?

Lab 13.51 *Troubleshooting the Internet Explorer installation*

You get a support call from a user who is attempting to install your pre-configured version of Internet Explorer. The user explains that when the installation is launched, the user gets an error after a few minutes of the install and the installation bombs out. Using the troubleshooting tools you learned about in Chapter 13, what tools would you use to troubleshoot this problem and what would you look for?

Lab 13.52 *Troubleshooting proxy server*

You have a group of new users that recently came on board with your company and are using a series of former employees' Windows NT Workstation computers. The users call and state that they cannot connect to any Web sites on the Internet. The error that the users are getting is that the page cannot be found. The site uses a proxy server for connectivity.

What would you use to troubleshoot this problem? Why would the fact that the users are new to the workstation have anything to do with the problem? How can you solve this problem?

Internet Explorer 5 Administration Kit Exam Objectives

This appendix lists the Microsoft objectives for exam 70-80, Implementing and Supporting Microsoft Internet Explorer 5.0 by Using the Microsoft Internet Explorer Administration Kit. When you pass this exam, you achieve Microsoft Certified Professional status. You also earn core credit toward Microsoft Certified Systems Engineer + Internet certification and elective credit toward Microsoft Certified Systems Engineer certification.

EXAM OBJECTIVES

Planning

Identify and evaluate the technical needs of a business unit. Types of business units include:

- Internet Service Provider (ISP)
- Internet Content Provider (ICP)
- Corporate kiosk-based site
- Corporate single-task-based site
- Corporate general business desktop

Design solutions based on business rules and organizational policies. Types of business units include:

- ISP
- ICP

- Corporate kiosk-based site
- Corporate single-task-based site
- Corporate general business desktop

Given a scenario, evaluate which components to include in a customized Internet Explorer package.

Develop the appropriate security strategies for using Internet Explorer for various sites. Types of sites include:

- Public kiosks
- General business sites
- Single-task-based sites
- Intranet-only sites

Configure offline viewing for various types of users. Types of users include:

- General business users
- Single-task-based users
- Mobile workers

Develop strategies for replacing other Internet browsers. Other browsers include:

- Netscape Navigator
- Previous versions of Internet Explorer

Given a scenario, decide which custom settings to configure for Microsoft Outlook Express. Types of settings include:

- Newsgroups
- SMTP mail
- POP3 mail
- Hotmail
- IMAP folders
- View settings
- Signatures
- Custom settings
- Custom content

Given a scenario, identify which custom settings to configure for Microsoft NetMeeting. Custom settings include:

- Audio and video
- Protocols
- File sharing
- Directory servers

Given a scenario, identify which custom settings to configure for the Internet Explorer Administration Kit (IEAK).

- Identify the type of installation, such as silent, hands-free, or interactive.
- Add or replace toolbar buttons.
- Decide whether to use a custom animated logo.
- Identify which URLs will be customized, such as search, home, or online support.
- Identify whether to customize favorites and links.
- Identify whether to customize channels.
- Identify whether to use a default, a custom, or no welcome page.
- Import desktop toolbars.
- Use a user agent string.
- Use security settings.

Develop a plan for implementing Install on Demand (IOD).

Develop strategies for using the Connection Manager Administration Kit (CMAK).

- Develop strategies for using the CMAK to configure PPTP.
- Develop strategies for using the CMAK to configure Dial-Up Networking.
- Develop strategies for using the CMAK to validate user security.

Given a scenario, identify which custom settings to configure for Internet Explorer.

Develop strategies for automatic configuration of customized browsers.

- Evaluate whether to use automatic or manual configuration.
- Evaluate whether to use the IEAK Profile Manager for managing deployed browsers.

- Choose the appropriate method for automatically configuring browser settings.
- Given a scenario, select the appropriate settings in the IEAK Profile Manager.

Given a scenario, plan an appropriate method for deploying multiple language versions of Internet Explorer.

Given a scenario, plan an appropriate method for deploying Internet Explorer on multiple platforms.

Installation and Configuration

Given a role, identify the key features of the IEAK that are available for that role. Roles include:

- Content Provider/Developer
- Service Provider
- Corporate Administrator

Download the IEAK.

Given a scenario, choose the appropriate method for deploying a customized version of Internet Explorer. Methods include:

- Multiple floppy disks
- Single floppy disk
- Single disk branding
- Download
- CD-ROM
- Flat

Configuring and Managing Resource Access

Maintain user configurations by using profiles, logon scripts, system policies, and the IEAK Profile Manager.

Create and assign various levels of security for security zones. Types of zones include:

- Internet
- Local intranet

o Trusted sites

o Restricted sites

Manage automatic configuration of connection settings by using various methods. Methods include:

o Microsoft JScript auto-proxy

o `.ins` files

o `.adm` files

Integration and Interoperability

Configure Internet Explorer to allow controlled access to an intranet by using the CMAK. Access methods include:

o Dial-Up Networking

o PPTP

Configure Internet Explorer to allow controlled access to the Internet. Access methods include:

o Dial-Up Networking

o Proxy server

o PPTP

Deploy a preconfigured version of Internet Explorer by using the IEAK. Deployment options include:

o Multiple floppy disks

o Single floppy disk

o Single disk branding

o Download

o CD-ROM

o Flat

Monitoring and Optimization

Manage the features of a deployed browser by updating user profiles.

Demonstrate an understanding of the licensing requirements for the IEAK.

Optimize a computer's cache settings and performance settings.

Troubleshooting

Diagnose and resolve connectivity problems. Types of connectivity include:

o PPTP

o Dial-Up Networking

o Proxy server

o TCP/IP

Use the IEAK Profile Manager to resolve configuration problems by modifying the registry settings of a remote client computer.

Diagnose and resolve the deployment failure of a preconfigured version of Internet Explorer.

Diagnose and resolve problems related to using the Internet Explorer Customization Wizard.

Diagnose and resolve connection failures of Outlook Express.

Diagnose and resolve connection failures of NetMeeting.

Diagnose and resolve failures of caching.

EXAM OBJECTIVES CROSS REFERENCE CHART

Table A-1 lists the objectives for exam 70-80, Implementing and Supporting Microsoft Internet Explorer 5.0 by Using the Microsoft Internet Explorer Administration Kit, in a cross-reference table for study purposes. Use this table to help you determine the specific sections of this book you should study.

TABLE A-1 IEAK Objectives Cross-Reference Chart

OBJECTIVE	CHAPTER	SECTION	LAB
Planning			
Identify and evaluate the technical needs of a business unit. Types of business units include:			
● Internet Service Provider (ISP)	Chapter 11: Pre-Deployment Planning	Gathering Deployment Data	Lab 12.45: Choosing security options
● Internet Content Provider (ICP)	Chapter 11: Pre-Deployment Planning	Gathering Deployment Data	Lab 12.45: Choosing security options
● Corporate kiosk–based site	Chapter 7: Running the IEAK Chapter 8: Using the Profile Manager	More CD Options Desktop	Lab 12.45: Choosing security options
	Chapter 13: Troubleshooting the Internet Explorer Suite	Windows NT Workstation Issues	
● Corporate single-task–based site	Chapter 11: Pre-Deployment Planning	Deployment Media	Lab 12.45: Choosing security options
● Corporate general business desktop	Chapter 11: Pre-Deployment Planning	Target Audience Representation	Lab 12.45: Choosing security options
Design solutions based on business rules and organizational policies. Types of business units include:			
● ISP	Chapter 11: Pre-Deployment Planning	Requirements Translation	Lab 12.45: Choosing security options
● ICP	Chapter 11: Pre-Deployment Planning	Requirements Translation	Lab 12.45: Choosing security options

Continued

TABLE A-1 *(continued)*

Objective	Chapter	Section	Lab
● Corporate kiosk-based site	Chapter 11: Pre-Deployment Planning	Requirements Translation	Lab 12.45: Choosing security options
● Corporate single-task-based site	Chapter 11: Pre-Deployment Planning	Requirements Translation	Lab 12.45: Choosing security options
● Corporate general business desktop	Chapter 11: Pre-Deployment Planning options	Requirements Translation	Lab 12.45: Choosing security
Given a scenario, evaluate which components to include in a customized Internet Explorer package.	Chapter 6: The Internet Explorer Administration Kit	Custom Components	Lab 10.40: Using Install on Demand
Develop the appropriate security strategies for using Internet Explorer for various sites. Types of sites include:			
● Public kiosks	Chapter 7: Running the IEAK	Security	Lab 12.45: Choosing security options
● General business sites	Chapter 7: Running the IEAK	Security	Lab 12.45: Choosing security options
● Single-task-based sites	Chapter 7: Running the IEAK	Security	Lab 12.45: Choosing security options
● Intranet-only sites	Chapter 7: Running the IEAK	Security	Lab 12.45: Choosing security options
Configure offline viewing for various types of users. Types of users include:			
● General business users	Chapter 8: Using the Profile Manager	Offline Pages	Lab 12.44: Configuring Offline Viewing

OBJECTIVE	CHAPTER	SECTION	LAB
o Single-task–based users	Chapter 8: Using the Profile Manager	Offline Pages	Lab 12.44: Configuring Offline Viewing
o Mobile workers	Chapter 8: Using the Profile Manager	Offline Pages	Lab 12.44: Configuring Offline Viewing
Develop strategies for replacing other Internet browsers. Other browsers include:			
o Netscape Navigator	Chapter 5: Internet Explorer Setup	Migrating From Netscape Navigator	Lab 5.19: Migrating from Netscape Navigator
o Previous versions of Internet Explorer	Chapter 7: Running the IEAK	Customizing Active Setup	Lab 5.19: Migrating from Netscape Navigator
Given a scenario, decide which custom settings to configure for Microsoft Outlook Express. Types of settings include:			
o Newsgroups	Chapter 2: Outlook Express 5.0	Newsgroup Rules	Lab 12.46: Configuring Outlook Express with the IEAK
o SMTP mail	Chapter 2: Outlook Express 5.0	The Servers Tab	Lab 12.46: Configuring Outlook Express with the IEAK
o POP3 mail	Chapter 2: Outlook Express 5.0	The Servers Tab	Lab 12.46: Configuring Outlook Express with the IEAK
o Hotmail			Lab 12.46: Configuring Outlook Express with the IEAK

Continued

Objective	Chapter	Section	Lab
TABLE A-1 *(continued)*			
● IMAP folders	Chapter 2: Outlook Express 5.0	The Servers Tab	Lab 12.46: Configuring Outlook Express with the IEAK
● View settings	Chapter 2: Outlook Express 5.0	The Outlook Express 5 Inbox	Lab 12.46: Configuring Outlook Express with the IEAK
● Signatures	Chapter 2: Outlook Express 5.0	The Compose Tab	Lab 12.46: Configuring Outlook Express with the IEAK
● Custom settings	Chapter 8: Using the Profile Manager	Wizard Settings	Lab 12.46: Configuring Outlook Express with the IEAK
● Custom content	Chapter 8: Using the Profile Manager	Wizard Settings	Lab 12.46: Configuring Outlook Express with the IEAK
Given a scenario, identify which custom settings to configure for Microsoft NetMeeting. Custom settings include:			
● Audio and video	Chapter 3: Microsoft NetMeeting 3.0	The View Menu	Lab 7.28: Configuring Microsoft NetMeeting
● Protocols	Chapter 3: Microsoft NetMeeting 3.0	The View Menu	Lab 7.28: Configuring Microsoft NetMeeting
● File sharing	Chapter 3: Microsoft NetMeeting 3.0	The View Menu	Lab 7.28: Configuring Microsoft NetMeeting
● Directory servers	Chapter 3: Microsoft NetMeeting 3.0	Directory	Lab 7.28: Configuring Microsoft NetMeeting

OBJECTIVE	CHAPTER	SECTION	LAB
Given a scenario, identify which custom settings to configure for the Internet Explorer Administration Kit (IEAK).			
● Identify the type of installation, such as silent, hands–free, or interactive.	Chapter 6: The Internet Explorer Admin Kit	User Interaction	Lab 10.42: Choosing Installation Types
● Add or replace toolbar buttons.	Chapter 7: Running the IEAK	Feature Selection	Lab 7.29: Working with the IEAK
● Decide whether to use a custom animated logo.	Chapter 5: Internet Explorer Setup	Files Used by Windows Update Setup	Lab 7.29: Working with the IEAK
● Identify which URLs will be customized, such as search, home, or online support.	Chapter 12: Some Real World Scenarios	Pre–Configuration Planning	Lab 7.29: Working with the IEAK
● Identify whether to customize favorites and links.	Chapter 12: Some Real World Scenarios	Pre–Configuration Planning	Lab 7.29: Working with the IEAK
● Identify whether to customize channels.	Chapter 12: Some Real World Scenarios	Pre–Configuration Planning	Lab 7.29: Working with the IEAK
● Identify whether to use a default, a custom, or no welcome page.	Chapter 12: Some Real World Scenarios	Pre–Configuration Planning	Lab 7.29: Working with the IEAK
● Import desktop toolbars.	Chapter 12: Some Real World Scenarios	Pre–Configuration Planning	Lab 7.29: Working with the IEAK
● Use a User Agent String.	Chapter 12: Some Real World Scenarios	User Agent String	Lab 10.41: Modifying the browser

Continued

TABLE A-1 *(continued)*

OBJECTIVE	CHAPTER	SECTION	LAB
● Use security settings.	Chapter 11: Pre-Deployment Planning	Information Gathering	Lab 12.45: Choosing security options
Develop a plan for implementing Install on Demand (IOD).			Lab 10.40: Using Install on Demand
Develop strategies for using the Connection Manager Administration Kit (CMAK).	Chapter 9: The Connection Manager Administration Kit	The Wizard	Lab 9.34: Deploying PPTP/VPN solutions Lab 9.35: Deploying dial-up networking
● Develop strategies for using the CMAK to configure PPTP.	Chapter 9: The Connection Manager Administration Kit	VPN Support	Lab 9.34: Deploying PPTP/VPN solutions
● Develop strategies for using the CMAK to configure Dial-Up Networking.	Chapter 9: The Connection Manager Administration Kit	Merging Service Profiles	Lab 9.35: Deploying dial-up networking
● Develop strategies for using the CMAK to validate user security.	Chapter 9: The Connection Manager Administration Kit	Realm Name	Lab 9.35: Deploying dial-up networking
Given a scenario, identify which custom settings to configure for Internet Explorer.			
Develop strategies for automatic configuration of customized browsers.	Chapter 7: Running the IEAK	Automatic Configuration	Lab 8.31: Managing your browser configuration
● Evaluate whether to use automatic or manual configuration.	Chapter 7: Running the IEAK	Automatic Configuration	Lab 8.31: Managing your browser configuration

Continued

OBJECTIVE	CHAPTER	SECTION	LAB
• Evaluate whether to use the IEAK Profile Manager for managing deployed browsers.	Chapter 8: Using the Profile Manager	Overview	Lab 8.30: Importing System Policies
• Choose the appropriate method for automatically configuring browser settings.	Chapter 7: Running the IEAK	Automatic Configuration	Lab 8.31: Managing your browser configuration
• Given a scenario, select the appropriate settings in the IEAK Profile Manager.	Chapter 8: Using the Profile Manager	System Policies and Restrictions	Lab 10.41: Modifying the browser
Given a scenario, plan an appropriate method for deploying multiple language versions of Internet Explorer.	Chapter 7: Running the IEAK	Language Selection	Lab 10.39: Selecting languages in Internet Explorer
Given a scenario, plan an appropriate method for deploying Internet Explorer on multiple platforms.	Chapter 7: Running the IEAK	Platform Selection	Lab 10.38: Platform deployment considerations
Installation and Configuration			
Given a role, identify the key features of the IEAK that are available for that role. Roles include:			
• Content Provider/Developer	Chapter 6: The Internet Explorer Administration Kit	Roles	Lab 6.25: Identifying roles and licensing
• Service Provider	Chapter 6: The Internet Explorer Administration Kit	Roles	Lab 6.25: Identifying roles and licensing

TABLE A-1 *(continued)*

OBJECTIVE	CHAPTER	SECTION	LAB
• Corporate Administrator	Chapter 6: The Internet Explorer Administration Kit	Roles	Lab 6.25: Identifying roles and licensing
Download the IEAK.	Chapter 6: The Internet Explorer Administration Kit	Getting the IEAK	Lab 10.37: Downloading the IEAK
Given a scenario, choose the appropriate method for deploying a customized version of Internet Explorer. Methods include:			
• Multiple floppy disks	Chapter 6: The Internet Explorer Administration Kit	Deployment Methods	Lab 11.43: Choosing deployment solutions
• Single floppy disk	Chapter 6: The Internet Explorer Administration Kit	Deployment Methods	Lab 11.43: Choosing deployment solutions
• Single disk branding	Chapter 6: The Internet Explorer Administration Kit	Deployment Methods	Lab 11.43: Choosing deployment solutions
• Download	Chapter 6: The Internet Explorer Administration Kit	Deployment Methods	Lab 11.43: Choosing deployment solutions
• CD-ROM	Chapter 6: The Internet Explorer Administration Kit	Deployment Methods	Lab 11.43: Choosing deployment solutions
• Flat	Chapter 6: The Internet Explorer Administration Kit	Deployment Methods	Lab 11.43: Choosing deployment solutions
Configuring and Managing Resource Access			
Maintain user configurations by using profiles, logon scripts, system policies, and the IEAK Profile Manager.	Chapter 8: Using the Profile Manager	System Policies and Restrictions	

OBJECTIVE	CHAPTER	SECTION	LAB
Create and assign various levels of security for security zones. Types of zones include:			
○ Internet	Chapter 11: Pre–Deployment Planning	Information Gathering	Lab 12.45: Choosing security options
○ Local intranet	Chapter 11: Pre–Deployment Planning	Information Gathering	Lab 12.45: Choosing security options
○ Trusted sites	Chapter 11: Pre–Deployment Planning	Information Gathering	Lab 12.45: Choosing security options
○ Restricted sites	Chapter 11: Pre–Deployment Planning	Information Gathering	Lab 12.45: Choosing security options
Manage automatic configuration of connection settings by using various methods. Methods include:			
○ Microsoft JScript auto-proxy	Chapter 10: Internet Explorer Maintenance	Auto–Configuration and Auto-Proxy	Lab 10.36: Adding auto-proxy scripts
○ .ins files	Chapter 7: Running the IEAK	Automatic Configuration	Lab 8.31: Managing your browser configuration Lab 10.41: Modifying the browser
○ .adm files	Chapter 8: Using the IEAK Profile Manager	System Policies	Lab 8.30: Importing System Policies

Continued

TABLE A-1 *(continued)*			
Objective	*Chapter*	*Section*	*Lab*
Integration and Interoperability			
Configure Internet Explorer to allow controlled access to an intranet by using the CMAK. Access methods include:			
● Dial-Up Networking	Chapter 9: The Connection Manager Administration Kit	Dial-up Networking entries	Lab 9.35: Deploying Dial-up Networking
● PPTP	Chapter 9: The Connection Manager Administration Kit	VPN Support	Lab 9.34: Deploying PPTP/VPN solutions
Configure Internet Explorer to allow controlled access to the Internet. Access methods include:			
● Dial-Up Networking	Chapter 9: The Connection Manager Administration Kit	Dial-up Networking entries	Lab 9.35: Deploying Dial-up Networking
● Proxy server	Chapter 10: Internet Explorer Maintenance	Auto-Configuration and Auto-Proxy	Lab 5.15: Configuring Internet Explorer for use with Proxy Server
● PPTP	Chapter 9: The Connection Manager Administration Kit	VPN Support	Lab 9.34: Deploying PPTP/VPN solutions
Deploy a preconfigured version of Internet Explorer by using the IEAK. Deployment options include:			
● Multiple floppy disks	Chapter 11: Pre-Deployment Planning	Deployment Media	Lab 11.43: Choosing deployment solutions

OBJECTIVE	CHAPTER	SECTION	LAB
○ Single floppy disk	Chapter 11: Pre-Deployment Planning	Deployment Media	Lab 11.43: Choosing deployment solutions
○ Single disk branding	Chapter 11: Pre-Deployment Planning	Deployment Media	Lab 11.43: Choosing deployment solutions
○ Download	Chapter 11: Pre-Deployment Planning	Deployment Media	Lab 11.43: Choosing deployment solutions
○ CD-ROM	Chapter 11: Pre-Deployment Planning	Deployment Media	Lab 11.43: Choosing deployment solutions
○ Flat	Chapter 11: Pre-Deployment Planning	Deployment Media	Lab 8.31: Managing your browser configuration
Monitoring and Optimization			
Manage the features of a deployed browser by updating user profiles.	Chapter 8: Using the IEAK Profile Manager	System Policies and Restrictions	
Demonstrate an understanding of the licensing requirements for the IEAK.	Chapter 6: The Internet Explorer Administration Kit	Getting the IEAK	Lab 6.25: Identifying Roles and Licensing
Optimize a computer's cache settings and performance settings.	Chapter 13: Troubleshooting the Internet Explorer Suite	Cache and Temporary Internet Files folder	Lab 5.24: Optimizing Internet Explorer
Troubleshooting			
Diagnose and resolve connectivity problems. Types of connectivity include:			
○ PPTP	Chapter 9: The Connection Manager Administration Kit	VPN Support	Lab 9.33: Troubleshooting VPN Connections

Continued

TABLE A-1 *(continued)*

OBJECTIVE	CHAPTER	SECTION	LAB
● Dial-Up Networking	Chapter 13: Troubleshooting the Internet Explorer Suite	Reach Out 5.0	Lab 9.32: Troubleshooting dial-up
● Proxy server	Chapter 13: Troubleshooting the Internet Explorer Suite	Proxy Server Issues	Lab 13.52: Troubleshooting Proxy Server
● TCP/IP	Chapter 13: Troubleshooting the Internet Explorer Suite	Utilities you can use	Lab 13.47: Using the Ping utility Lab 13.50: Using IP configuration utilities
Use the IEAK Profile Manager to resolve configuration problems by modifying the registry settings of a remote client computer.	Chapter 10: Internet Explorer Maintenance	Updating Configurations	Lab 7.27: Troubleshooting registry and permissions problems
Diagnose and resolve the deployment failure of a preconfigured version of Internet Explorer.	Chapter 13: Troubleshooting the Internet Explorer Suite	Active Setup	Lab 13.51: Troubleshooting the Internet Explorer installation
Diagnose and resolve problems related to using the Internet Explorer Customization Wizard.	Chapter 13: Troubleshooting the Internet Explorer Suite	Administration Kit	Lab 7.26: Troubleshooting the Internet Explorer Customization Wizard
Diagnose and resolve connection failures of Outlook Express.	Chapter 13: Troubleshooting the Internet Explorer Suite	Outlook Express	Lab 2.1: Troubleshooting Outlook Express
Diagnose and resolve connection failures of NetMeeting.	Chapter 13: Troubleshooting the Internet Explorer Suite	NetMeeting	Lab 3.12: Troubleshooting Microsoft NetMeeting
Diagnose and resolve failures of caching.	Chapter 13: Troubleshooting the Internet Explorer Suite	Cache and Temporary Internet files folder	Lab 5.18: Troubleshooting Internet Explorer content

Mini-Lab Manual

B

The labs in this book are important because they help you gain some hands-on knowledge of configuring applications within the Internet Explorer software suite. I strongly encourage you to use the labs and experiment with the applications to gain a better understanding of the features of the suite.

caution

By altering the configuration of your workstation, you could potentially render it inoperable, which could require you to reinstall the operating system. When you are experimenting, make sure that the workstation is not mission-critical.

Table B-1 lists all the labs in this book.

TABLE B-1 LABS IN THIS BOOK

LAB NUMBER	TYPE OF LAB	LAB TITLE	CHAPTER
2.1	Critical Thinking	Troubleshooting Outlook Express	2
2.2	Critical Thinking	Creating a Hotmail account	2
2.3	Hands-on	Using client-sided rules	2
2.4	Hands-on	Sending a mail message with Outlook Express	2
2.5	Hands-on	Creating an Address Book entry	2
2.6	Hands-on	Changing read marks on a mail message	2
2.7	Hands-on	Performing LDAP searches on the Internet	2
2.8	Hands-on	Recovering a deleted message in Outlook Express	2
2.9	Hands-on	Setting up another mail account	2
2.10	Hands-on	Changing port and mail server names	2
2.11	Hands-on	Creating and deleting folders	2
3.12	Critical Thinking	Troubleshooting Microsoft NetMeeting	3
3.13	Hands-on	Tuning your microphone and sound	3
3.14	Hands-on	Connecting and browsing an ILS server	3
5.15	Critical Thinking	Configuring Internet Explorer for use with Proxy Server	5
5.16	Critical Thinking	Configuring Internet Explorer for use on a standard workstation	5
5.17	Critical Thinking	Configuring advanced options in Internet Explorer	5
5.18	Critical Thinking	Troubleshooting Internet Explorer Content	5
5.19	Critical Thinking	Migrating from Netscape Navigator	5
5.20	Hands-on	Restoring an originally configured home page	5
5.21	Hands-on	Clearing the Temporary Internet Files folder	5

NUMBER	TYPE OF LAB	LAB TITLE	CHAPTER
5.22	Hands-on	Changing, modifying, and testing security changes in Internet Explorer	5
5.23	Hands-on	Changing cookie options	5
5.24	Hands-on	Optimizing Internet Explorer	5
6.25	Critical Thinking	Identifying roles and licensing	6
7.26	Critical Thinking	Troubleshooting the Internet Explorer Customization Wizard	7
7.27	Critical Thinking	Troubleshooting registry and permissions problems	7
7.28	Critical Thinking	Configuring Microsoft NetMeeting	7
7.29	Hands-on	Working with the IEAK	7
8.30	Critical Thinking	Importing System Policies	8
8.31	Critical Thinking	Managing your browser configuration	8
9.32	Critical Thinking	Troubleshooting dial-up	9
9.33	Critical Thinking	Troubleshooting VPN connections	9
9.34	Critical Thinking	Deploying PPTP/VPN solutions	9
9.35	Critical Thinking	Deploying Dial-Up Networking	9
10.36	Critical Thinking	Adding auto-proxy scripts	10
10.37	Critical Thinking	Downloading the IEAK	10
10.38	Critical Thinking	Platform deployment considerations	10
10.39	Critical Thinking	Selecting languages in Internet Explorer	10
10.40	Critical Thinking	Using Install on Demand	10
10.41	Critical Thinking	Modifying the browser	10
10.42	Critical Thinking	Choosing installation types	10
11.43	Critical Thinking	Choosing deployment solutions	11
12.44	Critical Thinking	Configuring Offline Browsing	12
12.45	Critical Thinking	Choosing security options	12
12.46	Critical Thinking	Configuring Outlook Express with the IEAK	12
13.47	Critical Thinking	Using the Ping utility	13
13.48	Critical Thinking	Using the Tracert utility	13

Continued

TABLE B-1 *(continued)*

LAB NUMBER	TYPE OF LAB	LAB TITLE	CHAPTER
13.49	Critical Thinking	Using the NSLOOKUP utility	13
13.50	Critical Thinking	Using IP configuration utilities	13
13.51	Critical Thinking	Troubleshooting the Internet Explorer Installation	13
13.52	Critical Thinking	Troubleshooting Proxy Server	13

Lab 2.1 *Troubleshooting Outlook Express*

Your boss comes to you and complains that she is unable to get to her e-mail using Outlook Express. She asks you to assist her in troubleshooting why she gets errors connecting to the POP server. She states that the error she receives says that the host cannot be found and something about POP Port 110. This is the only error message she receives. What configuration options would you check to see why she is having problems accessing her mail?

Lab 2.2 *Creating a Hotmail account*

Using Outlook Express, you are going to create a Hotmail account for yourself. Make sure that you are connected to the Internet and have installed Outlook Express 5. Select Tools ⇨ Accounts ⇨ Mail. Click Add and select Mail. Type Hotmail Account in the next field and click the Next button. At the next dialog box, select I'd like to sign up for a new account from Hotmail (there is no charge to do this). Click Next to continue to the sign up screen, and you will be asked to provide your information and create a unique ID for Hotmail. Once completed with the sign up, you will have created an account for Hotmail. Once you have created your account, send a hello e-mail message to `ieak5@netdatasys.com`. What happened?

Lab 2.3 *Using Client-Side rules*

1. Create a folder called Test Folder.

2. Select Tools ⇨ Message Rules ⇨ Mail.

3. Create a Rule that copies any mail message received from `IEAK5@NETDATASYS.COM` to your test folder. Ensure that you only copy, not move, the message.

Lab 2.4 *Sending a mail message with Outlook Express*

1. Open Outlook Express.

2. Select New Mail.

3. Send a mail message to `ieak5@netdatasys.com`.

4. Check your Inbox again in about five minutes; did you get a reply? Who was the reply from? (Do not delete the message, you will use it again later in the labs.)

Lab 2.5 *Creating an Address Book entry*

1. Open the Address Book in Outlook Express.

2. Create an Address Book entry for a user; first name is Test, last name is User. For the e-mail address enter `testuser@nowhere.net`.

3. Open a new message and type **testuser**.

4. What happened when you typed testuser?

Lab 2.6 *Changing Read Marks on a mail message*

1. Select the mail message that you received in Lab 2.4.

2. Select Edit ➪ Mark as Unread.

3. Select another mail message.

4. What changed in the view of the unread message?

Lab 2.7 *Performing LDAP searches in the Internet*

1. Using the appropriate feature, you are going to find a user on the Internet. The user's name is Bill Gates.

2. Using the Yahoo People Finder, how many e-mail addresses contain Bill Gates? (Do not delete the message, you will use it again later in the labs.)

Lab 2.8 *Recovering a deleted message in Outlook Express*

1. Find the message you received from `ieak5@netdatasys.com`.

2. Highlight the message and select Delete. Select Yes to delete if prompted.

3. You need to recover this message; how would you do that?

Lab 2.9 *Setting up another mail account*

1. Choose Tools ➪ Accounts.
2. Select the Mail tab.
3. Choose Add.
4. Select Mail.
5. Enter Test Account.
6. Enter your e-mail address.
7. Select whether your incoming mail server is IMAP or POP.
8. Enter your e-mail server's POP and SMTP addresses.
9. Enter your user name and password.
10. Enter Test Account again.
11. Select the I will establish my Internet connection manually option.
12. Select Finish.
13. Is the Test Account appearing in the Mail tab?

Lab 2.10 *Changing port and mail server names*

1. Select Tools ➪ Accounts.
2. Click the Test Account and select properties.
3. Click the Servers tab.
4. What are the server names?
5. Select the Advanced tab.
6. On which ports are SMTP and POP3 running?

Lab 2.11 *Creating and deleting folders*

1. Right-click the Inbox.
2. Select New Folder.
3. Call the folder Test Folder.
4. Select OK.
5. Right-click Test Folder in the Outlook bar.
6. Select New Folder.
7. Call the folder New Subfolder.
8. Did a plus sign (+) appear next to New Folder?
9. Right-click Test Folder again.
10. Select Delete.

Lab 3.12 *Troubleshooting Microsoft NetMeeting*

You are asked to solve a problem with a user's inability to connect to other Net-Meeting users. The user complains that he is unable to connect to other NetMeeting users with the NetMeeting client while other users in the same office are able to do so. What steps would you take to troubleshoot the user's problem?

Lab 3.13 *Tuning your microphone and sound*

1. Launch the tuning wizard.
2. Tune your microphone and speakers.
3. Which settings were you allowed to change and why?

Lab 3.14 *Connecting and browsing an ILS server*

1. Start Microsoft NetMeeting.
2. Select Call, and then select an ILS server from the directory, such as ILS.FOUR11.COM.
3. Find someone who is testing; you can find someone by looking in the Comments column for testing.
4. Double-click on the user's name.
5. Type a message to the person.

Lab 5.15 *Configuring Internet Explorer for use with a proxy server*

Your organization is deploying Internet Explorer, and at the same time is deploying an intranet site. The intranet site is behind your proxy server and is destined to become a major part of your organization's business. Which configuration option would you have to specify to enable every employee to start Internet Explorer at the intranet site?

Because your organization has already implemented a proxy server, what are the important considerations regarding proxy server configurations for Internet Explorer?

Lab 5.16 *Configuring Internet Explorer for use on a standard workstation*

Your company has decided to implement Internet Explorer as the standard browser. The organization wants to control access to Web sites that it deems inappropriate. The company also wants to allow unlimited access to its business partners' sites, thus allowing users to do what they please on these sites. Deploying a proxy server is not an option.

Which considerations and configurations would be the best approach for disallowing access to inappropriate sites? Which configurations would you have to change to allow unlimited access to the partner sites?

Lab 5.17 *Configuring advanced options in Internet Explorer*

Your company has recently signed a contract with a benefits manager to handle all of your company's benefit management. The benefits manager has written a Web-based application that handles benefits changes and lets employees review their benefits plan on the Internet. The site uses SSL 3.0 to ensure that the transactions are secure. Benefits plans are changed using several ActiveX controls for which the organization has obtained certificates. Because this is going to save your company several hundred thousand dollars a year, your boss wants you to ensure that Internet Explorer is configured properly for the enterprise to accommodate this application.

What changes would you implement to make the experience more appealing to users? What are some important considerations regarding your browser configuration to ensure that the employees can access and use the site without interruption?

Lab 5.18 *Troubleshooting Internet Explorer content*

You have a user who is complaining that when she visits sites on the Web, the content is outdated. She tells you that when she uses a co-worker's workstation, this does not happen. She also tells you that Internet browsing is extremely slow on her workstation as opposed to other users' workstations. What steps would you take to troubleshoot the problem?

Lab 5.19 *Migrating from Netscape Navigator*

You are in the final stages of the build for your browser configuration and getting ready to deploy one week from today. The CIO of your company walks into your office to express some concerns about your installation that have arisen from other departments. The users are concerned about replacing Netscape Navigator as their browser because they do not want to have to manually re-enter tasks and configuration information. The concerns are as follows:

1. The users do not want to have to re-enter their proxy configurations.

2. The users do not want to have to re-enter bookmarks from their old browser.

3. The users do not want to loose their cookies and plug-ins for Netscape Navigator.

4. The users do not want Netscape Navigator uninstalled until they are sure that Internet Explorer will work for them.

What can you safely tell the CIO about the users' concerns?

Lab 5.20 *Restoring an originally configured home page*

1. Launch Internet Explorer.
2. Choose the View menu on the toolbar.
3. Select Internet Options.
4. The General tab should be displayed; if not, select the General tab.
5. Select the Use Default option.
6. Select Apply and click OK.
7. Select the Home button on the toolbar. You should see the original home page.

Lab 5.21 *Clearing the Temporary Internet Files folder*

1. Launch Internet Explorer.
2. Choose the View menu on the toolbar.
3. Select Internet Options.
4. The General tab should be displayed; if not, select the General tab.
5. Select the Settings button in the Temporary Internet files area.
6. Choose the View Files option. These files are currently stored in your cache.
7. Close the dialog box and click OK.
8. Select Delete Files on the General tab/Temporary Internet files.

9. When prompted to delete all files in the Temporary Internet files folder, select Yes.

10. Select Settings again.

11. Choose View Files. The cache should be empty, with the exception of any cookies you may have (and any files that are open).

Lab 5.22 *Changing, modifying, and testing security changes in Internet Explorer*

1. Launch Internet Explorer.

2. Choose the View menu on the toolbar.

3. Select Internet Options.

4. Select the Security tab.

5. Scroll the Zone menu down to Internet zone.

6. Change the Internet security level to High.

7. View a few of your favorite Web sites. See the difference?

8. To correct the settings, select the Security tab again.

9. Scroll the Zone menu down to Internet zone.

10. Click Reset.

Lab 5.23 *Changing cookie options*

1. Launch Internet Explorer.

2. Choose the View menu on the toolbar.

3. Select Internet Options.

4. Select the Advanced tab.

5. Scroll down to the Cookies option, and change the selection to disable all cookie use.

6. Browse some of the big commercial Web sites. See how popular cookies are?

7. To reset back to the default, repeat steps 1 through 5 and select the Always accept cookies option.

Lab 5.24 *Optimizing Internet Explorer*

You can optimize the performance of Internet Explorer using the (Temporary Internet Files) cache settings.

1. Using these settings located in Tools ⇨ Internet Options ⇨ General, select the Settings button.
2. Now check the setting for Check for newer version of stored pages on every visit to page.
3. Close the browser and restart Internet Explorer.
4. Navigate to one of your favorite pages and then click on one of the links on the page.
5. Once you are on the next page, return to where you started.

Did you notice the browser running slower than normal? This is because you told the browser to reload the page every time you hit the page, no matter what. This means that every time you navigate to the site, all of the HTML and graphics have to be reloaded.

Lab 6.25 *Identifying roles and licensing*

Open your browser and navigate to `http://www.microsoft.com/Windows/ieak/en/licensing/courtesy/default.asp`. After reading the license agreement for the IEAK, which of the agreements would be applicable to the following scenarios?

1. Major cable modem provider, providing service to the general public.
2. Staff member of the IT department deploying Internet Explorer to the sales department.
3. Web portal providing a customized version of the Internet Explorer browser to their customers.

Lab 7.26 *Troubleshooting the Internet Explorer Customization Wizard*

You are creating your first build with the Internet Explorer Customization Wizard. After walking through Stage 1, you enter Stage 2 and get to the Automatic Version Synchronization page. After reviewing the versions of your components, you notice that all of your components are yellow. After trying to synchronize your files, you get an error stating that the server cannot be found. What do you think would cause this and what would you do to troubleshoot this problem?

Lab 7.27 *Troubleshooting registry and permissions problems*

You are tasked with installing Internet Explorer 5 in your user community that consists of mostly Windows NT Workstation users. What should you consider in deploying the software from a permissions perspective?

Lab 7.28 *Configuring Microsoft NetMeeting*

As a part of your Internet Explorer 5 deployment, you are going to deploy the latest version of Microsoft NetMeeting to allow your users to videoconference with each other. The server team has already set up an ILS server for you to use called `ils.widget.com`. The company is spread out among several locations across the country and has very fast WAN access to each site with only TCP/IP allowed across the WAN links and routers. Each desktop machine has been outfitted with a microphone and a video camera.

Using the IEAK as a reference, what features would you consider including in your configuration and why? What options do you need to set up based on the information provided?

Lab 7.29 *Working with the IEAK*

Using the IEAK, you will define configurations for the browser based on requirements set forth by the desktop team for your organization. Pay attention to the requirements and design a strategy for each requirement that would be the most effective means to accomplish the task.

1. Provide a means to launch Adobe Acrobat on the user's desktop. All installations of Acrobat are loaded in `C:\Acrobat3\Reader\Acrord32.exe`. Icons have been provided in the same path called `acrobatcolor.ico` and `acobatgrey.ico`.

2. Provide a means for the user to know if the browser is running a task using a graphic. The graphic is 22 × 22 and located in your `c:\graphics\ie4anim.gif` directory.

3. Add URLs for Support page, Home page, and a search page designed by your Web staff. The URLs are as follows:

   ○ Search: `http://search.widget.com`

   ○ Home: `http://intranet.widget.com`

   ○ Support: `http://ie5support.widget.com`

4. Add default links to the browser using the following URLs:

- `http://intranet.widget.com/humanresources`
- `http://intranet.widget.com/parking`
- `http://intranet.widget.com/security`

Make sure that no other links are included in the configuration.

5. Ensure that the default Active Channels are not included. Make sure that any existing channels from Internet Explorer 4 are deleted.

6. Add a welcome page to the user's configuration using the following link: `http://intranet.widget.com/ie5/welcome2ie5.htm`.

Lab 8.30 *Importing System Policies*

You are charged with creating and implementing system policies with your IEAK deployment. After a careful review of the policy settings, the organization feels that the policy file included in the IEAK called `inetcorp.adm` will be the best solution for your organization.

You have already configured the location and configuration script for your enterprise on your local intranet server. How would you go about creating the new `.ins` file and deploying the file for your already deployed browsers?

Lab 8.31 *Managing your browser configuration*

You plan to manage your users browser configurations using the IEAK Profile Manager. The person who had your job before you deployed the browser using the IEAK. The location for the `.ins` file was `http://intranet.widget.com/explorer/widget.ins`. If you wanted to change the file name, what options to do have to do this? If you changed the contents of the file, such as a configuration change, where would you make the change and how would you do it? Why do you think that using an auto-configuration script is prudent in large organizations rather than asking the users to make changes manually, by e-mail for example?

Lab 9.32 *Troubleshooting dial-up*

A user contacts you and states that he is having problems connecting to the dial-up server. You know after checking on the server that the server is fine and the user has a good dial-up account. What basic troubleshooting steps could you use to assist the user in troubleshooting his dial-up configuration?

Lab 9.33 *Troubleshooting VPN connections*

Late one afternoon, you get several phone calls from your remote users saying that they are unable to connect to the network over the Internet through their VPN connections. The error message that they are receiving states that they are unable to log in. With your knowledge of the basics of VPN, what would you logically consider checking before calling the VPN administrator?

Lab 9.34 *Deploying PPTP/VPN solutions*

Your organization is deploying a VPN solution using Microsoft technology. You are tasked with providing the browser and connection software to connect the users to the VPN using the IEAK and CMAK. Your organization has its own internal DNS servers that are not propagated on the Internet and are only internal addresses protected by a firewall. In addition, you need to be able to provide WINS access to your protected network to allow the users to connect to server resources inside the network.

Which software component would you use to provide this configuration? What considerations should you keep in mind when configuring the software? Using the software you have, can you accomplish the requirements as set forth to you? Look through the IEAK and CMAK software for solutions before you answer the question.

Lab 9.35 *Deploying dial-up networking*

Your organization is deploying a dial-up solution using Microsoft technology. You are tasked with providing the browser and connection software to connect the users to the dial-up RAS server using the IEAK and CMAK. Your organization has its own internal DNS servers that are not propagated on the Internet and are only internal addresses protected by a firewall. In addition, you need to be able to provide WINS access to your protected network to allow the users to connect to server resources inside the network.

Which software component would you use to provide this configuration? What considerations should you keep in mind when configuring the software? Using the software you have, can you accomplish the requirements as set forth to you? Look through the IEAK and CMAK software for solutions before you answer the question.

Lab 10.36 *Adding auto-proxy scripts*

Your firewall administrator has provided you with an auto-proxy script to include in your browser configuration. You are tasked with including this script in your browser deployment. Once you are provided with the script, answer the following questions.

1. In what stage of the IEAK will you provide the location of the script?

2. Once you have included the script, what else needs to be done to utilize the script when your browser is deployed?

Lab 10.37 *Downloading the IEAK*

You are asked to deploy Internet Explorer 5 in your organization. You will deploy the browser to your internal users using the IEAK, the platforms will be Windows 95 and Windows NT. Where would you go to download the IEAK software? Use your browser to locate the exact URL to download the software. Once downloaded, what else do you need to do? What role would you choose that would be compliant with the IEAK license agreement?

Lab 10.38 *Platform deployment considerations*

You are tasked with deploying Internet Explorer 5 in your organization. You will deploy the browser to your internal users using the IEAK; the platforms that you will have to deploy the browser to will include the following:

1. Sales department users running Windows 95.

2. Marketing department users running Windows 98.

3. Engineering department users running Windows NT Workstation 4.

4. Maintenance department users running Windows for Workgroups.

5. IT department users running Sun Solaris and HP UNIX.

Using the IEAK as a reference tool, how many builds will you have to create to deploy your software? If you are deploying the browser via CD-ROM, how many CD-ROMs will you have to create at a minimum?

Lab 10.39 *Selecting languages in Internet Explorer 5*

You are tasked with deploying Internet Explorer 5 in your organization. You will deploy the browser to your internal users using the IEAK. The various departments of your company are spread throughout the world and will require you to deploy the browser in various languages. The platforms that you will have to deploy the browser to will include the following:

1. USA-based Sales department users running Windows 95.

2. USA-based Marketing department users running Windows 98.

3. Japan-based Engineering department users running Windows NT Workstation 4.

4. Korea-based Maintenance department users running Windows for Workgroups.

5. Norway-based Support department users running Sun Solaris and HP UNIX.

Using the IEAK as a reference tool, how many builds will you have to create to deploy your software? If you are deploying the browser via CD-ROM, how many CD-ROMs will you have to create at a minimum?

Lab 10.40 *Using Install on Demand*

You are tasked with deploying Internet Explorer 5 in your organization. You will deploy the browser to your internal users using the IEAK. The various departments of your company are spread throughout the world and some do not have access to the Internet, but have access to the local intranet over your company's WAN. After talking with the desktop support department, you find that disk space on over 50 percent of the computers is at a premium. In addition, the offices throughout the world have very different functions and may need other components of the browser a few months from now.

In this case, would it be prudent to allow Install on Demand? What considerations would you consider in adding Install on Demand and why?

Lab 10.41 *Modifying the browser*

You are charged with modifying the configuration of your company's browsers. System policies have been included in your IEAK deployment. After a careful review of the policy settings, the organization feels that by using a User Agent

String, the company can identify the browsing habits of the user community more effectively. In addition, the company would like to use the User Agent String to identify the usage on some of the company's partners' extranet Web sites.

You have already configured the location and configuration script for your enterprise on your local intranet server. How would you go about creating the new .ins file and deploying the file for your already deployed browsers?

Lab 10.42 *Choosing installation types*

Given the following scenario, choose the best method to install the Internet Explorer browser by specifying the type of installation: silent, hands-free, or interactive.

1. A 250-user community that is receiving their first computers and is not experienced in installing software.

2. A group of network engineers with varying Web requirements.

3. A group of developers who need to have exactly the same browser settings.

Lab 11.43 *Choosing deployment solutions*

In the following lab, you will be asked to provide deployment solutions for a variety of scenarios. Pay close attention to the technical requirements of the scenario to arrive at the best answer. Use Chapter 7 to help you make the best selection for the requirement. The goal is to provide the quickest, easiest, and least expensive installation method.

1. A corporation whose employees are almost entirely sales staff. The sales people are always on the move and are equipped with laptop computers with a configuration consisting of dial-up access, and CD-ROM and floppy drives.

2. An ISP that is deploying the browser to its internal employees all over the US. The workstations have fast network access, and CD-ROM and floppy drives.

3. An ICP with Internet Explorer 5 pre-installed on its new workstations. The CIO would like to customize the browser for the organization to enable the browser to be more productive. The workstations have fast network access, CD-ROM and floppy drives.

4. A small office with 40 workstations and very slow Internet access — the browser will be used to view intranet information loaded on the local network. The intranet server hosts several applications that are Web-based and run at 90 percent CPU utilization all day long. The users have separate file servers that are not very busy during the day. The workstations have fast local network access, CD-ROM and floppy drives, but slow Internet access.

5. A major ISP that desires to do a bulk mailing to potential customers. The goal will be to provide new customers with their services along with their customized version of Internet Explorer. Since the customer base varies, the workstation configurations are not known.

6. A small, 20-person printing firm that wants to provide the new browser to eight sales staff using old laptops. The workstations have slow dial-up connections to the Internet, floppy drives only, and no local network access.

Lab 12.44 *Configuring Offline Viewing*

Your boss recently read an article in a popular computer magazine about Offline Viewing. Your boss has asked you to do a review of the organization and develop a plan to implement Offline Viewing for the user community. Following are listed the scenarios in which you could implement Offline Viewing. Describe whether or not you would choose to implement Offline Viewing for these users and why you would or would not. Use Internet Explorer 5 to assist you with your answer.

1. Company employees with very fast, local Internet access.

2. Satellite office employees with WAN access to the Internet that is somewhat slow.

3. Sales staff on the road most of the time with little or no Internet access.

4. Warehouse staff with a local LAN but no connectivity to any other office.

Lab 12.45 *Choosing Security Options*

You are given the task of deploying Internet Explorer 5 in your organization. You will deploy the browser to your internal users using the IEAK; the platform will be Windows 95 and Windows NT. You have been asked to provide a security solution for each scenario that will ensure that the workstation is as secure as possible, but will not impede the user's ability to work. Which features would you consider adding or restricting based on each given scenario?

1. Satellite offices with no Internet access.

2. Corporate offices with fast, reliable Internet access.

3. Corporate kiosks located in the main entrance of every office.

4. Corporate call centers with access to only one Web-based application.

Considering these scenarios, which tool would you use to enforce your security settings? Which features would you consider using to comply with the company's security concerns?

Lab 12.46 *Configuring Outlook Express with the IEAK*

You have been asked to incorporate Outlook Express into your browser configuration. Given the following requirements, describe where these requirements can be accommodated using the IEAK. Name specific locations within the IEAK to configure these options.

1. You will provide your users with access to the company's POP and SMTP mail server using the correct tools and make the server names read-only. You will include a configuration for a company news server and not allow the users to add any additional accounts.

2. You will use the `welcome.html` file provided by your Web developers as the welcome message when the users first install Outlook Express. Specify `ie5help@widget.com` as the sender and reply address.

3. Configure Outlook Express as the default mail and news program. Include a news server named `news2.widget.com` as one of the default news servers.

4. Disable the Tip of the Day from view.

5. Use the following text as a signature for your e-mail users, "This message from a user at Widget.com may not reflect the views or policies of widget.com. For more information, please contact webmaster@widget.com." Also, do not use HTML as the message composition default.

Lab 13.47 *Using the Ping utility*

What is the TCP/IP address of `www.microsoft.com`? Use the Ping utility to obtain it.

Lab 13.48 *Using the Tracert utility*

Use the Tracert utility to discover how many "hops" you are from `www. idgbooks.com`.

Lab 13.49 *Using the NSLOOKUP utility*

Use the Nslookup utility from a Windows NT server to find out what the TCP/IP address of `www.microsoft.com` is.

Lab 13.50 *Using IP configuration utilities*

Using the correct utility, open your IP configuration and note the default gateway. After you have obtained the TCP/IP address, ping the address from a DOS prompt. Which utility did you use, and what happened?

Lab 13.51 *Troubleshooting the Internet Explorer installation*

You get a support call from a user who is attempting to install your pre-configured version of Internet Explorer. The user explains that when the installation is launched, the user gets an error after a few minutes of the install and the installation bombs out. Using the troubleshooting tools you learned about in Chapter 13, what tools would you use to troubleshoot this problem and what would you look for?

Lab 13.52 *Troubleshooting proxy server*

You have a group of new users that recently came on board with your company and are using a series of former employees' Windows NT Workstation computers. The users call and state that they cannot connect to any Web sites on the Internet. The error that the users are getting is that the page cannot be found. The site uses a proxy server for connectivity.

What would you use to troubleshoot this problem? Why would the fact that the users are new to the workstation have anything to do with the problem? How can you solve this problem?

Answers to Instant Assessment Questions

CHAPTER 1: INTERNET EXPLORER

1. D is correct, the Links bar enables you to create pointers to Web locations.

2. C is correct, offline browsing enables you to use the Synchronization Manager to view content while you are not connected to the Internet.

3. B is correct, you can use over 26 languages in Internet Explorer using language packs.

4. D is correct, SCO is not a supported platform for Internet Explorer.

5. D is correct.

6. D is correct, Outlook Express is included with Internet Explorer 5.

7. C is correct, WebDAV is the standard created for drag-and-drop in Internet browsing.

8. B is correct, the radio broadcasts are live audio streams in nature and cannot be used offline.

9. B is correct, Microsoft FrontPage Express is installed as a separate application. Office 4.0 did not natively offer the capability to perform this function.

10. D is correct, a tag, such as this language tag specifies the language used to code the page.

11. A is correct.

12. C is the correct answer; answer B is just plain ugly; the word kludge comes to mind.

13. B is the best answer.

14. B is correct. The Quick Links feature allows you to navigate to Web locations.

15. C is correct.

16. A is correct, the LDAP protocol enables you to use the Find On the Internet option to access a search site to look for information on the Web.

17. C is the best answer; extranets are usually designed for information that is private in nature, but available to individuals outside your mainstream organization.

18. B is the best answer.

19. B is correct, Internet Explorer 5.0 is not supported on the Windows 3.0 platform.

20. A is correct, you can address an internal Web site with Internet Explorer without being connected to the Internet.

CHAPTER 2: MICROSOFT OUTLOOK EXPRESS 5.0

1. B is the correct answer.

2. A is correct, all you have to do is change the From field.

3. D is correct.

4. D is correct.

5. D is the best answer.

6. C is correct.

7. B is the best answer.

8. B is correct, this also affects Internet Explorer Security as well.

9. A is correct.

10. D is the best answer.

11. A is correct, you can configure this in the General tab.

12. B is correct; Internet addresses are ignored by default.

13. C is the best answer.

14. A is correct.

15. A is correct.

16. A and C are correct.

17. B is correct, you can configure this option in the Send Tab.

18. D is correct.

19. A and C are correct.

20. C is correct.

21. B is correct, you can save messages in your Sent Items folder, this is set by default.

22. D is correct.

23. B is correct, they must be configured by the administration kit or by the end user.

24. C is correct, the digital ID gives you the ability to encrypt messages.

25. D is correct.

26. A is correct, you can create multiple folders if you so choose.

27. A is correct.

28. C is correct, the address book allows you an easy way to connect to another NetMeeting user.

29. B is the correct answer, the contents of the ID are encrypted.

30. C is the best answer, the Lightweight Directory Access Protocol allows for directory searching.

31. B is the best answer, the carbon copy of the message sent to the Webmaster is not accomplished.

32. D is the correct answer, newsgroup filters will not help this situation.

Lab 2.1 *Troubleshooting Outlook Express*

The first thing to do is to open Outlook Express and see the error yourself. When troubleshooting, always try to see the error yourself before trying to troubleshoot the problem. Read it thoroughly and go from there. Based on the user's description of the problem, it sounds like there is a problem connecting to the POP server. Select Tools ⇨ Accounts ⇨ Mail and select properties of the mail server. On the Servers tab, check the name of the mail server.

Then, open a DOS window by selecting Start ⇨ Run and typing **command**. Using the Ping utility, ping the server name that was entered in Outlook Express. If there is no response, either the server is down or the name is incorrect. Check another user's workstation if you do not know the correct POP server name. If you can ping the server, open a Telnet session by typing **telnet** at the DOS prompt. Click Connect ⇨ Remote System and type in the POP server name or IP address in the host name field. In the port field, type 110 (the default for POP). After typing the port number, click on Connect. If you are able to connect, the server is responding. If you are unable to connect, but you can ping the server, you can conclude that the POP service on the server is not responding or is not available. Remember that if you are connecting to a POP server on the Internet and you have a firewall, your firewall must allow port 110.

Lab 2.2 *Creating a Hotmail account*

After a few minutes, you will receive a message from me thanking you for reviewing the book. If you received the message, you have installed Hotmail correctly. Good work!

CHAPTER 3: MICROSOFT NETMEETING 3.0

1. C is correct.

2. A is correct, this can be accomplished using the application sharing feature.

3. C is correct, the International Telecommunications Union defines this standard.

4. C is correct, an LPT port is required.

5. D is correct.

6. A is correct.

7. C is correct, the name was changed to ILS by Microsoft.

8. D is correct.

9. B is correct, half duplex cards can only send or receive, not at the same time.

10. C is correct.

11. B is correct.

12. B is correct.

13. B is correct.

14. C is the most likely cause.

15. A is correct, files can be directed to a group or to an individual user.

16. A is correct.

17. C is correct, the CODECS are individual compression algorithms.

18. B is correct, this was available under the 2.*x* version of NetMeeting.

19. B and D are correct.

20. C is correct, this will refresh the directory list.

21. B is correct; while expensive, the capture card also gives you the ability to edit video and audio clips.

22. A is correct.

23. B is correct.

24. D is the best method to solve the problem.

25. B is correct, you can block your information by selecting the option on the General tab.

26. C is the most likely cause of the problem.

27. B is correct, the Video tab gives the user the ability to tune the video settings.

28. D is correct.

29. D is correct, NetMeeting must know which video device you want to use.

30. A is correct.

31. B is correct, you can use the Internet Explorer proxy settings or denote specific settings for NetMeeting.

32. C is correct, ULS communications are provided on port 522.

33. A is correct.

34. C is correct.

35. C is correct.

36. A is correct, without a policy in place, enforcement and compliance are almost impossible.

Lab 3.12 *Troubleshooting Microsoft NetMeeting*

Remember that a lot of the time, connectivity problems are related to the TCP/IP configuration of the user's workstation. Cases where the users have static IP configurations, such as scenarios that do not use DHCP, usually require more support.

First, open a Telnet session using Start ⇨ Run ⇨ Telnet. Click Connect ⇨ Remote System and type in the ILS server name or IP address in the host name field. If you do not have a local ILS server, use one on the Internet, like ils.quicknet.net. In the port field, type **389** (the default port for LDAP). Remember that if you are connecting to an ILS server on the Internet and you have a firewall, your firewall must allow port 389. After entering the port, click on Connect. If you are able to connect, you can be fairly sure that the user does not have an IP connection problem. If you are not able to connect, you can use IP troubleshooting tools such as Ping and Tracert to verify IP configurations. On a Windows 95 or 98 workstation, click Start ⇨ Run, and then type **WINIPCFG**. Examine your IP address and default gateway. Once you have done so, click Start ⇨ Run, and then type **command**. At the DOS prompt, ping your own IP address by typing **PING 127.1.1.1**. If the ping is successful, your workstation is responding using the TCP/IP protocol. Next, try pinging the gateway. If the gateway responds, you can be fairly sure that your connectivity is okay. The next step would be to ping another NetMeeting user on your network to see if connectivity can be established with another NetMeeting user.

Remember the facts while you are troubleshooting. The user's co-workers can connect with NetMeeting. Verify that the other users are on the same TCP/IP segment. If they are, then you can be reasonably sure that the problem is isolated to the user's workstation. Verify that the user's workstation configuration is the same as the other users and move on from there.

CHAPTER 4: WINDOWS MEDIA PLAYER 6

1. C is correct, this is the file type for Microsoft Word.

2. D is correct.

3. A is correct.

4. C is correct, *Uni*, meaning one, allows connections from one host to another.

5. D is correct, Advanced Streaming Format is the format in which NetShow server presents streaming content.

6. C is correct.

7. B is correct, 10 seconds is the default, which can be modified.

8. C is correct, the Help/About Media Player selection will allow you to see the user's current running version of Media Player 6.

9. D is correct, additional buffering will allow the application more time to correct errors and dropped packets received over the network.

10. A is correct, NetShow can carry a live video feed when configured to do so.

11. B is the correct answer.

12. C is the best answer.

13. D is correct, the View menu gives you access to the Options menu to configure Media Player.

14. A is correct, the Options ⇨ Advanced menu allows you to configure RealVideo.

15. B is correct, NetShow is a one-way video streaming application. Microsoft NetMeeting would, however, accommodate this requirement.

16. A, B, and D are correct. An MPE is not a Macintosh file format.

17. D is correct.

18. D is the correct answer.

19. C is correct, the encoder includes some examples to get you started.

20. A is correct, you can control the protocols used by Media Player at your option.

CHAPTER 5: INTERNET EXPLORER SETUP

1. A is correct. The Windows Update Setup is based on Microsoft's ActiveX engine.

2. C is correct. The Internet Explorer 5 Administration Kit is used by administrators to customize how Windows Update Setup installs Internet Explorer 5.

3. D is correct. Internet Explorer 5 can be installed on all of the platforms listed.

4. B is correct. You need at least 32MB of RAM to install Internet Explorer 5 on Windows NT.

5. C is correct. Internet settings files are files with an `.ins` extension that are used by Windows Update Setup to configure option settings for Internet Explorer 5.

6. A is correct. The `Active Setup Log.txt` file is written to the operating system folder on the machine and records every action taken by the Windows Update Setup while installing Internet Explorer 5.

7. A is correct. If a download error or timed out connection event occurs, Windows Update Setup logs a Retry event as it attempts a "Smart Recovery" to continue the installation from a different download site.

8. D is correct. The user must accept the EULA prior to installing Internet Explorer 5.

9. B is correct. Minimal, Typical, Full, and Custom are the four installation types you can choose when installing Internet Explorer 5.

10. A is correct. To support the use of multiple browsers, Internet Explorer 5 can be installed without associating Web and Internet files with Internet Explorer 5.

11. A is correct. The time estimate in minutes was added to better gauge the time associated with installing Internet Explorer 5.

12. B is correct. Internet Explorer 5 can be installed and run on a machine already running a browser to support the use of multiple browsers.

13. A is correct. Cookies, favorites, and proxy settings are imported to Internet Explorer 5.

14. C and D are correct. All Add-ins and Plug-ins must be re-installed when upgrading to Internet Explorer 5.

15. C is correct. Microsoft recommends using the Netscape Switchers Guide when attempting to migrate to Internet Explorer 5 from Netscape Navigator 3 or Netscape Navigator 4.

Lab 5.15 *Configuring Internet Explorer for use with proxy server*

The home page configuration should specify the intranet site in the General tab/Home page selection. The proxy server should be specified in the Connection tab/Proxy server selection. If there are multiple proxy servers for different protocols, they can be specified in the Advanced button on the same page.

Lab 5.16 *Configuring Internet Explorer for use on a standard workstation*

Any sites that the company wants to block can be specified in the Restricted Sites Zone configuration. This will prevent the user from accessing these sites. Extranet or partner sites can be added to the Trusted Sites Zone to allow more flexibility in running Java and ActiveX applications.

Lab 5.17 *Configuring advanced options in Internet Explorer*

You may want to consider adding the benefits manager's site to the Trusted Sites Zone. By default, the Internet Zone prompts you when you download signed ActiveX controls. You may want to ensure that SSL 3.0 is enabled in your user's browser configuration. SSL 3.0 is enabled by default. If a proxy server is in use, you may also want to make sure that this site is not cached, because data changes frequently. Also, ensure that the proxy server can pass traffic with SSL encryption.

Lab 5.18 *Troubleshooting Internet Explorer content*

These types of problems are usually the result of caching problems. The first step in troubleshooting this problem would be to check the amount of disk space the user has left on her hard drive.

1. Launch Internet Explorer.

2. Select Tools ➪ Internet Options ➪ General ➪ Temporary Internet Files ➪ Settings.

In the center of the dialog box, locate the temporary Internet files. By default, they are located in `C:\Windows\Temporary Internet Files` on Windows 95 and 98. Then, use Windows Explorer to see how much space is left on the drive. If the drive space is low, this may be the cause of the slow browsing.

In the same dialog box, check the Check for newer versions of stored pages selection. If the selection is set for never, this may be why the content is not being refreshed.

Lab 5.19 *Migrating from Netscape Navigator*

Proxy configurations can be included in your custom install. In addition, any proxy settings in the Netscape browser will be migrated to the Internet Explorer browser as well. The Netscape bookmarks will be migrated to Internet Explorer favorites during the installation. The cookies and plug-ins will also be migrated to Internet Explorer. You should, however, explain that not all plug-ins will be migrated to the new browser as some may only work with Netscape Navigator. Internet Explorer does not uninstall Netscape Navigator during the installation, so this concern is not applicable.

CHAPTER 6: THE INTERNET EXPLORER ADMINISTRATION KIT

1. B is correct; the IEAK is downloaded or provided on CD-ROM. Internet Explorer can be installed via floppy disks.

2. C is correct.

3. D is correct.

4. D is correct.

5. C is correct.

6. A is correct.

7. B is the best answer; you can only utilize the Corporate Administrator features by using the appropriate customization code. The same concept applies to the ISP mode.

8. B is correct.

9. B is correct; this feature is designed for Internet Service Providers.

10. B is correct, the user will see the components being installed, but does not choose any of the options.

11. C is correct, Internet Explorer includes Authenticode 2.0.

12. B is correct, there are other Certificate Authorities, and you can also install your own certificate server.

13. C is correct.

14. B is correct.

15. D is correct.

16. B and C are correct.

17. C is correct.

18. B is correct; DLT or DDS would be a better answer.

19. B is correct.

20. C is correct.

Lab 6.25 *Identifying roles and licensing*

Based on the verbiage of the agreement, the cable modem provider would select the external license. Since the people receiving the browser are paid customers of the provider, the external license would be the best answer.

The staff member of the IT department should select the Internal License agreement. Since the customer being deployed to is a member of the same organization as the IT department, this would be accurate.

The Web portal is providing the browser to its customers. Even though the customers do not pay for the service, the customers are not employees of the organization and therefore, would be best categorized as external.

CHAPTER 7: RUNNING THE IEAK

1. A is correct. While this is true, you will have problems with the Windows Desktop Update.

2. All but D are correct, this is only for ISPs.

3. D is correct.

4. B is correct, this only can identify the platform by default.

5. D is correct.

6. D is correct.

7. C is correct.

8. D is correct.

9. A is correct.

10. C is correct.

11. D is correct.

12. B is correct.

13. B is correct, this was only available in Internet Explorer 4.

14. A is correct.

15. B is correct.

16. B is correct, you can also use FTP.

17. A is correct.

18. A, B, and C are correct.

19. B and C are correct.

20. D is correct. Silent install is not a option for an ICP.

21. D is correct.

22. D is correct, provided the browser was not installed in compatibility mode.

23. E is correct.

24. A is correct.

25. A is correct.

26. B is correct.

27. B is correct.

28. B is correct.

29. B is correct.

30. A is correct.

31. A is correct.

Lab 7.26 *Troubleshooting the Internet Explorer Customization Wizard*

When you launch the Automatic Version Synchronization, the IEAK checks Microsoft's Web site for the latest files relating to the options you choose. After contacting the server, the IEAK checks your versions against the versions on the Web site and indicates new versions by the yellow icon. If you have recently synchronized your files and you notice in a subsequent session that all icons are yellow, you can be fairly sure that you have a connectivity problem. Try connecting to Microsoft's FTP site by clicking on Start ⇨ Run and typing **command**. At the DOS prompt, type **FTP ftp.microsoft.com**. If you are able to connect to the server, your connectivity is most likely fine and you have a workstation-related problem, such as low disk space or corrupted source files. Try synchronizing each component one at a time.

If you are not able to connect, you can use IP troubleshooting tools such as Ping and Tracert to verify IP configurations. On a Windows 95 or 98 workstation, click Start ⇨ Run, and then type **WINIPCFG**. Examine your IP address and default gateway. Once you have done so, click Start ⇨ Run, and then type **command**. At the DOS prompt, ping your own IP address by typing **PING 127.1.1.1.** If the ping is successful, your workstation is responding using the TCP/IP protocol. Next, try pinging the gateway. If the gateway responds, you can be fairly sure that your connectivity is okay.

Lab 7.27 *Troubleshooting registry and permissions problems*

The biggest issue to remember is that the while the software makes changes to both the user's profile and the local machine, one of the biggest features of Windows NT Workstation is the ability to prohibit the user from making changes to the local machine. To make changes to the system sections of the registry, the user must have local administrator privileges. These changes are invoked upon the first reboot after the Internet Explorer installation. The RUNONCE registry key is read and instructions are invoked to make the final registry changes to complete the installation of Internet Explorer 5. To do this, the user must have local administrator privileges. You can use the Systems Management Server to install the software for you and create a script that logs the user in under another context to complete the installation, or you can create your own. Check TechNet for more details on Systems Management Server installations.

Lab 7.28 *Configuring Microsoft NetMeeting*

This is an ideal scenario where WAN speed is good, and the users have all of the hardware necessary to run NetMeeting. NetMeeting has some security concerns for your users, like desktop sharing and file transfer, for example. If someone wanted to, they could unknowingly transfer a virus-infected file or possibly damage another user's workstation by accident with remote sharing.

Another option you will need to configure is the default ILS server, in this case it is ils.widget.com. Since most of the other restrictions are not applicable due to the hardware and bandwidth, you can be reasonably sure that this will be a good start.

Lab 7.29 *Working with the IEAK*

In Stage 4, customizing the browser, you will first customize the title bar. Next, you will move on to adding a browser toolbar button.

1. For Acrobat, you can add a toolbar button for Acrobat. Select Add at the Browser Toolbar Buttons screen and type **Acrobat** in the caption window. Next, add the path to the Acrobat.exe file as specified in the requirement. Then, add the color and grayscale icons' paths in the respective windows. Select OK and Next to continue.

2. Next, you will add Animated graphics to the browser so that the icon in the upper left-hand corner of the browser will indicate when the browser is performing an action. Specify the path to the logos here in the 22×22 windows and specify the location to the file.

3. Skip the next screen, Static Logo, and select Next to move on to the Important URLs screen. Here, you will specify the Web locations for the Home page, Search page, and Support pages. Select Next to continue.

4. Here, at the Favorites and Links screen, you will add the links that have been requested. Use the Remove button to remove all of the default links and use the Add URL button to add the links as requested. Select Next to continue.

5. At the Channels screen, make sure that Turn on desktop Channel Bar by default is not selected. Then, select Delete existing channels, if present. Select Next to continue.

6. At the next screen, Welcome Page, select Use a custom welcome page and specify the URL to the file.

CHAPTER 8: USING THE PROFILE MANAGER

1. B is correct, the Profile Manager is used to change settings for the Internet Explorer suite of software.

2. D is correct.

3. D is correct, this is a change from Internet Explorer 4.

4. D is correct, My Computer cannot be removed.

5. A is correct.

6. A is correct, this will disable the cache from being loaded on the user's profile located on the file server.

7. C is correct.

8. B is correct.

9. D is correct, you can correct this with the Profile Manager.

10. B is correct, you can change the settings for proxies in the registry in HKEY\LM\SOFTWARE\MICROSOFT\ADVANCEDOPTIONS\HTTP\PROXY.

11. A is correct.

12. D is correct.

13. A is correct.

14. A is correct.

15. A is correct.

16. B is correct, you are only allowed one SMTP server per mailbox. Consider using a round robin or cost based algorithm in DNS.

17. B is correct, it will run much slower.

18. D is correct, none of these will solve the problem. The best resolution would be to update your .ins file with the boot menu enabled again.

19. B is correct, this is a security precaution.

20. A is correct.

21. A is correct.

22. B is correct, the autocomplete feature allows the browser to finish typing URLs for you.

23. A is correct.

24. A is correct, this can be done by specifying the proxy host name and port settings in the Windows Media Player section of the Profile Manager.

Lab 8.30 *Importing System Policies*

Using the IEAK profile manager, open your existing `.ins` file. Then, you would use the import feature located in Policy/Import in the Profile Manager application. The policy file is located in `Program Files/Ieak/Policies`. Select the import feature and then select the `inetcorp.adm` policy to import the file. When completed, save and copy the file to your intranet location of the existing file. Make sure that the file is the same name and that the file is in the same case, for example, `widget.ins`.

Lab 8.31 *Managing your browser configuration*

Changing the name of the file is difficult once the browser is deployed, and is not advisable. The user can change the name of the file at his or her workstation in the Tools ⇨ Internet Options ⇨ Connection ⇨ LAN settings page or you could put together a `.reg` file to change it. Once you put the file together, you could use SMS, a login script, or send it to the user in an e-mail message.

To make the change effective on your user's browsers, you would post the file on the Web site in the same location as the old file. When the workstation reached the update time of the pre-configured update cycle, the browser would pick up the changes in the file and install them on the user's local workstation. The biggest reason to use the auto-configuration script is configuration management. From one location, you can make changes to everyone's browser configuration. With this change, you can be reasonably certain that the configuration will be propagated throughout your organization the same way. By letting the users do it manually, you run the risk of the task not being done, being done incorrectly, or asking users who are not fluent enough to try to learn about the browser.

CHAPTER 9: THE CONNECTION MANAGER ADMINISTRATION KIT

1. B is correct, absolutes are almost never true with software.

2. A is correct.

3. B is correct, you can select this option in the Post-Connection options screen.

4. B is correct, you can run pre- and post-connect tunnel actions for VPN configurations.

5. B is correct, you can specify this information in the CMAK.

6. A is correct, the service profiles can co-exist with one another.

7. B is correct. Phone books are created with software located on the Windows NT Server Option Pak.

8. B is correct, this wording refers to pre- and post-connection actions.

9. A is correct.

10. B is correct, the realm name specifies the address that your users will utilize.

11. D is correct.

12. A is correct, this can be used to standardize file locations for your users.

13. C is correct.

14. B is correct, this takes place prior to the connection.

15. B is correct, these sizes are dictated by the application.

Lab 9.32 *Troubleshooting dial-up*

Always start with the basics. The most common problems are usually very obvious, and as professionals, we sometimes look deeper than we should to solve the problem. Try some of these basic dial-up troubleshooting steps to solve the problem.

1. Has the user ever connected to this dial-up number before?

2. Is the modem responding? Check the Diagnostics section of the Modem controls in Control Panel.

3. Is the phone number that the user is dialing long distance?

4. Does the user need to dial an 8 or a 9 from where they are to get an outside line? Is there a dial tone heard during the dial sequence?

5. Does the user hear a handshake (a really annoying screeching sound) when the user connects?

6. Examine the properties of a working dial-up connection to the same number and compare these settings to the user's configuration. Check the properties of the dial-up connection in My Computer/Dial-Up Networking. Are these settings the same?

Using basic troubleshooting steps, you will be able to solve the vast majority of user problems.

Lab 9.33 *Troubleshooting VPN connections*

VPNs are established over the Internet using the PPTP VPN client and a server acting as a VPN gateway. The VPN gateway is the user's tunnel point into your network. Since the user is getting an error logging in, this could mean that there could be a connectivity problem to the VPN gateway or that the gateway itself is not responding. You could try pinging the gateway to see if the gateway responds. Alternatively, the PPTP client can use the same user ID and password as the Dial-up Networking ID and password. The PPTP client ID and password can also be different depending on what was chosen at the time of implementation. You may want to check with the user to ensure that the correct ID and password are being used.

Lab 9.34 *Deploying PPTP/VPN solutions*

You can provide VPN access using the CMAK. The CMAK will allow you to provide the IP address of the VPN gateway, which will be an NT server providing RAS services. Before running the CMAK, you will need the IP address of the VPN gateway and the IP addresses of the internal DNS and WINS servers. The CMAK allows you to provide DNS and WINS services for a VPN session using the CMAK.

Lab 9.35 *Deploying dial-up networking*

You can provide dial-up access using the CMAK. The CMAK will allow you to provide the phone number of the RAS gateway, which will be an NT server providing RAS services. Before running the CMAK, you will need the phone number of the RAS gateway and the IP addresses of the internal DNS and WINS servers. The CMAK enables you to provide DNS and WINS services for a dial-up session using the CMAK.

CHAPTER 10: INTERNET EXPLORER MAINTENANCE

1. A is correct, User settings can be modified after installation by using the IEAK Profile Manager.

2. D is correct. All of the above files are created by the IEAK Profile Manager.

3. A is correct. Auto Detect is based on Web Proxy Auto Discovery (WPAD).

4. B and D are correct. While all are protocols/services, only DNS and DHCP support Auto Detect.

5. C is correct. Auto Configuration will run only when the user's machine is restarted.

6. D is correct. Auto Detect and Auto Configuration entries are in the [URL] section of the configuration file.

7. B is correct. Dynamic Host Configuration Protocol (DHCP) servers must support DHCPInfoForm messages to support Auto Detect with Internet Explorer 5.

8. A is correct. DHCP provides faster access time and more flexibility in LAN-only environments.

9. B is correct. 252 is the code number for the option type to support Auto Detect.

10. A and D are correct. Enabling Auto Detect on DNS involves creating either a host record or a CNAME "alias" record. These are then added to the DNS database file.

11. B is correct. *<host name>* IN A *<ip address of host>* is the correct syntax to add a host record.

12. A is correct.

13. A and B are correct. Only Proxy settings such as `.pac` files, JScripts (`.js`), or JavaScripts (`.jvs`), can be imported to the IEAK Profile Manager.

14. B is correct. An Add-On Components Web Site can be created to provide the ability to add components after Internet Explorer 5 has been installed.

15. A is correct. The full path must be provided to the IEAK Profile Manager for the Add-on Components Page.

Lab 10.36 *Adding auto-proxy scripts*

In Stage 4 of the IEAK, you will be asked to provide the location of your auto-proxy script. The auto-proxy script has to be located on a local Web server. You will need to know the server name and path to the file, such as `http://intranet.widget.com/scripts/proxy.js`.

Lab 10.37 *Downloading the IEAK*

The download location for the correct version of the IEAK is `http://www.microsoft.com/windows/ieak/en/download/bits/x8650.asp`.

Once you have downloaded the software, you will need to obtain a customization code from Microsoft. To obtain this, navigate to `https://ieak.microsoft.com/en/license/newlicensee.asp`.

You should choose the Corporate Administrator role for the most accurate description of your deployment.

Lab 10.38 *Platform deployment considerations*

You will have to create a least three installations. Sales, Marketing, and Engineering can use the same installation routing that covers Windows 95, Windows 98, and Windows NT 4. The Maintenance department users will have to use a build created for Windows 3.1/WFW/Windows NT 3.51. The IT department users will have to use the UNIX version of the browser.

Lab 10.39 *Selecting languages in Internet Explorer*

You will have to create a least four installations. Sales and Marketing can use the same installation routing that covers Windows 95, Windows 98, and Windows NT 4 in the English language build. The Engineering department is based in Japan, and will have their own build in Japanese. The Maintenance department users will have to use a build created for Windows 3.1/WFW/Windows NT 3.51 in Korean. Finally, The Support department users will have to use the UNIX version of the browser in Norwegian.

Lab 10.40 *Using Install on Demand*

It would make sense to include Install on Demand in this scenario. If you are going to send CD-ROMs to the offices or provide access to your intranet server to download the components, you should consider using this feature. To use the Install on Demand feature, you need to make sure that you synchronize all components before creating your build and also make sure that all components are selected to be included on the media in Stage 3, Components on Media.

Lab 10.41 *Modifying the browser*

Using the IEAK Profile Manager, open your existing `.ins` file. After you have opened the policy file, select User Agent String from the Wizard Settings and enter your User Agent String. When completed, save and copy the file to your intranet location of the existing file. Make sure that the file is the same name and in the same case, for example `widget.ins`.

Lab 10.42 *Choosing installation types*

For the 250-user community, the silent installation would be the best way to install the software to ensure that the user does not get involved in the installation and does not panic as the software is installed. For the network engineers, their requirements vary in need, so an interactive installation would be prudent so they can select their own options. Since the requirement for the developers is to have the same configuration, the hands-free installation would be prudent so that they cannot make any changes to the browser installation.

CHAPTER 11: PRE-DEPLOYMENT PLANNING

Lab 11.43 *Choosing deployment solutions*

1. The best answer here would be to deploy using the CD-ROM. Since dialing up the company would give them very slow downloads of the browser installation, the fastest method would be a CD-ROM.

2. Download would be the best method here due to the company's being spread out all over the country. This will give the organization a central point of installation and a low-cost distribution method. As a secondary solution, CD-ROMs could also be distributed.

3. Since the browser is already installed, the single disk branding option would be the best solution here. The existing browser could be branded with the CIO's desired configuration and accomplish the task in this manner.

4. The best solution for this company would be the flat installation. The installation can be placed on a file server and installed from there. Given that the intranet server is so busy, a download installation would not be advisable in this scenario. CD-ROMs could also be distributed as an alternate solution.

5. The single disk download is only available to ISPs. The ISP could mail out a single diskette to potential customers and have the customers download the browser from their Web site. The CD-ROM could also be used in this scenario as an alternative; the floppy disk option is, however, cheaper to deploy.

6. The floppy disk option is the best solution here. Since the laptops are old and do not have CD-ROMs, the floppy disk option would be the quickest method.

CHAPTER 12: SOME REAL-WORLD SCENARIOS

Lab 12.44 *Configuring Offline Viewing*

Offline Viewing enables the users to view Web pages when the workstation is not connected to the network. Company employees with fast Internet access do not really need this feature, other than possibly to preserve bandwidth. It would make sense for the satellite and sales staffs to use Offline Viewing, as their access is slow or non-existent in some scenarios. Using this feature, they could view the Web material when the connections were slow or not available. The warehouse staff cannot connect to anything; therefore, the Offline Viewing feature would not be of much use to them.

Lab 12.45 *Choosing security options*

The best solution here would be to define a global security configuration, where possible. Internet Explorer breaks the security zones down into Zones. For the offices that do not have Internet access, giving these offices a restrictive Internet security policy would have no effect on these users, since they cannot get to the Internet Zone. For the corporate users, the Internet Zone restrictions would be frequently used to protect the users from harmful Web content.

For the kiosks and call centers, I would suggest creating an .ins file for each scenario. For the kiosk site, you would want the most restrictive configuration possible. Using the Profile Manager, I would suggest locking down the desktop by hiding all icons, preventing logoff; prevent re-booting in a DOS window, and so on.

Since the kiosks are not normally staffed, the workstations need to be as bullet-proof as possible. As far as the call center goes, locking down the desktop is another valuable consideration. The call center users only use one Web-based application and nothing else. With that in mind, they do not need access to anything else. Using the Profile Manager, you can restrict their access to only one domain or site to only allow them access to the application.

Lab 12.46 *Configuring Outlook Express with the IEAK*

1. Using the Outlook Express Accounts Window in the IEAK, you will provide the POP or IMAP server name. Next, you will provide the SMTP server name and the news server name here as well. At the bottom of the page, you will select Make server names read-only and disable access to accounts.

2. Using the Outlook Express Custom Content screen, you will enter the path to the `welcome.html` file to be included. In the Sender and Reply-to fields, enter `ie5help@widget.com`.

3. In the Outlook Express Custom Settings screen, specify that Outlook Express is the default program for mail and news. In the newsgroups window, specify the news server name, `news2.widget.com`.

4. At the Outlook Express View Settings screen, uncheck the Tip of the Day from the basic views.

5. At the Outlook Express Compose Settings screen, check the Append a signature to each message and enter the text "This message from a user at Widget.com may not reflect the views or policies of widget.com. For more information, please contact webmaster@widget.com." Uncheck HTML as the message composition default.

CHAPTER 13: TROUBLESHOOTING THE INTERNET EXPLORER SUITE

1. D is correct, tracing a route to the router will tell you if the router is responding or not.

2. B is correct, the log allows you to troubleshoot problems with the Internet Explorer setup.

3. C is correct, Reach Out has known problems documented by Microsoft with Internet Explorer.

4. B is correct.

5. B is correct, these can also be changed within the NetMeeting application.

6. A and D are correct, these files are case-sensitive to these styles dictated by the Internet Explorer application.

7. D is correct, Network Monitor allows you to view utilization and statistics.

8. D is correct, Windows 95 does not have permissions on the file system like Windows NT.

9. B is correct, roaming profiles allow the user to retain custom settings for applications, such as Internet Explorer when the user goes to other workstations.

10. D is correct, you cannot run Internet Explorer from a server, it requires a local installation.

11. B is correct, DCOM is included in Windows 98. The DCOM installation is only necessary for Windows 95.

12. D is correct, the `smtp.log` logs errors encountered in SMTP transactions.

13. D is correct.

14. D is correct, this usually means that the link that was specified is incorrect.

15. B is correct.

16. B is correct, you need to synchronize your source files the first time you run the IEAK.

17. C is correct.

18. D is correct.

19. A is correct, this lists the name table for the machine specified by its address.

20. A is correct.

21. A is correct.

22. A and C are correct.

23. B is correct, patch 103792-09 is necessary at a very minimum to run the installation.

24. B is correct, Service Pack 3 is the minimum service pack.

25. B is correct, Nslookup is not available in Windows 98.

Lab 13.51 *Troubleshooting the Internet Explorer installation*

The cardinal rule in troubleshooting the installation is to check the `Active Setup Log.txt` file first. Have the user send you the file or review the file yourself. One of the biggest problems installing the software is the user's local disk. Examine the log for HRESULT errors that you learned about in Chapter 13. These errors will lead you in the right direction to solve the user's problem. Common problems are running out of disk space, virus scan software interfering with the installation, connectivity problems, and permissions problems.

Lab 13.52 *Troubleshooting proxy server*

The fact that the users are new and that they are using NT Workstation almost gives the problem out immediately. Since the profiles are new on the workstation, it is very likely that there is no proxy configuration. Select Tools ⇨ Internet Options ⇨ Connections ⇨ LAN Settings for the current proxy configuration. In the proxy configuration section, you will most likely see that there is no currently configured proxy server. To solve the problem, enter the proxy server name and port. Also, make sure that the Web sites that the user is attempting to connect to are not included in the proxy exception list by mistake.

Exam Prep Tips

The Microsoft Certified Professional Exams are *not* easy, and they require a great deal of preparation. The exam questions measure real-world skills. Your ability to answer these questions correctly will be enhanced by as much hands-on experience with the product as you can get.

 web links

Although the Exam Objectives in Appendix A were current when this book was published, you may want to ensure that you have the most current version of the exam objectives by accessing the Microsoft Training and Certification Web site at `www.microsoft.com/ train_cert.`

ABOUT THE EXAMS

An important aspect of passing the MCP Certification Exams is understanding the big picture. This includes understanding how the exams are developed and scored.

Every job function requires different levels of cognitive skills, from memorization of facts and definitions to the comprehensive ability to analyze scenarios, design solutions, and evaluate options. To make the exams relevant in the real world, Microsoft Certified Professional exams test the specific cognitive skills needed for the job functions being tested. These exams go beyond testing rote knowledge—you need to *apply* your knowledge, analyze technical solutions, solve problems, and make decisions—just like you would on the job.

Exam Items and Scoring

Microsoft certification exams consist of four types of items: multiple-choice, multiple-rating, enhanced, and simulation. The way you indicate your answer and the number of points you receive differ depending on the type of item.

Multiple-choice item

A traditional multiple-choice item presents a problem and asks you to select either the best answer (single response) or the best set of answers (multiple response) to the given item from a list of possible answers.

For a multiple-choice item, your response is scored as either correct or incorrect. A correct answer receives a score of 1 point and an incorrect answer receives a score of 0 points.

In the case of a multiple-choice, multiple-response item (for which the correct response consists of more than one answer), the item is scored as being correct only if all the correct answers are selected. No partial credit is given for a response that does not include all the correct answers for the item.

For consistency purposes, the question in a multiple-choice, multiple-response item is always presented in singular form, regardless of how many answers are correct. Always follow the instructions displayed at the bottom of the window.

Multiple-rating item

A multiple-rating item presents a task similar to those presented in multiple-choice items. In a multiple-choice item, you are asked to select the best answer or answers from a selection of several potential answers. In contrast, a multiple-rating item presents a task, along with a proposed solution. Each time the task is presented, a different solution is proposed. In each multiple-rating item, you are asked to choose the answer that best describes the results produced by one proposed solution.

Enhanced item

An enhanced item is similar to a multiple-choice item because it asks you to select your response from a number of possible responses. However, unlike the traditional multiple-choice item that presents you with a list of possible answers from which to choose, an enhanced item may ask you to indicate your answer in one of the following three ways:

- Type the correct response, such as a command name.
- Review an exhibit (such as a screen shot, a network configuration drawing, or a code sample), and then use the mouse to select the area of the exhibit that represents the correct response.
- Review an exhibit, and then select the correct response from the list of possible responses.

   As with a multiple-choice item, your response to an enhanced item is scored as either correct or incorrect. A correct answer receives full credit of 1 point, and an incorrect answer receives a score of 0 points.

Simulation item

A simulation imitates the functionality of product components or environments, complete with error messages and dialog boxes. You are given a scenario and one or more tasks to complete by using that simulation. A simulation item's goal is to determine if you know how to complete a given task. Just as with the other item types, the simulation is scored when you complete the exam. A simulation item may ask you to indicate your answer in one of the following ways:

- Review an exhibit (such as a screen shot, a network configuration drawing, or a code sample), and then use the GUI simulation to resolve, configure, or otherwise complete the assigned task.
- Based on information in the exam scenario, resolve, configure, or otherwise complete the assigned task.

   As with the other item types, you receive credit for a correct answer only if all of the requested criteria are met by your actions in the scenario. There is no partial credit for a incomplete simulation item.

Exam Formats

Microsoft uses two different exam formats to determine how many questions are going to be presented on the exam. The majority of Microsoft exams have historically used a fixed length exam, with between 50 and 100 questions per exam. Each time you take the exam, you are presented with a different set of questions, but still comprising an equal number of questions. Recently, Microsoft has attempted to increase the reliability of its testing procedures, and has implemented new strategies to that end. The newest format is called computer adaptive testing. A computer adaptive test (CAT) is tailored to the individual exam-taker. You start with an easy-to-moderate question; if you answer the question correctly, you get a more difficult follow-up question. If that question is answered correctly, the difficulty of subsequent questions continues to increase. Conversely, if the second question is answered incorrectly, the following questions will be easier. This process continues only until the CAT determines your ability. As a result, you may have an exam that comprises only 15 questions, but contains extremely difficult questions. Alternately, you may have an exam that contains 50 moderately difficult questions.

PREPARING FOR A MICROSOFT CERTIFIED PROFESSIONAL EXAM

The best way to prepare for an exam is to study, learn, and master the job function on which you'll be tested. For any certification exam, you should follow these important preparation steps:

1. Identify the objectives on which you'll be tested.

2. Assess your current mastery of those objectives.

3. Practice tasks and study the areas you haven't mastered.

This section describes tools and techniques that may be helpful as you perform these steps to prepare for the exam.

Exam Preparation Guides

For each certification exam, an Exam Preparation Guide provides important, specific information about what you'll be tested on and how best to prepare. These guides are essential tools for preparing to take certification exams. You'll find the following types of valuable information in the exam preparation guides:

- *Tasks you should master.* Outlines the overall job function tasks you should master.

- *Exam objectives.* Lists the specific skills and abilities on which you should expect to be measured.

- *Product resources.* Tells you the products and technologies with which you should be experienced.

- *Suggested reading.* Points you to specific reference materials and other publications that discuss one or more of the exam objectives.

- *Suggested curriculum.* Provides a specific list of instructor-led and self-paced courses relating to the job function tasks and topics in the exam.

You'll also find pointers to additional information that may help you prepare for the exams, such as *Microsoft TechNet*, *Microsoft Developer Network* (MSDN), online forums, and other sources.

By paying attention to the verbs used in the "Exam Objectives" section of the Exam Preparation Guide, you will get an idea of the level at which you'll be tested on that objective.

To view the most recent versions of the Exam Preparation Guides, which include the exam's objectives, check out Microsoft's Training and Certification Web site at www.microsoft.com/train_cert/.

Assessment Exams

When preparing for the exams, take lots of assessment exams. Assessment exams are self-paced exams that you take at your own computer. When you complete an assessment exam, you receive instant score feedback so you can determine areas in which additional study may be helpful before you take the certification exam. Although your score on an assessment exam doesn't necessarily indicate what your score will be on the certification exam, assessment exams give you the opportunity to answer items that are similar to those on the certification exams. The assessment exams also use the same computer-based testing tool as the certification exams, so you don't have to learn the tool on the day of the exam. An assessment exam exists for almost every certification exam.

TAKING A MICROSOFT CERTIFIED PROFESSIONAL EXAM

This section contains information about registering for and taking a Microsoft Certified Professional exam, including what to expect when you arrive at the testing center to take the exam.

How to Register for an Exam

Candidates may take exams at any of more than 700 Sylvan Prometric testing centers around the world. For the location of a Sylvan Prometric testing center near you, call (800) 755-EXAM (755-3926). Outside the United States and Canada, contact your local Sylvan Prometric Registration Center.

You can also take exams at any of the over 160 different Virtual University Enterprises testing centers around the world. To register for an exam at a VUE testing center in your area, call (888) 837-8616. Outside the United States and Canada, contact your local Virtual University Enterprises Registration Center.

Sylvan Prometric offers online registration for Microsoft exams at its registration Web site—`https://www.2test.com`. You can also register for an exam at a VUE testing center by visiting `http://www.vue.com/ms`.

To register for a Microsoft Certified Professional exam:

1. Determine which exam you want to take and note the exam number.

2. Call the Sylvan Prometric or VUE Registration Center nearest to you. If you haven't registered with them before, you will be asked to provide information to the Registration Center.

3. You can then schedule your exam at your choice of location. Once the exam is scheduled, you will be asked to provide payment for the exam. Both of the testing centers take major credit cards and offer pre-payment options for purchasing exam certificates for future or corporate use.

When you schedule the exam, you'll be provided instructions regarding the appointment, cancellation procedures, and ID requirements, as well as information about the testing center location.

Exams must be taken within one year of payment. You can schedule exams up to six weeks in advance, or as late as one working day prior to the date of the exam. You can cancel or reschedule your exam if you contact the testing center at least one working day prior to the exam.

Although subject to space availability, same-day registration is available in some locations. Where same-day registration is available, you must register a minimum of two hours before test time.

What to Expect at the Testing Center

As you prepare for your certification exam, it may be helpful to know what to expect when you arrive at the testing center on the day of your exam. The following information gives you a preview of the general procedure you'll go through at the testing center:

- You will be asked to sign the log book upon arrival and departure.
- You will be required to show two forms of identification, including one photo ID (such as a driver's license or company security ID) before you may take the exam.
- The test administrator will give you a Testing Center Regulations form that explains the rules you will be expected to comply with during the test. You will be asked to sign the form, indicating that you understand the regulations and will comply.
- The test administrator will show you to your test computer and will handle any preparations necessary to start the testing tool and display the exam on the computer.
- You will be provided a set amount of scratch paper for use during the exam. All scratch paper will be collected from you at the end of the exam.
- The exams are all closed-book. You may not use a laptop computer or have any notes or printed material with you during the exam session.
- Some exams may include additional materials, or exhibits. If any exhibits are required for your exam, the test administrator will provide you with

them before you begin the exam and collect them from you at the end of the exam.

- Before you begin the exam, the test administrator will tell you what to do when you complete the exam. If the test administrator doesn't explain this to you, or if you are unclear about what you should do, ask the administrator before beginning the exam.

- The number of items on each exam varies, as does the amount of time allotted for each exam. Generally, certification exams consist of about 50 to 100 items (unless you are taking a CAT exam) and have durations of 60 to 90 minutes. You can verify the number of items and time allotted for your exam when you register.

Because you'll be given a specific amount of time to complete the exam once you begin, if you have any questions or concerns, don't hesitate to ask the test administrator before the exam begins.

As an exam candidate, you are entitled to the best support and environment possible for your exam. In particular, you are entitled to the following:

- A quiet, uncluttered test environment
- Scratch paper
- The tutorial for using the online testing tool, and time to take the tutorial
- A knowledgeable and professional test administrator
- The opportunity to submit comments about the testing center and staff, or the test itself

The Certification Development Team will investigate any problems or issues you raise and make every effort to resolve them quickly.

Your Exam Results

Once you have completed an exam, you will be given immediate, online notification of your pass or fail status. You will also receive a printed Examination Score Report indicating your pass or fail status and your exam results by section. (The test administrator will give you the printed score report.) Test scores are automatically forwarded to Microsoft within five working days after you take the test. You do not need to send your score to Microsoft.

If you pass the exam, you will receive confirmation from Microsoft, typically within two to four weeks.

If You Don't Receive a Passing Score

If you do not pass a certification exam, you may call the testing center to schedule a time to retake the exam. Before retaking the exam, you should review the appropriate Exam Preparation Guide and focus additional study on the topic areas where your exam results could be improved. Please note that you must pay again for each exam retake.

One way to determine areas where additional study may be helpful is to review your individual section scores carefully. The section titles in your score report generally correlate to specific groups of exam objectives listed in the Exam Preparation Guide.

Here are some specific ways you can prepare to retake an exam:

- Go over the section-by-section scores on your exam results, noting objective areas where your score could be improved.
- Review the Exam Preparation Guide for the exam, with a special focus on the tasks and objective areas that correspond to the exam sections where your score could be improved.
- Increase your real-world, hands-on experience and practice performing the listed job tasks with the relevant products and technologies.
- Consider taking or retaking one or more of the suggested courses listed in the Exam Preparation Guide.
- Review the suggested readings listed in the Exam Preparation Guide.
- After you review the materials, retake the corresponding Assessment Exam.

FOR MORE INFORMATION

To find out more about Microsoft Education and Certification materials and programs, to register with a testing center, or to get other useful information, check the following resources. Outside the United States or Canada, contact your local Microsoft office or testing center.

- **Microsoft Certified Professional Program:** (800) 636-7544. Call for information about the Microsoft Certified Professional program and exams, and to order the *Microsoft Certified Professional Program Exam Study Guide* or the Microsoft Train_Cert Offline CD-ROM.

- **Sylvan Prometric Testing Centers:** (800) 755-EXAM. Call to register to take a Microsoft Certified Professional exam at any of the more than 700 Sylvan Prometric testing centers around the world, or to order the *Microsoft Certified Professional Program Exam Study Guide*.

- **Virtual University Enterprises Testing Centers:** (888) 837-8616. Call to register to take a Microsoft Certified Professional exam at any of the over 160 different Virtual University Enterprises testing centers around the world.

- **Education Program and Course Information:** (800) SOLPROV. Call for information about Microsoft Official Curriculum courses, Microsoft education products, and the Microsoft Solution Provider Authorized Technical Education Center (ATEC) program, where you can attend a Microsoft Official Curriculum course, or to order the *Microsoft Certified Professional Program Exam Study Guide*.

- **Microsoft Certification Development Team:** To volunteer for participation in one or more exam development phases or to report a problem with an exam, address written correspondence to: Certification Development Team, Microsoft Education and Certification, One Microsoft Way, Redmond, WA 98052.

- **Microsoft TechNet Technical Information Network:** (800) 344-2121. Call for support professionals and system administrators. Outside the United States and Canada, call your local Microsoft subsidiary for information.

- **Microsoft Developer Network (MSDN):** (800) 759-5474. MSDN is the official source for software development kits, device driver kits, operating systems, and information about developing applications for Microsoft Windows and Windows NT.

- **Online Services:** (800) 936-3500. Call for information about Microsoft Connection on CompuServe, Microsoft Knowledge Base, Microsoft Software Library, Microsoft Download Service, and Internet.

IEAK Checklist

E

When you are ready to begin your IEAK build, the best way to prepare is to know the options that you want to include beforehand. As you decide on which options to include and which to exclude, you can use this checklist to make your selections. The list of options is prepared in the order in which the selections are presented in the IEAK interface. Make your choices with the list, and run the IEAK.

IEAK SELECTION	SELECT? Y/N

Considerations during IEAK process

Default Browser?

Prompt User to Install IE5 during Outlook install?

Remove Windows Update?

Uninstall Options?

Compatibility Mode?

Windows Desktop?

Custom Title Bar?

Animated Logo?

Custom Home Page?

Custom Search Page?

Custom Online Support Page?

Links and Favorites?

Channels?

Welcome Page? Custom or Defaults?

Proxy Settings?

Custom Certificate Authorities?

Authenticode Security?

Security Zone Settings? (Low, Medium–Low, Medium, or High)

Content Ratings?

LDAP server for Windows Address Book?

Components

DCOM for Windows

Offline Browsing

MS Virtual Machine

IE Core Fonts

Dynamic HTML Data-binding

IE Browser Enhancements

Chat 2.5

Windows Media Player Codecs

IEAK Selection	*Select? Y/N*
DirectAnimation	
Vector Graphics Rendering (VML)	
AOL ART Image Format Support	
Macromedia Shockwave	
Macromedia Flash Player	
FrontPage Extensions	
Web Publishing Wizard	
Web Folders	
Additional Web Fonts	
MS Wallet	
Language Auto-Selection	
Policies and Restrictions	
Control Management	
Databinding	
RDS?	
TDC?	
XML?	
Internet Explorer Active Setup	
IE Active Setup Control	
Media Player	
Active Movie Runtime	
ActiveMovie Control	
MS NetShow Player	
Windows Media Player	
Extras	
Animated Button	
IE Label Control	
IE Menu Control	
IE Preloader Control	
IE Timer Control	

IEAK SELECTION	*SELECT? Y/N*
Menu Controls	
MCSiMenu	
PopupMenu Object	
MS Agent	
MS Agent Control 1.5	
MS Agent Control 2.0	
MS Chat	
MS Chat Control Object 2.0 – 2.5	
MS Wallet	
Webpost	
MS ActiveX Upload Control 1.5	
MSN	
Cache Preloader	
MSN Cache Preloader	
CarPoint	
CarPoint AutoPricer Control	
Install	
MSN Install Control	
MSN RegEdit Control	
MSN Version Control	
MSN.ini Control	
Setup BBS Control	
Investor	
MS Investor Ticker	
Stock Ticker	
MSNBC	
MSNBC News Browser Control 2.3	
NewsBrowser	
Music	
Evita Character	

IEAK SELECTION	SELECT? Y/N
Imixer 1.0	
Imixer 3.0	
Interactive Music Junior	
Quick View Access	
MSNViaDC Control	
Third Party	
InstallShield	
InstallFromTheWeb ActiveX Control	
Macromedia	
Macromedia Flash	
RSACi	
RSACi Ratings Control	
Microsoft Chat	
MS Chat	
Additional server list	
Default chat server	
Change default chat room	
Default chat room	
Default character	
Default backdrop	
User Profile String	
Show only registered rooms in room list	
Microsoft NetMeeting	
Restrict the use of file transfer	
Prevent the user from sending files	
Prevent the user from receiving files	
Restrict the use of application sharing	
Disable all application sharing features	
Prevent the user from sharing the clipboard	
Prevent the user from sharing MS–DOS windows	

IEAK Selection	*Select? Y/N*
Prevent the user from sharing Explorer windows	
Prevent the user from collaborating	
Restrict the use of the options dialog	
Disable the "General" options page	
Disable the "My Information" options page	
Disable the "Calling" options page	
Disable the "Audio" options page	
Disable the "Video" options page	
Disable the "Protocols" options page	
Prevent the user from answering calls	
Prevent the user from using audio features	
Restrict the use of video	
Prevent the user from sending video	
Prevent the user from receiving video	
Prevent the user from using directory services	
Set the Exchange Server property for NetMeeting Address	
Exchange Server Property	
Preset User Information Category	
Note: Only applicable for silent installs	
Set the NetMeeting home page	
NetMeeting Home Page URL	
Set limit for audio/video throughout	
Average audio/video throughout limit (in bps)	
NetMeeting Protocols	
Disable TCP/IP	
Disable null modem	
Corporate Settings	
Dial-Up Settings	
Use Automatic Discovery for Dial-Up connections	
Language Settings	

IEAK SELECTION	SELECT? Y/N
Default language for menus and dialogs	
Temp Internet Files (User)	
Check for newer versions of stored pages (Auto, Never, Every Visit to the Page, IE Startup)	
Set amount of disk space to use (in KBs)	
Auto-Proxy Caching	
Disable caching of Auto-Proxy scripts	
Temp Internet Files (Machine)	
Set amount of disk space to use (in KBs)	
User Profiles	
Disable Roaming Cache	
User Proxy Settings	
Make proxy settings per-machine (rather than per-user)	
Code Download	
Code Download Path	
Related Sites and Errors	
Disable the Show Related Links menu item and browser toolbar button	
Suppress the following errors	
400	
403	
404	
405	
406	
408	
409	
410	
500	
501	
505	

IEAK SELECTION	*SELECT? Y/N*

Office File Types

File types to NOT be browsed in same window

Excel Sheet 8

PowerPoint Show 8

Excel Chart 8

Word Document 8

Corporate Restrictions

Internet Property Pages

Disable viewing the General Page

Disable viewing the Security Page

Disable viewing the Content Page

Disable viewing the Connections Page

Disable viewing the Programs Page

Disable viewing the Advanced Page

Disable changing any settings on the Advanced Page

General Page

Disable changing homepage settings

Disable changing Temporary Internet files settings

Disable changing history settings

Disable changing color settings

Disable changing link color settings

Disable changing font settings

Disable changing language settings

Disable changing accessibility settings

Connections Page

Disable Internet Connection Wizard

Disable changing connection settings

Disable changing proxy settings

Disable changing Automatic Configuration settings

Content Page

Disable changing ratings settings

IEAK SELECTION	SELECT? Y/N
Disable changing certificate settings	
Disable changing Profile Assistant settings	
Disable AutoComplete for forms and saving of submitted strings	
Do not allow users to save passwords in AutoComplete for forms	
Programs Page	
Disable changing Messaging settings	
Disable changing Calendar and Contact settings	
Disable the Reset Web Settings feature	
Disable changing checking if Internet Explorer is the default browser	
Browser Menus	
File Menu	
Disable Save As... menu option	
Disable New menu option	
Disable Open menu option	
Disable Save As Web Page Complete format	
Disable closing of the browser	
View Menu	
Disable Source menu option	
Disable Fullscreen menu option	
Favorites Menu	
Hide Favorites menu	
Tools Menu	
Disable Internet Options... menu option	
Help Menu	
Remove 'Tip of the Day' menu option	
Remove 'for Netscape Users' menu option	
Remove 'Tour' menu option	
Remove 'Send Feedback' menu option	

IEAK Selection	*Select? Y/N*
Context Menu (Right Click)	
Disable Context Menu	
Disable Open in a New Window menu option	
File Download Dialog	
Disable Save this program to disk option	
Toolbars	
Toolbar Restrictions	
Disable customizing browser toolbar buttons	
Disable customizing browser toolbars	
Favorites and Search	
Favorites Import/Export	
Disable importing and exporting of favorites	
Search	
Disable Search Customization	
Disable Find Files via F3 within browser	
Persistence	
File Size Limits for Local Machine	
Per Domain (in Kbs)	
Per Document (in Kbs)	
File Size Limits for Intranet Zone	
Per Domain (in Kbs)	
Per Document (in Kbs)	
File Size Limits for Trusted Zone	
Per Domain (in Kbs)	
Per Document (in Kbs)	
File Size Limits for Internet Zone	
Per Domain (in Kbs)	
Per Document (in Kbs)	
File Size Limits for Restricted Sites Zone	
Per Domain (in Kbs)	
Per Document (in Kbs)	

IEAK SELECTION	SELECT? Y/N

Security Page

Use ONLY machine settings for security zones

Do not allow users to change policies for any security zone

Do not allow users to add/delete sites from a security zone

Trusted Publishers

Only allow content from Trusted Publishers

Software Updates

Automatic Install

Disable Automatic Install of IE components

Periodic Update Check

Disable Periodic Check for IE software updates and bug fixes

MS Logo5 Software Update Channel Notifications

Disable software update shell notifications on program launch

Startup Restrictions

Disable showing the splash screen

Maintenance Mode Settings

Disable adding IE components via Add/Remove Programs

Disable uninstalling IE5 and Internet Tools

Disable the IE5 Repair Utility

Internet Settings

AutoComplete

Use inline AutoComplete for Web addresses

Use inline AutoComplete for Windows Explorer

Use AutoComplete for Web addresses

Use AutoComplete for forms

Use AutoComplete for user names and passwords on forms

Prompt to save passwords

IEAK Selection	*Select? Y/N*

Toolbars

Default Toolbar Buttons

Show Small Icons

Back Button (default state, on, or off)

Forward Button (default state, on, or off)

Stop Button (default state, on, or off)

Refresh Button (default state, on, or off)

Home Button (default state, on, or off)

Search Button (default state, on, or off)

History Button (default state, on, or off)

Favorites Button (default state, on, or off)

Folders Button (default state, on, or off)

Fullscreen Button (default state, on, or off)

Tools Button (default state, on, or off)

Mail Button (default state, on, or off)

Font Size Button (default state, on, or off)

Print Button (default state, on, or off)

Edit Button (default state, on, or off)

Discussions Button (default state, on, or off)

Cut Button (default state, on, or off)

Copy Button (default state, on, or off)

Paste Button (default state, on, or off)

Encoding Button (default state, on, or off)

Display settings

Text Size

Default Size (largest, larger, medium, smaller, smallest)

General Colors

Background Color

Text Color

Use Windows colors

IEAK Selection	*Select? Y/N*
Link Colors	
Visited Link Color	
Use Hover Color	
Hover Color	
Advanced settings	
Enable Autodialing	
Browsing	
Disable script debugging	
Launch browser in full screen mode	
Show friendly URLs	
Use smooth scrolling	
Enable page transitions	
Browse in a new process	
Enable page hit counting	
Automatically check for IE Updates	
Underline Links (always, never, hover)	
Use Web Based FTP	
Show Go button in Address Bar	
Show friendly http error messages	
Display a notification about every script error	
Multimedia	
Show pictures	
Play animations	
Play videos	
Play sounds	
Smart image dithering	
Show image download placeholders	
Security	
Enable Profile Assistant	
Delete saved pages when browser closed	

IEAK Selection	*Select? Y/N*
Do not save encrypted pages to disk	
Warn if forms submit is being redirected	
Warn if changing between secure and not secure mode	
Java VM	
Java logging enabled	
Java JIT compiler enabled	
Printing	
Print background colors and images	
Searching	
Search Provider Keyword (Intranet for internal)	
When selecting from the Address bar (display results and go to the most likely site, just go to the most likely site, Just display the results in the main window, or do not search from the Address bar)	
HTTP 1.1 settings	
Use HTTP 1.1	
Use HTTP 1.1 through proxy connections	
URL Encoding	
Always send URLs as UTF-8 (requires restart)	
Component Updates	
Periodic check for updates to IE and Internet Tools	
URL to be displayed for updates	
Update check interval (in days)	
Help Menu > About Internet Explorer	
Cipher Strength Update Information URL	
Identity Manager	
Restrict Identities	
Prevent Users from configuring or using identities	
Web Desktop	
Disable Active Desktop	

IEAK SELECTION	SELECT? Y/N
Do not allow changes to Active Desktop	
Hide IE icon	
Hide Network Neighborhood icon	
Hide all items on Desktop	
Active Desktop items	
Disable adding ANY desktop items	
Disable deleting ANY desktop items	
Disable editing ANY desktop items	
Disable closing ANY desktop items	
Desktop Wallpaper settings	
Disable selecting HTML as wallpaper	
Disable changing wallpaper	
Desktop Toolbars settings	
Disable adding new toolbars	
Disable resizing ALL toolbars	
Start Menu	
Remove Favorites menu from Start menu	
Remove Find menu from Start menu	
Remove Run menu from Start menu	
Remove the Active Desktop item from the Settings menu	
Remove the Windows Update item from the Settings menu	
Disable Drag and Drop context menus on Start menu	
Remove the Folder Options menu item from the Settings menu	
Remove Documents menu item from Start menu	
Do not keep history of recently opened documents	
Clear history of recent opened documents	
Disable Logoff	
Disable Shut Down command from Start menu	
Disable changes to Printers and Control Panel Settings	

IEAK SELECTION	SELECT? Y/N
Disable changes to Taskbar and Start Menu Settings	
Disable context menu for Taskbar	
Add Run Dlg checkbox for New Memory Space (Win NT only)	

Shell

Disable File menu in browser window	
Disable context menu in Shell folders	
Only allow approved Shell extensions	
Do not track Shell shortcuts during roaming	
Hide Drives in My Computer	
Disable net connections/disconnections	

Printers

Disable Deletion of Printers	
Disable Addition of Printers	
Hide General and Details tabs in Printer Properties (Win 9.x only)	

System

Run only specified Windows applications	
Do not allow computer to restart in MS–DOS mode (Win 9.x only)	

Offline Pages

Disable adding channels	
Disable removing channels	
Disable adding schedules for offline pages	
Disable editing schedules for offline pages	
Disable removing schedules for offline pages	
Disable offline page hit logging	
Disable ALL scheduled offline pages	
Disable password caching for offline pages	
Disable channel user interface completely	
Disable downloading of site subscription content	
Disable editing and creating schedule groups	

IEAK Selection	*Select? Y/N*
Maximum size of subscription (in Kbs, zero disables)	
Maximum number of offline pages	
Minimum number of minutes between scheduled updates	
Time to begin preventing scheduled updates (in 60-minute increments)	
Time to end preventing scheduled updates (in 60-minute increments)	
Maximum offline pages crawl depth (0, 1, 2, or 3)	
Microsoft Windows Media Player	
Customizations	
Customize the Windows Media Player	
Prevent automatic Codec download	
Title bar of the Windows Media Player	
Button name on Windows Media Player navigation bar	
URL for button on Windows Media Player navigation bar	
Customize Network Settings	
Default number milliseconds to buffer data	
Enable HTTP protocol	
Enable Multicast	
Enable TCP protocol	
Enable UDP protocol	
Use Proxy	
Use custom Proxy settings (do not detect)	
Proxy Hostname	
Proxy Host Port	
Favorites	
Windows Media Player Favorites	
Do not install the default Windows Media Player Favorites in the Media folder	

Radio toolbar settings

Disable Radio toolbar (may require a reboot)

Disable menu for finding new Radio Stations

URL for finding new Radio Stations

Customizing Graphics

Table F-1 organizes the custom graphics you can create with the IEAK. Pay special attention to the size of each graphic. If you do not follow these guidelines in creating your custom graphics, you may experience unexpected or undesired results.

TABLE F-1 CUSTOM GRAPHIC PREPARATION

GRAPHIC NAME	WHAT IT'S USED FOR	SIZE/TYPE	PREPARATION
Static logo	To brand the Internet Explorer browser with your logo	38-by-38 pixel and 22-by-22 pixel .bmp files	Create two 256-color bitmaps. Save the files in the custom bitmap folder (CIE\Bitmaps).
Animated logo	To brand the Internet Explorer browser with your animated logo	38-by-38 pixel and 22-by-22 pixel .bmp files	Create two 256-color bitmaps. The bitmaps must contain a vertical stack of animation cell images that follow Internet Explorer animation rules (see below). Save the files in the custom bitmap folder (CIE\Bitmaps). When the browser isn't active, the first frame of the animated logo will be used as your static logo.
32 bit setup bitmaps (for Windows operating systems only)	For 32-bit versions of the browser	Left vertical: 162-by-312 pixel 256-color .bmp (on first Windows Update Setup wizard page). Top horizontal (on all but first page): 496-by-56 pixel 256-color .bmp	For 32-bit versions, the top horizontal banner needs to be light, like a "watermark," to allow text in the user interface to be readable.
16 bit setup bitmaps	For 16-bit versions of the browser	162-by-312 pixel .bmp	16-color recommended, with few or no background colors and patterns.

Graphic Name	What it's Used For	Size/Type	Preparation
Toolbar Background	Internet Explorer Toolbars	No specific dimensions	Background should be the size of the toolbar and light enough to show black text.
Internet Connection Wizard	Used to specify an icon for your version of the Internet Connection Wizard	Top image 49-by-49 pixel .bmp file. Left image 164-by-458 pixel .bmp file	Not available for serverless sign-up.
Browser toolbar button	Used to create a button for the Internet Explorer toolbar or a custom toolbar of your own	Two icon files, with black-and-white and color images for active and inactive states	For more information, see Designing Toolbar Icons for Internet Explorer 5.
Icons for Favorites list	Using this option, you can assign special icons to specific favorites that you preconfigure with the IEAK.	A 16-by-16 pixel .bmp file for each item you want to customize	None.
Autorun splash screen (Windows 32-bit platforms only)	To display a splash screen when the user inserts the CD	If you distribute your custom browser on a CD, you need to create a (540-by-357 pixel) bitmap for the Autorun splash screen that is displayed when the user inserts the CD	Before you create the splash screen, you need to convert any 24-bit images to 256-color identity palette.
Channels	Active Channels on the Internet Explorer Channel Bar	For each channel: 32-by-32 pixel icon, 80-by-32 pixel graphic for channel bar, and 194-by-32 pixel graphic for channel pane	The 80-by-32 pixel and 194-by-32 pixel graphics can be in .gif, .bmp, or .jpeg format. The channel category graphic is used in Windows 32-bit platform versions of Internet Explorer only.
LDAP service bitmap	Service background for LDAP implementations	134-by-38 pixel, 16-color .bmp file	None.

What's on the CD-ROM

The CD-ROM included with this book contains the following materials:

- BeachFront Quizzer exam simulation software
- Microsoft Internet Explorer version 5.0
- *Micro House Technical Library* (demo)
- Adobe Acrobat Reader
- An electronic version of this book, *Internet Explorer 5 Administration Kit MCSE Study System,* in .pdf format

The following sections describe each product and include detailed instructions for installation and use.

BEACHFRONT QUIZZER

The version of the BeachFront Quizzer software included on the CD-ROM gives you the opportunity to test your knowledge with simulated exam questions. The features of the BeachFront Quizzer product include:

- Study sessions, standard exams, and adaptive exams
- New exam every time
- Historical analysis

If you want more exam questions, you can purchase the full retail version of the BeachFront Quizzer software from BeachFront Quizzer. See the BeachFront Quizzer ad in the back of this book.

To install BeachFront Quizzer, follow these steps:

1. Open My Computer. Double-click your CD-ROM drive (usually D:). Double-click the BFQuiz folder. Double-click plain_quiz32a.exe. The BeachFront Quizzer setup program starts.

2. On the welcome screen, click Next to continue to the license agreement screen. Read the agreement, and click I Agree to continue.

3. On the Choose Destination Location screen, click Next to accept the default file location (C:\Quizzer). If you want to install the files to a different location, click Browse and select the file location. After you click Next, the installation begins.

4. After the installation, you will be asked to install Adobe Acrobat Reader. You need Acrobat Reader to enhance the BeachFront Quizzer product. The test questions are mapped to the contents of the book, which you access with the Acrobat (PDF) files. Click the check box marked "Install Adobe Acrobat Reader," and click Next.

5. The Acrobat Reader installation program starts. The Acrobat Reader welcome screen appears first. Click Next to continue. The License agreement screen appears next. Read the agreement, and click I Accept to continue.

6. The Choose Destination Location screen appears. If you want to choose a different location, click Browse and select the destination to install the files to. To accept the default, click Next to continue.

7. The Acrobat Reader installation program runs. After the installer is finished, a dialog box will appear that reads "Thank you for choosing Acrobat Reader." Click OK to finish.

8. You are returned to the BeachFront Quizzer installation process. The next screen gives you the option to install the online books. These are the Acrobat (PDF) files that contain the text of the book and are linked to the questions. You should install these to get the most benefit out of BeachFront Quizzer. Check the "Install supplied online books" checkbox, and click Next.

9. The online books install. When they're done, click Finish to complete the installation. You have the option of starting the BeachFront Quizzer engine now or later.

To use BeachFront Quizzer, follow these steps:

1. Start BeachFront Quizzer by selecting Start ⇨ Programs ⇨ BeachFront Quizzer. The select Exam Screen appears.

2. Select the exam you want to practice for and click OK. A legal warning window appears. Click OK to continue.

3. You will be asked for the CD key. The CD key can be found in a file named `Password.txt` within the BFQuiz folder. Enter the CD key and click OK.

4. The BeachFront Quizzer test engine starts. Select the category you wish to study, and the study mode you want to use, and click Start.

MICROSOFT INTERNET EXPLORER VERSION 5.0

A complete copy of Microsoft Internet Explorer is included on the CD-ROM. You can use Internet Explorer to browse the Internet if you have an Internet connection.

To install and run Microsoft Internet Explorer, follow these steps:

1. Start Windows Explorer (if you're using Windows 95/98) or Windows NT Explorer (if you're using Windows NT), and then open the `\Msie50` folder on the CD-ROM.

2. In the `\Msie50`, double-click `Setup.exe` and follow the instructions presented onscreen for installing Microsoft Internet Explorer.

3. To run Microsoft Internet Explorer, double-click the Internet Explorer icon on the desktop.

MICRO HOUSE TECHNICAL LIBRARY (DEMO)

Micro House Technical Library is a useful CD-ROM-based set of encyclopedias that contains hardware-configuration information. This evaluation copy of *Micro House Technical Library* includes only the Encyclopedia of I/O cards. Use this evaluation copy to determine whether or not you want to purchase the full version of the *Micro House Technical Library*.

To install and access the *Micro House Technical Library*, follow these steps:

1. Start Windows Explorer (if you're using Windows 95/98) or Windows NT Explorer (if you're using Windows NT), and then open the `Micro House` folder on the CD-ROM.

2. In the `Micro House` folder, double-click `Install.exe` and follow the instructions presented onscreen for installing the *Micro House Technical Library*.

3. To run the *Micro House Technical Library*, select Start ⇨ Programs ⇨ MH Tech Library ⇨ MTL Demo Edition.

THE ADOBE ACROBAT READER

Adobe's Acrobat Reader is a helpful program that will enable you to view the electronic version of this book in the same page format as the actual book.

To install and run Adobe's Acrobat Reader and view the electronic version of this book, follow these steps:

1. Start Windows Explorer, and then open the Acrobat Reader folder in `\\IDGBcert\software\acrobat`.

2. In the Acrobat folder, double-click `rs40eng.exe` and follow the instructions presented on-screen for installing Adobe Acrobat Reader.

3. To view the electronic version of the book, after you have installed Adobe Acrobat Reader, start Windows Explorer and open the Books folder.

4. In the Books folder, double-click the Acrobat (PDF) file for the chapter or appendix file you want to view.

Glossary

active caching Enables you to configure specific widely accessed Web sites for automatic caching on the proxy server's hard drive. Accessing data from the proxy server is much faster than going out to the Internet for every request.

Active Desktop Runs a mini-version of Internet Explorer on your desktop for displaying commonly used URLs, intranet sites, and Web applications. It also adds new integration features to the Start menu, the taskbar, and other configuration options.

Active Setup Wizard A series of dialog boxes that perform the Internet Explorer installation.

adapter address Also known as the MAC address, the adapter address assigned to your workstation is the workstation's unique identity on the network.

ANDing The process that determines which part of the address is the network ID and which part is the host ID. ANDing is done internally by TCP/IP. It checks the bit in the TCP/IP address and compares it to the corresponding bit in the subnet mask.

ARIN (American Registry for Internet Numbers) The organization that provides IP addresses to Internet service providers (ISPs). ISPs generally obtain IP addresses in very large blocks, much larger than most small to midsize corporations.

Authenticode This enables developers to obtain a digital signature for their applications from an organization, such as Verisign. Once a developer compresses an application, that individual can "sign" the code, which enables the application to be married with the digital signature, thus verifying that the code is genuine and won't harm a user's workstation.

Auto-Complete A feature of Internet Explorer that allows the browser to complete the typing of URLs by using the history feature.

Auto-Proxy The feature of Internet Explorer that allows for a script to be installed on a Web server and to be retrieved by the Internet Explorer browser to configure proxy settings.

Automatic Version Synchronization (AVS) This ActiveX technology checks source files against your most current downloaded site.

Basic Webcasting A simple information-gathering tool for users that also provides a lot of flexibility in mobile-computing solutions. Basic Webcasting is offered through the use of Favorites.

binary digits Ones and zeros that, once combined, translate to a decimal number.

capture cards Capture cards enable you to digitize video from a variety of sources such as VCRs, handheld video recorders, and television signals.

Connection Wizard A setup routine, geared toward users, for configuring Internet connection type. The Wizard follows users through a series of dialog boxes that determine how to set up Internet access.

Corporate Administrator One of the three roles chosen during IEAK setup, the Corporate Administrator has the most options for deploying Internet Explorer within an enterprise.

Desktop bar A representation of the icons and content displayed on the desktop itself. A handy feature for accessing applications, it is somewhat similar to the Quick Links bar.

DHCP (Dynamic Host Configuration Protocol) Enables Windows NT Server to act as a virtual TCP/IP address store. Workstations contact the DHCP server upon startup and ask for a unique address.

DNS (Domain Name Service) server Provides the host name to TCP/IP address resolution. Name resolution enables you to access servers and workstations by translating the host name into a TCP/IP address.

Dynamic HTML (Hypertext Markup Language) Enables developers to use HTML within the context of a user's browser, depending on the navigation that the user selected.

ECMAScript Developed by the European Computer Manufacturer's Association, ECMAScript is a scripting tool for Java.

encryption Enables the transmission of data to and from a browser in a scrambled format so that unsavory individuals cannot intercept sensitive data. The Internet Explorer browser offers 128-bit encryption.

Favorites Favorites are URLs and HTML documents that you can save as quick references to return to Web sites or view HTML documents.

FrontPage Express Enables users who have little or no knowledge of HTML to create large and effective Web sites in short order. The WYSIWYG feature enables you to immediately view the results of your development and facilitates quick deployment. FrontPage Express is included in Internet Explorer 5.

FTP (File Transfer Protocol) Based on TCP/IP, FTP offers an efficient, clean, and fast way to transfer files from an FTP server (also called an FTP daemon) to an FTP client. FTP services are included in Microsoft Internet Information Server (IIS).

History bar Catalogs the Web sites you visit, making it easy to navigate back to them. Your history is categorized by the day, week, and month for easy reference. The History bar actually views data stored in your `C:\Windows\History` folder.

host names Common names assigned to computers to give them logical names instead of numeric addresses.

HTTP (Hypertext Transfer Protocol) The method by which you retrieve most Web pages on the Internet. The browser and the Web server interact with each other and deliver documents to the client using this protocol.

IMAP4 (Internet Mail Access Protocol 4) The latest in a series of improvements to replace Post Office Protocol (POP) mail. One feature is that you can store mail on the server and access it from different clients without deleting the original message. IMAP also lets you read a message header without actually getting the entire message, which saves time.

Inbox Assistant Filters incoming e-mail based on the sender, size, and other information.

InfoPane A customized view where you can create personalized information, such as support and contact information, for your organization.

Internet content providers (ICPs) Organizations that provide Internet-based content and services to Internet users. This group also includes software and hardware vendors that sell and distribute products and services to the general public.

Internet service providers (ISPs) Organizations that have the capability to brand a browser and customize its distribution method: the single floppy disk. In addition to the single floppy disk, ISPs have the option of distributing Internet Explorer and signing up users for Internet access with the Internet Sign-up Server function of IEAK.

IPCONFIG.EXE Used on Windows NT Server and Windows NT Workstation, it displays various TCP/IP-related information at the command-line level.

Java A programming language derived from the C++ programming language, it enables applications to be developed independent of the operating system on which the Java application runs.

knowledge base A database with more than 60,000 documented issues with various Microsoft products. The knowledge base is the first stop for the resolution of most problems that you may experience with Internet Explorer and other Microsoft products.

LDAP (Lightweight Directory Access Protocol) Enables directory-based services on dissimilar operating systems to appear transparent to users. LDAP is an exciting new technology that facilitates easier administration for gurus and easier access for users — the best of both worlds.

Managed Webcasting With this, Web site developers can create rich, bold content specifically designed for delivery to a user's desktop. Managed Webcasting employs Extensible Markup Language (XML) to deliver HTML content across an intranet or the Internet.

Microsoft Exchange Server Microsoft's electronic mail server. The product provides internal and external mail services to clients and also offers an excellent platform for integrating mail-related services into applications on the Internet. Exchange Server also has a powerful collaboration tool for use in corporate intranets.

Microsoft FrontPage Microsoft's HTML editor, FrontPage is considered one of the best and easiest-to-use HTML editors on the market today. It enables both novice and expert users to create HTML documents easily and quickly.

Microsoft Index Server Microsoft's Web-search index tool. It runs as an application on top of IIS and offers powerful search tools optimized for Windows NT Server. You can search documents of many types with corresponding data, and you can search the bodies of some documents, such as a Microsoft Word document.

Microsoft Internet Information Server (IIS) Microsoft's Web server product, IIS offers the latest in Web server technology with a simple, easy-to-use administration tool. There are several tools included in the package; administration can be done with a provided HTML administration site.

Microsoft NetMeeting A multifunctional, real-time, video and audio collaboration tool. NetMeeting facilitates real-time videoconferences with audio support and a fully functional application-sharing tool.

Microsoft NetShow The application for receiving broadcast audio and video within the context of a user's browser. NetShow differs from NetMeeting because it is a one-way service.

Microsoft Proxy Server Microsoft's firewall product and proxy assistant. Proxy Server runs as an application on top of IIS and allows packet filtering for Internet traffic, clustering, and site-blocking services. For security purposes, most network engineers configure their Proxy Servers as the organization gateway to the Internet.

Microsoft SQL Server Microsoft's high-end database server. Although SQL Server is not specifically a Web product, you can easily integrate it with IIS, Exchange, and most Microsoft products to offer a full-circle solution to data storage. SQL Server can store IIS traffic information, access attempts from Proxy Server, and access error information from Exchange all at once on the same server.

Microsoft Visual InterDev Microsoft's development suite. This package combines some of the most powerful programming tools available today under one cover for the medium- to advanced-level developer.

Multipoint Data Conferencing This standard, used in NetMeeting, allows you to share applications, whiteboard features, file transfer, and chat functions.

NBTSTAT With this utility you can view remote servers and workstations and the NetBIOS name cache, and perform other NetBIOS-related troubleshooting tasks.

NetBIOS NetBIOS (Network Basic Input/Output System) enables the use of "friendly" names so workstations can communicate with one another on local area networks (LANs). A NetBIOS name consists of 15 characters.

NetShow encoder Provides the means to convert the analog live signal or the digital file-based video to a format you can stream.

Netstat.exe This utility enables you to view network protocol-related information at the command line.

newsgroups Databases of text and graphics on a wide array of subjects, from lawn care to space travel. USENET provides the majority of the newsgroup services, while newsgroups can be used on an intranet for information sharing.

NNTP (Network News Transport Protocol) The protocol used by Outlook to access newsgroups.

Nslookup The primary troubleshooting utility for DNS-related issues in Windows NT. Using Nslookup, you can locate host names and IP addresses for devices that have DNS entries.

octets A binary number, consisting of eight digits, that translates to a number between 1 and 256 in decimal notation.

offline browsing This feature of Internet Explorer enables you to view Web information and HTML when not connected to the Internet.

Outlook Express The light version of Microsoft Outlook; the full version is included in the Microsoft Office 97 suite of software.

Parallel Cameras Parallel cameras are very small cameras that connect to the workstation via the workstation's parallel port.

passive caching With this, data retrieved from Web sites can be cached on Proxy Server's hard drive. It differs from active caching in that there is no preconfigured cached site, and it is done dynamically depending on where your users are navigating on the Internet.

PICS Developed by the World Wide Web Consortium in 1995, PICS supplies the means by which you can rate Internet content according to various factors, including violence, racism, sexually explicit material, and nudity.

Ping.exe This utility sends a series of four Internet Control Message Protocol (ICMP) packets to a destination address.

POP3 (Post Office Protocol 3) POP mail is the standard for receiving e-mail on the Internet.

Private Communications Technologies (PCT) Enables you to create a secure channel to send and receive data from a PCT-enabled Web server. PCT is similar to the design and purpose of Secure Sockets Layer.

Quick Launch bar Enables you to configure frequently used applications with a shortcut on the taskbar itself. With it, you can more easily start an application when working in another application, without having to switch tasks.

Quick Links bar Used to more efficiently navigate to a user's favorite Web sites and frequently used URLs. This is also a good place to provide links to the Web-based applications your organization uses.

realm name A realm name allows for your users to be authenticated when they dial-up to an Internet POP or to your dial-up servers. For example, the realm `name@idgbooks.com` is read by the dial-up server when the user gets the dial-in handshake.

Resource kits Documentation that provides information on Microsoft products, such as reference materials, utilities, and other related documentation.

roaming profiles These enable a user to log in to different workstations within your network but retain the same desktop and Internet Explorer settings. Roaming profiles give the user a consistent, customizable interface.

Rules A feature of Outlook Express that allows you to enact processes based on conditions of an e-mail message, such as copying a message to a folder automatically.

RUNONCE Runs during the boot process after WININIT.EXE. Adds to the registry the path to a particular utility that you may want to run after installation.

Search bar A preconfigured pointer to a search site, which contains powerful Web-site indexing engines that help you find information.

SHDOCVW.DLL An ActiveX control that provides features for Internet Explorer, including Favorites, Navigation, History, and Visual Navigation buttons such as Home. The Web browser control can also be used in Visual Basic to create Web applications.

signatures This feature lets you append a disclaimer to a mail message to prevent users from sending mail that may not represent the beliefs or opinions of your organization.

silent installation Enables Active Setup to run within Internet Explorer without options for user intervention.

SMTP (Simple Mail Transport Protocol) The de facto standard for sending e-mail on the Internet.

Softboot This routine processes instructions located in the `Softboot.ini` file for information and instructions to process during and after the installation is complete.

Tracert.exe Used to determine the path that a packet takes to its destination.

True Webcasting A hardware- and network-based solution for delivering organized content to users. True Webcasting solutions, such as NetShow, accomplish the organized delivery of video and audio in one-to-one or one-to-many scenarios.

Universal Serial Bus (USB) USB is a class of hardware that makes it simple to add serial devices to your computer. Using USB Ports, you can chain together a series of devices, such as printers, cameras, drives, and other hardware on the same chain, similar to that of the SCSI capabilities. The advantage that USB has over SCSI is the number of devices that can be connected to USB.

User Agent String Enables content developers to identify several key factors about a user's workstation within HTML code. The User Agent String identifies the browser type and version, the workstation operating system, and a custom string that you can assign with the IEAK.

VBScript A simplified version of Visual Basic. It provides a lot of flexibility to an organization so that it can capitalize on existing Visual Basic programmers to assist in the development of Web applications.

Virtual Private Networking (VPN) VPNs allow you to connect to a network from another network using a secure, encrypted connection also called a tunnel.

Web views Facilitates the presentation of desktop folders in HTML format. The views are easily distinguishable, and the files have an .htt extension (HTML Template File) and can be edited in an HTML editor, Notepad, or any other text editor.

whiteboard The electronic version of a blackboard. It is also very similar to Microsoft Paint. Whiteboard enables you to collaborate with other NetMeeting/whiteboard users to create pictures, drawings, and text.

Windows Address Book Used to store frequently used addresses; also organizes addresses in a quick, logical fashion.

Windows IP Configuration (WINIPCFG) The WINIPCFG utility displays the TCP/IP information for your Windows 95/98 Workstation.

WININIT Checks the wininit.ini file for instructions put there by an installation program. Instructions included in this file may include instructions for registry changes, file copies, and other file updates.

Index

A

Continued

Continued

Continued

IDG Books Worldwide, Inc. End-User License Agreement

READ THIS. You should carefully read these terms and conditions before opening the software packet(s) included with this book ("Book"). This is a license agreement ("Agreement") between you and IDG Books Worldwide, Inc. ("IDGB"). By opening the accompanying software packet(s), you acknowledge that you have read and accept the following terms and conditions. If you do not agree and do not want to be bound by such terms and conditions, promptly return the Book and the unopened software packet(s) to the place you obtained them for a full refund.

1. **License Grant.** IDGB grants to you (either an individual or entity) a nonexclusive license to use one copy of the enclosed software program(s) (collectively, the "Software") solely for your own personal or business purposes on a single computer (whether a standard computer or a workstation component of a multiuser network). The Software is in use on a computer when it is loaded into temporary memory (RAM) or installed into permanent memory (hard disk, CD-ROM, or other storage device). IDGB reserves all rights not expressly granted herein.

2. **Ownership.** IDGB is the owner of all right, title, and interest, including copyright, in and to the compilation of the Software recorded on the disk(s) or CD-ROM ("Software Media"). Copyright to the individual programs recorded on the Software Media is owned by the author or other authorized copyright owner of each program. Ownership of the Software and all proprietary rights relating thereto remain with IDGB and its licensers.

3. **Restrictions On Use and Transfer.**

  (a) You may only (i) make one copy of the Software for backup or archival purposes, or (ii) transfer the Software to a single hard disk, provided that you keep the original for backup or archival purposes. You may not (i) rent or lease the Software, (ii) copy or reproduce the Software through a LAN or other network system or through any computer subscriber system or bulletin-board system, or (iii) modify, adapt, or create derivative works based on the Software.

  (b) You may not reverse engineer, decompile, or disassemble the Software. You may transfer the Software and user documentation on a permanent basis, provided that the transferee agrees to accept the terms and conditions of this Agreement and you retain no copies. If the Software is an update or has been updated, any transfer must include the most recent update and all prior versions.

4. **Restrictions on Use of Individual Programs.** You must follow the individual requirements and restrictions detailed for each individual program in Appendix G of this Book. These limitations are also contained in the individual license agreements recorded on the Software Media. These limitations may include a requirement that after using the program for a specified period of time, the user must pay a registration fee or discontinue use. By opening the Software packet(s), you will be agreeing to abide by the licenses and restrictions for these individual programs that are detailed in Appendix G and on the Software Media. None of the material on this Software Media or listed in this Book may ever be redistributed, in original or modified form, for commercial purposes.

5. **Limited Warranty.**

   (a) IDGB warrants that the Software and Software Media are free from defects in materials and workmanship under normal use for a period of sixty (60) days from the date of purchase of this Book. If IDGB receives notification within the warranty period of defects in materials or workmanship, IDGB will replace the defective Software Media.

   (b) **IDGB AND THE AUTHOR OF THE BOOK DISCLAIM ALL OTHER WARRANTIES, EXPRESS OR IMPLIED, INCLUDING WITHOUT LIMITATION IMPLIED WARRANTIES OF MERCHANTABILITY AND FITNESS FOR A PARTICULAR PURPOSE, WITH RESPECT TO THE SOFTWARE, THE PROGRAMS, THE SOURCE CODE CONTAINED THEREIN, AND/OR THE TECHNIQUES DESCRIBED IN THIS BOOK. IDGB DOES NOT WARRANT THAT THE FUNCTIONS CONTAINED IN THE SOFTWARE WILL MEET YOUR REQUIREMENTS OR THAT THE OPERATION OF THE SOFTWARE WILL BE ERROR FREE.**

   (c) This limited warranty gives you specific legal rights, and you may have other rights that vary from jurisdiction to jurisdiction.

6. **Remedies.**

   (a) IDGB's entire liability and your exclusive remedy for defects in materials and workmanship shall be limited to replacement of the Software

Media, which may be returned to IDGB with a copy of your receipt at the following address: Software Media Fulfillment Department, Attn.: *Internet Explorer 5 Administration Kit MCSE Study System*, IDG Books Worldwide, Inc., 10475 Crosspoint Blvd., Indianapolis, IN 46256, or call 1-800-762-2974. Please allow three to four weeks for delivery. This Limited Warranty is void if failure of the Software Media has resulted from accident, abuse, or misapplication. Any replacement Software Media will be warranted for the remainder of the original warranty period or thirty (30) days, whichever is longer.

(b) In no event shall IDGB or the author be liable for any damages whatsoever (including without limitation damages for loss of business profits, business interruption, loss of business information, or any other pecuniary loss) arising from the use of or inability to use the Book or the Software, even if IDGB has been advised of the possibility of such damages.

(c) Because some jurisdictions do not allow the exclusion or limitation of liability for consequential or incidental damages, the above limitation or exclusion may not apply to you.

7. **U.S. Government Restricted Rights.** Use, duplication, or disclosure of the Software by the U.S. Government is subject to restrictions stated in paragraph (c)(1)(ii) of the Rights in Technical Data and Computer Software clause of DFARS 252.227-7013, and in subparagraphs (a) through (d) of the Commercial Computer—Restricted Rights clause at FAR 52.227-19, and in similar clauses in the NASA FAR supplement, when applicable.

8. **General.** This Agreement constitutes the entire understanding of the parties and revokes and supersedes all prior agreements, oral or written, between them and may not be modified or amended except in a writing signed by both parties hereto that specifically refers to this Agreement. This Agreement shall take precedence over any other documents that may be in conflict herewith. If any one or more provisions contained in this Agreement are held by any court or tribunal to be invalid, illegal, or otherwise unenforceable, each and every other provision shall remain in full force and effect.

"Upset? Why should I be upset? So I couldn't reschedule my exam this weekend and still had to show up at precisely 8:00 Monday morning. And so what if it took till 10:39 before it was finally ready for me to take it. Does that bother me? Nooooooooooo. I'm just going to sit right here and drink my nice lovely cup of tea!"

my2cents.idgbooks.com

CD-ROM Installation Instructions

Each software item on the *Internet Explorer 5 Administration Kit MCSE Study System* CD-ROM is located in its own folder. To install a particular piece of software, open its folder with My Computer or Internet Explorer. What you do next depends on what you find in the software's folder:

1. First, look for a `ReadMe.txt` file or a `.doc` or `.htm` document. If this is present, it should contain installation instructions and other useful information.

2. If the folder contains an executable (`.exe`) file, this is usually an installation program. Often it will be called `Setup.exe` or `Install.exe`, but in some cases the filename reflects an abbreviated version of the software's name and version number. Run the `.exe` file to start the installation process.

3. In the case of some simple software, the `.exe` file probably is the software — no real installation step is required. You can run the software from the CD to try it out. If you like it, copy it to your hard disk and create a Start menu shortcut for it.

The `ReadMe.txt` file in the CD-ROM's root directory may contain additional installation information, so be sure to check it.

For a listing of the software on the CD-ROM, see Appendix G.